IN THE SWIM

Publisher: Swimming Times Ltd
Harold Fern House, Derby Square, Loughborough, Leicestershire, LE11 0AL

© 1996

First Published 1996

Designed by Leicester Printers Ltd
Printed in Great Britain by Leicester Printers Ltd

A CIP catalogue record for this title is available from the British Library.

ISBN 0-90052-43-0

In the Swim:
The Amateur Swimming Association from 1869 to 1994

By

Ian Keil and Don Wix

Swimming Times Ltd

This book is dedicated to all swimmers, organisers and voluntary helpers from the Districts and Counties who have kept alive the spirit of amateur swimming since 1869.

Foreword

Philip Jones
President of the ASA, 1996

A full history of the ASA has been long overdue. It is a pleasure to commend this book to all who have benefited from the ASA. It will provide a better understanding of why swimming has become the most successful sporting organisation in Great Britain today.

As early as 1962 a start was made on a history of the ASA so that the finished work would be available for its Centenary in 1969. Sadly, the death of Colonel Atherton, the key author, led to the abandonment of the project. In the Autumn of 1993 David Reeves raised the possibility of a history to mark the 125th anniversary of the Association in 1994.

The present authors began the task in January 1994 and found that this was a story of such weight and interest that it deserved to be properly researched and illustrated. They came to the task as historians without any ASA background. Therefore it is especially gratifying to draw attention to one of the themes which they have stressed, namely, the importance of the word *'amateur'*. This did not and does not imply bumbling inefficiency but true love of a sport which has attracted the great numbers of *amateur* swimmers and officials to participate in the ASA. This is pre-eminently a body which has depended of volunteers and our continuing success requires their selfless dedication.

The professional support of the ASA staff has facilitated the growth of our Association especially in the second half of the twentieth century. The very wide attraction of swimming for all ages has owed so much to the work of the ASA. This and much more is what this history has brought to light.

Philip Jones

Authors Introduction

When we began the task of writing this history in January 1994 we did not envisage its complexity. The work and activities of the ASA between 1869 and 1994 covered many aspects of swimming and its relationships with other sports. Changes in government educational policies and political attitudes have always coloured the background against which the ASA has striven to progress. Economic and social developments have also played their parts.

Our objective has been to show how the ASA adapted to the many changes which have occurred during the past century and a quarter. The contrasts and similarities between the year of its foundation and 1994 serve to underline the durability of this institution. The catalogue of differences may be seen in the material basis of everyday life: the availability of food, of entertainment, of employment and of health were tranformed by inventions of and discoveries. Some similarities between 1869 and 1994 include pollution in larger towns and poverty in central urban areas. Probably the most conspicuous feature in the history of sport has been the prowess of leading performers. In this respect swimming sports have shown very great developments in which the ASA has had a vital role to play.

There remain some issues which space and time did not allow us to pursue. We have covered those developments which the ASA's surviving records suggest were the most significant. The caprices of time have limited the survival of some archival categories which might have disclosed more about how the Association made decisions and why it made particular choices.

Amongst the questions which we had no opportunity to pursue were those which would reveal more about the people who made the ASA function. Little is recorded in the sources we had available about the education, working and social connections of the stalwarts who sat on ASA committees and attended the many events as officials.

We have not attempted to use this book either as a record of performances by individuals or teams in swimming, diving, synchronised swimming and water polo or as an exhaustive compilation of all who served on ASA Council, Committee or advisory bodies. Such listings would have contributed little to our purpose of showing how the ASA kept swimming in the forefront of sports activities.

The preparation of this book has placed us in the debt of many men and women who have enabled us to understand the ASA, warts and all. A full list of acknowledgements and the data about sources gives an indication of the help we have received. It has given us an appreciation of the qualities of friendliness and generosity which through the years made it possible for the ASA to achieve so much.

Needless to say we remain responsible for all errors and omissions in the book. We record our grateful thanks for their advice and comments on drafts of particular chapters to Hamilton Bland, J.M. Cameron, Helen Elkington, Gerald Forsberg, Jennifer Gray, Andy Morton, and John Wardley. The whole text benefited from readings by Austin Rawlinson, Peter Rawlinson and Norman Sarsfield. We owe a special debt of gratitude to Teresa Keil who has read the entire script and gave us valuable advice from the point of view of the non specialist reader. She has saved us from infelicitous expressions and guided us towards a clearer exposition of the complex story of the ASA.

Ian Keil and Don Wix

Acknowledgements

We acknowledge with gratitude the help we have received from the following people.

Gordon Alexander, Genevieve Applebee, Mavis Avery, Karen L. Batts, John Beswick, Hamilton Bland, S. Boothroyd, Neil Bramwell, Richard Brown, Paul Bush, Sarah Butlin, J. M. Cameron, Elizabeth Chalmers, Anne Clark, Wendy Coles, Jeff Cook, Margaret Coombs, M. Joyce Cooper (Mrs Badcock), Pat Coulson, Alan Donlan, Helen Elkington, The Misses Fern, Viv Firman, John Fisher, Gerald Forsberg, Stephen Freeth, Ron Germany, Ian Gibson, Karen Glendenning, Susan Glyptis, Josie Grange, Jennifer Gray, Ann Green, Joan Gurney, Colin Hardy, Peter Hassall, Jill Hawes, Tony Holmyard, Pat Holmyard, Samantha Howlett, Philip Jones, Margaret Kelly (Mrs Hohmann), A. D. (Bert) Kinnear, Cathy Lambert, John Lawton, Andy Morton, Thelma Phelps, Tony Purvis, Austin Rawlinson, Peter Rawlinson, David Reeves, Brian Relf, Ann Reynolds, Amanda Richards, M. C. Lee Robinson, Marl Rutter, Norman Sarsfield, Mrs Shaikh, Jane Sheard, Susan Sloman, David Smith, David Sparkes, John Stitt, Derek Stubbs, Keith Thomson, Alan Towse, Alfred Turner, Richard Underwood, John Wardley, Sydney Ward, Aline Williams, Joy Woodward.

Sports Organisations:

N. Bramwell, Hon. General Secretary, English Schools Swimming Association, Hollowell, Northamptonshire. J. Plumridge, British Paralympics Association, Croydon. M.C.L. Robinson, Swimming Teachers Association, Anchor House, Birch Street, Walsall, West Midlands.

Archive Depositories and Libraries:

The editor of the *Swimming Times* and the librarian of the Amateur Swimming Association at Loughborough for access to the collections of illustrations in their care.

City Archivist, Solicitor and Secretary's Department, Guildhall, Bath.

The Head of Service and Staff, Bath Museums and Historic Buildings, Bridge Street, Bath.

The Head of Libraries and Information Services and the staff of the Archives Office, Central Library, William Brown Street, Liverpool.

The Librarian and Staff of the Pilkington Library, Loughborough University, Loughborough.

The Guildhall Librarian and Director of Libraries and Art Galleries, and the Keeper of Manuscripts, Guildhall Library, Aldermanbury, London.

The Librarian and Staff of the Bodleian Library, Oxford University, Oxford.

Photographs and Illustrations

We have contacted owners of copyright directly for permission to reproduce items. Although we have taken care to trace owners of copyright we should be pleased to hear from any owner who has been overlooked.

Text Preparation

We thank Mrs Gloria Brentnall for help with wordprocessing part of the text from manuscript and for assistance in making two wordprocessing systems compatible to produce the final text.

The index was prepared by Ms Suzanne Pattinson.

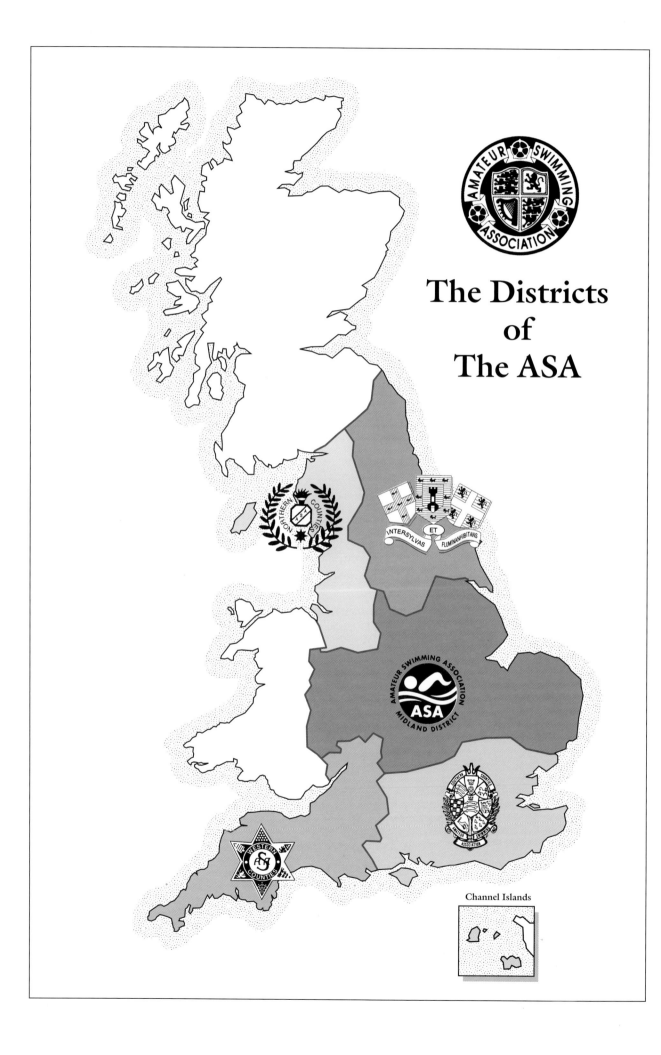

The Districts of The ASA

Channel Islands

Contents

Abbreviations

Various abbreviations are commonly used in the world of swimming and sport and below are those used in this book. Some titles of organisations are given in full on the first occasion that they appear in the text together with the appropriate commonly used abbreviation.

AAA	Amateur Athletic Association
ADA	Amateur Diving Association
ASA	Amateur Swimming Association
ASAMD	ASA Midland District
ASFGB	Amateur Swimming Federation of Great Britain
ASU	Amateur Swimming Union
BBC	British Broadcasting Corporation
BLDAS	British Long Distance Swimming Association
CCPR	Central Council of Physical Recreation
CSA	Channel Swimming Association
ESSA	English Schools Swimming Association
FINA	Fédération Internationale de Natation Amateur
IOC	International Olympic Committee
ISTC	Institute of Swimming Teachers and Coaches
ITV/ITA	Independent Television Authority
LEN	League Européenne de Natation
MSA	Metropolitan Swimming Association
NASI	National Association of Swimming Instructors
NCASA	Northern Counties ASA
NCU	National Cycling Union
NECASA	North Eastern Counties ASA
NUT	National Union of Teachers
SC	Swimming Club
SCASA	Southern Counties ASA
STA	Swimming Teachers Association
TV	Television
WCASA	Western Counties ASA

Chapter 1:
Swimming towards organisation

Comment by A. Sinclair and W. Henry in 1894.

'Prior to the year 1869 there was very little if, indeed, any distinction between amateur and professional swimmers. The baths were few in number, ill constructed, and badly ventilated and the race meetings of a rough and ready character which beggars description. There were very few clubs to control racing, and the swimmers were allowed any amount of latitude.'

Introduction

Swimming in the 1990s is the leading leisure activity in Britain. Whether swimmers recognise it or not, this situation has been achieved largely through the work of the Amateur Swimming Association (ASA). Its campaigns for the provision of facilities and sound teaching opened up to large numbers the opportunity to learn to swim and enjoy all aspects of swimming, including safety and survival in the water. The task of this book is to explain how, when, where and why the ASA came into being and its progress in identifying and achieving its aims until the end of its 125th year. In doing so, it is intended to put the Association in its rightful place as a major sports organisation.

Since this book is devoted to explaining how the ASA has contributed to making swimming what it has become for so many people in Britain today the history of swimming skills or the attainments of particular swimmers are discussed only when they have relevance to the history of the ASA. However, for readers who wish to extend their knowledge of swimming in more detail or in the broader context, a list of sources together with a bibliography have been provided.

During the twentieth century many historians of sports have either ignored or chosen to exclude swimming and related water sports from their studies. For example, one the most recent detailed studies of sport which excluded swimming was *Sport and*

1

English pearl fishers at work. One presents a shell to the boatman. Another, in the shoal of fish, swims towards the viewer. This picture decorated a fifteenth-century manuscript. (Copyright: The Bodleian Library, Oxford. Ms. Bodley 264 (III) fol. 265 r)

the British, A Modern History by Richard Holt published in 1989. The author explained that his decision to exclude water sports was in order to make his subject more manageable. One of the exceptions is The *Oxford Companion to British Sport* edited by John Arlott in 1985; however, the attention to any one sport was necessarily of a summary nature. It is also the case that most popular histories of specific sports focus on the record holders rather than on the administration, social organisation and economic structures which have made it possible for large numbers of people to participate. Among the few to have received such attention to their underlying structures have been cricket and association football.

This account of the emergence and development of the ASA over the century and a quarter since 1869 has demanded the use of a wide range of sources of information as the references and acknowledgements indicate. These sources have been used to trace the interplay of the Association with educational, political and other social institutions, and to show the way in which the ASA responded to changes in values, attitudes and technologies by creating an organisation capable of achieving its underlying goals. The details of this development are set out in the following chapters. However, before this fuller account focussed on the ASA it is useful to place in context swimming as an unregulated activity.

Before the nineteenth century

Evidence of the emergence of swimming seems to be available from many parts of the world but it seems impossible to say where swimming began. Western historians usually outline the known references to swimming in the civilizations of the Mediterranean basin and the Middle East. During the later nineteenth century anthropological evidence and narratives from other parts of the world indicated that humans had learned to swim without the benefits of cultural diffusion from the Mediterranean area, once seen as the only cradle of civilisation. Thus, it is probable that the peoples of the British Isles possessed knowledge of swimming in prehistoric times. However, many modern historical narratives draw upon printed books, in particular those produced in the British Isles, to repeat accounts of swimming in Classical Greek and Roman times and the evidence for its re-emergence in the guides to swimming in printed instruction books of the Renaissance.

Reappraisals of the evidence about swimming suggest that it had its origins long before the creation of any written record. For example, it has been established that new born babies have the innate ability to swim even though the skill disappears very rapidly unless it is deliberately encouraged. In parts of the world near rivers, lakes and the seas, people have retained and developed their swimming skills for pleasure and to meet various needs and challenges of their environment.

Written records tell us that the Romans organised the teaching of soldiers to swim in the River Tiber. It is not known how extensive this practice was amongst the imperial army units recruited and trained far from Rome, or, whether it had any importance for the British provinces. However, illustrations of swimming in British manuscripts from the era prior to printed books, survive today. One example from the fifteenth century shows that the value of pearls encouraged swimmers to search for these treasures (Pearls formed part of the jewelry of the English royal regalia). Swimming for pleasure did not seem to attract the attentions of early artists. However, cases of drowning featured in legal records of the fourteenth and fifteenth centuries when summarised evidence often pointed to death arising not from the inablity to swim but from getting into difficulties when swimming.

We do not know how many people swam in any century before our own or who their teachers were. How the skills of swimming were used or transmitted seem to have been unrecorded before the publication in 1531 of *The Governour* by Thomas Elyot. This author advocated swimming as an art valuable in time of war. ,The first book to give instructions about the methods of swimming, which was published in England, was *De Arte Natandi (Of the Art of Swimming)* by Everard Digby in 1587. Digby took some risks because the University of Cambridge by a decree of 1571, had forbidden any of its members to swim anywhere in the county. The decree gave no specific explanation for the prohibi-

tion beyond saying that it was for *'serious and grave'* reasons. Digby, himself, believed that teaching the art of swimming would reduce the loss of undergraduate life as a result of boating accidents on the Cam. His work was written in Latin and began by lamenting that swimming was not as much practised as in earlier times and that the decline was especially marked amongst the aristocracy. The work was translated into English by Christopher Middleton in 1595 and translated into other languages during the seventeenth century. Relatively few printed references to swimming occurred in English in the late sixteenth or early seventeenth centuries although William Shakespeare, in his less well-known play, *Henry VIII* (III, 2, 358) commented on 'little wanton boys that swim on bladders'. Francis Bacon, the polymath and courtier, advocated swimming in his *Historia Vitae et Mortis* of 1623, and at the end of the seventeenth century Thomas Randolph of Queens' College, Cambridge, wrote:

> *'When bashful daylight once was gone*
> *And night, that hides the blush, came on,*
> *Six pretty nymphs, to wash away*
> *The sweating summer's day,*
> *In Cam's fair stream did gently swim*
> *And naked bathe each curious limb'.*

The workaday need for fishermen to swim, and for sailors and shipwrights at sea to inspect or repair vessels remained largely unchronicled. Many eighteenth-century mariners of the Royal Navy lacked the ability to swim and drowned when vessels caught fire or were shipwrecked. For example, in 1758 Rear Admiral Broderick spent over an hour in the water when his flag ship the

Woodcut illustrations in Everard Digby's De Arte Natandi show a man floating in a river cutting his toe nails whilst another formed part of an explanation of 'circumvolution'.

This sea bathing machine at Scarborough appeared in a print produced by Setterington in 1735. A naked gentleman stands at the door which is held open by a liveried servant. (Copyright: Local Collections, Scarborough Public Library)

Prince George sank and only 256 of the crew of 721 had survived, the rest being presumed drowned because they were unable to swim. These tragedies did not cause the Admiralty to encourage all who went to sea to learn to swim. That responsibility was a matter left to the individual of whatever rank.

Soldiers able to swim had tactical value, although we have no records of how many possessed such skills. Ironically, one episode during the civil wars indicated that the ability to swim might be a mixed blessing. During a Royalist uprising in 1654 in the Trossachs of Scotland, Royalist supporters took shelter on an island in Loch Katrine. The Parliamentarians needed to transport their soldiers to the island so one soldier swam to the island to collect a boat seen tied-up there. As the soldier attempted to loose the boat from its moorings a highland woman beheaded him with a sword! In *An Essay Upon Projects* published in 1697, when Great Britain was at war with France, Daniel Defoe (author of *Robinson Crusoe*) advocated the creation of a Royal Academy for Military Exercises to improve the capability of the nation to defend itself. Amongst subjects in the suggested curriculum of the Academy was 'Swimming, which no soldier, and indeed no man whatever, ought to be without'.

Swimming in specially constructed baths rather than in the sea or in rivers and lakes seems to have begun in England during the eighteenth century. For example, the baths of the spa facilities at Bath were used by swimmers. Fashionable visitors for medicinal purposes are recorded to have been intrigued by mixed bathing and the kinds of costumes worn in the water. Nonetheless swimming remained popular and by 1829 the Spa's entrepreneurs had employed Decimus Burton to design a tepid bath for swimmers which was fed from the hot springs. One of the earliest purpose built swimming baths was in existence at Pearless Head, Shoreditch in north London, by 1743. Several other swimming baths had been constructed in the London area by the end of the century. We do not know the extent to which swimming was taught or learned dur-

ing this period, but newspapers and magazines reported deaths by drowning and often emphasised the swimming skills of those who rescued people in danger of drowning.

Fashion also played its part in sustaining the popularity of sea bathing. Scarborough boasted of its facilities for taking a dip in the sea and there survives a print depicting a bathing machine which dates from the mid eighteenth century. In the later years of the eighteenth century Dr Russell of Brighton argued that sea water contained all the properties once claimed exclusively for spa waters. This opinion came to dominate fashionable medical opinion and contributed to the upsurge in the popularity of swimming at seaside resorts. Benjamin Beale has been claimed to have invented the bathing machine (a mobile hut enabling the shy to undress unseen and to enter the water without being observed) which was in use at Margate before the end of the century. The fashion of sea bathing for health gained momentum during the blockades of the Napoleonic Wars (1803-1815) when the embargoes on trade and travel between the warring countries came into effect in 1807 and the well-off no longer took holidays on the European continent.

The nineteenth century

Swimming like many other physical sports and pastimes became more organised in the nineteenth century. Moves from the casual enjoyment of swimming to specialised clubs and systematic teaching and competitions seem to have arisen for several reasons. One of the most powerful was the development of reliable and rapid transport over long distances, particularly as a result of the creation of a basic railway network by 1850. It transformed the British Isles from a series of localities and self-regarding regions into an increasingly unified state. In turn this rapid means of transport gave impetus to the growth of local, regional and nationwide competitions. This could occur because railway timetables permitted reliable schedules of events to be drawn up and it had become practical for games and sports to be played at venues attracting sportspeople and supporters from over much of the country. In turn these developments required agreements about how games and sports should be played and on what terms. Guarantees of fairplay were crucially important in competitions and, for those who enjoyed gambling, there existed a strong impetus for clarity about rules and conditions relating to performance in each sport.

During the nineteenth century the commercial aspects of games and sports became increasingly dominant. Businesses associated with sport and entertainment catered for an expanding urban population with incomes to enjoy leisure. Entrepreneurs invested in building venues, for example for horse racing, cricket and boxing. These attracted competitors and spectators because they gave opportunities for the participants to demonstrate prowess, to gain prestige and to earn large purses. Railway companies not only carried crowds to events but they owned hotels to lodge players, officials and spectators away from home. Other companies sold food and drink to the pleasure-seeking visitors. Press reports of events added to the knowledge and enthusiasm of the general public. Swimming benefited from this coverage from the middle of the nineteenth century and largely in local newspapers. The London *Times* only gave occasional reports, and these were sometimes at second hand. For example, 3 July 1866, *The Times* reported on a gala, which signals the interest in medals, distances and times, held in the Serpentine in Hyde Park, London, although it did so by reproducing the following from the *Pall-mall Gazette*:

'Swimming. - The match for the gold medal open, to all who have never before won a similar, was swum yesterday in the Serpentine from the rails to the Kensington-Bridge, a thousand yards. There were 22 entries, and 21 started, Mr John Latey, the Hon. Secretary of the London Swimming Club, acting as referee, vice Mr Williamson, the President, who was unavoidably absent. There was a capital start, Mr W. Cole having the best, and Mr D.J. Aviss, of Coventry, the worst of it, but when a third of the distance had been "done", the last named gentleman went ahead at a strong pace, and won easily by 40 yards. Mr. J. Cole beat Mr W. Crinian for second place by five yards, and Mr W. Cole as fourth man, headed a very straggling division as placed thus:- Mr G. Parrott, Mr C. Whyte, Mr W. Long, Mr S. Hicks, and others coming in the course of the morning. The winner did the distance in 18 minutes 29.25 seconds, and the second and third divided the entrance money, Mr Crinian preferring a medal to the coin. There was an enormous assemblage of spectators'.

Sports and games raised many questions about the social values of all those who were involved. Prominent contributors to the debates were Evangelical Christians who sought to glorify their faith by advocating the constructive use of leisure. A trite but very significant summary of their position was expressed as *Cleanliness is next to Godliness*. For them, freedom from the taints of time-wasting and dissipation of resources of all kinds gave swimming a leading place among acceptable sporting activities. Swimming had the virtues of not only emphasising cleanliness but of promoting healthy bodies. Swimmers could save life when the need arose, certainly their own and possibly someone else's. Side by side with these concerns, was the wish of many middle and upper

class evangelicals to extend the benefits of spiritual and physical health to the working classes who were less well educated and so assumed to be less able to use their time constructively. Thus, evangelicals were amongst the pressure group which sponsored the Baths and Wash Houses Acts of 1846, 1847 and later additions. Many boroughs adopted the powers available through these laws in subsequent years.

During the same period leaders in public school education and in the armed services repeatedly asserted the advantages of sports, including swimming, in forming physically fit people with high moral values. One of the first public schools to take swimming seriously was Eton College which, after 1839, employed an instructor and made use of a special enclosure beside the River Thames. The advance of formal teaching of swimming was limited to privately financed schools for boys. It was not until the second half of the century that steps were taken to extend physical education (which might include swimming) to state schools in some areas of the country (This is discussed at greater length in chapter 2).

The rise of swimming clubs

A letter in *The Amateur Swimmer* of 1926 suggested that a case for the earliest date for the foundation of a swimming club in England could be made for the Huddersfield and Lockwood SC which was said to have held a gala at the Lockwood baths in 1825. Certainly there is good evidence that swimmers organised clubs in some large towns during the first half of the nineteenth century, although it is not always easy to give a precise date for their establishment. An early, well-documented example was the St George's Club in Liverpool whose members swam in the first municipally owned baths built in Britain. These were erected in 1828 and the Club began in the same year. Once in being, swimming clubs did not necessarily last for any length of time. Membership waxed and waned depending on the organisation and funding as well as on the programmes which attracted members support. Undoubtedly financial pressures obliged the more ambitious clubs to devise programmes of events which would attract paying spectators. There seems little doubt that contests between individual swimmers or teams proved popular where purses rather than medals were on offer. The prizes were in goods rather than money as for example, a leg of mutton and a cask of beer at the first gala of the Jersey SC in 1866. The Jersey SC has been continously active since its foundation. A number of clubs claim a similar continuity of activity since the 1860s, before the formation of the ASA. Those with continuity of records included Brighton (1860), Newcastle upon Tyne, and Durham City (1861).

Swimming clubs were influenced by the climate of competition which their members enjoyed. Many of these people belonged to other sporting organisations and the leading members of clubs often came from the middle or even upper classes who had the time and the managerial skills to form bodies to regulate their sports. For example, in September, 1868, *The Times* reported on a swimming gala held at the Royal Military College of Sandhurst, Surrey, which had adopted swimming as a sport in the 1860s and possessed facilites of a high standard. The gala comprised a series of competitive races for the cadets with prizes awarded by the professors. The organiser, Captain Webb, was complimented on the

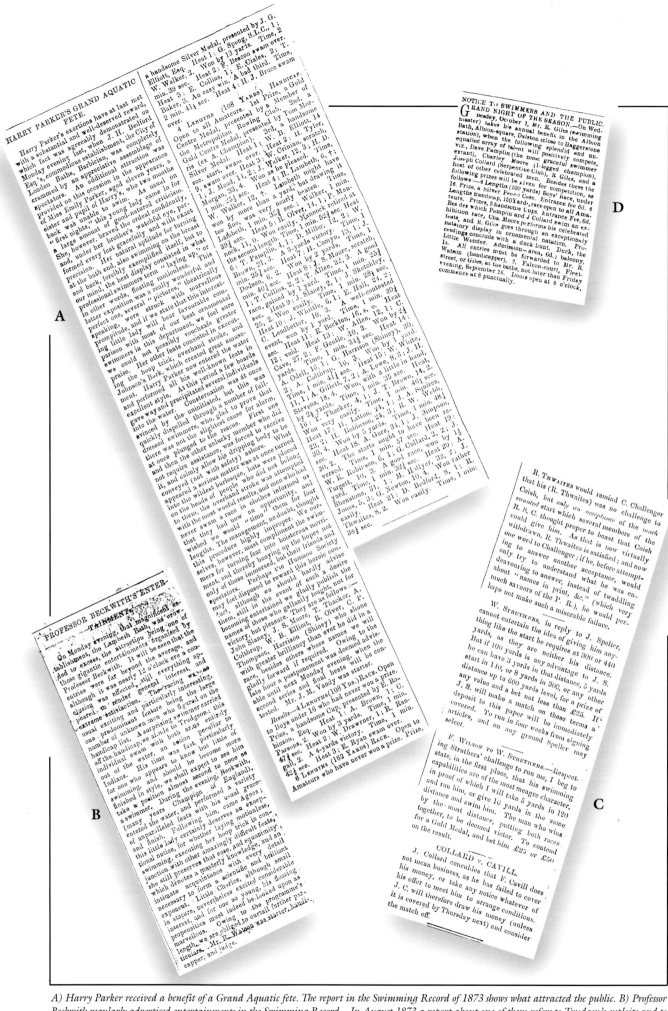

A) Harry Parker received a benefit of a Grand Aquatic fete. The report in the Swimming Record of 1873 shows what attracted the public. B) Professor Beckwith regularly advertised entertainments in the Swimming Record. In August 1873 a report about one of them refers to Trudgen's exploits and to ornamental and scientific swimming by Beckwith's family. C) Betting and professionalism. Challenges such as these listed in 1873 threatened the highest ideals of amateurs. Bookmakers encouraged gambling by giving odds on such contests. Cheating was said to be rife and results did not reflect the true prowess of the swimmers. D) Professional's held benefit nights such as Giles's in 1873.

safety precautions to prevent mishaps and on the entertaining interludes for the spectators.

A further feature of the more systematic approach to swimming which was developing during the middle of the nineteenth century was the appearance of teachers of swimming. They were more likely to be associated with particular pools than with specific clubs and advertised as freelance professors offering to teach their skills for a fee. Some were themselves extremely successful competitive swimmers, for example Professor Beckwith who won considerable prize money in competitions. In October 1861 *The Times* reported that Deerfoot, the champion American runner, intended to race against Beckwith at Lambeth Baths, the purse to be £10 with a further £20 deposited on the night. The challenge was to swim 20 lengths with Deerfoot, described as 'the tawny son of the prairie', being given a 15 second start. 'Betting is going on very briskly between friends of the contending parties......' continued *The Times*. report. However, the outcome was never decided since Deerfoot withdrew two days before the contest and forfeited his pledge to Beckwith.

The growth of swimming facilities

Swimming in the sea for pleasure had always been a feature of coastal life. Organised sea racing had emerged by the middle years of the nineteenth century. For example, *The Times* carried a report of an event held at Plymouth in 1867 which gives information about the racing speeds of the time. Henry Gurr of London was first, completing 1000 yards in the time of 13 minutes 21 seconds. River swimming also continued. Even as late as the 1870s swimming championships were still organised in the Thames but had to be moved upstream to more salubrious surroundings. However, most expansion took place in the provision of swimming pools in inland towns and cities

Municipal investment in a range of provision for urban dwellers, together with private investment in leisure facilites for the increasing social groups with disposable incomes, combined to make the second half of the nineteenth century a period when the number and quality of swimming pools grew steadily. The private investor hoped to make money from the new enthusiasm for swimming. The municipal corporations were prompted to build baths and swimming pools in the interests of public health. The quality of the water in rivers deteriorated as this became a convenient way of disposing of wastes. Pollutants from industrial processes and outflows of sewers were known to make swimming hazardous.

Precise details of the first swimming baths are difficult to establish. The Cleveland Swimming Bath at Bath, built by a private company, was said to have opened in 1815 but surviving documentation suggests that in fact it was erected in about 1823 or 24 as an open air pool fed from cold springs on the site at Hampton Row adjacent to Sydney Gardens. Liverpool Corporation built

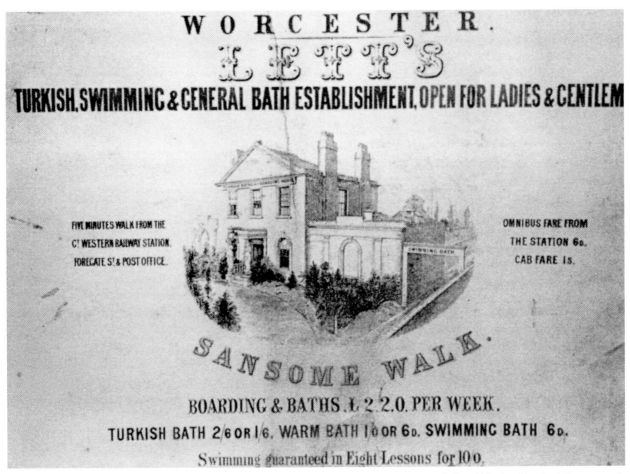

By the early 1860s Worcester had developed as a spa as well as being the county town. The advertisement implied a middle class clientele willing to pay to be pampered in a luxurious Turkish bath and wanting to enjoy swimming.

the first public baths in England at St George's Pierhead in 1828 with the specific intention of providing facilities for the teaching of swimming in the context of a debate about avoidable loss of life at sea. Concerns about public health had less importance at that time. The baths drew their salt water from the tidal River Mersey. Interestingly Liverpool Corporation only built the baths and left the management to the swimming clubs which leased them.

Few descriptions of the interiors of swimming baths survive. However the following description by Granville in *Spas of England and Principal Sea-bathing Places* of one of the baths in Bath during the 1840s indicates the standards which could be reached:

> 'Contiguous to the Royal Private Baths is that elegant oval piscina, or swimming bath, sixty feet long, twenty-one wide, holding thirty-six thousand gallons of water, the heat of which is kept at what is called a tepid temperature, by admitting the thermal water from the source of the King's Bath at the same time with other water from the same spring, previously cooled in a reservoir. ..... A series of windows and a dome-lantern light the interior, around which are openings leading to separate and convenient dressing rooms, whence the bathers descend by steps into the baths'.

The needs of women swimmers were ignored by the reformers of the public health laws during the 1840s and early 1850s. Arguments for change appeared in various quarters. The Ladies' National Association for the Diffusion of Sanitary Knowledge, an organisation devoted to promoting women's health, urged that women be taught to swim. Harriet Martineau, a prominent advocate of reforms on behalf of the evangelical movement, published

an article on 'How to Learn to Swim' in the magazine *Once A Week* in 1859. Some progress was being made. *The English Women's Journal* of the previous year, 1858, described the opening of a bath for ladies. In the same year the magazine *Work and Leisure* reported that St Marylebone opened its baths to the *'feminine public'* and commented:

> '........though the cost of admission is very moderate, being only eight pence, this is a higher price than is charged for any other bath in the establishment, and therefore quite sufficient to keep it select'.

The charge for women equalled an average working woman's daily earnings at this time and was several times that levied on men who came from the better off working class. Women users who could afford such charges were likely to come from the middle class.

A further indication of the way in which women swimmers were ignored is that fact that separate accounts of the activities of women swimmers rarely appeared in newspapers and general magazines. Journalists of the mid nineteenth century, invariably men who reported on women's sporting activities, often did so in terms suggesting that the events were a *curiosity*, either to be regarded as extraordinary, or to be mocked.

Movements for organisating swimming

Recognition of the advantages of orderly development and the establishment of a national focus for swimming occurred as early as 1836. In that year Mr J. Strachan at Dean Street, Westminster, established the National Swimming Society for *teaching and promoting swimming throughout the empire*. The reference to the imperial dimension echoed what was happening in other sports where there existed a growing consciousness of taking English, if not British, cultural activities to all parts of the world where the flag flew. The British Swimming Society, formed in 1840, had rather different objectives, namely to '*promote health and cleanliness by encouraging swimming, and by gratuitously giving instructions in the art*'. An insight into the society's activities comes from the report in *Bell's Life in London* about their third annual dinner on Tuesday, 5 September 1843. The secretary reported that the Society had increased support and that more people were swimming in the Serpentine. At the conclusion of the speeches prizes were awarded to competitors. At the meeting, Thomas Wakley, M.P. was in the chair. Wakely had founded *The Lancet*, a medical journal, which campaigned for many reforms including the removing corrupt practices from the work of the Royal College of Surgeons and stopping the addition of harmful adulterants to food and drink. His concern for swimming placed particular emphasis on clear and fair rules for competition.

Difficulties faced those seeking to translate their intentions of making swimming a nationwide competitive sport into reality. For example, in 1843, the newspaper, *Bell's Life in London*, reported of the experience of the National Swimming Society which had:

> '.... sent free to Plymouth, two years ago, by Mr F. Bellamy, of that town, a set of silver medals etc, to be competed for by the numerous youthful swimmers of that great seaport, under the immediate superintendance of Mr Bellamy and

B. Wyon designed the medal for the National Swimming Society founded by John Strachan on 30 June 1837. Although it was called 'national' the society did not survive beyond the 1840s.

friends. The prizes have, nevertheless, to the chagrin of the Society, been returned uncontended for, and in all probability have never been heard of by the youths of that locality. The medals, we learn, are engraved, and, of course, inapplicable to any other place. As the fine weather, which is well suited for such healthful sport, cannot long continue, we would recommend the swimmers of Plymouth to wait immediately upon some public-spirited gentlemen, admirers of the art, who could instantly have again the prizes, "bring off the races", in fair play, and award them to the winner, that Plymouth may, like other towns, through her "swimming representative", be entitled to contend for honour, in the approaching grand national struggle in the Serpentine river, Hyde-park'.

The choice of Plymouth as a centre must have appeared to make good sense even though communications were relatively slow. Not only was it a major naval base and an international commercial port but it was the most important town in the south west. Its leading position in the region had been recognised in 1841 when the British Association for the Advancement of Science selected it for one of their early annual meetings. *Bell's* report implied that other centres had competitive swimming events with a prospect of a national race in London, though it is not clear how extensive such activites were elsewhere in England.

The existence of two bodies concurrently claiming to represent swimming throughout the country probably diminished their validity and impact on swimming and on public opinion. They seemed to have disappeared from the record within a short time. A successful attempt to organise swimming on a national basis had to wait for a further twenty years.

In 1868 a group of leaders in some of the London swimming clubs took the initiative to advertise in the newspapers *Bell's Life in London* and the *Sporting Chronicle* calling a Swimming Congress with the aim of forming an organisation to improve competitive swimming. They chose as the venue the recently opened Turnhalle in Kings Cross, London. The Turnhalle was a purpose built gymnasium, originally opened in 1866. It was established by Ernest Ravenstein for German residents in London wishing to continue to enjoy the pleasures of indoor physical exercises similar to those available in Germany. The clientele rapidly grew, attracting large numbers of British men and women, with Mrs Ravenstein holding special classes for women. The ambience of this venue favoured new sporting ventures and the first meeting of the Swimming Congress met with Mr Ravenstein in the chair.

The meeting at the Turnhalle held on 7 January 1869 may be viewed as the beginning of the Amateur Swimming Association although there were some changes in name and organisation before it can be recognised as the Association we know today. The name adopted at its February meeting was *Associated Metropolitan Swimming Clubs*. It had already established a group to formulate a constitution and when this was adopted on 24 June, the title was changed to the *London Swimming Association* (LSA). There seems to have been some debate about the use of London in the title, possibly because of the need to have support from swimming clubs elsewhere in England. A further, unminuted alteration of name occurred, so that from the beginning of

The Turnhalle, in 1995 at Kings Cross, London, was the meeting place of the Swimming Congress which set up the London Swimming Association, soon to rename itself the Metropolitan Swimming Association. The German Gymnastics Society erected the building in 1864-5 to the design of Edward Gruning.

1870 the organisation became the *Metropolitan Swimming Association* (MSA) and the accounts presented for 1870 bore that name. Early in 1870 the meetings of the MSA moved to the London University Hotel for an annual rent of 10 shillings. Only a small number of London clubs joined the MSA even though the body tried to strike a more authoritative tone in the news items it sent to the press. Comments in the sporting press made mock of their ambitious ideas and were rarely sympathetic.

The following swimming clubs were founder members of the LSA: Alliance; North London; Serpentine; National; West London; and St Pancras. In order to provide financial stability each guaranteed to pay 5 guineas payable over 3 years. In its first year, 1869, the LSA had an income of £19 10s 6d, of which £10 11s 9d was carried forward to the following year. Subscriptions accounted for £13 9s 0d. Prizes for the championship cost the LSA £3 5s 6d. One of its earliest promotions was the amateur English Men's Mile Championship. The first of this annual event took place in 1870; the course ran along the River Thames from Putney Aqueduct to Hammersmith Bridge. However, in 1873 the venue was changed to the Serpentine because of the problems of allowing for the currents in the river and its unpleasant pollutants.

From the beginning the Association was concerned with the development of all swimming sports, including what later became known as Water Polo. A Notice of Motion by Mr J. Daniels dated 14 April 1870 suggested that '*a committee of four be appointed by the association for the purpose of drawing up a code of rules for the management of the game of football in the water*'. The next meeting carried this motion and the four nominees included Daniels. Although Daniels stated that the proposals would be brought before the Association in the winter months, the project, like many other attempts to draw up regulations, seemed to have been delayed and there is no further reference to it.

METROPOLITAN ASSOCIATION.

We have received several letters respecting the stability and existing apathy displayed by the many gentlemen who are intimately connected with this amalgamation. It is not our province to suggest or imply motives one way or the other, but we certainly think that it seems a pity to see an institution so prolific of good results disappear entirely from amongst the many creditable institutions of our metropolis. The latter result will most positively be the Association's fate ere long, unless some additional interest becomes infused into it. We shall sincerely look forward to a little more activity amongst the delegates, who ought at this period to be exerting themselves towards organising the Amateur Championship, which will if swam this year, produce excitement and contention far beyond previous events for that honour.

The MSA received unfavourable press coverage as in the June 1873 Swimming Record. Clubs sent any available members to the meetings who were often unfamiliar with the business. Decisions made at previous meetings were often overturned.

The MSA stated formally in its constitution that its principal purpose was to 'promote and encourage the art of swimming', this in context of 'the highest values associated with the "amateur"'. Arriving at an acceptable definition of *amateur* took many years and culminated in what was to be a final change of name to the Amateur Swimming Association. Practices current in the 1860s and 1870s blurred the lines between the professional and the amateur. In the Association much time was spent in the years between 1869 and 1874 in trying to clarify what was exclusively amateur and exclusively professional and establishing how practical criteria could be monitored and policed effectively. Such debates as well the conflicts of personalities and purposes with the MSA resulted in it being described at this time as 'a tempest tossed institution' in the memories of R. P. Watson. At one meeting a member even proposed that that MSA should organise an athletics match but this gained no support, being contrary to the purposes of the Association.

Inspite of these difficulties the MSA took some important practical steps to assert and implement its claim to be the main organiser of national swimming. It kept its clear focus, for example, and moved towards systematic assessment of performance, agreed descriptions of swimming strokes, and the achievement of fair standards. As with other sporting organisations such as those associated with cricket, golf and horse racing, the MSA sought to provide leadership in achieving the objectives of promoting and encouraging swimming in a framework of agreed regulations. The story of how the Amateur Swimming Association grew from such beginnings to the organisation which it is today is the subject of the remainder of this book.

METROPOLITAN ASSOCIATION.

According to promise, we, this week, publish the laws of amateur swimming, with the view of placing before our provincial readers, a subject which will better enable them to grapple more satisfactorily with the Amateur *versus* Professional Question. In order to successfully decide this moot point, we will gladly publish the views of any correspondent. Owing to the pressure upon our columns we are obliged to refrain from enlarging upon the Association, but intend, next week, to give the number of years it has been established, officers, the various amateur champions, clubs comprising it, and the number of prizes given to those who have swam second and third.

LAWS OF AMATEUR SWIMMING.

1.—Persons who have competed for money prizes, for wagers, for public or admission money, or who have otherwise made the art of swimming a means of pecuniary profit, shall not be allowed to compete as amateurs.

2.—Any amateur competing against a professional swimmer shall be disqualified from all future amateur contests.

3.—Winners of club prizes shall not be disqualified from open competitions.

4.—Application for entry to any competition to be made to the persons appointed by the donor or donors of the prize, and to contain the applicant's correct name and address; and if a member of any recognised swimming, gymnastic, athletic, or similar club, the name of the club also, and to be accompanied with the amount of entrance fee.

5.—If it be proved that a person has entered in an incorrect name, or under any other false pretence, he shall forfeit the amount of his entrance fee, and be disqualified from entering any open competition for a period to be determined upon by the Association.

6.—Any objection to the qualification of a competitor must be lodged with the umpire or hon. sec. of the Association, within fourteen days.

7.—When the qualification of any competitor is objected to, the umpire or hon. sec. shall inform him of the same.

8.—When any person, other than an officer of the Association, lodges an objection against a competitor, he shall be required to deposit the sum of five shillings with the umpire or hon. sec.; and if unable to prove the same, shall forfeit the sum deposited to the Association.

9.—An umpire and a judge shall be appointed for each competition by the donor or donors of the prize; if necessary, the duties of umpire and judge may be combined in one official.

10.—At the time appointed for the start, the umpire shall read over the names of those entered for the competition, and any person not answering to his name at that time, shall be considered a non-starter, and shall forfeit the amount of his entrance fee.

11.—The choice of stations at starting shall be determined by ballot, except in handicaps, when the umpire shall place the competitors in their respective positions.

12.—The umpire previous to the start, shall describe, in the hearing of all the competitors, the course of the competition and the spot where it shall end. Should they be required to round any object, he shall also describe in what manner it shall be rounded. If a boat be the goal, it (where practicable) to be secured moored at both ends.

13.—The start to be directed by the umpire who, when he is satisfied that all competitors are ready, shall sim give the word "go."

14.—Any start made before the umpire order, shall be deemed a false st and the competitors be required return to their stations. Any competitor failing to do so to be qualified.

15.—Any competitor rounding an ob contrary to the umpire's direction and not turning back, shall also disqualified.

16.—If there be more competitors than sufficient for one heat, they sha divided by ballot.

17.—If in any competition a dead ensues, the competitors shall contend at such time and place umpire may direct.

18.—The umpire shall be sole judge foul that may take place.

19.—It is the province of the umpire, appealed to," to decide a for any competitor refusing to ob order shall be disqualified from competitions, for a period to be mined upon by the Association

20.—Any competitor "swimming must complete the entire from start to finish, in order to himself as the winner.

21.—If a competitor shall become fied, the umpire shall forw name, address, &c., together disqualification, to the h within ten days: these re all cases, to be made in wri signed by the umpire.

22.—In the event of a dispute ari none of the foregoing l upon, the Association shall power to deal with any su they may think fit.

23.—That no new law be made, or foregoing laws amended, rescinded, unless with the a majority of the membe at a general meeting spec for that puposo.

'Laws of amateur swimming' were publicised in the Swimming Record after the agreed code was made in November, 1873. These laws did not end the controversy about the meaning of amateur.

IMPORTANT MEETING OF THE ME-
TROPOLITAN ASSOCIATION.

One of the best meetings ever held in
connection with this amalgamation took
place last Monday evening at the Yorkshire
Grey, Fitzroy-street, Fitzroy-square, under
Mr. H. G. Smith's (Regent S C.) presidency.
Amongst those present we observed Messrs.
W. J. Everton (Alliance S.C.), hon. sec.,
A. Colthrup (South London S.C.), W. Kent
(Regent S.S.), E. Watts (St. Pancras S.C.),
C. A. Challenger (hon. sec. Regent S.C.),
and W. E. Robinson (Alliance S.C.) The
minutes having been read and
and confirmed, it was unanimously agreed to
call a special general meeting for the revision of the laws of amateur swimming,
which will take place on Monday, December
8th. Every swimmer is particularly requested to attend, the patronage and opinions
of provincial swimmers being earnestly
solicited. At this juncture a discussion
arose respecting the subscription cards
issued in the interests of the Amateur Championship; and it having been proved that
many gentlemen were anxious to hand over
the proceeds, which amounted to something
considerable, Mr. W. Kent proposed, and
Mr. W. E. Robinson seconded, that all subscription cards be at once called in, so that
the amount could be submitted to those who
assemble on December 8. A rather animated
debate now ensued on the propriety o
transforming the title of Metropolitan Association into something more general, which
would embrace the provinces and country
throughout. Mr. Everton argued that
" countrymen " were entitled to a deal of consideration, were a most powerful body, and
providing they could be induced to co-operate
with the association's members, he felt sure
an amicable and just reconciliation of the
amateur *versus* professional question could
be very readily brought about. To this Mr.
Smith, in reply, expressed his concurrence.
He was confident that the time had now
arrived for prompt and decisive action, considering, therefore, the overwhelming majority of swimmers outside London compared
with this city he felt sure that provincial
support ought to be solicited. Mr. A. Colthrup, in dilating upon this necessity, advocated a branch, which was generally acceded
to. In dismissing the subject Mr. Everton
gave a notice of motion, which will come on
at the next " hearing," that the title of
" Metropolitan Association " undergoes a
metamorphosis. The question of an entertainment was now mooted. It will, perhaps,
be remembered that for this purpose Mr. J.
H. Bedford, proprietor of the City of London Baths, kindly offered to place his establishment at the Association's disposal, but
through some unforeseen circumstance the
favour, although gladly accepted, was aban-
doned. It was now proposed by Mr. W.
Kent, and seconded by Mr. R. Watson, that
a letter be at once written to Mr. Bedford
containing the association's high opinion of
his generosity, paramount desire to enhance
swimming, and above all for his kind and
liberal offer. The Excelsior and Leander
Medals, won by Messrs. Davenport and Cot-
tam for swimming second and third in the
Amateur Championship, are now being engraved, and will shortly be ready for presentation. Owing to the majority, if
not all, of our provincial subscribers
being entirely unacquainted with the present
laws of amateur swimming, we beg to state
that on Saturday next we will publish them
in their integrity: after which we hope to
hear more upon the subject, when a portion
of these columns will be religiously devoted
to the opinions of those who may favour us
with their views. The proposition that the
letter given below be published, came from
Mr. C. A. Challenger, seconded by Mr. E.
Watts :—

To THE EDITOR OF THE SWIMMING RECORD.

SIR,—Will you kindly insert the following proposition, which was duly carried at a
general meeting of the M.S.A., held on the
10th instant.

Gentlemen interested in the subject are
particularly requested to attend at the next
meeting of the Association, on Dec. 8th.
Yours,
W. J. EVERTON,
Hon. Sec.

NOTICE.

[We beg to inform our readers that we do not
hold ourselves responsible for the views expressed by correspondents. Our columns are
open to the ventilation of any subject, good,
bad, or indifferent, in order that a friendly and
successful termination may be arrived at.—
ED.]

THE LATE AMATEUR CHAMPION-
SHIP.

To THE EDITOR OF THE SWIMMING RECORD.

SIR,—
Having seen your valuable paper to-day
(Sept. 6th), I was rather surprised to find my
name published in connection with Mr. Wilson's ; that the latter should be barred from
swimming in an amateur race I consider a
shame, particularly when there are others
who transgress with impunity. It is perfectly
true that Mr. Wilson did compete against a
professional, and I myself am open to swim
any man in the world scientifically, either
above or under water the Marquis Bibbero included. It appears rather strange to me that
the latter did not answer my last challenge,
which was issued through the *Sporting Life.*
I am yours, &c.,
J. W. BIRKS, Liverpool.

[We beg to inform Mr. Birks, in answer to
a question not published, that the Metropolitan Association obtained their knowledge
entirely through this journal.—ED.]

To THE EDITOR OF THE SWIMMING RECORD.

SIR,—
It would be more satisfactory if the laws
of amateur swimming were better known
through your columns. If swimming against
Birks constitutes a man a professional, it is
difficult to know where this imperial code
begins or ends. We have boys at 15 years
of age in this town who have swum for, and
won, money; pray, does this consti-
tute them professionals, exclude all from
contesting against amateurs, and if by mere
chance some other boy should swim against
them, would he be debarred from amateur
competition? Such absurdities are merely
contemptible, and such laws quite unworthy
of being respected. Pray, what are the
names of this self-constituted authority, who
make laws to edge themselves round for
protection from the overwhelming superiority of country amateurs, who have no
ambition to be dubbed professional. Let the
laws be known, and the framers of such laws
also, that country bumpkins may consider
whether to respect them or not; and if such
laws are only applicable to the Metropolitan
district, and not universal (of course, Metro-
politans may make such laws as they please
for self-protection), then let a geographical
line be drawn, outside of which they have
no power, where country men will make
their own laws and interpret them, without
the interference of any self-constituted
hierarchy.
I am, Sir, your obedient servant,
WM. MILLIGAN,
Superintendent of the Rochdale Baths,
Lancashire.

CORRESPONDENCE.

NOTICE.

[We beg to inform our readers that we do not
hold ourselves responsible for the views expressed by correspondents. Our columns are
open to the ventilation of any subject, good,
bad, or indifferent, in order that a friendly and
successful termination may be arrived at.—
ED.]

THE LATE AMATEUR CHAMPION-
SHIP.

To THE EDITOR OF THE SWIMMING RECORD.

Sir,—My attention has been called to the
revision of the law of Amateurs *versus* Professionals. For years it has been held that
an amateur could contest with a professional
without forfeiting his title, always with the
understanding that with the money so won,
he bought some article of plate or adornment
for which he was bound to produce a receipt
if required.

By the new regulation, many country
swimmers are placed *hors de combat.* No
previous notice was given them, and the matter presses very heavily in many individual
cases ; for instance, J. Wilson, of Liverpool,
as good a gentleman amateur as can be, but
because he contested with Birks, he is disqualified. This I consider is very unfair ;
nor is the Association consistent in the
alteration made. They have allowed this
thing to go on for years to suit one of their
own clique, but, as that state of affairs no
longer suit their purposes, they suddenly revise their law to exclude good men like the
party I name, and I think that in a matter
so momentous as this, there ought to have
been a congress of swimming men from all
England, who could then have settled the
matter once for all, and to the satisfaction of
every party. I write in good faith.
Yours respectfully,
MARQUIS BIBBERO,
A lover of the life saving art.

---

*Defining Amateur. In September 1873 a letter in the Swimming
Record from the Superintendent of the Baths at Rochdale, Lancashire,
contributed to the great debate about definitions of amateur and professional. Letters from professionals such as Marquis Bibbero emphasised their hostility to stricter definitions of amateur because these
would limit open competitions for prizes. In November the MSA
decided to reform.*

London Swimming Association.

At a meeting of the Swimming Congress held at the German Gymnasium, King's Cross, London, on January 7th 1869; E. G. Ravenstein Esq in the chair; it was

Proposed by Mr. W. Ramsden & seconded by Mr. J. Morris.

"That, in the opinion of this meeting, it is desirable that an Association, to be composed of the various clubs in London, & having for its object the promotion & encouragement of a knowledge of the art of Swimming, should at once be formed."

Carried—

Proposed by Mr. W. Ramsden & seconded by Mr. H. Cawley.

"That to give practical effect to the foregoing resolution, a provisional Committee be now appointed to draw up a Code of Rules, the same to be submitted for approval at a future meeting"

Carried.

Proposed by Mr. H. Cawley & seconded by Mr. James Cole

"That the Committee consist of Messrs. E. G. Ravenstein, J. Warrington, J. Jaques, J. Morris & W. Ramsden.

Carried.—

Minutes of the first meeting of the London Swimming Association held in January 1869.

Chapter 2:

Making the ASA effective - 1874 to 1920

Comment by George Pragnell,
Honorary Secretary of the ASA, 1902.

' The healthiest of English exercises, the purest of our national pastimes, and the most useful of all our recreations is probably the worst supported and has more general apathy, criminal negligence and crass stupidity to contend with than with all the rest put together. The opportunities afforded by our rivers are passed over, whilst the facilities along the sea coast are antiquated and uninviting. New baths are built with the same anomalies and defects as those erected 40 years ago, and there are many large towns which cannot boast any swimming baths or bathing places at all. ...... The great City of London, in spite of ceaseless agitation, does not possess a proper swimming bath, and an enlightened Education Department has quite recently decided to teach school children to swim on land! How truly the words of the Colossus apply "So little done, so much to do."'.

Introduction

Records of the early years of the ASA are less detailed than those of more recent times. Nonetheless it is possible to use these, together with a range reports and information from the sporting press, to give an account of the development of the Association until after the First World War. Some of the details are set out below and through them it is possible to trace a series of changes. These include the formation of and evolution of the constitution of the ASA. They define the underlying values in relation to amateur status as well as in relation to finances. Also covered are the Association's responses to external social and economic changes.

Debates about the definition of *amateur*

Most historical accounts of the ASA have assumed that many difficulties relating to defining the aims of the Association and decision making processes had their origins in the clashes of personalities of the men who took the most active part in the debates. However, such an interpretation conceals or seriously diminishes the important and distinctive values about the interpretation of 'amateur' held by many of these men. These may be seen as the

'Swimming in the Serpentine in 1874' gives an artist's view of a gala and its entertainments in the Illustrated London News.

basis of most of their serious arguments particularly in the struggle to devise laws (that is, rules and regulations), which could win the acceptance of the great majority of swimmers and their club representatives. Modifying laws or introducing new ones often touched on the fundamental values held by the legislators, and contemporary accounts of the debates drew attention to the vigour with which they were conducted, and noted that these were sometimes soured by intolerance.

Debates about the definition of *amateur* were taking place in British society during the nineteenth century wherever attempts were made to regulate sporting activity. They revolved round the issue of financial rewards. At one extreme the term *amateur* in Victorian Britain conveyed the ideal of achievement to the highest standards without any remuneration. In contrast to the twentieth century the word carried neither the pejorative implication of the inferior efforts of the novice nor the unskilled performance of an enthusiast resulting in indifferent quality. The word amateur had originated as a synonym for lover and its use implied playing the best game possible for its own sake. Another definition saw the amateur as a committed sporting enthusiast who might receive some reward, though the nature of the reward, whether financial or decorative, itself caused further debate.

The Evangelical Christians of the time spoke out against any form of financial reward for success in competitive sport. They believed that moral imperatives required the best use of gifts and skills for the attainment of heavenly grace. Simultaneously they condemned immoral time wasting and frivolity and betting.

They believed that the performances of swimmers or other athletes were corrupted with the lure of financial rewards in that competitors might be tempted to underperform deliberately. Moreover they asserted that betting was associated with other vicious practices or outcomes. Placing wagers impoverished the betting man, who might otherwise have used his resources more constructively. Money for wagers might be the fruit of other crimes. Additionally associated with betting might be those criminals who threatened or encouraged violence.

In the middle years of the nineteenth century the amateur ideal was used to define performance to the highest standard. Such achievement had to be in a context which was free from any hint or taint of corruption. Thus, the player or swimmer sought to reach the best possible standard by observing the spirit of the laws and not just the letter. Hence the importance of ensuring that laws provided the framework where all participants were aware that fair play was to be sustained. The dedicated sports lover played for the sake of the nobility of the game; winning or record breaking were mere incidentals which came to those who reached their true potential in appropriate conditions. Dr R. Holt observed in *Sport and the British* that the Corinthian Football Club in the later nineteenth century expressed this sentiment in its most pure form. The Club's rule required the goal keeper to leave the goal unguarded if a penalty kick was awarded against the side since the Corinthians believed that the award of a penalty indicated that the standard of fair play had been breached.

Intimately involved with the amateur concept were the ideals of *sportsmanship* and of *manliness*. Sportsmanship had at its heart the notions of fair play but it contained, too, beliefs about the importance of losing gracefully and behaving with courtesy to opponents. These social aspects of playing games and participating in sport found their expression in handshakes between competitors before and after contests in full view of any other participants and any of the public present. To act with honour derived from teachings about manliness. This depended on the integration into the personal life of the sportsman that good behaviour, for example in the swimming pool, was but one aspect of the character and conduct of the participant in any transaction in home life, business or public affairs. The attributes of manliness included keeping as fit a body as possible and developing a healthy mind: *mens sano in corpore sano*. These ideals were promoted in universities, public schools and increasingly in publicly funded schools with games as an integral part of their achievement.

Such ideals helped to shape the rules of virtually all sporting bodies which came into being or were developing during the second half of the nineteenth century. The predecessors of the ASA (London Swimming Association, Metropolitan Swimming Association and Swimming Association of Great Britain) drew upon them in shaping their laws, probably influenced by those members of their committees who had been either pupils at public schools or shared the attitudes which had become current in them. The ASA itself made agreements in 1886 with the Amateur Athletic Association and with the National Cycling Union. Each organisation accepted the membership definitions and adjudications of the others with the consequence that an agreed definition of amateur status was common. Any infringement brought automatic sanctions from the other two organisations.

Interpretations of the laws were very strict, the treatment of swimming teachers provided a good illustration of this strictness. Teachers who accepted payment for instructing people of any age to swim were defined as professionals and could not be members

'The Builder' in March 1879 gave prominence to the newly erected Manchester Hotel, Aldersgate Street, London. It was a frequent venue for meetings of the SAGB and the ASA.

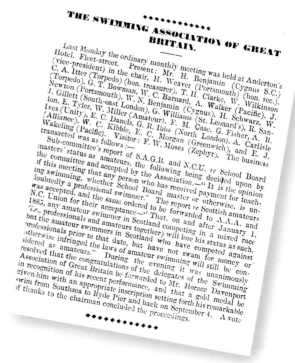

The SAGB faced continuous challenges concerning the meaning of 'amateur' and these were reported in Swimming Notes during 1884. The Mile Championship race at Manchester showed that the professionals and amateurs were segregated for the contest.

of any amateur sports association. This judgement even defined the teachers in publicly financed Board Schools as professionals even though most of their duties involved general classroom subjects. So too were the entertainers whose livelihoods came from performances. Swimming teachers and entertainers responded by setting up the Professional Swimming Association in 1881, although the Association, which had the aims of increasing the esteem of and social contacts between its members, seems to have collapsed during the later 1880s. Competitors in galas were deemed to have lost their amateur status if they accepted prizes in cash or were involved in events which were the subject of publicly advertised gambling. As may be imagined the definition of amateur and adjudication on individual applications for membership caused the ASA many problems.

Formation and evolution of the constitution of the ASA

As its name indicates the MSA comprised clubs solely from the London area. To increase its authority and in particular to enhance its claims to control amateur competitive swimming in Britain, it convened a meeting in 1874 where it was agreed to change the title, and by implication the scope of the organisation, to the Swimming Association of Great Britain. Once established SAGB made great efforts to encourage clubs from all over the country to join although it met with limited success. By 1880 the SAGB had made little progress in recruiting member clubs from outside of the London area. The major stumbling block appeared to be the vexed question about what constituted amateur status, and in particular the lack of clarity about the application of the rules in particular cases. It was probably no comfort to those who had been excluded to know that exclusions or arbitrary reversals of earlier adjudications probably arose from the rapidly changing composition of the Council where club representation at each meeting varied, depending on illness, pressure of other work or other reason.

Such chaotic indecisiveness seriously weakened the SAGB and 7 April 1884 the Otter SC of London, led by Dr Hunter Barron, decided to withdraw from membership and, with a small number of other clubs, agreed to form the Amateur Swimming Union (ASU). Disputes about the relative jurisdiction of the ASU and SAGB demonstrated the ineffectual position of both bodies. On 3 March 1886 the two bodies came together and agreed that they would establish the Amateur Swimming Association. In defining its constitution the new association drew up 135 laws which covered its procedures for handling suspensions and appeals, the conduct of Council meetings and race meetings together with the organisation of championship competitions. Inevitably, the constitution included a definition of *amateur*. Thus, the ASA came into being on 12 April 1886.

Prominent amongst the contacts the ASA had at this time with the highest levels of society was Lord Charles Beresford, politician, naval officer, sportsman and a close friend of the Prince of Wales. He served as an aide-de-camp to the Queen and ultimately became an Admiral. He was also Member of Parliament for Marylebone between 1885 and 1890. He was elected President of the ASA for the three years 1887 to 1889. He obtained royal patronage for the ASA in 1887, Queen Victoria's Golden Jubilee

year. It was at this time that the ASA adopted the badge which is still in current use. By 1888 the ASA had as Patrons: the Duke of Portland, Lord Randolph Churchill and Lord Wolseley. The Duke of Portland served in the Conservative administrations of 1886 and 1895. Lord Randolph Churchill became Chancellor of the Exchequer in the Marquess of Salisbury's cabinet formed in 1886. Lord Wolseley ultimately became a Field Marshal whose major contribution was to modernise the army. It had six vice-presidents: H.L.W. Lawson M.P., Dr Hunter Barron, W.J. Innes, H.W. Fisk, A. Clark and G.H. Rope. Of these, the most interesting to contemporary readers is Lawson who, when he had achieved the title of Lord Burnham, chaired the committee which adjudicated on school teachers pay and whose name continues to be associated with educational issues.

By the beginning of the twentieth century, the ASA had changed the way the president was elected and no longer invited prominent members of society to hold the office of vice-presi-

AMATEUR SWIMMING RECORDS.

IT is an age of records. They seem to follow one another as fast as new pape almost as regularly as Ravensbourne Galas. These are the latest in the swi world up to the hour of going to bed—or, as it is generally put by less t writers—"the hour of going to press." They all stand to the credit of J. H. Ty Manchester.

100 Yards, 1 min. 1 2.5 sec.; 150 Yards, 1 min. 42 2.5 sec.; 220 Yards, 2 min. 41 sec.; 300 Yards, 3 min. 56 1.5 sec.; 5 min. 53 1.5 sec.; 500 Yards, 6 min. 45 sec.; 880 Yards, 13 min. 20 sec.; 1,000 Yards, 15 min. 2 sec.; One Mile, 26 min The above are the only distances recognised by the A.S.A. Records must be made in A.S.A. costume, and in still water, a distances, up to and inclusive of 500 yards, in baths not less than 25 yards long, above 500 yards, in open water, over course than 220 yards in length.

Some of the foregoing may be altered soon, and others may be altered often; bu is one record which deserves to stand. At Leamington Spa, on March 30th, 18: Annual General Meeting of the Amateur Swimming Association lasted twelve ho from 4 p.m. until 4 a.m.—and the prophetic artist of *Swimming*, a week prev sketched a scene which, under the circumstances, ought surely to find a place National Gallery, if not in the Chamber of Horrors.

AN ALL-NIGHT SITTING OF THE A.S.A

A meeting of the ASA Committee illustrated in the Souvenir Programme of the Ravensbourne Gala in 1896. The cartoon by Salaman (signed 'Sally') belonged to George Pragnell, then Honorary Secretary of the ASA and concurrently Honorary Secretary and Treasurer of the Ravensbourne SC. He sits wearing a silk top hat next to a chairman having difficulties. The life belt hangs about the shoulders of William Henry, a founder of the Life Saving Society (later Royal), and the devil carries a document labelled 'Plunging' - then a debated issue.

"nd more District Associations."

"Nailed to the Mast."

"Bloodless Annexation."

"Prepared for Peace, but armed for War."

The Ravensbourne Souvenir Programme of 1896 gave prominence to the activities of the ASA. George Pragnell (top left) was a reforming organiser of the ASA and of his club. The honorary secretaries of the, then, three Districts into which England was divided were E.J. Tackley (South, top right), H.Thomsett (Midlands, bottom left), and F.R. Edwards (North, bottom right).

other expenses when participating in national competitions. Provincial clubs also noted the financial benefits from gate money and other sources of income from national championships. This atmosphere of injustice gained further weight in the general context of the rapid expansion of the London based newspapers into territories previously dominated by the local or regional press. Londoners reported events from a perspective which fed the notion that what was of national importance in most sports only had prestige when the venue was London.

Leading the opposition to the continuance of London as the principal arbiter in swimming matters were the large clubs in Liverpool and Manchester. In 1889 they convened a meeting of clubs in northern England with the purpose of debating possible moves to establish their own organisation. In the same year the Midland Aquatic Polo Association called a meeting in Birmingham to seek greater autonomy. Simultaneously the

dent. This occurred when constitutional reforms took place and the Districts became an integral part of the government of the ASA. The presidency rotated between the districts on an annual basis. From this time the ASA no longer indicated any patron on its stationery other than the sovereign.

The establishment of Districts

The increasing numbers of clubs joining the ASA indicated its success in governing swimming sports. Uniformity of rules for competitive contests sustained and enhanced all aspects of swimming. By 1888, 65 clubs were affiliated to the Association, rising to 135 in 1890 and by 1894 the tally had reached 300. This increase in the number of member clubs brought its own problems to the ASA and prompted the emergence of a movement for devolution into Districts.

The origins of this movement lay in the resentment felt by those outside London of the metropolitan focus of the ASA. At the outset of the Association in 1886 *The Swimmer* newspaper carried an editorial drawing attention to the unfairness to those who lived at a distance from London in that almost all of the national swimming championships took place in the London area and provincial centres were ignored as possible venues. Certainly 'out of Town' swimmers incurred greater travelling costs and

VOTE IN SUPPORT OF THE
SOUTHERN COUNTIES' A.S.A.

The Gentlemen whose names are printed below are your supporters.

PLUMP! PLUMP FOR THEM ALL!!

If you do not PLUMP you will be outvoted.

If you will VOTE SOLID and PLUMP, the day is yours.

Yours faithfully,
ARCHD. SINCLAIR.
WILLIAM HENRY.

P.S.—The Clubs in all parts of the Southern are with you.

We hate these methods, they are not calculated to be beneficial to the Sport; but, in defence of the Association, they are compulsory. Hoping that such methods will never again be needed.

President.
Benjamin, H.
One wanted, one proposed, therefore elected.

Vice-Presidents of S.C.A.S.A.

Davenport, H.	Payne, E. H.
Griffin, H. H.	Pragnell, G.
Henry, W.	Sachs, F.
Hunter, C. Val, C.C.	Sinclair, A.
Innes, W. J	Rope, G. H.

Ten wanted, ten proposed, therefore all elected.

Vice-Presidents of A.S.A.
PLUMP FOR THE FOLLOWING SIX—

Davenport, H.	Sachs, F.
Henry, W.	Sinclair, A.
Payne, E. H.	Rope, G. H.

Executive.
PLUMP FOR THE FOLLOWING—

Baker, C. A.	Payne, G. H.
Benjamin, W. N.	Plumbridge, E. J.
Bull, W. E.	Styer, A. St. John.
Crafter, T.	Gardner, J. E.
Cufflin, A. St. P.	Poole, A.
Hankins, W. S.	Jones, Norman C.
Hudson, A.	Du Parcq, E. R.
Lister, G. D.	Haes, D.
Mawbey, H. F.	
Norton, F. H.	
Norris, W. B.	

Official Handicappers.

Hudson, A.	1.	Metropolitan district, 20 miles from Charing Cross.
Bruce Jones, H. ...	2.	Rest of Essex, Middlesex, Kent, Surrey and Sussex.
Bartlett, C. W. J. ...	3.	Berks, Hants, Wilts and Channel Islands.
	4.	Somerset, Dorset, Devon, Cornwall and South Wales.

Representatives to A.S.A., 1896.
PLUMP FOR THE FOLLOWING, and history is yours—

Norris, W. B.	Plumbridge, E. J.	
Barclay, H. J.	Crafter, T.	Du Parcq, E. R.
Lister, G. D.	Hudson, A.	Payne, G. H.
Benjamin, W. N.	Cufflin, A. St. P.	Bull, W. E.
Gray, G. H.		Poole, A.

The creation of the Districts aroused strong feelings as shown in this poster.

ASA itself had called a meeting to review the constitution in the light of its expanding work, though it seems likely that hints of potential difficulties of maintaining the existing system made the issue more urgent. In fact the ASA sent Mr Henry, Mr Sinclair and Mr C. Val Hunter to the Manchester meeting as its delegates. They explained that there was no opposition from the ASA to devolution of decision-making on many issues, subject only to the invariability of the laws relating to competition. The ASA recognised the advantages of districts taking responsibility for their own affairs where local or regional factors had importance. The meeting in Manchester coincided with the ASA meeting in London, and these meetings used the technology of the telegraph service to confirm the agreement to establish districts. The first idea was to divide England along the line of 53° of latitude into two areas but this arbitrary concept was replaced by a proposal for three districts: North, Midland and South, each being represented on the ASA committee. The division between the Northern District and the Midland District followed the 53° of latitude which required the partitioning of Staffordshire and Derbyshire along the line of latitude, except that Stoke and Longton were assigned to the North.

By 1900 the ASA had established its Commission on the Constitution to examine evidence from clubs from the West of England and from Yorkshire about the practical advantages of redrawing the boundaries of the Districts. At its meeting on 28 September 1900 the Commission voted by eight to three to recommend that Council create five Districts to replace the current three.

From 1901 the ASA comprised five districts: Southern, Western, Midland, Northern and North Eastern. Their names and their geographical composition were partly pragmatic answers, appropriate to conditions in the later 1890s and partly arbitrary, in that a core of clubs made a focus for development of competitions. On this basis the new system worked. The precise assignment of some counties to one district rather than another depended on the relationships of the clubs with the association. However, there seems little doubt that the convenience of railway passenger train routes had played a part in the processes involved. This was because rapid, easy and low cost transport were vital for the maintenance of competitions and for the personal contacts which ensured lasting co-operation.

By 1904 the sizes of the Districts and their contributions to the work of the ASA demonstrated their importance. Many of the ASA national competitions took place in Districts as the table showed:

Table 1.1: ASA Districts and Competitions in 1904

District	No. of Clubs	National Competitions
Midland	124	440 yards, County Water Polo, Schoolboys
Northern	120	150 yard back, 220 yards, mile
North-Eastern	90	100 yard ladies, 100 yards
Southern	293	200 yard Breast, 500 yards, Long Distance, Club Water Polo
Western	48	Half-mile, Plunging

Competitions within localities, Districts and the nation depended at that time on finding the money for transport. Expanding these activities was limited by the willingness and ability of competitors to pay for their own travel to venues. It seemed to the ASA in 1906 that its programme of events, whilst vital to its endeavours, undoubtedly brought significant returns to the railway companies. Thus, Council entered into negotiations to arrange lower fares for swimming competitors. These failed initially despite their delegation having the formidable skills of the young Harold Fern at its disposal. A partial victory came in May 1907 when the Secretary of the Railway Clearing House wrote to agree that from June of that year parties of four swimmers could have the concession of paying one and a quarter fare instead of the full cost of a return ticket. Shortly afterward the Railway Clearing House, the organisation which handled all ticketing arrangements in Great Britain, explained that only swimmers and life savers qualified for the concession. Mr Pragnell had the task of seeking similar advantages for water polo teams whose case, as he pointed out to the ASA, had formed an integral part of the original arguments with the Railway Clearing House.

The Officers

The newly established ASA continued to follow the pattern of its predecessors and relied upon volunteers to undertake all aspects of its work. Members of the Council, elected by each club, were required to undertake the considerable range of work at each meeting since items relating to policy and its execution invariably appeared on agendas. Once the Districts had been established, a solution was proposed by George Pragnell, later Sir George, who proposed the creation of a Committee with the task of undertaking the execution of policy and the preparation of business proposals for Council. The composition of the managing committee comprised two members elected by each District together with the elected honorary officers. The Committee made the management decisions of the ASA. In practice the day to day work depended upon the honorary officers and particularly the honorary secretary.

The documentation of the early ASA reveals the work of a dedicated series of unpaid officers. For example, much work was undertaken by Arthur Cook who served for some years as Assistant Secretary. He worked from his office at 10 John Street, Adelphi, London which became the usual venue of meetings of the Committee. George Pragnell contributed first as a member of Council and then as Honorary Secretary from 1891 until 1903 in which year he became Honorary President. An outline of his contribution provides evidence of the extent and quality of commitment these officers were prepared to give to the ASA.

George Pragnell was born at Sherborne, Dorsetshire, in 1863 and made his career in the City of London at the wholesale dry goods business of Cook, Son and Company where he rose to be managing partner. His services to swimming included membership of the first Committee of the Life Saving Society and active support for water polo in London. He received a knighthood in 1912 for his public services and died in 1916 whilst holding the office of Deputy-Lieutenant of the City of London.

As its Honorary Secretary, he contributed significantly to the evolution of the ASA. He dealt single-handed with a growing correspondence both within Britain as well as overseas. He travelled widely on behalf of the ASA, largely at his own expense. He recorded his expenditure in order to document the cost to the individual of serving the ASA and he estimated that he spent between £50 and £100 a year for fares and incidentals. Immediately before becoming Honorary President George Pragnell wrote a memoire about his period as an elected officer to the then President, Mr Thomsett. He seems not to have suffered fools gladly and refers somewhat contemptuously to the lengthy arguments about 'making amateurs professional' and vice-versa. Acrimonious debates had been and remained a characteristic of the conduct of some of the ASA's business. However, the objectives of the ASA were very important to him and in the Memoire to Mr Thomsett, he refers to the initiatives which he had taken as Honorary Secretary. He stated that at the outset of his term of office he had hoped to achieve twenty objectives. These were: (1) instituting a Committee of the ASA; (2) an increase in the number of District Committees; (3) earlier general meetings of Council; (4) annual presidents; (5) perpetual challenge trophies; (6) application of the laws of the ASA to both sexes; (7) inauguration of ladies' championships; (8) formation of an ASA for Wales; (9) a complete series of international matches; (10) improved ASA certificates; (11) international costumes; (12) caps; (13) an additional objective for the ASA to favour more baths and bathing places being established; (14) a list of existing baths and bathing places; (15) lifesaving to be exempt from amateur laws; (16) certificates for reliable professional teachers of the art; (17) decent recognised costumes for ladies and gentlemen; (18) improved regulations for entertainments; (19) tabulated amateur records and rules; (20) a combined ASA year-book showing the progress and position of the art in each district. Commenting on his twenty propositions George Pragnell noted:

> *'To my great astonishment, every one of these has been more or less bitterly opposed; and now that the last one is agreed to, and all are in working order, I intend retiring at the next annual general meeting, and I am writing thus early in order to give Council plenty of time to find a successor'.*

As is indicated by his remarks about his struggle, the proposals took effect at different times. For example, the annual *Handbook* of the ASA, began life in 1893 although no complete set of the *Handbooks* seems to have survived for the first seven years.

The example of the work of Sir George Pragnell is possible because it is better documented. Much other crucial work on behalf of the ASA was done by a great many committed supporters.

Finances

Systematic records of the finances of the ASA and its predecessors have not survived continuously from 1869. However, we gain some glimpses of the difficulties which beset the early years of creating a coherent organisation for swimming. For example, the SAGB was supported by only a small number of clubs whose affiliation fees comprised the greater part of its annual income. The total income in 1877 was £84 12s 4d. Such an impoverished state reflected its limited authority. In 1876 when Horace Davenport won the SAGB cup for the mile for the third time, he found himself paying for half the cost of the trophy. Such a parlous state of affairs did not change until after the reforms which created the ASA in 1886. This did not produce a flood of money but sufficient to give it stability.

The crisis year of 1889, when the northern clubs came near to leaving the ASA, showed the organisation had a membership of 96 clubs of which 40 were provincial. The latter included two Irish clubs and the accounts indicated that eight formed the core of the Midland ASA and ten, the Northern ASA. The annual revenue was £87 16s 1d. Separate funds, raised largely from competitors' fees, met the expenses of the Amateur Championship meetings, including water polo, amounting to just over £117. Other assets, such as badges and cups were valued at about £25 but were not included in the annual accounts.

Reforms in organisation and growing membership improved the ASA's position to the extent that the accounts of 1894 showed more activity and a total revenue of £119 1s 10d. Even so, there were deficits in the International Polo account of £11 1s 8d and in the revenue account of £14 1s 10d, the greater part being the loss from the Polo account. The affiliated districts had club memberships respectively of 131 in the Southern, 107 in the Northern and 27 in the Midlands. In 1900 the numbers of clubs affiliated had risen in all the three Districts: to 243 in Southern, to 128 in the Northern, and to 98 in the Midland. The revenue account showed receipts of £181 14s 4d.

The first year of the new five Districts, 1902, showed club affiliations as follows: 106 in the Midland, 110 in the Northern, 80 in the North Eastern, 250 in the Southern and 49 in the Western. This made a grand total of 595.

The financial statements showed that by the year 1904 club subscriptions were referred to as 'the call'. It stood at 4s and amounted to £135 for the 675 clubs. For the same period the revenue account showed a turnover of £240 15s 6d. The ASA's balance sheet showed assets of £58 10s 2d indicating a gain in 1904 of £7 18s 0d. The revenue account showed that the Districts not only collected the individual club call but each District paid for medals awarded for its selection to national championships whose overall cost in 1904 amounted to £92 17s 0d. Moneys relating to International Water Polo matches were noted in a separate account and amounted to £42 12s 0d.

The last full year of peace, 1913, indicated that the ASA had 1409 affiliated clubs and the annual revenue account showed receipts of £490 1s 4d. The District sizes varied greatly in the numbers of member clubs: 225 in Midlands, 215 in Northern, 173 in North Eastern, 718 in Southern, and 78 in Western. Activities during the war time years 1914 to 1919 were low key and were funded by the affiliation fees paid in 1914 and such other income as had come into the ASA. The war had a severe impact on the number of affiliations to the Association which by 1920 had declined to 874 clubs. All Districts had suffered, with the numbers of clubs in membership being: 173 in Midland, 130 in Northern, 119 in North Eastern, 405 in Southern, and 47 in Western, a total of 874. The years immediately following the end of the war suffered from inflation so that the call on clubs rose to 6s each. The revenue account showed receipts totalling £549 16s 9d of which £63 1s 10d was a loss. Amongst the special expenses was the support needed for the British Swimmers at the Antwerp Olympic Games of 1920.

Amateur Swimming Association.

PRESIDENT.
*J. F. HERBERT.

PAST PRESIDENTS.
H. DAVENPORT.
*W. J. READ.
H. E. CASHMORE.
G. H. ROPE.
J. H. FISHER.

HON. TREASURER.
*J. H. FISHER.
9, South Parade,
Manchester.

HON. SECRETARY.
*GEO. PRAGNELL.
53, Drayton Gardens,
London, S.W.

E. A PAGE, *President M.C.A.S.A.*
F. H. THOMAS, *Hon. Treas.* ,,
*H. THOMSETT, *Hon. Sec.* ,,

MIDLAND REPRESENTATIVES.
J. S. BIRD.
H. R. AULTON.
S. G. CANNING.
G. D. HAZZLEDINE.
G. A. POTTER.

R. WILLIAMS, *President N.C.A.S.A.*
G. E. MARSHALL, *Hon. Treas.* ,,
F. R. EDWARDS, *Hon. Sec.* ,,

NORTHERN REPRESENTATIVES
*F. BAXTER.
R. BEATTIE.
S. DAWSON.
J. DERBYSHIRE.
W. SMYTH.
R. M. WHITEHEAD.

E. J. TACKLEY, *President S.C.A.S.A.*
C. E. MACRAE, *Hon. Treas.* ,,
V. M. MANSELL, *Hon. Sec.* ,,

SOUTHERN REPRESENTATIVES
H. BENJAMIN.
*W. E. BULL.
A. St. P. CUFFLIN.
W. HENRY.
*R. C. BEALE.
H. T. BRETTON.
A. HUDSON.
W. N. BENJAMIN.
G. MARSHALL.
G. H. GRAY.
A. St. J. STYER.
A. J. TUCKER.

*COMMITTEE.

53, DRAYTON GARDENS,
SOUTH KENSINGTON.

March, 9th, 1900.

DEAR SIR,

The **Annual General Meeting** will be held on Saturday, March 24th, at the **Grand Hotel, Manchester,** commencing at 2 p.m. prompt.

I enclose a copy of the Report and Agenda together with a chart shewing proposed rotation of Championships including **International** Water-Polo matches. The latter are included on the supposition that each District will in future take them in turn, but this point, as also the question of defraying the cost of out and home Internationals will be discussed under Clause 54 of the Report.

I have not yet received any notices of Amendments to proposed new Conditions for the County Water-Polo Championship (*see Handbook, p.* 70), nor to the existing International **Water=Polo Rules** (for the guidance of English representatives on the International Board).

Upon the Report, attention will be called to the absence of any minute or information relating to two important objects of the A.S.A., and of each District thereof, viz. : (*a*) the promotion and encouragement of the Art of Swimming and the game of Water-Polo amongst **ladies,** and (*b*) the stimulation of public opinion in favour of providing **proper accommodation** and facilities for acquiring and practising the art of Swimming.

As the first International Match will take place during August, the three **Inter District** Trial Games should be played on three Saturdays in July this year. The proposed **dates** for these and for all Championships should be sent to me without delay so as to avoid clashing, and if possible have the list complete by the 24th inst.

The Records and Minute Books of the Association will be on the tables for the use of all representatives, but I shall be glad to have **notice** of any question involving references thereto, both as a matter of courtesy and in order to save the time of the meeting. Kindly **bring** your A.S.A. Handbook for 1899 as I have no spare copies.

The Northern District will entertain the delegates at **Dinner** at 6.30 p.m. It is expected that some Members of the Manchester Corporation will be present. Social at 8 p.m. The Honorary Treasurer will be pleased to secure **beds** for any who write to him not later than March 22nd. (Bed and Breakfast, 6/6)

In the event of an elected representative being unable to attend he may appoint a **substitute** in his place, but this Rule does not apply to the sixteen ex-officio members of the Council.

Yours thoroughly,

GEORGE PRAGNELL,

Hon. Secretary,

NOTE.

The International Competitions in connection with the Paris Exhibition will take place on Sundays, August 19th & August 26th.

The range of activities

From its earliest days the ASA and its immediate predecessors had a clear image of their task. Even in the context of disagreements about organisational structure, the definition of amateur and the detail of policy, there was general agreement with the aims of promoting swimming in all its forms for recreation, health and for competition, as well as for working for the provision of good facilities available to the entire population. There was also agreement with the aim of placing the ASA as the defining body for the non commercial development of swimming activity. Efforts to achieve these aims during this period set the pattern for the future and were maintained through the difficult times leading to the First World War and after.

Promoting swimming between 1874 and 1914

One of the fundamental aims of the ASA was to promote swimming and the associated sports of diving and water polo. It was self-evident that the only way that the association could achieve its intentions was by persuasion because it lacked the funds to do more than publicise its cause. This in turn required attracting public support so that politicians both at local and national levels recognised the attractions of meeting some of the wishes of constituents.

Circumstances gave the ASA opportunities to make some of its aims realisable in its early years, particularly in respect of swimming baths as is discussed more fully in chapter 5. One of the important openings for the ASA was in larger towns which had chartered borough status. These boroughs had powers or could adopt the provisions of permissive legislation to erect baths and wash houses which included swimming pools. Arguments for building pools were that these facilities provided all classes, particularly the working classes, with convenient places for recreation. Boroughs met the capital expenditure of construction from the general rates and offset most of the running costs by charging users prices they could afford. Moreover, the authorities chose locations convenient to the larger concentrations of people so that access was easy. Removing people from idling on the streets, particularly the young and able bodied, and encouraging them to enjoying themselves, attracted the decision makers in town halls. From the stand point of the ASA the more swimming clubs used these facilities, the more people would become involved in swimming sports.

The ASA regarded the formation of swimming clubs as essential for the extension of its work. To this end it encouraged, as far as it could, groups of like-minded people to found swimming clubs whose purposes chimed with those of the ASA. Effective and efficient organisation was the essential for success and these depended on the self sacrifice of dedicated people who gave their time and skills for the sake of the club and swimming. The ASA published guidelines for those setting up clubs. Its own organisation reflected the unstinted sustained support which its officers gave for no rewards other than serving the sport of swimming.

Left:- In 1900 the Minute Book of the ASA included this notice from George Pragnell. He conducted the business of the ASA from his own home.

Women and swimming

Any discussion of women and swimming must recognise the divisions which existed, even amongst the most enthusiastic advocates. Some wanted equal opportunities with men, whilst others argued that women differed from men and should have separate facilities and approaches to sport. *Sportsmanship* had its counterpart in *sportswomanship*. It, too, emphasised the moral virtues of fair play and the duty to strive to reach the highest standard of performance. This latter aspect had its supporters who wanted the teaching and coaching of women to be exclusively for women and to use such techniques as seemed appropriate for the preservation of femininity. One of the strong advocates of this position was Martina Ollenberg. She received government support in 1916 when she became head of an institute to train women to teach girls swimming.

PROVINCIAL NEWS.

MINNA WOOKEY'S SWIM.

On Friday evening, July 24, this famous little West country swimmer accomplished a feat in natation in the River Avon, unparalleled in the local historical records of this city. Some few weeks ago a gentleman, well-known in Bristol as being a patron of swimming, offered Mr. Wookey a gold medal if he could find any one in the City of Bristol to swim from Bath Bridge to Bedminster Bridge in the River Avon, a distance of half a mile, with hands and feet tied. Mr. Wookey at once accepted this on behalf of his daughter, Minna, and commenced to make the necessary arrangements. Miss Wookey, who was neatly attired, having been taken on the boat, in which were the press and some of the committee of the Leander Swimming Club, was securely tied by Mr. J. M. Longney, hon. sec. Bristol Leander S.C., at the wrists and ancles, the palms of the hands being close together, the same being examined by the officials of the press in Bristol and found to be secure. The boat was then rowed to the starting place, where Miss Wookey dived into the water amidst the ringing cheers of the thousands of people who lined both sides of the banks of the river. She commenced very fast swimming on her side, but, from instructions received from her father, altered her style alternately, and went steadier, first on the side and then on the chest and back. Fully 20,000 people were there, the cheers being something deafening all the way. A boat, with several members of the Leander S.C., rowed alongside of Miss Wookey, and were ready to render assistance, and Mr. Stansbury, of the same club, was in costume ready in Mr. Wookey's boat, so that every precaution was taken to prevent an accident. But it is needless to say that their services were not required, for Miss Wookey glided through the water without any unnecessary trouble, and passing the foot of the bridge in the sharp time of 5 min. 21 sec., finished the whole distance, half a mile, with the tide, in 13 min. 21 sec. Miss Wookey was then untied, and after being presented with several bouquets of flowers dived into the water and swam down to the landing stage, about a quarter of a mile, to show the large concourse of people she was not tired. There were several bets lost and won over this feat, as the general public thought it was impossible for her to do it, but those who knew Mr. Wookey knew he would not allow his daughter to undertake a task which she could not accomplish. Miss Wookey did not appear the least exhausted, and could no doubt have swam a couple of miles with her hands and feet tied. She was afterwards presented with the gold medal at her father's house, the Clarence Hotel, Bedminster. Bristol, by Mr. J. Longney, hon. sec. Leander Club, and subsequently several members of the club spent a jolly evening. We almost forgot to mention that Miss Wookey is only 11 years of age, her birthday being the 31st of October next.

Outstanding women swimmers who attracted press notice were usually professionals such as Minna Wookey whose performance took place in July 1885.

Girls and women were perceived by many late Victorian and early twentieth century medical experts 'as weaker than men'. The great majority of these experts were men, whose opinions were based on assertions rather than systematic physiological study. These perspectives survived without serious challenge well into the twentieth century. They had consequences for the ways in which competitors prepared themselves for events, there being a view in some quarters, both male and female, that muscular exercises would distort and damage the delicate anatomy of women. The consequences were seen in the design of competitions at all levels of swimming. The opposition to women's participation in the Olympics owed some of its support to such fears, as well as to the misogyny of some of the leaders of the Olympic movement itself.

The ASA accepted, though somewhat anxiously, the rise of women's swimming clubs and the importance of teaching girls to swim. Apprehension about women took various forms. *Swimming Notes* recorded the fears of one male swimmer of using water in which women had swum as a reason for excluding them from baths. Some women established separate swimming clubs of their own, one of the earliest being at Rochester, Kent, which was holding annual general meetings at least as early as June 1884. At that meeting it was reported to members that one of the club's employees taught any members who needed assistance with improved swimming techniques. Accounts of women's events in the press were often written by men who did not take them seriously. Their tone was jokey and patronising. Not all women wanted to use baths built for men and, in some districts, purpose built baths were erected for women. One such example was the Amphitheatre in Islington, London, built in 1901. Among the women's clubs founded in this period were the Birmingham Ladies founded in 1884 and Croydon Ladies founded in 1891.

There were also anxieties about women as spectators as well as swimmers. At first the presence of women at events worried some people that men's costume, or the lack of costume, might shock ladies. To meet this anxiety, costume was the subject of ASA laws which varied to reflect circumstances such as at galas where events were arranged for both men and women. A fuller discussion of this aspect of the work of the ASA is located in chapter 6. The Association gave its first formal recognition to women as competitive swimmers in 1901 when it organised the 100 yards national competition. The 200 yards competition began in 1912.

Rochester Ladies Swimming Club was the first to be reported in the Swimming Notes in June 1884. Its activities received further mention in October. A special entertainment for 'ladies only' was noticed later in the same month.

Some swimming clubs in the later nineteenth century organised events for women which differed from men's. Thus, for example, the reports about the annual sea gala of the Portsmouth Swimming Club referred to these activities. These had begun in 1880 when an annual 88 yards handicap race was organised. One variant included a 'Siamese twin' race where two competitors were tied together. In 1885 Portsmouth SC employed Miss Helga Lassen of Copenhagen to act as its 'lady instructress'. At the club's gala she gave a display of ornamental swimming. Elsewhere in August 1885, ladies gave both a swimming entertainment and took part in competitions at the Marble Baths, Junction Road, in North London.

During the nineteenth century the ASA had no official policy about mixed bathing. It assumed that the arrangements of separate facilities and times of availability were matters for the proprietors of the baths whether local authority or private company. ASA law required swimmers to wear costumes where spectators of the other sex were present, at galas or other events. The issue of mixed bathing emerged as a matter of public debate early in

In November 1884 the 'En Passant' columnist of Swimming Notes and Record found that a mixed audience had novelty value.

the twentieth century. Newington, a local authority facility, permitted mixed bathing in 1904. Access to baths by whole families was seen as desirable by some members of the ASA, such as Harold Fern. They expected that such a change in the use of pools would encourage swimming. However, there was no decision to promote mixed bathing before the First World War.

Swimming and education

Swimming as part of physical education had a long history before the formation of the ASA but the case for physical education in publicly financed schools became part of the debates about the curriculum only during the last quarter of the nineteenth century. In the later nineteenth century most senior officials of the Board of Education and their political masters had received their own education at one of the major public schools where physical education formed a vital part of their development. In these, the ASA addressed an audience whose own experiences and those of their children included swimming as an important part of physical education.

Swimming for girls and women had a history as long as that for men although it lurks in shadows created too often by historians whose principal focus was the achievements of men. This bias reflected the interests of the majority of journalists who wrote about sport during the nineteenth and early twentieth centuries. Nonetheless society was not homogenous during the second half of the nineteenth century. In parallel with the moves to improve the status of women through the Married Women's Property Acts were the foundations of independent girls' boarding schools, those established by the Girls' Public Day School Trust and girls' grammar schools. The curriculum for the education of middle and upper class girls attending these new or refounded schools resembled closely that for boys of similar backgrounds.

LADIES ENTERTAINMENT.

Misses Humphrey's the daughters of one whose name is still a household word with Serpentine bathers, and who, during his lifetime did so much to elevate the tone of swimming, and promote its welfare, celebrated their annual entertainment in the St. Marylebone Baths, on Wednesday, October 15th, and attracted a large and very select audience, composed entirely of ladies. Besides a number of interesting races, which bore unmistakeable evidence of the wonderful proficiency attained by the performers and the masterly tuition received from the Misses Humphreys', the following events were contested, viz.: chariot race, consolation race, contest in tubs, and mussock riding, in addition to which Miss Humphrey and Miss Jenny Humphrey gave a remarkably clever display of ornamental swimming. The proceedings were watched with the keenest possible interest, and were managed very satisfactorily by the following officials :—Starter, Miss J. Humphrey ; judge and whip, Miss Beatrice Foot ; stewardesses, Miss Foot, Miss Forty, Miss Classey, and Miss Jefferies ; timekeeper, Mrs. A. E. Foot. Details :—

ONE LENGTH (25 yards) RACE.—Miss J. Batchelor 1, Miss E. Jones 2, Miss L. Hess 3, Miss A. Stark 3, Miss K. Aldridge 3 ; won by two yards.

ONE LENGTH RACE (for Marylebone bathers under 17 years of age).—Miss De Rivay 1, Miss R. Halliday 2, Miss B. Hood 3, Miss Maud Calcutt 0, Miss J. Orr 0 : won by a yard and a half. Time. 25 seconds.

50 YARDS (two lengths) HANDICAP (Miss J. Humphreys' pupils).— Miss B. Green 8 1, Miss M. Parker scratch 2, Mrs. Sanders scratch 3, Miss Eloch scratch 0, Miss Merrick scratch 0, Miss Weatherby scratch 0 ; a good race, won by half a yard, a moderate third.

75 YARDS (three lengths) RACE (lady pupils of Miss Humphreys).— Miss Wrapson 1, Miss Adams 2, Miss M. More 3, Miss Scott 0, Miss E. K. Scott 0 ; won by two yards, half as much between second and third. Time, 1 min. 30 sec.

50 YARDS (two lengths) RACE (for Paddington bathers under 16).— Heat 1 : Miss E. Anderson 2 : Miss Cridland 2, Miss Dolly Taylor 3, Miss Ingham 0 ; won by a yard. Heat 2 : Miss E. Cridland 1, Miss T. Bell 2, Miss M. Cridland 3 ; won easily. Final heat : Miss E. Anderson 1, Miss Cridland 2, Miss E. Cridland 3 ; won, after a good race, by a foot, a yard separating second and third. Time 60 sec.

25 YARDS (one length) RACE (girls under 14).—Miss E. Chater 1. Miss G. Wrapson 2, Miss H. More 3, Miss F. Brown 0, Miss D. Brown 0, Miss M. Ingham 0 ; won by two yards.

25 YARDS (one length) RACE (for Marylebone bathers).—Miss E. Propert 1, Miss Grimes 2, Miss Price 3, Miss E. Propert 0 ; won by three-quarters of a yard, third well up. Time, 30 sec.

75 YARDS (three lengths) HANDICAP (for Marylebone bathers).— Miss Parker scratch 1, Miss S. Taylor scratch 2, Miss Weatherby scratch 3, Miss Green 8 0, Miss H. Murphy 10 0 ; after a well contested race, Miss Parker took the lead in the last length, and won by half a yard, about a yard separated the second and third. Time, 1min. 17 sec.

50 YARDS (two lengths) ALL-COMERS' RACE (under 17).—Miss E. Weatherby 1, Miss A. Libby 2, Miss Maud Calcutt 3, Miss Calcutt 0, Miss Rutby 0, Miss E. K. Scott 0 : won by three yards, a yard between second and third. Time, 57 sec.

75 YARDS (three lengths) ALL-COMERS RACE.—Miss S. Taylor 1: Miss B. James 2, Mrs. Lee 3, Miss Lloyd 0, Miss H. Murphy 0 ; a capital race, won by a foot. two yards between second and third. Time, 1 min. 22 sec.

PLUNGING.—Miss B. Barber 33 ft. 1, Miss Lloyd 0, Miss Murphy 0, Miss Kirby 0.

PLATE DIVING.—Miss Rutley 1, Miss Bacon 0, Miss Lloyd 0 : the winner brought up twenty-three plates out of twenty-four thrown in.

CHILDREN'S RACE (under 12).—Miss E. Stoneham.

RACE for pupils of Middle-class School.—Miss R. Yates.

PUPILS of Miss J. Humphrey, beginners in 1884.—Miss A. Roberts.

CHILDREN'S RACE.—Miss D. Brown.

EXHIBITION SWIMMING AT PORTSMOUTH.

At the recent Police Regatta held at Southsea, Mr. John Stanley, professional instructor to the Portsmouth Club, gave an exhibition with the object of showing the ease with which a swimmer, heavily clad, can keep afloat.

Illustration 1 : High dive 22 feet and rescue—Clothes—University costume—boots, drawers, woollen trousers woollen waistcoat, shirt, collar, tie, thick cloth coat, strong flood tide, and drowning man 40 yards from shore. Illustration 2 : Adding to above another pair of trousers, and winter overcoat lined with woollen mixture, he swam about for sometime with evident ease. Illustration 3 : Plate swimming, clad as above ; the pace was good considering the heavy clothes he wore. Illustration 4 : Undressing in the water, scientific and trick swimming. Illustration 5th: Confidence—The Monte Cristo trick—in 14 feet of water with strong flood tide, the first time performed at Southsea. Mr. H. W. Fisk, Captain and hon. sec. of the club, arranged and superintended the exhibition. Stanley's efforts were rewarded by repeated rounds of applause. and at the finish he received quite an ovation from the thousands who lined the beach.

✦✦✦✦✦✦✦✦✦
THE BATHING SEASON.

To the Editor of the " Daily Chronicle."

SIR,—The bathing season—or as some call it, with reason, the drowning season—draws attention to the facilities offered for learning to swim. Doubtless it may surprise a great many to know that after several hours' search of the " London Directory " I succeeded in finding one teacher noted therein. Perhaps there may be more. I count much for my own stupidity, though I searched under every possible head of reference. Nevertheless, it could do no harm to advise teachers and secretaries of clubs to see that their names and addresses are inserted in the " Directory " in a way that would be plain even to your humble servant,

A DULL ONE.

Deptford, Aug. 18.

DEAR SIR,—I beg to inform you that I have answered the above, and trust that it will appear in the *Daily Chronicle* to-morrow. As I am particularly anxious that a list of all the London and country teachers of swimming, and the baths they instruct at, should be printed, I have written to the daily press to the effect that any person of either sex anxious to acquire the natant art can have a list of all the London and country teachers. Of course this list will be only made up from members of the Professional Swimming Association. I therefore cordially invite all professional non-members to join at once : country subscription, 7s. 6d. ; town subscription, 5s. ; and, for the purpose of obtaining professional names of each sex, ask for letters to be sent to my address, so that I can propose same next meeting, Wednesday, 27th inst., at the Northumberland Arms, Charing-cross, W.C.

Yours truly,

T. C. EASTON, Hon. Sec. P. S. A.

4. Derby-street, Mayfair, W.

✦✦✦✦✦✦✦✦✦
THE PROFESSIONAL SWIMMING ASSOCIATION.

At a meeting held on Wednesday at the Northumberland Arms, Northumberland Avenue, Charing-cross, a four lengths (160 yards) handicap was fixed to take place at the Lambeth Baths on Wednesday, September 3.

Above:- Campaigning for swimming tuition included letters about the availability of information in Swimming Notes of August 1884.

Left:- A report on Exhibition Swimming at Portsmouth in the Swimming Notes of September 1885.

Thus, swimming became part of the physical education of more and more women. The consequences of this movement include the participation of girls' schools in events and qualifications organised by the London Schools Swimming Association. However, this body included some of the local board schools within its membership.

The provision of free swimming lessons to children owed much to the pioneering work of H.J. Johnson, a member of the Leander SC. In 1883 he began his attendances on Monday evenings at the Northwood Street Baths in Birmingham to teach anybody wishing to learn. Subsequently Johnson moved to Leeds where he joined the Leeds SC and devoted much of his leisure to teaching swimming. His reputation in Leeds encouraged the Leeds School Board to appoint him to advise their staffing committee on the suitability of applicants for posts of swimming teacher. This Leeds initiative was a part of efforts to increase the numbers of swimmers in England.

The National Union of Teachers supported the Leeds venture and joined with the ASA in an appeal to the Board of Education to encourage the teaching of swimming as part of Physical Education in schools. Mr Johnson acted as the representative of the joint committee and met Lord Londonderry to discuss the arguments. The government refused to provide a special grant to encourage such a development but it conceded that a school board could use part of its rate income to cover the costs of teaching swimming as a component of physical instruction.

The ASA succeeded in persuading the Board of Education to include swimming as a formal part of the *Code of Education* in the 1890s. However, this was a qualified victory because the Code had the status of being a document expressing aspirations and was not prescriptive. The application of the Code depended on the funds made available by school boards who were elected by local ratepayers. The basic needs of literacy and numeracy absorbed the lion's share of the education budgets so that in most board schools physical instruction was confined to providing drill, or Swedish drill, neither of which involved expense. These exercises improved some muscular development of children but in limited fashion. Such exercises were taught by general subject teachers whose own knowledge of what was beneficial to the pupils often came from the outline information issued by the Board of Education. The ASA offered, free of charge, to the Board of Education the services of members who were competent to teach swimming. In this way the Association hoped to foster swimming in state run schools. In 1891 the London School Board agreed to accept the ASA offer.

The ASA in conjunction with the Royal Life Saving Society lobbied the Board of Education at various times between 1890 and 1914 but made little impact on public spending to improve swimming education and related facilities. They hoped to improve the code for physical education to make swimming and life saving compulsory but their moves achieved little.

A certificate issued by the London Schools Swimming Association, a forerunner of ESSA, and a body affiliated to the ASA, made awards for swimming prowess. This is an early example from 1905, and it shows how swimming was encouraged.

Collaboration with the National Union of Teachers seemed to give an important opportunity for persuading the state education system to embrace the changes in the physical education curriculum which the ASA believed to be essential for promoting swimming. Consequently, Council in 1914 appointed a subcommittee to conduct the necessary negotiations with the NUT and, if appropriate, to arrange a meeting with J.A. Pease, M P, President of the Board of Education and the responsible cabinet minister. This meeting was held in September 1914 and the ASA sought government support for a series of changes. These included:- the encouragement of local education authorities to provide facilities for swimming and, where facilities existed, to ensure that swimming formed a part of physical instruction; that 'drill' should include land exercises for teaching swimming and life saving; and that the Code of Education issued in 1905 by the Board of Education should include the suggestion that, where public baths were available, swimming and life saving should be taught. By that date the war had started and all that could be achieved was the expression of support from the minister for the principle of including swimming in the school curriculum.

Qualifications

Although the ASA held strenuously to the ideal of the amateur, it regarded the contribution of professionally qualified teachers as essential for increasing the numbers of people who could be taught to swim. The 1904 *Handbook* included a notice stating that:

> *The aim of the ASA is to raise the status of professional teachers and to bring under the notice of Schools, Institutions, and Bathing Authorities the importance of having a properly qualified and properly paid teacher appointed in the future'.*

To this end the ASA had instituted its Professional Certificate in 1899. By 31 December 1900 the ASA had awarded 26 Professional Certificates to male and female candidates from all over England.

The Professional Certificates were granted to teachers on application providing candidates had satisfied the executive committee of the District where they lived.

> *The District Executive shall be satisfied as to the character and antecedents of an applicant as well as to his ability as a professional teacher before recommending him for the Certificate of the Association'.*

By 1909 minimum age limits for eligibility for this certificate were specified as 21 years for men and 18 years for women. By 31 December 1909 the ASA had awarded 293 Professional Certificates.

In 1910 the ASA law on the award of the Professional Certificate was thoroughly revised. The reference to antecedents was deleted, but much more significant, were the requirements that candidates should pass both a theoretical and a practical examination. The theory was tested by demonstrating how to instruct the breast stroke, the back stroke, and breathing. The practical was to emphasise style rather than speed of various strokes including, for men only, the *'Trudgen'*. All candidates had

About 1900 Holbein, a professional swimmer, defrayed some of the costs of his book on swimming by including advertisements from several companies who saw the value of reaching this special readership.

to possess the bronze medallion of the Royal Life Saving Society in order to satisfy the ASA's concern about safeguarding pupils. The new rules did not seem to reduce the numbers of people qualifying for the award, for in the year ending 31 December 1910 there were 19 successful candidates. By the end of 1913 the total number of Professional Certificates awarded had risen to 383. It was possible for candidates who scored more than 80% to have Honours awarded for their prowess.

As a consequence of the disruption of the First World War and the low level of ASA activity, the Committee decided to appoint a Reconstruction Sub-Committee which reported on 16 November 1918. Among its recommendations, which became ASA law, was further reform of the Professional Certificate. In 1919, as a result of the reframed law 71, the Certificate for Teachers, was available to professionals and amateurs showing proficiency in teach swimming. These certificates were graded by syllabus as Elementary and Advanced with Honours available in the latter case if the candidate gained at least 80% of the marks in each test and satisfied the examiners as to their ability to teach the crawl stroke.

25

For those familiar only with modern swimming strokes some clarification of the origin of the 'trudgen' is appropriate. The innovations of the trudgen stroke, sometimes spelt *trudgeon*, was attributable to one man, John Trudgen who was born in Poplar, 2 May 1853. He was a self-taught swimmer who acquired his knowledge watching Amerindians swimming in the River Plate in South America. His style was described in *The Swimming Record* of August 1873. The stroke was accepted by the ASA. However, the style was specifically excluded for women to learn or teach.

Discipline

The ability of the ASA to enforce its laws was crucial for its success. The definition of amateur status remained a continuing concern after 1886 and the code of criteria for judging amateur status seemed to cause some headaches. For example, adjudications about the standing of Board School teachers whose duties included instructing their pupils to swim, led Council to deem them professionals because they received a salary for teaching even though only a small part of the working day might be spent on swimming instruction. Sailors in the Royal Navy received similarly strict treatment.

The minutes of the SAGB and the ASA showed that many hours were spent discussing the status of swimmers and whether they had disqualified themselves as amateurs. Appeals against such rulings, with the necessity of producing evidence of amateur

Poor discipline attracted coverage in October 1884 in the Swimming Notes

intent, illustrated the continuing concerns of the ASA with protecting amateur status. Interestingly the Association had ruled that its own officers did not endanger their amateur standing by claiming expenses for officially approved business. For all others, the acceptance of pecuniary rewards in any way earned from swimming, called into question their amateur status. The ASA spent much time in the years between 1884 and 1914 in Council seeking ways of excluding from membership those competitors or officials who had accepted rewards from any source whatsoever. Occasionally, the rulings by the ASA Committee and later confirmed by Council, have a bizarre quality. Such a one was made in 1908 which forbade amateurs to sell picture post cards at galas. The Western District had requested clarification of this matter but the extent and nature of the abuse remains hidden from us.

Competition

Making laws which effectively ensured fair play in all competitions was one of the fundamental objectives of the ASA. Its predecessor bodies had begun the task of crystallising what was acceptable for diving, racing, and water polo. More detailed accounts of the disciplines of diving, water polo and long distance swimming are covered of chapters 7, 9 and 10 respectively.

By initiating national championships the ASA encouraged competition and an increasing number of events stimulated competitions in clubs, localities, counties and districts. The laws of the

John Trudgen, an outstanding swimmer, invented and popularised a new stroke.

SWIMMING.

—o—

WEEK'S FIXTURES.

April 27.—Mr. J. H. Bedford's Handicap, City of London Baths, Barbican; 8.15.
„ 28.—The "Swimming Record's" Handicap, City of London Baths, Barbican—8.30.
„ 29.—Alliance Club, Four Lengths Handicap, City of London Baths, Barbican—8.30.
„ 29.—Regent Club, Third Class Race, King-street Baths, Camden Town—8.30.
„ 30.—Atlantic Club, Final Heat of Four Lengths Handicap, City of London Baths, Barbican—8.30.
May 1.—Swimming Entertainment at the East and West India Docks.

NOTICE.

Reports of the North London, and Alliance clubs together with the Swimming Association stand over until next week for want of space.

NOTICE TO SUBSCRIBERS.

We must request our Subscribers to forward their subscriptions, failing which no copy of the paper will be forwarded from this date to any gentleman in arrears.

THE HANDICAP OPEN TO ALL COMERS.

The pen, which glibly commits to paper the writer's thoughts, steals with joyousness across its spotless and unruffled surface, and in doing so, betrays an unusually active disposition, arising from the knowledge that for once during its novitiate the wielder enables it to acquaint the public of a remarkable performance, and an equally remarkable man. In the last edition of this paper we, undoubtedly, prepared our readers for the intelligence which it is our lot upon this occasion to place before them. The present subject refers to a handicap, which was commenced at the City of London Baths, on Monday week, and terminated last Monday evening. The principal attraction displayed itself in the appearance of J. Trudgeon, who swam in his preliminary heat uncommonly fast, this coupled with the liklihood of a fine race, and exceptional ability on Trudgeon's part, no doubt enticed a very considerable concourse of spectators, who crowded into the establishment and betrayed intense excitement. Without harassing our readers with any further details it behoves us to state that our expectations were verified and a performance accomplished which must ever rank as one of the fastest on record.

The winner of the handicap, J. Trudgeon, was born at Poplar, London, on May 2nd, 1853, and accordingly will have reached the age of 21 next month. He is self-taught, and acquired the knowledge of swimming in the River Plate, South America, at which place the subject of our memoir informs us there are many swimmers much faster than himself. Previous to this race the winner has only contested one event, which was swam in the Lambeth Baths on Monday, August 11, 1873. The distance traversed was 160 yds., Trudgeon being in receipt of 25 secs. start from W. Cole (100 yards amateur champion). The time he occupied in each essay (there being a second series and final heat) was as follows: 2 min. $12\frac{3}{4}$ secs.; 2 min. $18\frac{3}{4}$ secs.; and 2 min. $17\frac{1}{4}$ secs,; and respecting each trial we must not forget to state that the victor won easily.

The sporting and daily papers it is well known rarely fail to acquaint their readers of the fulfilment of any prediction, and the writer therefore begs the privilege of following in their "mighty" footsteps, and in doing so culls from the "Swimming Record's" early productious the appended prophecy as regards Trudgeon. In our introductory remarks on August 11, 1873, concerning Trudgeon's first essay at Lambeth, will be found the following:—

"A surprising swimmer carried off the handicap, we allude to Trudgeon; this individual swam with both arms entirely out of the water, an action peculiar to Indians. His time was very fast, particularly for one who appears to know but little of swimming, and should he become more finished in style, we shall expect to see him take a position almost second to none as a swimmer."

In the "Retrospect" of the same date will be found the appended information;—

"The event was eventually won by a complete stranger, named Trudgeon, who was in receipt of 25 seconds start. I question indeed if the swimming world ever saw a more peculiar stroke sustained throughout a 160 yards race. I have seen many fast exponents retain the action for some distance, but the great exertion compels them to desist, very much fatigued. In Trudgeon, however, a totally opposite state of things existed, for here we had a man swimming apparently easy, turning very badly, and when finished appeared as though he could have gone at least another 80 yds. at the same pace. His action reminds an observer of a style peculiar to Indians; both arms are thrown partly sideways, but very slovenly, and the head kept completely above water. Placed in the hands of a man like Beckwith, I most unhestatingly declare that we should have in Trudgeon, if not the best, at least one of the fastest swimmers extant."

From the date mentioned above up to the present time little was heard of Trudgeon, and many were the enquiries as to his exact whereabouts and probability of ever appearing again.' In alluding to the time it must not be forgotten that W. Cole swam a similar distance in the same bath on May 5, 1873, occupying in doing so 1 min. $17\frac{3}{4}$ secs., which is $2\frac{1}{2}$ secs. faster than Trudgeon's performance, it must; however, be remembered that Trudgeon turns badly, and would undoubtedly swim much faster in a bath like the Wenlock, or better still in the Serpentine. In our opinion it is the easiest task possible to name the four fastest swimmers in the world over a distance of 120 yards; they are as follows:—J. B. Johnson, E. T. Jones, W. Cole and J. Trudgeon.

With respect to Monday's race the description given below, together with the time, speaks volumes, and bears us out in the opinion expressed, viz., that unless Trudgeon proved himself very little inferior to W. Cole the race would terminate in a dead heat, with Page about a foot behind. Mr. R. Watson was starter, judge, and handicapper.

RESULT—108 YARDS (4 LENGTHS) HANDICAP.—Prize 2 Cups. Second Series. Heat 1, J. Trudgeon (Alliance Club) scratch, 1; J. Giles, 3, 2; J. Howe (West London Club) 12, 3. This race was one of the finest exhibitions of swimming ever witnessed. On Giles receiving his dismissal he at once commenced swimming at a marvellous pace, and so fast did he swim that he passed Howe on traversing $1\frac{1}{2}$ length, and ere two had been concluded Trudgeon was still about $1\frac{1}{2}$ yards behind. The winner appeared rather taken aback at Giles's lead, and on turning for the next length improved his speed, which enabled him to get on level terms on turning for the fourth. A magnificent struggle now ensued to the goal, and although Giles swam in the most dogged and praiseworthy manner, Trudgeon finally defeated him after a brilliant finish by a little over one yard.

TIME.

		min.	sec.
Trudgeon	..	1	$20\frac{1}{4}$
Giles	..	1	$24\frac{1}{3}$

Heat 2, J. Stynes (Bartholomew Club) 20, 1; J. Slaney (Atlantic Club) 2, 2; W. E. Robinson (Alliance Club) 4, 3. Stynes led throughout, Slaney seeing that pursuit was hopeless ceased to persevere with his accustomed energy, the leader consequently won easily. Slaney and Robinson finished in close proximity. Time 1 min. $45\frac{1}{4}$ sec. Heat 3: W. Page (Alliance Club) 12, 1; H. Litten (Atlantic Club) 20, 2; A. Gore (Atlantic Club) 26, 3; M. Hollyer (Atlantic Club) 21, 4. This heat was well contested, and although Page swam rather erratic he was awarded first position by about $1\frac{1}{2}$ yard. Time 1 min. $42\frac{1}{4}$ sec.

FINAL HEAT.

Trudgeon	..	1
Stynes	..	2
Page	..	3

Stynes was sent away amidst profound silence, which was only broken when Trudgeon departed on his journey. About ten yards from the end of the second length the leader crossed over, and on turning for the third pushed off into Pages's water, he however, finding his mistake, once more regained his own station, meanwhile Trudgeon was swimming in the most astonishing manner, nevertheless, to all appearance, victory rested with Stynes, who entered the fourth length with a most commanding lead. At this juncture the excitement grew most intense, and in the most gallant manner each fought out the struggle with great energy. Trudgeon now perceptibly diminished his youthful opponent's lead, and five yards from the goal shot up alongside him and finally won one of the finest and most interesting races ever witnessed by a little over one yard. Same distance separating second and third.

TIME.

		min.	sec.
Trudgeon	..	1	$21\frac{1}{4}$
Stynes	..	1	$43\frac{1}{4}$
Page	..	1	$36\frac{1}{2}$

The prizes were presented at Mr. Webb's, the Rodney Head, by Mr. R. Watson on the same evening.

The Trudgeon Stroke, used by its originator in races held in April 1874, attracted the attention of the Swimming Record.

THE 220 YARDS CHAMPIONSHIP

WILL TAKE PLACE AT

LIVERPOOL,

ON

Monday, July 4th, 1898.

PERPETUAL CHALLENGE CUP,

PRESENTED BY G. H. ROPE, Esq. (Pres. A.S.A. 1897-98), 1895.

Holder—J. H. TYERS, Farnworth S.C.

Originally promoted by the S.A.G.B., 1880.

Previous Winners.

1880	E. C. DANELS.	1888	T. JONES.
1881	E. C. DANELS.	1889	W. EVANS.
1882	E. C. DANELS.	1890	W. EVANS.
1883	T. CAIRNS.	1891	J. H. TYERS.
1884	T. CAIRNS.	1892	J. H. TYERS.
1885	J. NUTTALL.	1893	J. H. TYERS.
1886	J. NUTTALL.	1894	J. H. TYERS.
1887	J. NUTTALL.	1895	J. H. TYERS.
		1896	J. H. TYERS.
		1897	J. H. TYERS.

English Amateur Record, 2 min. 38¼ sec., made by J. H. TYERS, at Nottingham, June 26th, 1897.

Standard Time, 3 min. 15 sec.

Entries (5s. each) close to GEO. PRAGNELL, Hon. Sec. A.S.A., Rathavon, Eltham, on June 27th.

THE 100 YARDS CHAMPIONSHIP

WILL TAKE PLACE AT

NOTTINGHAM,

ON

SATURDAY, JULY 9th, 1898.

PERPETUAL CHALLENGE CUP,

PRESENTED BY THE OTTER S.C., LONDON, 1895.

Holder—J. H. TYERS, Farnworth S.C.

Originally promoted by the South-East London S.C., 1878.

Previous Winners.

1878	J. S. MOORE.	1888	J. NUTTALL.
1879	J. S. MOORE.	1889	C. J. LENTON.
1880	W. R. ITTER.	1890	W. EVANS.
1881	G. BETTINSON.	1891	J. H. TYERS.
1882	C. DEPAU.	1892	J. H. TYERS.
1883	W. BLEW JONES.	1893	J. H. TYERS.
1884	L. MAYGER.	1894	J. H. TYERS.
1885	L. NUTTALL.	1895	J. H. TYERS.
1886	J. NUTTALL.	1897	J. H. TYERS.

English Amateur Record, 1 min. 1 2-5 sec., made by J. H. TYERS, Manchester Osborne S.C., at Burslem, on June 11th, 1896.

Standard time, 1 min. 12 sec.

Entries (5s. each) close to GEO. PRAGNELL, Hon. Sec. A.S.A., Rathavon, Eltham, on July 2nd.

THE MILE CHAMPIONSHIP

WILL TAKE PLACE AT

SOUTHPORT,

ON

SATURDAY, JULY 16TH, 1898.

PERPETUAL CHALLENGE CUP,

HORACE DAVENPORT, Esq. (Pres. A.S.A. 1890-95), 1896.
Presented by J. A. JARVIS, Leicester S.C.

Holder—J. A. JARVIS, Leicester S.C.

Originally promoted by the Metropolitan Swimming Association.

Previous Winners.

1869	T. MORRIS.	1883	E. C. DANELS.
1870	H. PARKER.	1884	G. BELL.
1871	H. PARKER.	1885	S. SARGENT.
1872	D. AINSWORTH.	1886	C. SCHLOTEL.
1873	H. DAVENPORT.	1887	J. NUTTALL.
1874	H. DAVENPORT.	1888	I. STANDRING.
1875	H. DAVENPORT.	1889	H. BOWDEN.
1876	H. DAVENPORT.	1890	S. W. GREASLEY.
1877	H. DAVENPORT.	1891	S. W. GREASLEY.
1878	J. P. TAYLOR.	1892	J. H. TYERS.
1879	J. P. TAYLOR.	1893	J. H. TYERS.
1880	J. P. TAYLOR.	1894	J. H. TYERS.
1881	J. P. TAYLOR.	1896	J. H. TYERS.
1882		1897	J. A. JARVIS.

English Amateur Record, 26 min. 46¾ sec., made by J. H. TYERS, on July 11th, 1896, at Walsall.

Standard Time, 35 minutes.

Entries (5s. each) close to GEO. PRAGNELL, Hon. Sec. A.S.A., Rathavon, Eltham, on July 9th.

THE LONG DISTANCE Championship

WILL TAKE PLACE AT

LONDON,

(Anglian Boat House to Putney Pier—5 miles 60 yards),

ON

SATURDAY, JULY 23rd, 1898.

PAIR OF CHALLENGE CUPS,

Presented by W. J. INNES, Esq. (late President S.C.A.S.A.), 1888.

Holder—P. F. CAVILL, East Sydney S.C., N.S.W.

Originally known as "Lords and Commons' Race" (1877 to 1879), the First Cup having been presented by a number of Members of Parliament.

Previous Winners.

1877	H. DAVENPORT.	1887	A. E. FRANCE.
1878	H. DAVENPORT.	1888	A. E. FRANCE.
1879	W. R. ITTER.	1889	H. BOWDEN.
1880	W. R. RICHARDSON.	1890	W. HENRY.
1881	E. W. HUNTINGTON.	1891	A. IBBOTT.
1882	W. R. ITTER.	1892	M. DRAKE.
1883	G. BELL.	1893	J. H. TYERS.
1884	G. BELL.	1894	Race void.
1885	A. E. FRANCE.	1895	W. GREEN.
1886	A. E. FRANCE.	1897	P. F. CAVILL.

Standard Certificates are given to those finishing within 10 minutes of the winner.

Entries close to GEO. PRAGNELL, Hon. Sec. A.S.A., Rathavon, Eltham, on July 16th.

THE HALF-MILE Championship

WILL TAKE PLACE AT

LEICESTER,

ON

TUESDAY, AUGUST 2nd, 1898.

PERPETUAL CHALLENGE CUP,

Presented by The Surbiton S.C., 1896.

Holder—J. H. DERBYSHIRE, Manchester Osborne S.C.

Originally promoted by the "SPORTING LIFE," 1881.

Previous Winners.

1881	D. AINSWORTH.	1889	J. F. STANDRING.
1882	D. AINSWORTH.	1890	W. EVANS.
1883	D. AINSWORTH.	1891	S. W. GREASLEY.
1884	G. BELL.	1892	S. W. GREASLEY.
1885	H. C. SCHLOTEL.	1893	J. H. TYERS.
1886	H. C. SCHLOTEL.	1894	J. H. TYERS.
1887	H. NUTTALL.	1895	J. H. TYERS.
1888	H. BOWDEN.	1896	J. H. TYERS.
		1897	J. H. DERBYSHIRE.

English Amateur Record, 13 min. 20 sec., made by J. H. TYERS, July 13th, 1895, at Bradford.

Standard Time, 16 Minutes.

Entries (5s. each) close to GEO. PRAGNELL, Hon. Sec. A.S.A., Rathavon, Eltham, on July 26th.

THE 440 YARDS SALT WATER Championship

WILL TAKE PLACE AT

WEYMOUTH,

ON

Wednesday, August 31st, 1898.

PERPETUAL CHALLENGE CUP,

Presented by HORACE DAVENPORT, Esq. (Pres. A.S.A. 1890-95), 1896.
P. F. CAVILL, East Sydney S.C., N.S.W.

Originally promoted by the Portsmouth S.C., 1884.

Previous Winners.

1884	T. CAIRNS.	1891	W. EVANS.
1885	H. C. SCHLOTEL.	1892	W. EVANS.
1886	H. C. SCHLOTEL.	1893	J. H. TYERS.
1887	J. NUTTALL.	1894	J. H. TYERS.
1888	W. HENRY.	1895	J. H. TYERS.
1889	W. EVANS.	1896	J. H. TYERS.
1890	W. EVANS.	1897	P. F. CAVILL.

Standard Certificates are given to those finishing within 30 secs. of the winner's best time in this race.

Entries (5s. each) close to GEO. PRAGNELL, Hon. Sec. A.S.A., Rathavon, Eltham, on August 24th.

The Handbook for 1898 advertised all the ASA's championships.

ASA validated championships and ensured that the great majority of entrants for competitions were of appropriate minimum standard for each event. The following table lists the ASA championships in existence by 1900.

By 1920 the organisation of ASA Championships had changed so that each district had a share of the major events at venues under its control. These arrangements had come into being with the creation of the five Districts. The increase in the number of championships reflected the more competitive nature of the swimming scene. Since that time more championships reflecting the more competitive nature of the swimming scene had come into being. The institution of women's championships marked a major development in the sport, the first of these being established in 1901. A number of the older Cups and Trophies were given perpetual status and these are indicated with an asterisk in the table below which lists the ASA championships in existence by the year 1920.

Comparisons of performances over long periods of time raise many problems about the conditions in which races took place, methods of judging and time measurement. These reservations circumscribe too fine a use of the statistics but there is no doubt that in most competitions performances in terms of faster times improved during the years between the formation of the ASA and 1920. There were no ASA national championships between 1914 and 1919 because of the disruptions caused by the First World War. However, in all other years national events were open to competitors from overseas and these swimmers, especially from Australia, contributed to the achievement of faster times.

In the 100 yards ASA Free style national competition for men there were fluctuations between one year and the next but the overall trend was towards a reduction in the time. At its inception in 1878 J. Moore swam the distance in 1:16.75. During the following twenty years there were increasingly faster times so that the comparable result in 1898 by J. Derbyshire of Osborne SC was 1:00.80. For many of the subsequent years accelerations continued. The fastest time was that of 1920, when I. Stedman, from Australia, won in 0:58.00.

The first ASA Free Style National Championship for women took place in 1901 when H. Thorp of Leeds SC won the race in

1:30.40. Thereafter until 1920 timings speeded up with the fastest time of 1:13.60 being achieved by I. Steer of Cardiff SC in 1910 and by D. Curwen of Westminster SC (Liverpool) in 1913. The ASA introduced its 220 yards Free Style National Championship for women in 1912 and the times were all above 3 minutes.

The men's ASA 220 yards Free Style National Championships began in 1880 with a win by E. Danels of North London SC in 3:09.75. In 1901 the winning times had been reducing and in that year the time was 2:42.00 by J. Derbyshire of Osborne SC. By 1912 J. Hatfield of Middlesbrough SC had the championship for swimming the race in 2:30.20. In 1920 the fastest time of the period was achieved by F. Beaupaire of Australia in 2:29.20.

The first 440 yards ASA Free Style National Championship for men was won in 1884 by T. Cairns of Everton SC in 6:33.00 and during the nineteenth century no English competitor did better than W. Henry of Zephyr SC in 1889 whose time was 6:04.00. Between 1901 and 1920 the fastest English competitor to win the event was H. Taylor of Chadderton SC whose time was 4:43.00.

In 1878 the first 500 yards ASA Free Style National Championship for men took place and was won by J. Taylor of Newcastle SC in 8:07.25, the slowest time before 1920. In the early 1890s the winning times fell to just over 7 minutes and after J. Jarvis of Leicester SC won in 6:47.60 winning times were never above 7 minutes and the fastest time was in 1905 when the Australian B. Kieran won in 6.07.20.

The ASA's National Half Mile Championship began in 1881 when D. Ainsworth took the title with a time of 14.31.50 and the trend for faster times before 1920 reduced the winning times in the early twentieth century by about two minutes. In 1905 Kieran swam the distance in the best time of the period of 11:28.00.

The oldest of the National ASA Championships, the Mile took place in the River Thames. It began in 1869 when T. Morris of National SC of London won the race in 27:18.00. Because of varying conditions the race took over 30 minutes in some years the slowest being 35:20.00 in 1881 by J. Taylor. The faster times of under 30 minutes became the norm after 1900 when the loca-

Table 1:2 ASA Championships by 1900

Distance	Promoter/Originator	Date of first Competition
The Mile	MSA later SAGB – Cup presented by Otter SC (1895)	1869
The Half Mile	Sporting Life	1881
The 100 Yards	South East London SC – Cup presented by Otter SC	1878
The 220 Yards	SAGB – Cup presented by W.J. Innes	1880
The 500 Yards	North London SC – Once called 'Lords and Commons Race'	1878
Long Distance (Between 5 and 6 miles direct)	Challenge Cup Cup presented by W.J. Innes, President of SCASA	1890
Other Championships:		
The Salt Water	Portsmouth SC – Challenge Cup property of club	1884
The Plunging	SAGB – Cup presented by W.J. Innes, President of SCASA	1883
The Water Polo	ASA	1888

tion of the race had moved to a different part of the river. The fastest time was by H. Taylor, then of Hyde Seal SC, whose time was 23:35.50.

Entertainment and swimming

The ASA and its antecedents regarded the gala as the principal means of the exposure of swimming to the general public. It is not surprising to find that such prestigious activities should be the subject of Association laws. In the case of newly established or affiliated clubs, ASA advice was available on as many aspects as possible so that swimming had the most favourable public image.

Order and security at swimming baths and other locations posed problems during the second half of the nineteenth century.

One of the features of comments in the swimming press of the 1890s was the proud boast that during the previous twenty years thefts of swimmers' clothing and other belongings had almost ended thanks to club vigilance. Similarly, fights and unseemly conduct had become rarities at public events. The latter owed much to the effective management of events, clarity in making decisions and announcing results, and of club members acting as stewards where the need arose.

Attracting the general public and the press to galas called for careful management of events and adequate advanced publicity. Although competitive races and stylish diving appealed to the connoisseurs, the general public lacked the knowledge of the finer points of performances needed to fully appreciate the achievements of performers. Thus the ASA advocated holding demon-

Table 1:3 ASA Championships by 1920		
Activity	*Trophy*	*Date*
Club Performance	*The Henry Benjamin National Memorial Trophy* Presented by the Five Districts of ASA	1910
100 yards	Perpetual Challenge Cup★ Presented by Otter SC	1895
220 yards	Perpetual Challenge Cup★ Presented by G.H. Rope, President ASA 1897-98	1895
440 yards Salt Water	Perpetual Challenge Cup Presented by Horace Davenport, President ASA 1890-94	1896
500 yards	Perpetual Challenge Cup★ Presented by Sir George Pragnell, Hon. Sec. ASA 1890-1902, Pres. 1903	1896
The Half Mile	Perpetual Challenge Cup★ Presented by Surbiton SC	1896
The Mile	Perpetual Challenge Cup★ Presented by Horace Davenport	1896
The Long Distance	Perpetual Challenge Cup★ Presented by W.J. Innes, Pres. SCASA	1901
200 yards Breast Stroke	Perpetual Challenge Cup Presented by Dr Morgan Dockrell	1903
150 yards Back Stroke	Perpetual Challenge Cup Presented by J.T. Hincks, President ASA 1907	1903
100 yards Ladies'	Perpetual Silver Challenge Vase Presented by Ravensbourne SC	1910
220 yards	Perpetual Challenge Trophy by ASA called *Sir George Pragnell Trophy*	1912
Plunging	Perpetual Challenge Cup★ Presented by Horace Davenport	1901
Diving	Perpetual Challenge Cup Presented by A.StP. Cufflin, President of ASA 1919	1907
150 yards Ladies' Back Stroke	No Trophy – Instituted in	1920
200 yards Ladies' Breast Stroke	No Trophy – Instituted in	1920
Ladies' Long Distance	No Trophy – Instituted in	1920
Schoolboy Team Swimming	*Barker Memorial Trophy* Perpetual Challenge Shield presented to ASA by NCASA in memory of G.H. Barker, Hon. Secretary of NCASA	1896
Club Team Swimming	*Webb Memorial Trophy* Perpetual Challenge Trophy in memory of Captain Webb	1909
Club Water Polo	Perpetual Challenge Shield Presented by Ravensbourne SC	1896
County Water Polo	Perpetual Challenge Shield Presented by W.J. Read, President of ASA 1895-6	1896

strations and spectacles to draw supporters to events. This became of greater importance once the lure of gambling diminished or disappeared.

Common events in a gala were demonstrations of life saving so that the practical importance of being able to swim had due emphasis. Often the larger clubs arranged a water polo match or diving, where possible, and perhaps a display of ornamental swimming. This was one of the most popular events at galas in the period between 1870 and 1914. Sometimes known as *scientific* swimming its prime purpose was to demonstrate less common skills in swimming baths. Illustrations from the later nineteenth century indicated the range of strokes and motions through the water:

> '*treading water, swimming like a dog, sculling, somersaults, marching on water, swimming on the breast feet first, the propeller and the pendulum, the plank, the porpoise, the torpedo, the spinning top, and various tricks such as swimming with feet and hands tied, undressing in the water, smoking and drinking under water*'.

Making a gala and spectacle, as reported from Whitehaven in 1885.

WHITEHAVEN CLUB.

This club held an amateur aquatic entertainment and sports, in the Baths, Duke-street, on Monday night. The bath was crowded by most of the leading tradespeople of the town and their families. By kind permission of Captain Atkinson, the Whitehaven Artillery Volunteer Band was in attendance, and played a selection of airs during the evening. Mr. John Jackson occupied the chair, at the request of the Swimming Club Committee, and introduced the programme by a short speech. He congratulated the young men and yonths—in fact the whole of the population of Whitehaven, on having such a sweet bath in which to pursue a health-giving occupation and amusement, and to qualify themselves in the art of natation, so that they might in case of emergency not only be able to save their own lives but those also of their fellow creatures. They never knew when an occasion of that kind was going to arrive. Those who had seen the papers that morning, would see that without any notice a pier collapsed entirely, and the whole of the people who were on it fell into the water. In such cases, if it were not for baths and opportunities of learning swimming, there would be many more drowned than there were. He had been requested by the committee to observe that this was their first entertainment and to ask that the company should be charitable in their judgment. (Applause). He could not say, from his own knowledge and observation that that appeal was scarcely necessary, because he believed they would come up to the mark in every respect. (Applause.) The following programme was then gone through, Captain Atkinson acting as starter, and Mr. G. H. Liddell as judge:—

One Hundred Yards' Race (six lengths of the bath).—There were twelve entries, but only eight competed. These swam in three heats. In the first heat, Mr. A. Mathieson, Dr. Muir, and Mr. A. Gibb started. These three adopted the breast stroke. Mathieson fell in the rear, and gave up at the fourth length. Muir kept a slight superiority over his remaining opponent until the last length, when his reserved energy brought him to the front. In the second heat, C. Milligan, J. Peat, and R. Newall swam. This trio went off with the side stroke. Milligan went off at a magnificent rate, and before more than half the distance was done first Peat and then Newall retired. Heat 3: C. Bondsey and W. Thornber were the only competitors, these adopted the side stroke also. Bondsey had a slight advantage in the fourth and fifth lengths, bnt in the last, amid great applause, Thornber struck out more vigorously, and his greater sustaining power brought him in first. Muir, Milligan, and Thornber were left for the final. Milligan's swimming was greatly admired. With a most powerful side stroke he rushed along at an astonishing rate, and won by better than half a length. Time 1 min. 28 secs., Muir beat Thornber by two or three yards.

Four Lengths' Race (boys under 15).—Masters J. Brown, G. Nairn, and James M'Gowan were the competitors in this race, which was also a very interesting one. M'Gowan and Nairn had the race pretty

much to themselves, the one swimming side-stroke and the othe breast-stroke. The former had the greatest staying power, ane although the two kept together fairly well until the last length, the final spurt enabled him to distance Nairn easily.

Hurdle Race.—Two stout poles tied at the ends to the sides of the bath, obstructed the course, and it was required that the competitors should alternately go under and over the impediments. There was sixteen entered, but only five competed; these swam in two heats. Messrs. W. Brockbank, J. Kessell, and J. Peat formed the first heat, and Newall and Bondsey the second. The difficulty proved to be to remember whether it was under or over the pole that one was required to go. Kessell lost a lot of time by a mistake of this kind, and Brockbank won the first heat, which would otherwise have been his. Newall's staying power proved too strong for Bondsey. The final between Newall and Brockbank was a pretty close race, the former winning by a yard or two.

Tub Race by Members of the Club.—This was a farcical performance solely for the amusement of the company. There was no attempt at any competition. Those who entered were seated in tubs, the diameter of which was just sufficient to enable them to seat themselves on their haunches, and they were required to propel themselves by paddling the water with their hands. Messrs. W. Mulcaster, Kessell, Gibb, and Bondsey entered. They were all dressed in extravagant attire. Gibb having a top hat, while Mulcaster and Kessell were made up as females. The fun consisted in the overturning of the tubs, and the antics of their owners. It caused great amusement.

Blindfold Race (for boys under 15).—Here there was also great fun, although this time there was real competition. Masters H. H. Brown, J. H. Brown, Jas. M'Gowan, and G. M. Nairn entered. The course was two lengths of the baths. M'Gowan was the only one who kept on a straight course, and he won. The others all went diagonally, ultimately reaching one of the sides, whereupon they turned round and kicked off in the opposite direction, landing against the other side, and so on, finally giving up the attempt and putting off their bandages to find themselves furthest away from the place they imagined they might be.

Clothes Race (two lengths, minimum weight of clothes 6lb).—Messrs. Muir, Kessell, E. Boyd, and I. Kitchin competed; Muir was first. Kessell second.

Exhibition of Life Saving, &c.—The members of the club then gave an exhibition of life saving, fancy swimming, and object diving. Dr. Fisher and Mr. Feldtman illustrated life-saving operations, and quite a crowd went in for the other parts of the performance. Among the divers, Shippen distinguished himself by diving from the top of the balcony railings. Mulcaster turned somersaults backwards from the low spring board. Newall turned five successive somersaults in the water, and performed a variety of extraordinary feats, such as drinking milk under water, writing on both sides of a slate under water, eating a piece of bread under water, smoking a cigar under water, and so on. The performances of Newall were especially admired. The bath was illumined by the electric (incandescent) lamps, one of which was placed in the water at the bottom of the centre of the bath.

Blindfold Race.—Seventeen were entered for this event, but only eight competed, and these smam in heats—(1) Messrs. Kessell, Brockbank, Mathieson, and Bondsey; and (2) Messrs. Muloaster, Thornber, Wake, and E. Boyd. As in the previous race for boys, victory was not necessarily to the strongest nor to the swiftest, but to the one who could swim from one end of the bath to the other, and return with the least deviation from a straight line in his course. Mathieson managed to win the first heat, while Wake won the second; the collisions and confusions of the various other competitors caused roars of laughter. In the final. Mathieson was being cheered on his return journey, in prospect of a win, in the midst of which Wake veered of the straight and arrived at one of the sides, and was much astonished on uncovering to discover his position.

Tug of War.—Messrs. Peat, Milligan, Newall, Gibb, and Kitchin, pulled against Messrs. Boyd. Bondsey, Muir, Shippen, and Brockbank. The result was a draw, the one team winning at one end and the other when ends were reversed.

Aquatic Football.—Nearly the whole of the members who took part in the programme entered for this event, forming sides one of which was distinguished by red neckerchiefs. The game was to hit a football with the hand, or throw it, so as to make points as in the game of football, the two ends of the bath forming the goal lines.

Presentation of prizes.—Mrs. Whittle kindly consented to present a number of prizes provided for the successful competitors in some of the events.

A vote of thanks was awarded, on the motion of the chairman, to the ladies and gentlemen who lent flags to decorate the bath-room; to Captain Atkinson and Mr. Liddell, and to Mrs. Whittle; and a vote of thanks to the chairman, on the proposition of Dr. Fisher, brough a most successful entertainment to a close.—*Whitehaven News.*

Most frequently these events were undertaken by professional swimmers, both male and female. Occasionally music accompanied a water dance as part of a programme intended to amuse rather than to show artistic interpretations. Essentially all these ornamental activities were staged for their novelty value and to hold the interest of a public which might become bored by racing or diving competitions. The performance of novelty swimming tricks of Professor Beckwith and his daughter attracted the attention of the swimming press. Amateur swimmers took part in such events as *duck hunts,* an event where one swimmer was chased by others. Team events included *crocodile races* which required four swimmers in a team to remain in contact with each other whilst challenging others.

One of the aspects of swimming clubs which gave them their vitality was the social activity which their members organised to enjoy good fellowship. The close association of the ASA with the AAA and the NCU undoubtedly owed much to their overlapping memberships in that many members of swimming clubs took a broad interest in sports and games. Information about this range of activities was often included in swimming publications.

British swimming and overseas connections

Few aspects of British life in the nineteenth century took place without the consciousness of the nation's position as a world wide power. Amongst the more potent influences was the Empire. Throughout the period from 1874 until 1920 imperial sporting connections expanded. One of the attributes which the British claimed to bring to all parts of the world where it exercised sway was a high regard for sporting activity. Naturally swimming had its role in this spread of British culture, although it did not lead to competitive fixtures of representative teams from overseas. Undoubtedly, the major inhibitions to this were the costs of travel and subsistence for competitors. The ASA had insufficient funds to do much for British entrants to the Olympic Games.

Closer relations with neighbouring countries to Britain were fostered when the ASA made agreements with several of its European counterparts. The agreement with the Union des Sociétés Françaises de Sports Athlétiques (USFSA) was made in 1907, whereby the ASA and USFSA recognised each others competitions and conditions for entry. In the next year similar agreements were negotiated with the Deutscher Schwimm Verband of Germany and with the Fédération Belge des Sociétés de Natation of Belgium in the same year. These alliances increased the international sporting competitions of the years immediately prior to the outbreak of the First World War.

One of the concurrent developments in the decade before the outbreak of war in 1914 was the formation in London on 19 July 1908 of the Fédération Internationale de Natation (FINA). In its early years the ASA *Handbooks* referred to it as the International Amateur Swimming Association. Council welcomed these developments because international competition brought like-minded people together to enjoy the sport. In this period the achievements of British swimmers brought much prestige. The close links between FINA and the ASA are demonstrated by the appointment of George Hearn as FINA's first Honorary Secretary. He had served as President of the ASA in 1908, and remained a member of the ASA Committee. His involvement

with the Association had included being its Honorary Secretary and holding the same office for the Western District ASA, and he was one of the members of the International Board which organised water polo competitions between England and Scotland.

ASA and the Olympic Games, 1896 to 1920

The first Olympic Games of the modern era were held in Greece in 1896 where its small range of swimming competitions took place in a course set out in the sea. No British swimming team took part. Four years later the organisers organised swimming events in a pool to ensure less variable conditions for competitors. In that year J. Jarvis of Leicester won the 1000 metres free style and the British team won the water polo competition.

Evidence of the way the ASA supported the Olympic movement appeared in the terse report to Council in 1907. The report referred to the supplementary Games held at Athens in 1906 was so designated because the 1904 Games had not included some of the swimming events. The report mentioned that

> '*The arrangements made by W. Henry for the convenience and comfort of the travellers were admirable, and J.A. Jarvis filled the dual parts of Captain and Honorary Treasurer*'.

Even this brief comment gives some insight into the organisation and the expectations of 'Olympians' in the early years of the movement. It reflected the spirit of amateurism where participants paid for their own sport, largely from their own pockets and were independent of other support. There was no sponsorship beyond the grant of £69 6s 8d from the British Olympic Association 'towards the expenses of four swimming representatives'. The ASA contributed £37 16s 4d from its funds. The total expenditure on rail and boat fares, hotel expenses and special costumes amounted to £107 3s 0d. W. Henry, a competitor and team manager, met all his own costs. All swimmers paid for their own training and took responsibility for their health needs.

On this occasion the ASA was invited to select the team to represent Britain after trials. The team selected comprised: G. Melville Clarke (diving), J. H. Derbyshire (100 metres and team race), H. Taylor (400 metres, 1600 metres and team race), J.A. Jarvis (400 metres, 1600 metres and team race). The fourth place was taken by W. Henry (team race). Oddly he was one of the Swimming Jury at the Supplementary Olympics at Athens. Before departure Jarvis had the task of obtaining costumes '*strictly in accordance with regulations*' with the Union Jack as team badge. Jarvis, who came from the centre for knitwear, Leicester, had links with the trade so his task might have proved less onerous than for other potential nominees.

The ASA was also invited to select the swimming team for the Olympic Games held in London in 1908 and again for the Games in Stockholm in 1912. In the 1908 games H. Taylor won gold medals in the 400 metres free style and 1500 metres free style, H. Haresnape of Liverpool won the bronze in the 100 metres back stroke and F. Holman of Exeter and W. Robinson of Liverpool were respectively winners of gold and silver medals in the 200 metres breast stroke. British swimmers won the team race and the water polo gold awards. Although a limited programme of events was arranged for women there were too few participants to make

EX-AMATEUR CHAMPION
SWIMMER OF THE WORLD
EXHIBITOR AT GALAS

PROF J. A. JARVIS

5, DERBY STREET, KING'S CROSS,

WINNER OF 108 CHAMPIONSHIPS.
INSTRUCTOR IN ALL STROKES

LONDON. W.C

John Arthur ('Jack') Jarvis was born in Leicester in 1872 and died in London in 1933. He dominated many events at the very end of the nineteenth and at the start of the twentieth century. In the 1900 Olympic games he won the 1000 metres and 4000 metres. He won various international long distance events and held ASA records when he triumphed in ASA championships.

Henry Taylor, the outstanding British Olympian, competed in all the Olympic Games from the Athens Supplementary of 1906 to the Antwerp of 1920 and he won 4 Gold, 1 Silver and 3 Bronze medals. His tally of ASA national championships was fifteen in the same period.

The start of the 1908 Olympics final of the 200 metre breaststroke which was won by F. Holman of Great Britain.

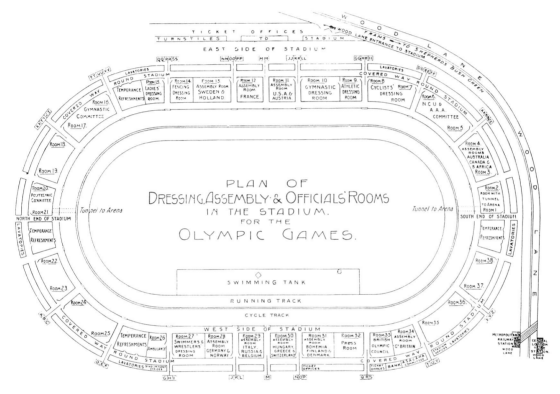

The stadium erected at Shepherds Bush, London, followed the plan which located the swimming events in the tank within the arena.

The British team won the 200 metres swimming race at the 1908 Olympic Games and they were from left to right: P. Radmilovic, W. Foster, J.H. Derbyshire, H. Taylor and their trainer W. Brickett.

it an official competition. At the 1912 Games J.G. Hatfield won the silver medals in the 400 metres and 1500 metres free style; P. Courtman of Old Trafford SC won the bronze in the 200 metres breast stroke. At Stockholm women competed fully. J. Fletcher of Leicester won the bronze in the ladies' 100 metres, and I. (Belle) White of Ilford won the bronze in the ladies' plain diving. The British team won the bronze for the 800 metres team race, and golds were won in the ladies' team race and in water polo. The ASA's report of 1912 reflected on the differences between in the achievements in the two Olympiads and reported as follows:

> *'While not equalling our successes at the Olympiad of 1908, the results, although somewhat disappointing, were not disheartening, as two first, two second, and four third positions were secured, representing 14 points out of a possible 75 with 18 nations competing'.*

After the First World War the Olympic Games were resumed at Antwerp. The outcome in 1920 was clearly disappointing to George Hearn the ASA's Honorary Secretary for the Olympic Games. He reported that:

> *'Reviewing the results attained during the Games we have little to be proud of.*
> *1st in Water Polo,*
> *2nd in Ladies' Team Race,*
> *3rd in Men's Team Race and*
> *2nd in Ladies' High Diving,*
> *Miss Armstrong being the only individual competitor to get placed'.*

This change of fortune seemed to echo the diminished power of Great Britain in a world of increasingly strong competition.

The ASA accounts for 1920 showed that the greater number of events and hence competitors, cost more than four times the figures for 1906. The receipts were £497 14s 3d, of which Southport Corporation, which had hosted the initial trials at its resort, donated £150, *'The Old Olympian Fund'* £227 14s 3d, and the British Olympic Association £120. The expenses showed that the trials for swimming and diving cost £256 9s 4d, and that the ASA had to find £17 16s 5d from general funds to balance the excess of expenditure over receipts. International competition had become expensive.

ASA and the First World War

The ASA, in common with many other organisations, adapted in a piecemeal fashion to the changing conditions created by the war in August 1914. In this the ASA followed the lead of the government whose propagandists had promised an end to hostilities by Christmas. In October the ASA championships were suspended. By March 1915 the continued warfare and reappraisals prompted the ASA to consider closing down its activities for the duration of the war. However this did not happen and it continued its activities at a diminished level.

No Council was held until 1919 when the ASA Committee gave an account of its activities during the war years. Efforts to foster swimming education had continued and in 1917 the Schoolboy Team Championship was held. Women's events con-

The British team in 1912 with the officials at the Stockholm Olympiad. The women competitiors all wore the regulation robes over their costumes.

This group at the Coventry Swimming Baths in 1919 were awarded certificates 'in recognition of Honorary Services to the ASA in demonstrating the correct methods of swimming'. During the war years the Committee had continued to promote swimming and relied on these participants. Back row (l to r) Bessie Kneen (Ladies' secretary and chaperone), Alan Mann, William Joy, Austin Rawlinson [Olympic Backstroke finalist in 1924 and later president of the ASA], Harry Philips, William Owen, William Howcroft (Honorary Secretary and Coach) [member of the ASA education committee and journalist]. Seated row (l to r) Marjorie Finch, May Spencer [held records for Back and Breast strokes], Lilian Bennett [one of the first holders of the ASA Advanced Certificate], Charlotte Radcliffe, Hilda James [Seven times world record holder of Free style and silver medallist at 1920 Olympics]. The seated front row (l to r) Robert McKenzie [silver medallist at Olympics, 1924], James Edwardson, Joseph Crowther. Three people were not present for the photograph taken at the baths in Coventry: Freda Turner, James Mason and William Taylor.

tinued where pools were still accessible in spite of wartime restrictions. Indeed some records were broken. The determination to avoid association with financial awards for swimming was maintained by the Committee in that a request to use War Savings Certificates (each with a face value of 16s 0d) as prizes was rejected.

Only a few Committee meetings were held and no *Handbook* was published between 1915 and 1918. Once the war ended two slim volumes covered the war years. The revival of the ASA began in 1919 following most of the policy recommendations of the Reconstruction Sub-Committee appointed in October 1918 and which had reported five days after the Armistice of 11 November. The clock could not be put back. *Normality* had to take into account the experiences and losses of the war as well as the extent to which new circumstances existed in Britain and overseas. As noted earlier, the full impact of overseas competition became apparent at the 1920 Olympic Games where British results did not compare with those of earlier meetings. It was clear that the ASA had to respond to the needs of swimming in a changed social environment.

External relations

ASA and kindred organisations

Two bodies had particular interests which impinged on swimming: the Royal Humane Society (RHS) and Royal Life Saving Society (RLSS). The ASA sought to make common cause with the RHS by encouraging people to learn to swim both to save their own lives and to help others in difficulties. The interest in life saving had been prompted by tragedies such as the sinking on the River Thames in 1879 of the Princess Alice with the loss of more than 700 lives. The subsequent publicity suggested that there were only a small number of survivors because only a few passengers were able to swim. No less than 339 females drowned but one only swam to safety. Approaches in 1887 between the Association and the RHS did not develop further because the RHS did not wish to enlarge its activities beyond suggesting that the ASA promote swimming to save life.

William Henry who was born in London in 1859 and died in 1928. He founded the Royal Life Saving Society. He worked tirelessly for the ASA and was an outstanding swimmer. At the age of 47 years he won a bronze medal in the 4x250 metres relay at the Athens Supplementary Olympics in 1906.

The life saving issue was very important because of the numbers of people who drowned each year in circumstances where the ability to swim would have saved lives. Preventing these tragedies became such a preoccupation of Mr William Henry that he and some of his fellow members of the ASA decided to organise the Life Saving Society (later Royal) in 1891. Its title *Royal* was granted soon after 1893 when the Duke of York became its President, and the Duke of Teck, its Vice President. The only aspect of swimming with professionals which was acceptable to the ASA was that of giving demonstrations of life saving to the general public. The RLSS made common cause with the ASA in arguing for swimming to be a part of the educational experience of all children at school.

The RLSS began publishing *The Swimming Magazine* as its official organ in 1914. In every issue it covered matters relating to the ASA and its interests, and 'The Ladies' Section' indicated the expansion of women's participation in all aspects of water sports. This journal appeared monthly and one of its active contributors and organisers was William Henry whose advocacy of swimming education ensured that the topic had prominence throughout the war years.

The ASA also enjoyed cordial relationships with the Amateur Diving Association, founded in 1900, which is discussed in Chapter 7.

Publications about swimming

Specialised magazines and newspapers proliferated during the second half of the nineteenth century. The abolition of all taxes on newspapers and magazines in 1855 lowered prices. Expanding numbers of literate people thirsty for knowledge coincided with ever more businesses seeking to advertise goods and services. Politicians and publicists took their chance to appeal to the growing range of particular interest groups gaining support amongst voters. Popular sports attracted enterprising publishers hoping to make a living within this expanding market. Sales to sports people and access to a defined market gave potential for drawing advertising revenues. Organisations making sporting codes of practice, which claimed nation-wide authority, emerged during this period. Thus, it is not surprising that swimming became one of the activities which encouraged the launch of a specialist magazine at the time of the emergence of the SAGB from the MAS.

Robert Watson issued the first number of *The Swimming, Rowing and Athletic Record* on 10 May 1873. This weekly cost one penny and comprised four pages, of which the major part was devoted to swimming news. A fortnight later the number of pages increased to six and the masthead title changed to *The Swimming Record and Chronicle of Sporting Events*. The paper carried reports of meetings of the MAS, a swimming entertainment organised by the Rochdale (Lancashire) Board of Health, and among the advertisements was one for a swimming teacher for ladies. In August the paper reported on the opening of the Clapham and Brixton Baths by the Lord Mayor of the City of London, Sir Sydney Waterlow, who commented that: '*He was pleased to find excellent accommodation had been provided for the ladies.*' In the same month it reported on a swimming entertainment at the Crystal Palace which included a *Duck Hunt* . In October the Parkers, Harry and Emily, demonstrated *Ornamental Natation* in an entertainment.

Watson's paper carried a lively correspondence about the relationship of professionals with amateurs in swimming and the problems of definitions of status. It was evident from editorial comments that his own position was equivocal. His paper carried news of professionals and challenges which involved cash prizes and undoubtedly gambling on the side.

Watson's first venture seemed to have failed. He returned to the same publishing field in 1884. By this time the effects of Forster's Education Act of 1870 had gone far towards nation-wide basic literacy among the young. In 1884 Watson published *Swimming Notes* which appeared at first on octavo sized sheets as a weekly, but after a few issues it was printed in a much larger format. Two years later Watson changed the name of his publication to *The Swimmer,* made it a fortnightly publication, and maintained the price at one penny. The subtitle was *A Journal Devoted to Natation* and it appeared on 1 February 1886. The first editorial in *The Swimmer* called for swimming to form part of the school curriculum in view of the *Princess Alice* tragedy. In April 1886 the paper reported on the diversity of certificates awarded for swimming competence and a letter from Edward Wakeling called for the SAGB to set standards for certificates.

Swimming Notes and its successor *The Swimmer* carried news of the problems confronting the SAGB and its breakaway group known as the Amateur Swimming Union. The tone adopted by Watson in his papers suggests that he regarded debates about the meaning of amateur as a matter of irritating semantics. His paper carried news of professional activities including the Professional Swimmers Association. During its relatively short period of pub-

PORTSMOUTH CLUB.

On Monday morning the **fourth annual** contest for the ladies' cham-
ship was swam in the sea off Southsea Beach, nearly two
usand spectators attending. The distance was 88 yards, and Mr.
H. Fisk officiated as starter, the judge being Dr. C. Knott. Miss
een, the champion of last year, won the championship and the
guinea gold medal in 1 min. 12 sec. Miss Nellie Thompson
am second, her time being 1 min. 23 sec.; a second behind came
ss Alice Gore. Miss Mabel Green was fourth, and a foot only
parated her and Miss Ida Wynhall. The others who finished were
ss Lilly Flowers, Miss Rose Flowers, Miss Blanche Mildred Barrow,
iss Fanny Cousens, Miss Ruth Jelks, and Miss Catherine Friend.
he time of last year's race was 1 min. 37 sec. Times of previous
ears : 1881, 1 min. 50 sec ; 1882, 1 min. 35 sec. ; 1883, 1 min. 37 sec. ;
884, 1 min 12 sec.
The Senior Championship 500 yards Scratch Race, by residents
ook place on Wednesday last, when S. Sergeant beat C. White, E
Eason, and H Burton.

PROVINCIAL NEWS.

SOUTH COAST RACES.

PORTSMOUTH FESTIVAL (CONCLUDED).

The club's events, which owing to the number of entries could not
be contested on the August Bank Holiday, were brought to a most
successful conclusion on Saturday afternoon. and formed the conclu-
ding item in the programme of the Southsea Regatta week. The
races started at 3 o"clock. sharp and were not concluded till 6. 30.
Judges, Mr. Horace Davenport, Ilex S. C. (Ex-Champion Amateur);
and Messrs. R. J. Jones, H. M. Dockyard. Portsmouth, and G. T
Carter (hon. instructor. P.S.C.) : handicapper and starter, Mr. H. W"
Fisk.

88 YARDS LADIES SIAMESE TWIN RACE.—The Misses Nellie
Thompson, and Rose Flowers. 1 : the Misses Mabel Couzens Ander-
on Green and Blanche Mildred Barrow. 2 : the Misses Ida Louise
Vynhall and Edith Totterdell. 3: the Misses Catherine Mary
riend and Elizabeth Dempsey, 0 ; the Misses Ruth Jelks and
illy Flowers, 0 ; the Misses Esme Wynhall and Fanny Couzens. 0 ;
ne Misses Chontal Brown and Lilly Cox. 0; the fair competitors
ter using a number of arguments in order to induce the hon. sec. to
ad all completed the distance. the spectators crowding every avail-
le portion of the beach in order to obtain a good view of the race.
88 YARDS BOYS RACE UNDER 14 (carrying banners with a strange
vice).—Heat 1 : W. H. Hooper, 1 ; W. Francis, 2 ; L. Harrison, 3 ;
. Johnson, 0 ; W. Sandall, 0 ; R. V. Ogilvie, 0 ; A. Lewis, 0 ; D.
Johnson, 0. Heat 2 ; G. H. Andrew. 1 ; J. H. Parker, 2 ; T.
rent, 3 ; R. Webb, 0 ; J. Briant, 0 ; H. Cook, 0 ; L. Harding, 0.
nal heat : Andrew, 1 ; Parker, 2 ; Hooper, 3 ; the strange device
on the banners of " The Grand Old Man, Francis the Tailor," was
oductive of some little chaff and amusement.
88 YARDS FOR MEMBERS (who on August 5th, had never won a
ze for fast swimming in an open amateur race, brought out 28
rants, and was contested in four heats, the placed men being):
at 1 : F. Batchelor, 1 ; A. Lush, 2 ; A. W. Blake, 3. Heat 2 ; E.
Eason (penalised 12 sec.) 1 ; H. Sprent, 2 ; John Aitkin, 3. Heat
E. R. Prior, 1 ; W. G. Graham, 2 ; James Aitken, 3. Heat 4.
H. Andrews, 1 ; R. G. Kirk (pen. 5 sec.), 2 ; J. G. Barrows. 3.
al heat : Final heat : Eason, 1 ; Graham, 2 ; Batchelor, 3 ; a
worth seeing. won by Eason by virtue of his length of arm.
ham, a small youth. not being able to reach out quite so far,
chelor also swam remarkably well.
YARDS CHAMPIONSHIP (Portsmouth Schools, for two prizes
ented by Portsmouth School-board).—G. Cheeseman (Oliver's
ning College). 1 ; E. H. Parry (Gloucester House Academy). 2 ;
eseman. profiting by his experience in the race for the Junior
mpionship, swam right away from the first, and never stopped
I Mr. Davenport had recorded his name in the official list as
pion for the ensuing year. The pace was far to warm for any
others, but Harris, Parks, and the rest of the boys deserve to be
oned for the determined manner in which they struggled to
Parry for second place.
YARDS HANDICAP.—Heat 1 : A. F. Cooke. 10. 1 ; W. M
ham, 9, 2 ; F. G. J. Wright. 20, 3 ; A. Sargeant. 5. † ; H. H.
on, 3. † ; E. R. Prior, 16, 0 ; F. Batchelor, 14, 0 ; G. H
ew. 14. 0 ; J. Andrew, 12. 0 ; W. G. Graham, 11. 0 ; B. Ward.
J. Moore. 7. 0 ; a splendid race. Heat 2 : W. R. P. Winni-
, 1 : W. Anderson, 15. 2 ; G. Cheeseman, 5, † : W. C. Reed.
E. Sigrist, 25. 0 ; W. Francis, 22. 0 ; J. H. Parker. 20, 0 ;
Hooper. 20. 0 ; G. Gould. 16. 0 ; W. E. Hobson. 15. 0 ; C.
all, 14. 0 ; J. R. Holley, 5, 0 ; a good race. Final heat :
, 1 ; Bingham, 2 ; Wright, 3.
SOLATION SCRAMBLE IN SACKS.—A. Sargeant, Arthur Cooke,
erman. A. Lush, J. Moore, E. R. Prior. J. Aitken. E. Sigrist.
T. Dyer : Moore was first to reach the Curiosity Box. but he
to find the " toggle." Sargeant was more successful and at
t pull of the rope Britannia seated on her car and holding aloft
earing the inscription. " Success to the Portsmouth Swimming
rose majestically from the deep blue sea to the height of
above her throne amidst the loud cheers of the spectators.
re delighted with this clever invention of Mr. Baker. A foot-
tch between Messrs. Sigrist's and Armstrong's Teams ended
of the former by one goal to love.

---

lication Watson made attempts to attract readers from all types of
people interested in water sports. In the event, these innovations
did not save the paper and it closed in 1886.

The next attempt to publish a magazine specifically devoted to
swimming was *Swimming* which had as its subtitle *'with which is
incorporated City of London and West End Sport'* which was produced by *English Sports* in 1895. This weekly carried advertisements from costume makers offering ASA style costumes, and the
front cover showed water polo players apparently climbing from a
bath to seek out Bovril, as a warming and restorative drink. Most
news items dealt with reports on local London competitions. It is
not clear how long this publication survived. As noted earlier, ASA
matters had been reported in the *Swimming Magazine* published
by the RLSS beginning in 1914. This monthly journal appeared
to have established a more stable readership and lasted until 1919.

Press coverage of swimming had appeared in that period,
though it is difficult to trace the details. Galas and competitions
were popular in both London and provincial papers. These are
glimpses of the pattern of activities of swimming clubs with galas
and competitions alongside club meetings in the summer. Clubs
usually held their annual general meetings during the winter
months, often in association with a *Smoker* or Smoking Concert.
The winter season was often a time when it was not possible to
swim because pools were unheated. Social events kept club members in contact. These usually depended on the more extrovert
members who could sing, recite or in other ways entertain their
friends. As the name implies, tobacco was consumed and, since
the venues were hotels or public houses, alcoholic beverages as
well. Some clubs organised more elaborate winter events such as
annual dinners, to which members brought their spouses and
sometimes other guests to listen to worthies toast the Queen, the
Club, and the Guests. Such events were usually the occasion for
entertainments often from professional musicians and singers.
These accounts of social activities read as very familiar in that they
parallel club social activities which continue to the present time.

Similarly the ASA benefited from publicity in local newspapers
on the occasion of swimming competitions and galas. There is no
systematic study of the relationship of publicity to swimming in
the period of this chapter. One indicator of the success of the ASA
in gaining both press coverage and the achievement of some of
its aims appeared in local newspapers. One such example was *The
Tipton Herald* of 1913. This carried a report of the activity of the
Dudley Swimming Club's Ladies' Gala. It gave details of races as
well as of events such as diving for plates and *'cork bobbing competitions'*. The youngest winner was Ena Morris aged 6 years who
had begun to swim 3 years earlier. All the judges were men
although the competitors and visitors had assistance from stewardesses. This paper referred to a cup being offered for swimming
achievements of former pupils of the Dudley Higher Elementary
School to encourage them *'to keep up their swimming practice
after leaving the day school'*.

---

*The Portsmouth Festival held on August Bank Holiday (the first Monday of
the month) attracted large crowds to its competitions.
Such was the growth of the event that some of the programme was transferred
to the programme of the Southsea Regatta week.
Events for women formed part of the schedule as these extracts from
Swimming Notes for 16 and 23 August, 1884, showed.*

Swimming Notes

CLUB RECORD.

Turkish, Vapour, and Electric Bath and Bathing Guide.

[No. 88, Vol. II.]   SATURDAY, OCTOBER, 17, 1885.   Price One Penny.

TO OUR READERS.

THE proprietors have much pleasure in announcing the permanent enlargement of this journal to four more pages as soon as the necessary arrangements can be made, and thus in multiplying our clientecle by some thousands, members of Swimming Clubs will still find room for their very able and interesting reports. In the meantime we will just glance at the work we have cut out to do, and with the kind help, advice, suggestions, and co-operation of our friends, we hope to make SWIMMING NOTES worthy the support, in all parts of the Country, of the noble women and men who strive by precept and example to make popular the graceful, artistic, and life-saving art of swimming.

We hope in a few weeks to give the work of clubs in all parts of the Country, and by thus recording the progress of the art the country friend will be stimulated and encouraged by the work of the Londoner. These, in their turn, cannot help being interested in the exertions of their friends at a distance bringing on public opinion, so that all may desire a speedy recognition of the art of swimming as a part, and very necessary part, too, of the education of every boy and girl in the Country. Without for one moment desiring to increase the expenditure of the new school boards, we trust the time is not far distant when every board-school will possess a swimming bath for girls and boys, and half-an-hour's bathing each morning would add very much to the virtue of the girls, the honour and bravery of the boys; at the same time adding considerably to the stamina and robustof the next generation.

Doubtless some falling off will take place during the winter months in the usual reports of clubs; but we would advise them to keep up their meetings regularly, and finding many worthy deeds to do in preparing for the next season—arranging matches with Country friends, and pleasant days' outings for the Londoners—papers could be prepared and read before members, and if considered valuable send on the MS. to us, so your suggestions and experience may be made known through the length and breadth of the land, as well as your own club. The Editor would be glad to receive such, and also short stories by members of swimming clubs, illustrating the art of swimming its advantages, educational, sanatorial, and life-preserving. Should the Editor receive any such paper or tales that would do for a *Grand Xmas Double Number*, and if so used the Editor will forward a reward of £5 for the same.

The short, pithy, and saucy remarks that have adorned this page in the past are this week conspicuous by their absence, but we have something in store for our readers that could not possibly be done at any other house in the kingdom, and to prove that, we should be glad to shew any friend calling over our establishment. If we state that some ten thousand newspapers or more, let alone magazines, quarterlies, &c., are read—aye, carefully read—by a staff of fifty hands, some thirty being young ladies, who are specially trained for the work. Many thousands of acres of printed matter are looked through every day, for anything relating to swimming now, in addition to some thousand or more other subjects they have hitherto been doing.

These journals, newspapers, and magazines come from all parts of the World, and you may rest assured a scramble will take place every day after these blessed morsels, for we have offered a beautiful swimming costume to the young lady that discovers the most in any week between now and next June.

We hope to take you, dear readers, week by week in our council, and we have every confidence you will not only bring to the notice of all friends in London, but you will kindly send sample copies to friends in the provinces. Make this journal the Swimmer's Friend and Guide, get schools and friends to subscribe, and do all you can to strengthen our present very weak backbone (scarcity of advertisements). For this week, then—*Farewell.*

QUEEN'S CLUB.

Trial heats of the fifth competition for challenge watch. Results :— Heat 1 : H Clarke 43 1, A Wildman 28 2, A Lavers 38 3, W Wheeler 63, did not finish ; won by three yards, three yards divided second and third. Heat 2 : H Neal 19 1, W Morriss 24 2, E Bailey scratch 3, J Jones 34 4, did not finish ; won by a foot, three yards divided second and third.

The third annual supper takes place at the One Swan Inn Bishopsgate-street, E.C., on Saturday, November 28th.

A new approach by a struggling newspaper.

THE CRAZE for "HARDENING."

●●●●●●●●●

Many years ago a species of leaderette appeared in the *Pall Mall Gazette*, dealing with the Serpentine Club's Christmas Morning Handicap. At this distance of time the readers of SWIMMING NOTES and RECORD will probably feel a pleasure in perusing the extract, which in its present form is like Brian O'Lynn's nether garments "all tattered and torn":—

"On the morning of Christmas Day the winter bathers in the Serpentine held a grand festival. First they had a swimming match, the course being 100 yards, and the competitors thirty in number; then they all had some rum and milk out of a pail. Having emptied the pail by drinking her Majesty's health, it was replenished by "the kind and genial superintendent of the Royal Humane Society," and the hardy bathers drank with fervour to the health and speedy convalescence of the Prince of Wales. So far as regards the rum and milk there can be no doubt that the bathers spent a most enjoyable morning, but it is difficult to imagine that any persons in their senses, but for the pride of the thing, can really feel any pleasure in stepping into the Serpentine on a raw winter's morning. Yet one old bather, it is stated, when the lake is covered with ice, comes each morning with a hatchet, with which he smashes the frozen surface, and thus slowly, inch by inch, works his way into the water. The hideous sufferings he must endure when the thermometer is several degrees below zero are too terrible to contemplate, and the utmost sympathy is due to the Humane Society's boatmen, whose duty compels them to witness his agony. It is doubtful whether it is good policy to draw attention to this winter bathing, for weakly persons are often strangely moved to follow the example set them by their hardier brethren, and probably many lives are annually sacrificed owing to the erroneous idea that bathing in cold water at all seasons is conducive to health. Some people are so insane on this point that, not content with injuring their own health, they insist on their children being thoroughly frozen in a cold bath each morning before breakfast, without any reference to constitution or temperament; whereas any sensible doctor would tell them that tepid water is, in nine cases out of ten, far preferable to cold in a sanitary point of view, and that for cleansing purposes it is much better. The cold-water-at-any-price maniacs, when remonstrated with on the intolerance they exhibit towards those who prefer baths of a higher temperature, invariably retort by boasting of what they call "the glow," alluding to the warmth alleged to be diffused over the bodies of those able to withstand the first shock of immersion: but they entirely forget that in many cases, more especially of children, the powers of the body are too languid to bring on a reaction, and the shock, instead of being followed by "that glow," is followed by a fit of shivering and general chilliness, sowing frequently the seeds of consumption and other diseases. However meritorious, therefore, may be the conduct of the old gentleman, who, with the help of a hatchet, manages to get into the Serpentine in all weathers at an early hour in the morning, it is advisable that he and his companions should be content with their own enjoyment, without attempting to induce others to share with them. They have had a merry Christmas, and we wish all of them a happy new year."

[I swam in the handicap alluded to, so I suppose I am a maniac.
Ed. S.N. and R.]

●●●●●●●●●

BATHERS' CRAMP.

——

To the Editor of SWIMMING NOTES AND RECORD.

SIR,—In your SWIMMING NOTES of the 10th inst., I find an article on "Swimming Cramp." I have often read about bathers being seized with cramp and being drowned, but I never yet read of a bather having cramp and being rescued from drowning so as to tell the tale of this much-talked of Bathers' Cramp. The only sort of cramp I have seen swimmers take has been in the legs or in the fingers, and in every case the swimmer has left the water without assistance, and in some cases the persons have kept on swimming until the cramp has left them. I heard H. G. Dunlop, of Manchester, tell a nice tale about E. T. Jones, the Champion, taking cramp in a race at Hollingworth some years ago. Jones, Dunlop and several others were swimming in a handicap. Dunlop had a start from Jones, and when Jones caught Dunlop he said "Grey, I have got the cramp, and he replied "swim to the side and leave the water," and he answered "No, not until I have won the race," and Dunlop says he lashed out with his legs at a double speed, and nearly drowned the other swimmers with his back water as he passed them. Dunlop concluded by saying that whenever Jones is swimming a race and he takes cramp he will be sure to win, for he swims a deal faster with cramp than without it In conclusion, I have been a swimmer and a member of the Bolton Club for about ten years, and "I never knew a swimmer to have cramp so as to interfere with his safety, nor have I ever known a swimmer that ever knew a swimmer to have cramp so as to interfere with his safety." Whenever I read about persons drowning near land when they can swim I conclude that it is not cramp, but that they must have "got water in their windpipe," and become exhausted, for I have often seen swimmers in a bath get water in their windpipe and thus "cause them to rest and cough violently" for some time, and my opinion is that there are "more swimmers drowned this way than with cramp.

I remain, yours respectfully,

JOHN SMITH.

77, Latham-street, Bolton, Lancashire, Jan. 26th, 1885.

◆◆◆◆◆◆◆◆◆

Above:- During the 1880s entertainments had become increasingly popular in the London area. Examples included promotions by the Beckwiths in May 1884, and again in October 1885. Other item from Swimming Notes show offers by full time professionals to teach swimming and to manage baths. Left:- Health and fitness had occasional notices in Swimming Notes such as the account of the Christmas Day swim in the Serpentine, London, and a letter on cramp both appeared in January 1885.

41

Overview

Between 1874 and 1920 the ASA developed in several important ways which influenced its later structure and organisation. These developments can be summarised in relation to three major themes. The first relates to the internal organisation of the Association. This changed from a London to a national focus and the establishment of the District framework strengthened the representation of its members. Finances were placed on a sound footing and a system of honorary officers became taken as given. The second relates to the range of activities carried out. These covered the attempt to achieve the aims of the Association of promoting swimming, encouraging the provision of facilities for all, and controlling the rules of competition as well promoting for pleasure and entertainment. The third theme relates to the Association and the wider society where links were developed with other sporting associations and every effort was made to publicise and obtain publicity for swimming. The tragedy of the First World War cast its shadow on all the ASA's aims and activities. However, as with all similar bodies it attempted to face the new challenges of the inter war years with a stronger and better organised structure.

In 1898 Ravensbourne SC proclaimed its ASA membership.

The programme for 1898 showed Ravensbourne's support for swimming for children and women.

Chapter 3:

The Harold Fern Era, 1920-1970

Comment by H.E. Fern, Honorary Secretary of the ASA, 1926.

'The sport - the Amateur swimming Association - needs a constant flow of enthusiasts; men and women with new ideas and new methods, and willing to work for their attainment.'

Introduction

This chapter happily fits the long period of Harold Fern's occupancy of the Honorary Secretaryship of the ASA. In that sense it certainly reflects the impact which he made upon the multifaceted developments of that era. It may be food for thought that he was in power for so long.

The main sources for this chapter were the ASA annual *Handbooks* which contain a wealth of detail along with minutes of meetings, monthly copies of the *Swimming Times* magazine, the ASA collection of memorabilia, and a number of interviews with veterans who were familiar with the scene.

The story opens as the First World War ends and seems to mark the beginning of a continuing upsurge and expansion of ASA activity. The basic structure of the Association's administration already existed. Now was the time to build on this and to consolidate and rationalise procedures. Experience would dictate what changes would occur while initiative, innovation, determination and the quality of management would play their parts. Throughout this period, many other national sporting organisations were also expanding. It was partly in the strength of the agreements existing between all of these organisations that the solid wall of amateurism was to hold firm against many challenges.

These were times when the changing level of national and world competition was to be a continuing spur for the ASA to do everything possible to raise standards. As travel became easier so could the volume of competition increase and perhaps access to facilities would be less difficult. Transport also played a part in the growth of 'swimming for pleasure' and the ASA's interest in this side of the sport was always to be included in its efforts to teach swimming properly, to teach survival and to provide the optimum swimming environment.

The acceleration of women's participation in swimming, both at club level and in competition, added new dimensions and challenges. As this aspect grew so new glories were added to the record list.

Twentieth century technological progress was sometimes born out of demand and necessity, such as the filtration and chlorination of pool water. Other technology such as television, which was imposed from outside the ASA structure, at first appeared a threat. When properly 'managed' its introduction proved to be a catalyst, a publicity boon and a source of income. Likewise, a number of innovations were viewed with great caution until the ASA management was 'assured beyond reasonable doubt'. The increase in technological advances led to a need for professional appointments to cope with their introduction. Thus the engagement of National Technical Officers was a recognition of the ASA's wish to disseminate the latest technical features to as wide a public as possible. It was also a reflection of the need to expand the influence of the Education and Scientific Advisory Committees. This period of ASA history was to experience a huge increase in the output of educational materials - books, films, posters, etc. Alongside this, the 'Awards' schemes were to provide great incentive to the young and not-so-young to reach standards and targets. Not only did many dreams thus become reality for eager swimmers, but the ASA's financial situation was to be enormously improved in the process.

Much of the ASA's expansion had taxed the efforts of the management structure. The increase in club affiliations and the many new tasks with which the organisation had surrounded itself had put a great burden on the shoulders of the many voluntary managers and workers. As 1970 approached it was necessary for the Martin Committee to work out the way forward in detail. The need for the ASA to adjust to the needs of the 1970s was clearly recognised.

The Post First World War Picture

1920 was the last of the eight years for T.M. Yeaden as ASA Honorary Secretary. The ASA was still recovering from the First World War when many baths had been closed by lack of fuel, but already many activities seemed to be happily back on course. In the 1920 *Handbook* report, Yeaden typically commented on the success of the Education Committee's demonstrations and exhibitions, on water polo success, the Antwerp Olympics, three new events for ladies in the ASA Championships and the award of 151 Amateur Certificates and 21 Teacher's Certificates.

ASA Time-Tests had been instituted prior to the War as part of a scheme to promote swimming and to improve standards. The results were published in the *Handbook* each year. The Districts supervised the tests which awarded gold, silver or bronze badges to those swimmers who could complete the various distances within the scheduled time scales for Free Style, Breast Stroke or Back Stroke events. Another incentive scheme was the award of Swimming Scholarships which picked out the more promising school swimmers. This gave them free bathing facilities and free club membership so that they would be encouraged to continue swimming instruction for up to three years after leaving school.

The Call (or annual subscription per member club to the ASA) was raised in 1921 by one shilling to 6s 6d per club with the extra shilling being allocated to the ASA Education Committee to fund its increasing activities.

Harold Fern's first report as Honorary Secretary was made for 1921. Apart from his praise for the creation of ten new ASA records there were three administrative matters being negotiated. These reflected the ever-increasing function of the ASA to act as a pressure group to government and other organisations. The representations made to the Railway Commission to grant cheaper rail fares for parties of club members travelling to matches had little success at that time and so the pre-war concessions were not renewed. The Association's efforts to stop the Customs and Excise action to tax club membership tickets, *where such tickets also admitted holder, free of charge to galas, etc.* resulted in the calling of a conference of all Governing Bodies of Amateur Sport to discuss a strategy. Thirdly, there had been concern that the Baths and Wash Houses Act of 1878 would be altered to allow local authorities to close swimming baths for more than five months a year. This fear resulted from the Government's need to *'wield the Geddes Axe'* to cut public expenditure and the longer period of bath closure would thus have helped to cut baths running costs. Answers were given from the Minister of Health that no such changes were imminent.

The ASA in 1924 was able to praise the wonderful progress of ladies' swimming reflected in seven out of eight of the 1923 records. The standard of men's sprint-swimming had far to go to reach American levels. There was much regret also that middle- and long-distance swimming was almost at a standstill. Clubs were urged to train swimmers for events over 220 yards. W.G. Howcroft, newly appointed Olympic Coach, toured ten swimming centres throughout England and commented that his visits had stimulated the 200 swimmers whom he had tested. He had helped to co-ordinate and systematise the work and methods of the best coaches in Britain and noted that the crawl stroke was being generally adopted for free-style swimming. The results of the Paris Olympics gave little consolation - *'only a little better results than in Antwerp four years before'* and *'the first time a British Team had ever been defeated at Water Polo'*. In speed swimming we were found to be in the same position as in our

The 'Sunday morning mixed bathing parade' at Bradford in July 1928. The Swimming Times caption stated that 'The absence of unnecessary restrictions has made mixed bathing a success. It can be indulged in every day except Friday'.

ST. PANCRAS SWIMMING CLUB.

Affiliated to the Southern Counties Amateur Swimming Association.

LADIES' SECTION.

A long felt want in the Borough of St. Pancras has now been fulfilled by the formation of a Ladies' Section to the above Club, and it is felt that there must be many ladies in the Borough who will welcome this opportunity of becoming members of what is recognised as one of the foremost Swimming Clubs in London.

SWIMMING is now firmly established and widely acknowledged as one of the finest physical exercises and pastimes women can indulge in, bringing as it does nearly all the muscles into play without straining any of them.

The Club will meet every Wednesday throughout the year in the Prince of Wales Road Baths, at 7 p.m.

Members are admitted to the Bath at a reduced rate of admission at all times on production of Membership Card.

Professor Walter Brickett, the famous Olympic swimming trainer and coach, has been engaged to improve those who can, and teach those who cannot, swim.

Races will be held, all on handicap terms, and a good Programme of social events is being arranged.

The Section is open to both Seniors and Juniors and the Subscription is: Seniors, 5/- per annum; Juniors (under 16 years of age), 3/- per annum.

For further particulars. write the Hon. Secretary,

A. C. PRICE,

1, Earl's Court Square, S.W.1.

To Acquire GRACE OF MOVEMENT and RHYTHM, SWIM.

Join the LADIES' SECTION of the St. Pancras Swimming Club.

Maker of Champions.
Well-known Swimming Instructor and Coach.

HOLDER WORLD'S ATHLETIC RECORD, Aug. 15th, 1919. Walking 1 mile, Running 1 mile, Running 1 mile over Hurdles, Cycling 3 miles, Rowing 1 mile, Swimming 1 mile, all in 1 hour. Time occupied for the 8 miles, 55 mins. 34 1/5 secs.

British Olympic Swimming Trainer, 1908 1912.   Present Antwerp 1920
Address—101, Gaisford Street, Kentish Town, N.W.5.

The new St Pancras Ladies' Section were fortunate enough to have the services of Professor Walter Brickett.

In 1925 the two oldest all-the-year-round swimmers in England were A. Ledger, aged 75, Captain of the Serpentine SC, and G. Webster, aged 78, President of the St Pancras SC. For 30 years they had swum daily either in the Serpentine or Hampstead Pond, breaking the ice when they had to. Here they are about to carry on the good work with some of their followers.

The Olympic Games in Paris in 1924.

good days of 1908, while the Americans had meanwhile vastly improved. Another concern in the late 1920s was the lack of support for the Association's Championship events. To stimulate some improvement the ASA reduced standard times required for all championships. The 1925 events were thus somewhat better supported but there was still the paradox of some veteran swimmers beating the young opposition and this situation was to continue. However, rays of hope were appearing as District Coaching and Training Committees were revealing some new and promising talent. The 1920s and 1930s was a period of expansion for women's swimming, both in events and quality. Improved coaching was obviously paying off.

As a shining example Joyce Cooper represented, along with others, the ascendancy of women at a time when all British swimmers were finding it difficult to keep pace with the world's improving standards. As a member of the Mermaids SC she was fortunate to be coached by W.J. Howcroft and in 1927 won the Ladies' 220 yards event in the ASA Championships. In 1928 she held the British native records for 150 yards, 220 yards, and 300 yards. By 1930 she had added the 100 yards, 440 yards, 500 yards and the 150 yards backstroke to her record list and held most of these until 1935. In 1932 and 1933 she won the ASA Long Distance event. At her peak in 1931 she gained the World Record for the 150 yards backstroke and in the 1932 Olympics came fourth in the 400 metres freestyle and sixth in the 100 metres backstroke. This fame led her to be invited to tour European countries and to produce regular illustrated articles on the crawl and back crawl in the *Morning Post*. Joyce Cooper's legendary achievements have more recently been honoured by the Swimming Hall of Fame at Fort Lauderdale in the USA. The ASA also invites her as an honoured guest to top events where, no doubt, she must reflect on the vast differences which exist between the 1930s and the 1990s.

The new ASA Teacher's Certificate qualification also bode well for the future. In 1925, 339 certificates were awarded out of a total of 579 to date - a great boost for ASA policy. At the same time a new ASA Teacher's Certificate for Diving was in preparation with the aid of the Amateur Diving Association, and in 1926 the latter brought out a Certificate for Proficiency in Diving, of which 18 were awarded in the first year.

The ASA Committee was also keen to further the interests of university swimming and entered into discussions with the Universities Students Athletic Union to see how swimming facilities might be extended and to suggest that Oxford and Cambridge universities should consider *full colours* for swimming as with a range of other sports. In 1927 K.C. Wilson, Captain of Cambridge University Swimming Club, commented on the state of university swimming: *'Oxford's cramped space in Martin Street Bath was inadequate and at Cambridge there was little real activity'*. Neither university had full use of a bath and neither had a resident coach. Both universities even had to teach student beginners to swim and to coach those who could swim a little. Even a Combined Oxford and Cambridge team took a lowly place in the hierarchy of student sport. Mr. Wilson saw new improvements in the future with increased public interest in bath construction by both municipal and education authorities. He recognised also, that schools with their own new baths would produce swimming material for later university life. In 1932 the

THE WORLD'S RECORD BREAKER.

Miss JOYCE COOPER
(Mermaid S.C.)

Joyce's records this year are as follows:

February, in Paris. Lowered European record for 100 metres from 71 4/5secs. to 70secs.

April, in London. Lowered her own British record for 300 yards from 3mins. 57 3/5secs. to 3mins. 50 1/5secs.

June, in Scotland. Lowered Scottish record for 220 yards to 2mins. 44 1/5secs. (Her own British record is 2mins. 46 2/5secs.)

Lowered World's record for 150 yards backstroke from 1min. 54 4/5secs. (Bonnie Mealing, Australia) to 1min. 54secs.

The record-breaking Joyce Cooper in 1931.

UAU applied to affiliate directly to the ASA but this was not favourably received. Harold Fern supported an amended draft, *'to affiliate to the District in which the University is situated and to allow representatives on to the Council and Executive of that District and to hold competitions under A.S.A. laws'*. This amendment too was lost.

The ASA was always keen to use the medium of the silent film as a teaching aid and in 1924 contracted for such footage to be produced. This was to be updated in 1926 and the *Handbook* minutes included authorisation for the Treasurer to *'pay for a pair of flippers purchased for the making of the original film'*. A subcommittee in 1926 saw many defects in the film and considered that it lacked educational value and so it was withdrawn.

The *Swimming Times* was a vehicle for ASA hierarchy and others to suggest how clubs could improve their administration. F.A. Unwin in 1926 pleaded for clubs to take more interest in junior members. He conceded that Junior Committees had been formed as a first step but stressed the need *'for more practical interest and improved supervision of practice for boys and girls'*. A weekly social evening on a bath night was not good enough. *'Older experienced members should help to follow up the coaches' work; otherwise too much of what a coach has taught is almost immediately forgotten'*. Captain B.W. Cummins gave advice on *how to run a swimming club* and suggested that the need was not so much for more clubs but to make the existing ones work properly. He identified the problem that those clubs restricted to business houses, church or social club groupings had to fight against great odds to establish themselves. *'If our well-established clubs could foster these groups and take them under their wings as 'sectional elements' and encourage them, much talent could be better used.'* In this way, perhaps, a large club could also gain more officials. Captain Cummins saw the need to give best ASA advice to those who wanted to form clubs where new baths had been constructed. His advice list included - *'use the press to advertise'*, *'get a good organising secretary'*; *'keep good contact with your local bath'*; *'engage a trainer'*; *'encourage competition for time-test medals'*; and *'send a team to the local gala'*.

Harold Fern in 1926 gave his views on a typical ASA Annual General Meeting. He confirmed that this meeting was mainly for alterations and additions to rules and regulations by honorary officials and delegates, each of the latter representing 60 clubs and having previously been a member of the executive of his own District. Fern stressed that for the two-day meeting firm chairmanship was essential -

> *'Repetition of some delegates is painful to listen to: they reiterate much of which has been said to better advantage by a previous speaker and bore other delegates to desperate remedy of sleep, for it is no uncommon feature to see delegates peacefully having a nap, particularly after lunch or late at night.'*

He criticised the fact that rarely was there talk of the educational work of the Association -

> *'nearly all the time it was rules and regulations'*. Also, *'District proposals often get short shrift and often receive and deserve ridicule'*.

Alderman Harold Fern OBE JP.

Changes in ASA laws could get through a District Council Meeting but as these often reflected local needs usually did not pass at national level.

The positive side of the AGM as far as Fern was concerned was *'the happy reunion of old friends with a social side well catered for'* and

> *'probably the only man who would abolish the AGM is the Honorary Secretary to whom it is a form of purgatory, relieved only by the presence of meeting so many old and valued friends'*.

Fern may have wished that his AGMs were able to be shortened in line with the Scottish ASA which, in 1927, announced that it got through all of its business in three hours because members were encouraged to think on *'national'* and not on a *'district'* basis. This must have given the delegates much more time for refreshment!

Harold Fern

Harold Fern's influence on the development of the ASA between 1920 and 1970 was of legendary quality. His extreme organising ability, his foresight, his love of the sport and his ability to deal with *'all manner of men and women at all levels'* have earned him an unrivalled place in the history of swimming in this country and in the world. None was better qualified for the task of rebuilding swimming after two world wars. For most men one war would have been enough. His decisive part included producing schemes to extend swimming as an activity throughout our population; his recognition of the need for *education*; his concern for improving our competitive ability at home and abroad; and his sharp sense of the need for good *'connections'* and good publicity - all have placed him at the forefront of ASA progress and have marked his name indelibly as builder extraordinaire.

Mr. Fern was a formidable secretary of committees, preparing for meetings thoroughly and guiding chairmen and members through many knotty issues where feelings sometimes ran high. His attitudes became entrenched in later years to protect what he believed to be the ethos of the ASA. In consequence he was intolerant of some proposals for change or innovation. Inevitably there were clashes of personalities from time to time and such may have contributed to the difficulties which arose in the relationship of the ASA and RLSS.

Harold Fern's *'swimming history'* goes back long before 1920. In 1903 he was on the Executive of the Southern Counties ASA and at the age of 24 became its Secretary in 1905. It was in that capacity that he first showed his strengths. Against a variety of opposition he fought to make sure that the education aspect of swimming became a reality, and thus that children were taught to swim instead of lip service being given to the aim. His educational promotions included public lectures, publications, demands for more bath facilities and campaigns to encourage swimming for schools. During his period as Secretary from 1905 to 1921 the number of clubs affiliated to the SCASA more than doubled. Concurrently he was a founder member and committee member for some years of the Amateur Diving Association. He became a founder member of Holloway United Swimming Club in 1898 and it flourished with his help. Harold's initial interests were not just in swimming. For three years he was Honorary Secretary of the Albion Rowing Club and also ran for Highgate Harriers and Herne Hill Harriers. Later he turned to football and founded the Islington Football Club. These links with other sports were to put him in a very knowledgeable position in later years when it came to negotiation.

In 1909 Mr. Fern challenged the ASA Council against spending money on sending two English swimmers to Australia when the money could be better spent on promoting swimming at home for schoolchildren and in getting public opinion to demand more and better facilities. He won his case. This was the first real turning point for the ASA which then started to focus more attention on the educational aspect of its aims. His inclusion in a deputation to meet the President of the Board of Education in 1918 for the purpose of including the teaching of swimming in the curriculum of elementary schools was the beginning of meetings with government throughout his life.

Harold Fern was also a keen advocate of 'mixed bathing' but there were many who did not agree with him and the Southern Counties ASA were in two camps over it. He won the day with them but it was perhaps harder to persuade local authorities to make mixed bathing facilities available.

MIXED BATHING IN HYDE PARK

NEW REGULATIONS IN FORCE ON MONDAY

Mixed bathing in the Serpentine will be allowed as from 4.30 p.m. next Monday. The extended hours during which bathing will be permitted to adults will be from 6 a.m. to 10 a.m., and from 4.30 p.m. to 8.30 p.m. on week-days. On Sundays bathing will be permitted from 6 a.m. to 10 a.m. only.

Children under 14 years of age will be permitted to bathe between 4.30 p.m. and 6 p.m. on Mondays, Tuesdays, Wednesdays, Thursdays, and Fridays. On Saturdays and every week day during the school holidays children will be permitted to bathe between 1 p.m. and 6 p.m.

While bathing is in progress, the bathing enclosure will be reserved for bathers, and, in view of this, railings and gates were being erected yesterday.

Those who wish to bathe should approach the bathing area from the newly-constructed path at the back of the new pavilion. A charge of 3d. will be made for the use of the pavilion or cubicles, but free accommodation will be provided for children in separate marquees.

These arrangements are tentative and liable to alteration as experience of their working dictates.

A 1930 news extract.

Mr. Fern joined the ASA Council in 1905. By 1912 he was elected as one of the two representatives of the SCASA on to the ASA Committee. In 1921 he was elected Honorary Secretary of the ASA and continued so until 1970. At that time the ASA had 875 affiliated clubs. This grew to 1,210 in his first year and to 1,629 in his retirement year.

Harold Fern held a string of titles in his swimming career - 1924 President of SCASA; 1907 President of London Water Polo League; 1909 President of Middlesex County Water Polo Association; from 1913 ASA representative on the British Olympics Association and in 1928 Chairman of the Finance Committee of that Association and served as its treasurer for many years. An extraordinary accolade, not only for Mr. Fern but for the standing of swimming in this country, was his appointment as President of FINA in 1936, a position he retained until 1948. Thereafter he served FINA as its treasurer until 1960. This was crowned with an Honorary Life Presidency of FINA in 1960, the only one then awarded in the world. He was also made Honorary Life President of the European Swimming League. All of Harold Fern's work was done on an unpaid voluntary basis. He had full-time professional work as a qualified Chartered Secretary and Accountant as a partner in his own firm which had dealings on the Metals Exchange in London. His faithful secretary, Gladys Writer, conducted his voluntary and professional business for him for 45 years.

As if the foregoing catalogue of achievements were not enough, H. Fern worked tirelessly for the municipal interests of his local Barnet Urban District Council of which he was both a member and later chairman. There followed 18 years as Chairman of the Finance Committee; Chairman of Hertfordshire County Council and Chairman of its Education Committee; his election as an Alderman in 1934; Justice of the Peace; Chairmanship of the two local Queen Elizabeth Schools from 1929 to 1965 and Chairmanship of Hatfield Technical College (later Hertfordshire University).

In 1944 his services were recognised by the award of OBE, followed in 1960 by CBE.

When the new £60,000 ASA Headquarters was opened in Loughborough in 1973 Harold was thrilled that it was named Harold Fern House in his honour. When he retired in 1970 the ASA's balance of £141,500 reflected the Association as one of the wealthiest amateur governing bodies in Britain.

Two quotes from the press may serve to précis the quality of Harold Fern's efforts on behalf of swimming:

'His was a greater contribution to swimming than anyone else in the world in the 20th century.'

and

'British children owe their right to be taught swimming at school more to Harold Fern than to anyone else.'

One of the final accolades bestowed on him, but posthumously, was the honour of being recorded in the Swimming Hall of Fame at Fort Lauderdale in the USA.

The Amateur Situation 1920-1970

In 1920 the ASA *Handbook* contained pages of samples of amateur case-laws to help in the understanding of how these laws were interpreted. Some of these cases dated back to 1905, 1907, etc. and showed that little change had occurred in the intervening years:

European Championships officials in Magdeburg, Germany, in 1984. Harold Fern seems to be the focus of interest.

Quote 1907   *'Does a man lose his amateur status by competing against a professional wrestler at a musichall, and not taking any money that he may win?' The Council ruled that until such a man had applied for and received reinstatement as an amateur from the National Wrestling Association, he was disqualified as an amateur swimmer.'*

Quote 1907   *'It was ruled that an amateur may not sell picture postcards at galas.'*

Quote 1909   *'A club may not present a Railway Season ticket to a swimmer living more than 20 miles distant.'*

Quote 1911   *'A swimmer does not have to forfeit his amateur status by accepting a monetary present for saving a life.'*

Quote 1919   *'An amateur swimmer does not lose his amateur status by joining a professional Rowing Club for boat practice only, and not for competition.'*

Quote 1919   *'It is not permissible to accept War Savings Certificates as prizes.'*

The ASA's continuing aim was to keep the Association an amateur body in every way. This did not mean that it was anti-professionals. Indeed it had catered for the professional from the beginning of the century when it had set up the Professional Swimming Teachers Certificate as part of its programme to improve the quality of swimming teaching. It was in 1919 that the scope was widened to make it the Amateur or Professional Certificate so that a greater range of teachers would be available.

The *Amateur* ethos pervaded all aspects of swimming administration and was fiercely defended, strictly controlled and seldom altered without a struggle. Thus the control of prizegiving, monetary prizes, expenses, broken time, entries for competitions and galas and many other aspects of organisation were covered by the Amateur Laws and were strictly interpreted by the Committee. The occasional pleas in the *Swimming Times* to loosen or adjust various laws tended to have little effect and, if they did then the wheels of change turned very slowly. Any potential financial gains for any winners were gathered into the ASA's coffers or were directed to benefit the individual's club. Bath superintendents and bath attendants had to know where to draw the line between their amateur and professional functions.

After the First World War all sporting bodies were growing, changing and consolidating. The general call from all of them was for *amateurism* and so they strengthened their individual positions by affiliating to each other for the benefit of recognising each other's amateur laws. In this way, a suspension of an amateur in one sport would be recognised by other sporting bodies as well. There was no hiding place for a *culprit*. In 1920 a Conference on *amateur status* was organised between all sporting governing bodies and this helped to form a united approach.

The effect of FINA rulings on the ASA was really a two-way affair. The ASA had to abide by collective FINA rulings but it was also able to modify some of FINA's thinking by the imput of its own deliberations.

One of the most important decisions of the ASA was made in 1922 -

> *'School teachers, organisers and games masters and mistresses, recognised and paid by an Education Authority, and giving instruction to pupils of schools and colleges, do not, because of their duties, endanger their amateur status as swimmers.'*

This historic ruling obviously greatly extended the ability of schools to produce swimmers but it was to prove a difficult law to justify at various times in the future when comparisons with other amateur laws were made.

In 1924 the British Olympic Association sent a questionnaire to the ASA as part of the search for a *Definition of Amateur.* Highlighted among the responses were comments such as: (a) the amateur swimming against a professional should lose his status; (b) there would be no universal definition of an amateur for all sports; (c) there can be no compensation for broken time; (d) professionalism should be legalised; (e) the National Association (i.e. the ASA) should be responsible for the status of its representatives (and not depend on the Olympic Amateur oath-taking).

The following are a series of rules or elucidations published in the ASA *Handbooks* of the 1920s and 1930s. They should serve to illustrate the current thinking.

Quote 1925   *'Agreement for mutual recognition of suspensions authorised to be entered into with the National Cyclists' Union and the Amateur Athletic Union have been completed.'* [In 1927 the Royal Air Force, Royal Navy, and Royal Marines completed their affiliations to the ASA and this of course implied obeying ASA laws.]

Quote 1925   *'New Rules for Souvenirs or Prizes -*

> (a)   *These must be purchased before the date of the event and presented on the day.*
>
> (b)   *No clothes or consumables may be presented as prizes.*
>
> (c)   *Money may not be accepted in lieu of a prize.*
>
> (d)   *First time prizes in handicaps must not exceed one guinea in value.*
>
> (e)   *Prizes above the value of £5 must be engraved with the name and date of the meeting.'*

Quote 1925   *'(a)   Souvenirs may only be accepted with the authorisation of the ASA.*
>
> (b)   *Souvenirs shall not exceed one guinea in value.'*

Quote 1927   *'All swimmers travelling in parties of not less than four adults to take part in any swimming competition or exhibition may be issued with 1st or 3rd class cheap tickets in exchange for vouchers signed by the secretary.'* [A post-war agreement with railway companies.]

Quote 1929   *'A swimmer would not retain his amateur status if he competed as a dirt-track rider for money prizes.'*

Quote 1930   *'The NARA and ASA will mutually respect each other's suspensions, disqualifications and reinstatements. The ASA will not debar NARA members who are "occupied in boats as an occupation", from swimming as amateurs.'*

Quote 1932   *'If a swimmer referees a boxing-match and gets paid he loses his amateur status.'*

The fiercely-defended amateur stance was thus clearly marked out. The *Swimming Times* in 1929 concentrated on the need for great numbers of amateur coaches. It was apparent that there would never be enough professional coaches to cater for the expanding swimming world and, that on balance, many institutions or clubs could not afford them anyway.

Bath attendants received good news in 1931. They were still to be considered as amateurs unless, as part of their duties, they gave instruction in swimming. This was a bonus to those who wished to compete while working in an area where they could probably improve their own standards.

The changes made to rules in the late 1920s and 1930s continued with very few amendments after the Second World War. Occasionally a particular query would be highlighted to help in the interpretation of the laws, e.g.:

Query   (a)   *'Could a teacher of health-exercises who would be paid be regarded as an amateur?'* Answer - yes.

Query (b)   *'Can a teacher swim at a gala for a fee which would be paid to charity remain an amateur?'* Answer - yes.

Query   (c)   *'Can a teacher who gives a series of swimming lessons for a charity fee remain an amateur?'* Answer - yes.

In 1942 Harold Fern had discussions with Lord Kindersley, Chairman of the National Savings Committee, concerning the ASA's attitude to *'Savings Certificates or Stamps as prizes for amateur competitions'*. As expected, the outcome was that the offer was not permissible. Subsequently the Secretary urged all sports bodies to recommend that no prizes at all be given in wartime. *'Swimmers should be content to compete without the necessity of a prize being dangled before them'*, he said.

As part of the consideration of the post-war structure of swimming administration there was much questioning of existing ASA law.

In 1945 R.H. Harbidge suggested that those who took up posts as swimming instructors at public baths, hesitated to do so because of losing amateur status and being debarred also from sitting on their District executive committee. If school teachers who also teach swimming could keep their amateur status - why not bath instructors also? The Baths department would not be getting the instructors of the quality so badly needed. Why should a champion swimmer who becomes a bath instructor not be allowed to continue in competitions? The ASA were standing in the way of progress here!

E.J. Scott also in 1945 looked at the question of amateurs being allowed to compete with professionals without losing status. In baseball, basketball, cricket, golf, handball, hockey, tennis, etc. an amateur could compete with a professional without monetary reward and with no problem, but not so in swimming. The amateur who turned professional was also more or less ostracised by the swimming world.

The ASA's answers to such suggestions stated that, *'the potential for corrupt practices was far greater with joint amateur/professional exhibitions and competitions'*. The Association also doubted the implication that professionals tended to be ostracised. *'Professionals were busy people with their own work to do'*. The ASA's answer about the difficulties of getting good bath instructors was that this was a wartime shortage problem which all baths were having to face and, also that the idea of *'good competitors making the best instructors'* was a false premise.

In 1946 F. Marshall Kendrew found that he had stirred things up when he wrote to the *Swimming Times* suggesting that the ASA amend its amateur law concerning instructors. The reaction to this was that if such laws were altered, it would be of detriment to NASI by *'flooding the world with incompetent instructors - a free-for-all of those "capable or incapable" and "qualified or unqualified"'*. What Mr. Kendrew was really concerned with, however, was the potential loss to the ASA of some good instructors who may turn professional; and the ill-effects to the professional ranks of some good or bad swimmers who may be incompetent as instructors. The line of demarcation was unclear. The ASA said, *'Break the rules and thou shalt cease to be an amateur'*. The culprits would then be *'non-amateurs'*. NASI would only accept those who could satisfy certain conditions. In between the ASA and NASI there would be many people who belonged to neither camp. Mr. Kendrew suggested that there needed to be a differentiation between the *'real professional'* and the *'suspended swimmer'*. To this end both the ASA and NASI should make joint efforts to ensure that **all** professional instructors held either the ASA or NASI qualifications.

In 1946 the ASA Board of Examiners expressed grave concern that the ASA Committee had rescinded a 1939 proposal *'that persons giving lectures to teachers of swimming may receive payment without losing amateur status'*. This proposition had been accepted to bring lecturers in line with schoolteachers' terms of reference. The Board unanimously requested that, *'If the ASA is hoping to develop approved classes for intending teachers of swimming, it is essential that payment of suitable specialists be allowed.'*. At first the ASA refused to reconsider but, in November of the same year, gave way as a result of further representations by the Ministry of Education.

In 1947 an ASA sub-committee was appointed to redraft the Amateur Law. When the draft appeared in 1948, parts of it caused

controversy. The revised definition of an amateur was the one adopted by the International Olympic Committee:

> *'An amateur is one whose connection with swimming is, and always has been, solely for pleasure and for the physical mental and social benefits he derives therefrom and to whom swimming is nothing more than recreation without material gain of any kind, direct or indirect.'*

Some ASA committee members objected to various clauses: (a) the omission of the clause *'that a professional in other sports shall be regarded as a professional in swimming,'* (b) the omission that *'an amateur swimmer shall not write articles for the press, or broadcast for the BBC for payment (unless he be a full-time employee of a newspaper, press-agency or BBC)'* and (c) the proposal that *'the amateur status of a swimmer shall **not** be endangered by lecturing for remuneration to classes of teachers of swimming'*. It seems that with part (c) in mind the ASA had gone back on their deliberations of 1946.

One aspect of amateurism was that of *broken time*. This was concerned with the period when a competitor was away from his usual place of work and thus was perhaps not being paid. In 1948 an Olympic water-polo player applied for payment for loss of time and was advised by the ASA to approach his employers and, in the case of payment being granted, *'he should reapply to the ASA for permission to accept'*.

In 1948 the ASA Council met to consider the redraft of the Amateur Law. After three hours they accepted it. In particular they agreed (a) that professionals in other sports should be able to compete with amateur swimmers and (b) payment for *broken time* - i.e. for loss of wages when training for or attending international swimming competitions.

However, surprisingly, the Council rejected *'payment to amateurs giving lectures to teachers of swimming - i.e. they would lose their amateur status'*.

Amateur Laws always needed the reinforcement of public airing. In 1948 the *Swimming Times* gave a timely warning to those who were being asked to participate in the Aquacades or gala spectaculars. Juniors were particularly vulnerable as shown by a number of them losing their amateur status after performing at a large Earls Court Aquacade. It was no good being wise after the event.

Throughout the 1950s and 1960s the ASA Districts continued to receive requests for clarification of points of ASA Law, particularly the amateur aspect. The requests were always passed to the ASA Committee; e.g. in 1952.

> *'Can a person who qualified under the Emergency Teachers Training Scheme and who takes various subjects at school during the day, but who 'voluntarily' teaches an evening class for other remuneration retain amateur status?'*
> Answer - no.

The rights of professionals were also the source of decision-making; e.g. in 1953 -

> *'A professional is permitted to act as a judge, timekeeper or starter in any school competition or competition confined to members of an affiliated club, but he is not permitted to officiate in an **open** competition'*. This was changed in

1965 to *'permit the professional to act as an official in **any** swimming contest held under ASA Laws'*.

The list of items permitted to be given as prizes was also gradually extended to include an ASA teaspoon (value 12s 6d), swimming costumes, training suits and ties.

In 1956 an ASA Appeals Committee met to decide between Mrs. P. Nievens (better known as the journalist Pat Besford) and the Southern Counties ASA. The latter's decision had been, *'that Mrs. Nievens has contravened ASA Law 29 by capitalising on the reputation she has derived from swimming and that accordingly she has forfeited her amateur status'*. The Committee, however, found a difference between *athletic fame* (as in the wording of the law) and *reputation*. As Mrs. Nievens was not possessed of *athletic fame* she thus won her appeal.

The status of the professional footballer was scrutinised in 1957 and was decided by FINA Law - *'A professional in any athletic sport shall be considered to be a professional in swimming'*. Thus the footballer could not take part in an amateur swimming competition.

Sometimes the result of a query was opposite to that expected.

'Does an amateur swimmer, acting as a voluntary lifeguard who accepts a free season ticket, admitting him to the bath all year round, endanger his amateur status, as this was, the equivalent of payment for his services?'

The Committee ruled to the contrary as there was a pressing need to encourage swimming.

Both the ASA and local education authorities wanted answers about amateur coaches teaching evening classes. The ruling given in 1959 was that the coach should be paid a normal fee but should sign a form permitting the LEA to pay that fee to the governing body, i.e. the ASA. The latter would then arrange the reimbursement of expenses and keep the balance in its own coaching fund.

In 1959 the ASA again revised the whole of its amateur laws partly with the aim of simplifying them. The Districts were asked to express their opinions about the redrafting. This time the lecturers were to be permitted to receive their payment. It is interesting also to note that the ASA were sending a copy of their new laws to FINA with the possibility that these could affect or help FINA thinking and even effect changes to FINA laws.

Bert Kinnear, ASA National Technical Officer, added his weight in 1964 to the arguments for greater *across-the-board* participation by professionals in the administration of swimming. He suggested that these laws were out-of-date and that farcical situations resulted. His assessment of the professionals was that they were true experts with a vocation just as all other professionals and that their standing abroad was more highly recognised than at home. He highlighted the fact that the *'current attitude to amateur sport was that it was a competitive situation - not as much earlier when the matter had solely been "playing the game for the game's sake"'*. The paradox and lack of justice that *'a professional can be an official and a member of an affiliated club but not act as a delegate to any organisation concerned in the direction or government of swimming'* was clearly unacceptable. There was an implication that a professional was not to be trusted.

As 1970 approached, Harry Littlewood, Principal Technical Officer of the CCPR, suggested that the amateur/professional barriers showed signs of breaking down and inferred that the sports world was increasingly in need of the high standard of professional competence of the coaches of his day. He stressed that it was incumbent on all the great amateur sporting bodies to become more professional in their outlook if they were to progress in the world of competition. He foresaw the huge development of multi-sports centres with each sport represented by a professional coach. Hamilton Bland and Helen Elkington, after a world tour, backed Harry Littlewood's proposition by comparing the coaching environment abroad with that at home. Abroad, champions were produced almost as a direct result of the willingness to pay for professional coaching of a high standard.

There was no doubt about the need for professional excellence or for the need for funding for it. As an organisation in pursuit of amateurism the ASA had always recognised this. The ASA's main goals in its first hundred years as an amateur administration had been to do everything possible to increase the facilities for swimming, to improve and extend standards of swimming education and to maximise the competitive standards of all swimmers, including our internationals. To do all this while protecting the amateur ethic and while gaining sufficient funding for the increasing costs of running a large administration was a great achievement, especially when we consider that most of the ASA hierarchy were not in a professional capacity.

Education: 1920 to the Second World War

Harold Fern's huge efforts to highlight the *Educational Function* of the ASA were to be the continuing hallmark of his long period in office. Educating the Government, Ministries, the Local Authorities, the Districts, the teachers or the public took a variety of forms. The ASA made use of some progressive although still rather primitive forms of technology such as the silent film to transmit ideas and methods. It pressured governments which wanted the people to be fit but which were still feeling their way about how to best achieve fitness. The Association attempted to put in place its own internal structures to improve the training and competitiveness of its swimmers. As an *Amateur* Association where most of the work was effected by part-time, voluntary, administrators, the ASA surely achieved great measures of success although it was natural occasionally to receive a prod or critique by the professionals or even by its own members.

The need for Education was sharpened not only by an earnest hope that everyone would learn to swim but also by the urgent need to raise national competitive elements to the high positions where once they had led the world.

Throughout th{s 1920-1939 period it must be remembered that a variety of national hurdles lay in the path of progress. The end of the First World War was in itself a concentration on reconstruction and rehabilitation and the ASA had to pull together the strands of pre-war developments and attempt to plan for a brighter future. The period of Depression especially from 1930 to 1934 acted as a brake on progress especially on the bath-running and bath-building programme. The Government's good intentions of sanctioning loans for building nationwide baths and washhouses were once more realised in 1934 and the following years when grants were multiplied. No doubt there was a realisation of providing work for the unemployed in the construction of so many baths.

There was, therefore, the will to educate but the administration, even for an amateur body, required funding to become a reality. Funding from the annual District clubs' *'call'* (or subscription) was but one aspect. In the long term the aim would be to encourage both local and central government to identify with the aims of the ASA and other sporting bodies with the hope that additional monies for administration and loans for new pools would be forthcoming. The ASA's *know-how* would guide the process.

The post-war ASA Swimming Teacher's Certificate which had developed from the pre-war ASA Professional Teacher's qualification was to be a flagship of educational progress between the two world wars. Every year in his report Harold Fern commented with pride on the increased numbers issued. He also praised all those who organised and conducted the examinations. By 1930 Mr. Fern commented that education authorities were by then recognising the value of the ASA Teacher's Certificate and that it was an essential qualification for vocational appointments. It was stated also in 1928 that 75 per cent of the total certificates were gained by ladies, a reflection of its introduction to Ladies' Training Colleges as part of the curricula. The names and addresses of all certificated persons were published annually in the *Handbook* for the convenience of public contact.

ASA Teacher's Certificates Issued between 1923 and 1939

Year	Issued	Running Total
1925	339	578
1926	380	958
1927	358	1316
1928	495	1811
1929	518	2296
1930	260	2502*
1931	246	2748
1932	271	3019
1933	254	3273
1934	273	3546
1935	322	3868
1936	311	4179
1937	290	4469
1938	365	4834
1939	641	5475

*In this year the exam. was made more difficult.

In 1928 Sir George Newman, Chief Medical Officer of the Board of Education gave three pages to swimming in his annual report: *The Health of the School Child.* He praised swimming as an

exercise, an enjoyment and a *whole body* activity and quoted statistics to show how often school children were visiting the baths:

'e.g. Sheffield 1926.	*191,933 pupil visits in school hours.*
	132,956 out of school hours.
Liverpool 1926.	*286,000 pupil visits in school hours.'*

In country districts, e.g. East Suffolk, there were now 40 bathing centres for children in rivers or on the sea coast. Oxfordshire had only two enclosed baths - *'but suitable stretches of stream have been selected'*. In Calgarth, Cumberland, people were making their own bath.

Sir George's report at this high level was good for swimming. It must have helped to prod those local authorities which needed to do more and it gave many folk an incentive to build baths.

In the report, the teaching of swimming was criticised as *'often careless and unscientific'* and if good instruction were not available then the recreative and competitive aspects would not easily follow. The ASA was praised for its publications on strokes and methods and for its efforts to educate public opinion. Teacher Training Colleges were improving the country's swimming instruction levels with the inclusion of swimming as part of the courses.

This was the sort of government interest which Harold Fern relished as much as he did when His Majesty's School Inspectors, on visiting schools, were in the habit of criticising the fact that swimming was not part of the curriculum.

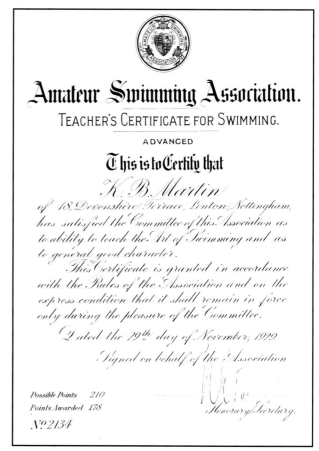

K.B. Martin's ASA Teacher's Certificate for Swimming awarded in 1929.

In the early 1920s the ASA had a separate *Education Committee* with a brief to *'exercise control over funds specially donated for educational and propaganda work'*. There was a short annual report and a financial statement in the *Handbook*. The duties of the Committee were

> *'to use every means to increase and improve the teaching of swimming to children and adults: to bring pressure to bear upon Educational Authorities to install baths and to maximise their usage: to co-operate with naval, army and air services and with youth organisations in the promotion of swimming'.*

Each District also had its own Education Committee, and annually presented very comprehensive reports in the *Handbook*. In the late 1920s the Education Committee disappeared and its functions were subsumed by the main ASA Committee. One of the ASA's educational innovations was the introduction of Swimming Scholarships to be supervised by the Districts. To facilitate this it was suggested that Local Committees should be supervised by the Districts. It was suggested that Local Committees should be formed to liaise with Bath Authorities to encourage them to co-operate in the scheme. The aim of the scholarships was to pick out the more promising swimmers among school children and provide them with free bathing facilities and club membership for up to one, two or three years after leaving school. It was obvious that this new scheme was to answer the many complaints about *Drop-outs* from the sport at school leaving age. After *junior* swimming finished there was no organised competition available for over 16's and these youngsters were often not fast enough to enter senior teams. It was calculated that at least 1,500 youngsters a year were being lost to other sports. Some clubs such as Old Trafford at Manchester had instituted a race for Under 18's, while Liverpool had formed a District League for Under 19's. Some blamed the drop-out on the need for more competent instruction and also on the need for more modern methods. Carl Wootton suggested that the 1,400 clubs in England, in the main, failed their duty by concentrating on a handful of promising boys instead of giving *'full instruction to all'*. He also suggested that too many men were *'burying their noses in committee rooms instead of being on the poolside - "Strepticoccus Legislandii" the virulent germ of too much legislation and not enough action'*.

We can see here that the ASA and others were not oblivious to problems and gaps in the total system. No doubt the Scholarship efforts were successful in areas where local committees were strong and where bath managers were enlightened.

W.J. Howcroft, writing in the *Morning Post* in 1930 commented on England's swimming decline. He said that our standards had improved but not so rapidly as other countries. We had failed to keep in line with the latest developments in instruction methods, stroke analysis and progressive training.

> *'Great Britain is the only country where the governing associations have attempted to control instructional methods by textbooks and certificate exams. The A.S.A. have dallied on the path to progress. Their recent record is one of apathy and procrastination'.*

Howcroft then criticised various ASA publications which were much in need of revision and praises other books. He showed

concern too that Training Colleges were using texts *'which should have been scrapped years ago'*. In 1935 Howcroft expressed concern for the administration of Olympic training. He suggested

> *'the appointment of a national organiser, that new blood was needed in the administration and that the place to raise standards was in the training pool and not in the racing arena'.*

Howcroft was himself a successful author of swimming books and no doubt his criticisms called for idealistic solutions not always to be easily expedited in an organisation run mainly by volunteers. However, the ASA had formed a Publications Committee in the late 1920s and a variety of new and updated books were issued with very high sales records. The ASA also reacted to the need for publications where none already existed, e.g. a new book on the subject of bath design as a basis for advice to local authorities.

1937 advertisement for swimming books.

In the mid-1930s the ASA continued to build on its interest in the film as a medium for education and as a stimulus for a public which was gradually becoming used to being entertained by cinematography. The *talkie* film was growing in popularity and the addition of a soundtrack greatly enhanced the potential of the earlier silent editions. The *News Chronicle* sponsored a *Learn to Swim* film which the ASA commended. It depicted the crawl, back crawl and breast-stroke. That newspaper also produced a *Learn to Swim* booklet for 6d. A film of the 1932 Olympics was also in circulation.

Ciné-Kodak was much advertised as a method of feeding back information about a swimmer or diver when a single frame series of moving pictures could be analysed at leisure. The ASA advised clubs that the Film Evening was a good way of entertaining and educating their members on winter evenings.

The *Swimming Times* frequently gave copious advice, much of it from the ASA, about how to improve the organisation of events. Any club secretaries who were receptive to such advice could make their annual gala events much more acceptable to both swimmers and spectators. Diving, trapeze artists, water comedians, champion-canoeists and water ballet girls, all added to the gala attractions. Another innovation was *Organise a Swimming Week in 1934*. Bristol and Croydon had experimented with such weeks in 1932 and 1933 respectively and were longing to pass the message on. Their planning had involved co-operation with bath authorities and the press, special *News Chronicle* coaching sessions, diving tuition, lifesaving demonstrations, parades, mannequin costume displays, shop window dressing and films. This was public education on a grand scale and it worked.

The value of the press and propaganda was increasingly recognised as a tool for spreading the word. The ASA President, R.A. Colwill, in 1929 appealed to club secretaries to *'get the press to give space to swimming club reports'*. He also praised the *Public Lecture* as a way of arousing interest in swimming. One can imagine that a one-hour lecture by an eminent swimmer, with magic lantern slides support, would stimulate interest rather more than *political meetings*.

An important professional swimming development occurred in 1932 when the National Association of Swimming Instructors was founded *'to improve teaching standards via conferences, etc., to protect the status of the Professional Swimming Instructor and to elevate the standard of tutorship'*. The idea that the ASA in 1930 should set up such a body, had not taken root. Nevertheless, at the first AGM of NASI, Harold Fern not only attended, but was elected as Vice-President. Ross Eagle, the famous professional coach and exponent of the crawl stroke, was a founder member. His experience of the 1928 Olympics helps to illustrate the problem of the professional/amateur gap. He was, in 1928, given the backing of Croydon Swimming Club to attend the Olympics in Amsterdam. There it was hoped he could pick up many ideas about swimming strokes and be able to pass them on to others later. At the same time he offered voluntary service to our own competitors in Amsterdam and was met with a curt refusal. This situation was part of the spur which led to the formation of NASI so that professional instructors could express their views and enhance good practice.

In 1936 Ross Eagle was still highlighting what he saw as the lack of concerted action between NASI and the ASA. He commented on the progress of the crawl stroke from 1907 until 1911 which he called the *'Experimental Speed Age'* and suggested that we had never reached the *'Advanced Speed Age'*. His reasoning was that professionals were not enough involved and that the ASA had done little to encourage those responsible for producing advanced swimmers. He praised the ASA's efforts to get amateurs

A visit of the London Schools' Swimming Association teams to compete in Nottingham in September 1931. The Duke of Portland stands to the left with his stick. These are the grounds of Welbeck Abbey.

to acquire the ASA Teacher's Certificate but thought that the NASI and the ASA should work more closely together in developing the talents of the most promising swimmers. In 1937 Oliver Stanley MP, Minister of Education, talked of the need to improve the health and physique of the people.

> *The object was not to create specialists or great athletes but to inculcate into all citizens the desire to keep their bodies fit. Physical Training would enable all citizens to do their work better, enjoy leisure more, and more competently bear the burden of citizenship.'*

Stanley suggested that swimming clubs would be a natural extension of the keep-fit movement. The ASA grasped this idea and confirmed that much scope existed for making *health centres* of our public baths. Harold Fern decided to confer with the Minister of Health, Sir Kingsley Wood, on these general proposals.

Both the Ministers of Health and Education were playing their part in furthering the ASA plans. In 1936 the Minister of Health urged all local authorities to keep pools open in winter, prepared model byelaws concerning water purity and cleanliness, and sanctioned £1,602,242 increased expenditure on pool building. Loans in 1933 had been £638,058 and in 1934 £312,237. Also the Board of Education was preparing to sanction grants for the provision of school swimming baths to the extent of 50 per cent of capital and running costs.

In 1936 Parliament introduced the Public Health Bill with the object of consolidating many Acts of Parliament passed since 1875. The 1925 Public Health Act had decreed that Local Authorities would close their baths between the end of October and 30 April each year. Urban Districts were currently asking the Government to extend this period. Obviously they had other winter uses for the baths and could also save fuel on heating the water. Harold Fern made representations to Parliament against the closing time extension. He said that it was reasonable to close open-air baths but that at least one covered bath in each area should remain open throughout the winter for schoolchildren to learn *throughout the year*.

1936 was also the year when the ASA administration realised how low were school affiliations to the ASA. To remedy this it was proposed to reduce the annual group subscription to five shillings, to inaugurate a schoolboys championship and to encourage coaches to visit schools. This would take some time to show results.

The 1937 Physical Training and Recreation Act was an important piece of legislation. Its most salient feature was the decision to appoint a *National Advisory Council* to act in an advisory capacity to the Government. Harold Fern was appointed as a member of the Council. Area committees were to be set up all over the country for the assessment of local needs with the object of apportioning government funds. Mr. Fern commented:

> *For nearly 70 years the A.S.A. - (handicapped by lack of financial resources) - and its army of voluntary workers, have been making the claim with ever-increasing success. Now the opportunity presents itself of taking advantage of a propaganda campaign on a scale only possible with government resources.'.*

£2,000,000 was set aside by the Government for all sport and recreations and the new Advisory Council was there to spend it. Fern was as ever guarded - *'Don't ask how much you can get out of the £2,000,000 but how much service your club can give'.*

In fact initially the ASA received an annual £2,000 in 1938 and this was a great boost to the administration. The ASA Committee chose to spend the money on the appointment of two organisers, one for the North and North-East Counties, the other for the Midlands, South and Western Counties. Their duties were

> *'to assist and advise in the formation of classes for the ASA Teachers Certificate; to arrange the showing of ASA films; to press for the extension and improvement of facilities; to enlist the support of Local Authorities and to be link between the National Futures Council and the ASA.*

Mrs. E. Burton (South) (later Lady Burton) and Miss M. Laxton-Lloyd (North) were the successful appointments from 142 applicants. They subsequently communicated the success of their work via the *Swimming Times.*

Mrs. Burton formulated a scheme for training the leaders in six centres throughout the country (three London, one Midlands and two North). In each centre 20 to 30 young men or women would train for one night a week for six months towards the ASA Elementary Teacher's Certificate and the RLSS award. Each candidate would only be charged five shillings with the balance from the new funding. In 1938 Mrs. Burton also conducted an experiment at Victoria Park Lido in the East End of London to prove to London County Council that recreative keep-fit work and swimming coaching could be combined in the new lidos as the best way to improve the nation's fitness. The LCC was convinced and recommended the appointment of two leaders *'fully qualified for recreative keep fit work and the coaching of swimming'* to each of three lidos for that summer. Mrs. Burton was very active in setting up coaching classes and in negotiating with town councils to maximise the use of their bath facilities.

Miss Laxton-Lloyd was keen to extend a scheme at Thornaby, Yorks, where the bath manager had started a *Duckling's club for 3 to 12 year olds.* The ducklings were taught by the qualified manager and some keen fathers. For a fee of 2s 6d the children also received a badge. The membership of 50 had a waiting list. Miss Laxton-Lloyd saw the potential here for bath managers to make such good use of a slack period of the day. Also the mothers would later be in the bath with their children to practice what had been learned.

Miss Laxton-Lloyd found that one of her main functions was to convince local authorities to be more favourable to swimming in general. She certainly had temporary success in convincing Darlington County Borough Council that pools were built for swimming and not for dancing. She enrolled the help of many Darlington organisations to pressurise the authorities. Consequently Darlington had its winter swimming; had cheap winter season tickets and block rates for Scouts, Guides, etc.; had winter swimming for schools, lifesaving classes and ASA Teacher's Certificate classes. This success story was repeated in many areas with the organisers' support but the scenario changed at the outbreak of the War.

Miss Laxton-Lloyd quoted another project of targeting two counties - Lancashire and Cheshire - with an ambitious propaganda and publicity campaign backed up by the National Fitness Council. Exhibitions, films, demonstrations and free coaching opportunities were staged with the organisation of a variety of more permanent activity to follow. Such activities included establishing junior branches of clubs, classes, Certificate Classes and the Scholarship Scheme for school leavers. Blackburn, Farmworth, Colne, Accrington and Radcliffe were the centres for the project. Miss Laxton-Lloyd commented that the Mayor, Town Clerk and other dignitaries should be on the committees for the campaign as this ensured success. There is no doubt that the work done by the two ASA National Fitness Organisers was effective and that their function of liaison with local authorities and communicating via courses, demonstrations, etc. was successful. The War seemed to put an end of this initial surge of activity.

A National Fitness Campaign Review was instituted in 1939 to assess progress, and statistics were taken from the 22 area committees.

A report was published and it praised the *'imposing number of persons taking part in sports and games but highlighted a lack of provision available in many areas'*. About one million active members were reported to be under the umbrella of the ASA but 50 towns each with a population of over 25,000 contributed a total of two million people who had no swimming bath available. One quarter of such towns had proposals to build baths. Another statistic was the 1¾ million people were now served by baths

towards which grant-aid had been provided. Although this proved the value of the grant-aid, the challenge for the future was obvious.

The War Years (September 1939 - August 1945)

1939 was assessed to be the ASA's best year to date - a peak in almost every way. The accumulated balance was £2,310, - the highest yet. The General Account had a surplus of £223 and the Education Account's surplus was £168, substantial amounts at the time. Although the ASA's administration had only functioned effectively for eight months of that year, the Districts had still paid their *'call'* for the whole year. This had helped the funds. Also, ASA publications sales were very high; swimming records were being created; and the work of Miss Laxton Lloyd and Mrs. E. Burton as organisers was bearing much fruit. It was unfortunate that their services had to be dispensed with in wartime because the grants ceased. The ASA was also proud of its part in the Ministry of Health having sanctioned a total of £4,227,940 expenditure on public baths and washhouses over the previous five years.

The War curtailed most activities. Almost all affiliated clubs closed down. Many baths were closed and were used instead for Civil Defence Headquarters, mortuaries, dressing-stations, and air-raid shelters. Those which did not close had to be *blacked-out* before swimming continued. Officials were drafted into the

---

Johnny Wilkes—His Essay on the History of the A.S.A.

Mr. Paul Herbert has very kindly furnished "The Swimming Times" with the undermentioned extracts from the essay of a schoolboy on the history of the Amateur Swimming Association, but he does not say whether the boy was a pupil of Messrs. Perring, Newton, Atherton, Jordan, Darke, or Martin.

SWIMMING clubs were formed as early as 1820, their chief function being to form a suitable background for officials.

The growth in number of clubs was only equalled by the growth of strife amongst them.

This necessitated the formation of an association in 1863 to give officials proper facilities for the noble art of viturpation.

The Association's first achievement was to draw up a law governing regulation costumes.

Care was taken to ensure that the costume was approved by nobody

The costume quarrel lasted 50 years, and was only solved by the combined intelligensia of the international federation, led by the nose by Alderman Fern.

This year officials were delighted to learn that the warfare would shortly be renewed over regulation trunks.

The formation of clubs and associations was secretly encouraged by publicans. . . . They realised that innumerable abortive committee meetings called for adequate refreshment.

In 1884 a rival organisation was formed to give officials wider scope for disagreement.

Two years later they amalgamated to form the A.S.A.. whose five Districts were devised to make agreement impossible.

By common consent, the favourite pastime of officials is guerilla warfare upon the A.S.A. Committee and the Selection Committees.

In 1938 the A.S.A. faced its biggest problem—President John Hodgson, Man of Peace.

Floreat Gloria Britannica.

Some amusing 'tongue-in-cheek' comments about the ASA in 1938.

Services or essential war work. There was virtually no competitive swimming and where clubs did continue to operate it was to concentrate on the progress of younger members. Every issue of the *Swimming Times* had a *Sea Lions* page for the younger members. The ASA was concerned that these youngsters should still learn the right strokes in the right way. In 1942 the ASA offered to find volunteers to give swimming instruction to youth clubs and pre-service organisations and this offer was quickly accepted by the Board of Education. There were no ASA Championships and all trophies were stored in London vaults. Even the badge and chain of the President were put away in a safe place. The ASA *Handbook* ceased publication for the duration. The *Swimming Times* suspended publication for two months, as Captain Cummins was put on Civil Defence work. Miss Janet Bassett-Lowke then stood in as wartime editor but special subscription appeals were needed to keep the magazine going as a slimmer version due to paper shortages and rationing. Harry Koskie suggested a *patrons list* and this was published in the wartime editions which became leaner as the War progressed. Many servicemen received their *Swimming Times* via the forces mail throughout the War.

The ASA did not close down in the War. There were no Council Meetings or AGMs, but Harold Fern still led a crusade to make the most of the facilities which remained open in the country and to pressurise and familiarise the Government and local authorities wherever interests of swimming could be extended. Thankfully, there was also early recognition that government could play the main part in future legislation which would help to bring to fruition most of the ASA's cherished aims.

It was the War, above all, which highlighted the need for everyone to learn to swim. The hasty evacuation from Dunkirk in 1940 with the inevitable drownings of many servicemen was only one of many *Swimming Times* articles suggesting that neither the services nor the country had yet succeeded in saving life by sufficient and proper swimming instruction. Each of the services had to face criticism but it was good for them. It seemed to focus the attention of their administrators on to the need for additional swimming instruction, for instruction by recognised methods and for the encouragement to swim longer distances. On occasions the Army let ASA observers see how they did things, and it was obvious that not all criticism was deserved. All of the services consequently liaised with the ASA to the benefit of all and became affiliated to the ASA in all five Districts.

The ASA's wartime policy to keep as many baths open as possible, and to run as many gala activities as possible, fitted well with the Government's *Stay at home holiday policy*. There was a recognition that industrial fatigue emanating from the war effort needed corresponding recreational facilities to compensate the workforce for not taking out-of-town holidays. Local Authority permits were required to hold galas but these did not seem difficult to acquire.

Almost all galas were run to raise funds for a variety of wartime causes, especially for comforts for the services. Many galas were run for or in conjunction with the services. Minehead in 1942 ran three large events with thousands of spectators. Diving was a main attraction next to the racing and water polo, but antics on the greasypole and diving for pennies added to the fun. The Canadian Tank Corps Swimmers also participated, while at the Bath Gala

A wartime effort to keep the public entertained.

the RAF and Army Water Polo Teams vied with the home competitors. The local hospitals, the Duke of Gloucester's Red Cross and St. John Fund and the Nursing Association all benefited financially. Croydon's Gala, organised by the local swimming clubs, attracted packed audiences and included demonstrations by the Army Physical Training Corps in full battledress. These were all brave ventures in the middle of a war. Not all areas had the facilities they needed. Coventry had one bath destroyed and another was hastily repaired, all except for the filtration plant which nobody in the local government could seem to put on the priority list. Northampton's bath usage was quoted as an example for others to follow. In a June week of 1941 the indoor baths took in 1,150 people, the slipper baths 3,000, the medicinal baths 100 and the outdoor pool 6,000.

One ASA function which did not close down in war was the encouragement given to those who wanted to pass the ASA Certificate for Teachers of Swimming. The courses and examinations were fostered and organised by the Districts and results confirmed by the ASA. The examination papers were revised by the examiners in 1945. Successes were: 1940-132; 1941-164; 1942-126; 1943-78; 1944-114; 1945-148. The ASA was pleased that some candidates were also tested for *swimming* as part of the Central Council for Physical Recreation's *National Test for Leaders in Physical Recreation*.

United Nations Swimming Committee

INTER-ALLIED GALAS
taking place before next publication

JULY 15th (Saturday).
At Marshall Street Baths. Belgium Sports Committee. 6 p.m.
Ticket enquiries to A. Meuwis, 78, Eaton Square, London, S.W.1

JULY 29th (Saturday).
At Marshall Street Baths. London Transport S.A. 6 p.m.
Ticket enquiries to G. E. Kenzie, 122, Ridley Road, Forest Gate,
London, E.7.

JULY 29th (Saturday).
At Twickenham. Thames Valley Ladies' S.C. 6 p.m.
Ticket enquiries to R. J. Millard, 23a, King Street, Twickenham.

AUGUST 5th (Saturday).
At Marshall Street Baths. French Forces in Great Britain. 6 p.m.
Ticket enquiries to Lt. du Moulin, "Amis des Volontaires Francais,"
Queensbury Way, London, S.W.7.

AUGUST 10th (Thursday).
At Hornsey Open-air Pool. Hornsey "Holidays-at-Home". 7 p.m.
Ticket enquiries to R. W. Mills, Superintendent, Hornsey Swimming
Pool, Hornsey, N.8.
NOTE. Kingsbury Gala (July 15th) is cancelled.

SPECIAL NOTICE
All swimmers who desire to compete at any of the galas should notify
Mr. S. T. Hirst at 242, Dollis Hill Lane, London, N.W.2 (phone Gladstone
1818), at least ten days beforehand. Where it is desired to enter for the
remaining galas of the whole series, to avoid correspondence one letter will
be sufficient.

PROCEEDS TO DATE
Romford Road, May 20th	-	£61	0	0
Hounslow, May 22nd	-	£21	0	0
Marshall Street, June 3rd	-	£128	0	0
East Ham, June 10th	-	£42	0	0

Wartime swimming helped to boost morale. These events took place in 1944.

By 1941 Harold Fern, as ever with an eye to the future, wrote of the urgent need, not only to plan ahead, but to consider the current state of the ASA. He posed eight points for discussion:

'1. Is the crawl stroke the primary movement to be taught in schools instead of the breast stroke? (It was so abroad.)

2. How do we maintain the interests of those who have left school? (i.e. the Youth)

3. What is the consensus of opinion about having a liaison committee of the ASA and the 'professional instructors' in order to improve standards?

4. How can the status of the professional instructor be raised?

5. Should County Associations be given greater powers because of the tendency of District organisations to become unwieldy? Should some District Funds thus go to County Associations?

6. Are the current ASA Laws in keeping with current needs?

7. How can Water Polo standards be improved and the game made more popular?

8. Can the lack of ASA financial resources be remedied?'

As one might imagine, this list provided the basis for much positive and fruitful discussion and was not biased by Mr. Fern's personal views. This type of discussion was to be the springboard for much of the ASA's workings in the latter part of the War and the later years of peace.

By 1943 the Government was crystallising its thinking concerning the need for *everyone to be taught to swim*. Many lives of servicemen may have been lost unnecessarily in the War. The RAF had just produced a new regulation that *'all aircrews must be able to swim'*. Pressure was put on MPs for the Board of Education to undertake to amend the new Education Bill *'to impose on Local Education Authorities the duty of providing School swimming baths instead of the "permissive power" already provided'*. When the Education Act of 1944 was delivered the following clause was included:

'It shall be the duty of every L.E.A. to secure that facilities for Primary, Secondary and Further Education provided for their area, include adequate facilities for recreation and social and physical training, and for that purpose an L.E.A., with the approval of the Minister, may establish, maintain and manage, or assist the establishment, maintenance and management of camps, holiday classes, playing fields, play centres, and other places (including playgrounds, gymnasiums and swimming baths not appropriated to any school of college) at which facilities for recreation and for such training as aforesaid are available for persons for whom primary, secondary or further education is provided by the authority ...'.

The natural follow-up to this was for the ASA to tell its disciples to go forward and pressurise the LEAs to carry out their new duties and also to plan the provision of new baths in all new large secondary schools and colleges.

The ASA were also pleased with a report issued in 1944 by the Research Board for the Correlation of Medical Science and Physical Education. The report recommended that school facilities for swimming should be made available, that every pupil should be taught swimming and lifesaving and that specialist teachers of swimming should be in all PE departments of secondary schools. Such a report added weight to main arguments.

There were two other areas where the ASA pressed for improvement. The first was to urge the Minister of Education to improve the status and rewards for professional swimming instructors employed by schools. The second was the on-going efforts, in conjunction with the CCPR, to get the Chancellor of the Exchequer to eliminate entertainment duty relating to amateur sports promotions. More efforts in this direction were to be made in 1945.

When the war ended in 1945 the ASA seemed pleased with its wartime achievements. It looked forward to the release of swimming baths from their Civil Defence purposes. However, some baths were still being used as British Restaurants, the government-run institutions for the provision of cheap, wholesome food, and these were not easily prised out. District and County Associations were being revived and the ASA Committee met in September for the first time since 1939. Plans were made for reprints of various ASA publications but paper shortages would rule the quantities.

The number of galas increased and on 30 June 1945 the United Nations Swimming Committee organised a *Victory Aquacade* as a celebration.

It was a time to rejoice, to look forward and to remember. Winifred Gibson of the NABS recalled the hardships:

'baths commandered; loss of men from the PE staff of schools; government clothing coupons needed to buy costumes; no rubber available for bathing caps; reduced water temperature due to lack of coal'.

Few swimming pools remained, especially in the bombed towns and cities. The Borough of Croydon only had three baths remaining out of a pre-war total of 39. When reconstruction began it was obvious that housing must come before baths but the plans were there.

The ASA finances were not good. The 1939 position had been reversed as the war years' expenditure had no income to balance it. To improve this position the Association had requested a special *'call'* of five shillings for each 1939 affiliated club and consequently the current account was just in surplus. The future of the financial side did not promise much improvement in the light of rising paper costs, an increasing number of committee meetings and other expenditure.

Very soon after the War the ASA had planned its first Championship dates for 1946 and with Harold Fern in his 25th year as Secretary he noted, *'All is set fair for a complete revival of the Association's activities in the coming year'*.

Perhaps innovation was in the air when George Creighton of Scotland on behalf of all the National Associations asked, *'Can we have a Swimming Summer School with lectures, films, coaching and exhibitions?'*

Post-Second World War

As with all institutions, the ASA faced an uphill task in post-war England, but there was no doubt that the wartime lobbying of Government and the continual exhortations to the Districts to organise galas and to keep up as many of their activities as possible, had kept the flame alight.

There was the realisation that change was in the air and that aspects of ASA administration and activity should be subjected to the sort of scrutiny which Harold Fern had advocated from 1941 onward. In 1946 Captain Cummins identified some of the areas to pick up on progress: clubs, dormant since 1939, needed the help of any swimmer with administrative experience to awaken them; the many servicemen who had learned to swim in wartime needed to be encouraged to join these swimming clubs; local authorities should be encouraged to provide swimming instructors wherever baths were still open; a completely new breed of water-polo players needed to be trained if the sport was to survive; and full use should be made of the divers who had given such excellent wartime gala displays. Cummins acknowledged the great work being done by NASI to produce more qualified instructors.

The first ASA Council Meeting since 1939 was held in Hanley, Stoke-on-Trent, in 1946. It was there that Harold Fern was presented with an expensive television set to mark his 25 years as Honorary Secretary of the Association. In thanking the members Mr. Fern said that he was disappointed at seeing his work destroyed twice by war but believed that it would be easier for the Association to get back to its pre-war position now than it was in 1920. Council decisions reflected the times: presentation of

THE SWIMMING TIMES

Hon. Editor : Capt. B. W. Cummins, 4, Waddon Pk. Ave., Croydon.   *Croydon* 5673.
Hon. Sub-Editor : Miss Janet Bassett-Lowke, 18, Albion Place, Northampton.

| Vol. XXIII. No. 5. | JUNE, 1946. | Price 6d. |

Amateur Swimming Association
(FOUNDED 1869)

NATIONAL APPEAL

With the approval and encouragement of the Government, the Olympic Games are to be held in London in two years time, and it is essential that the swimmers of England shall make an adequate contribution. To produce a team worthy of the country will cost a lot of money, and six years of war and no income have left the Association very impoverished. On the occasion of the Annual Meeting at Hanley in March last, this situation was fully realised, and it was decided by the representatives that an immediate effort must be made to provide money. In view of the very substantial sums raised during the war years for charity—now, fortunately, no longer needed—it is clear that if our Clubs make a determined effort, the problem can be solved. To show what can be done, the A.S.A. representatives there and then made a silver collection, and raised several pounds to start a fund.

After fully considering the matter, the Council decided to ask every Club in the country, big and little, to make an effort. This can be a Gala, where it is hoped swimmers will be willing to compete without prizes, or some social function, if more money is thought likely to be raised in that way.

Clubs are asked to talk about it to their members, and to explain that the preparation of an Olympic team should begin right now. All sorts of activities come under this heading—classes of instruction for teachers, summer schools for swimmers, coaching for swimmers, divers and water polo players. All these things are part of the preparation and would be helped by the fund. In addition, of course, other international activity would have to be financed.

We feel sure you will play your part. The A.S.A., as the national body, is powerless to act without money. The A.S.A. cannot appeal to the individual. That is the job of the Club. In short YOU are the A.S.A.; and the A.S.A. Committee and Council are but the instruments carrying out the schemes you make possible.

THIS IS AN URGENT MATTER. We want money as soon as possible. Will you make your effort soon? Make your cheque payable to the "Amateur Swimming Association" and send it either to the Hon. Sec., Mr. H. E. Fern, Springhaven, Barnet, Herts., direct, or through your District Association. And please make it as big as possible. If we put enough enthusiasm into this, we can do something worthy of the great sport in which we are interested.

B. W. Cummins President

Reginald A. Colwill Hon. Treasurer

H. E. Fern
          Hon. Secretary

The 1946 appeal for funds to support the home swimming team for the Olympics of 1948.

prizes to national champions should be resumed but certificates had to replace statuettes which were unobtainable; *standard times* would remain the same for a year because war had not helped to improve competitive swimming; the Long-Distance Championships in the Thames were to be suspended for a year due to expense and they were to be transferred to the Serpentine Lake in Hyde Park. Captain B.W. Cummins was elected President of the ASA.

A groundswell of opinion was making itself heard in favour of a *Summer School of Swimmers*. In 1946 it was proposed to hold a Swimming Course as part of Scarborough's Summer School and this was approved. Loughborough College already had a thriving Summer School encompassing a wide variety of subjects and activities. Mr. Creighton gave great praise to an existing Swimming Summer School Course at Loughborough organised by Mr. W.H. Downing. The 28 student coaches were treated as children for part of the course so that they should understand how children learned the process of swimming. They were examined by ASA and RLSS officials and were awarded medals and certificates. Specialist lectures were given in mechanics and hydrostatics. Students also learned how to teach the blind to swim and to help those whose limbs were weakened by infantile paralysis. The facilities of the indoor pool were described as magnificent and the underwater observation windows were used to detect faults. Mr. Creighton's final accolade: *'For shaking the complacent instructor out of his bed of laurels I can recommend no better tonic'*.

Both Loughborough College and the ASA were quick to realise the potential for innovative swimming courses and in 1947 an experimental Advanced Swimming and Coaching Course was set up parallel to Loughborough's existing courses. Swimming history was made with this *pre-Olympic Games preparation fortnight*. Harry Koskie, as the ASA's Chief Swimming Adviser, planned the schedules to include all aspects of aquatic training. He had combed the country for the talent. District Coaches and chaperones attended in addition to the 47 swimmers. Max Madders, lecturer in Physical Education at Birmingham University, attended as Physical Fitness Adviser. The swimmers from 14 years of age to seniors participated in a programme of physical fitness and relaxation exercises, intensive water training, a time-trials gala, resting, walking, lectures and discussion. Profitable publicity was also achieved through many press visits, over 1,000 photographs being circulated, and by BBC and European broadcasting. A.D. Kinnear (Bert) attended for a week at his own expense and was to continue to give voluntary demonstrations and lectures over the years. He was obviously thrilled at the Loughborough developments which were, in latter times, to be part of his raison-d'être.

Harry Koskie as ASA President in 1962.

The 1948 ASA Olympic Games Management Committee recommended that *'a residential course should be held each year at Loughborough College, for at least two weeks duration, at which nominated swimmers and coaches of both sexes should be invited for one week'.*

Max Madders as Director of the Loughborough Course in 1951.

LOUGHBOROUGH COLLEGE
Principal - Dr. H. SCHOFIELD, M.B.E.

SIXTEENTH SUMMER SCHOOL
Head of School: J. W. BRIDGEMAN, B.Sc.   **Duration: August 3rd-31st**
Courses will be held in
Physical Training   Swimming   Crafts   Teaching of Art   Education
A prospectus can be obtained on application to:
The Registrar, Loughborough College, Leicester

Swimming was already part of the Loughborough College summer programme before the ASA made use of this facility.

A.S.A. Advanced Training Course
Loughborough College Summer School

Tutor i/c Mr. MAX MADDERS,
Lecturer in Physical Recreation, Birmingham University.

Medical Officer : H. NOEL BLEASDALE, M.B., Ch.B.

Duration : August 12th to 26th, 1950.

Places :

   (i) *Swimmers* 30, allocated as follows : England four per district; Wales four; Scotland six. Trainees must be potential champions of either sex between the ages of 14 and 17 years in August, not necessarily the same swimmers who were on last year's course. The selection of trainees is left entirely in the hands of districts.

   (ii) *Coaches* 30, allocation on same basis as swimmers. Wherever possible Associations are asked to nominate coaches whose pupils will be on the course. The course is a strenuous one; consequently coaches of the younger generation are to be preferred. Either sex.

Fees, etc. :

   Tuition fee 3½ guineas for the fortnight.
   Residential charge: Single study bedroom, 7 guineas per fortnight; Rooms for two, three or four trainees, 6 guineas per fortnight per person.

   (i) *Swimmer trainees*: National Associations will be responsible for tuition fees and residential charges, no contribution being asked from trainees. Trainees will, however, be responsible for their own travelling expenses unless assisted by their respective Associations.

   (ii) *Coach Trainees*: National Associations will be responsible for tuition fees. Coaches will pay their own residential charges through their Associations and also their own travelling expenses. District Associations may wish to assist financially coaches, who can be either amateur or professional.

Discipline : Trainees will be required to give an undertaking that they will conform to all rules and regulations which may be in force at the College, and that they will attend for the full 14 days.

Closing date : Associations will make their nominations on official forms not later than May 31st. Vacancies will be filled by Management Committee: Associations are therefore invited to submit at least one additional name for a waiting list.

Syllabus outline :

   Morning: Physical and relaxation exercises for all trainees, half hour periods in the bath, coaches working with their own swimmers under the supervision of Tutor i/c, and massaging them before or after waterwork.

   Afternoon: Walks, a game, or swimming in outdoor pool. 4 p.m. tea. 5 to 6.30 p.m. all in the indoor pool for sectional work, dives, turns, etc.

   Evening: Game, walk, lecture, or films for all.
   For coaches: Lectures. The principles involved in (a) Training; (b) Diet; (c) Massage; (d) Preparing a swimmer for an event; (e) Swimming technique, practical massage and physical exercises

BERTRAM W. CUMMINS,
Hon. Administration Officer.

A)

B)
D)

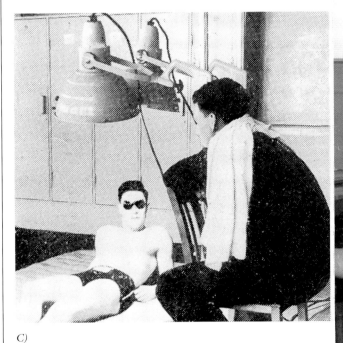

C)

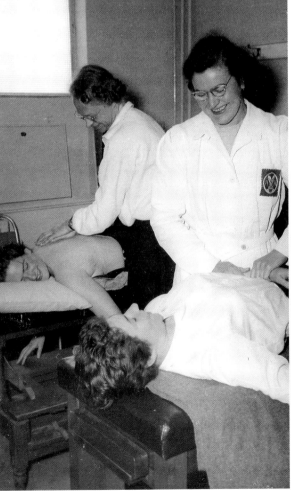

A) *Details of the 1950 ASA Advanced Training Course.*
B) *Pictures from below water level taken from the viewing gallery at the Loughborough pool.*
C) *The sunray treatment room at Loughborough.*
D) *The physiotherapy room in action. Lorna Frampton, who was also chaperone to the girls is the lady to the left.*

Harry Koskie trains potential members of Britain's 1948 Olympic Team at Loughborough. Left to right: Margaret Girvan, aged 14; Eleanor Gordon, aged 14; Margaret Wellington, aged 19; and Cathie Gibson, aged 16.

Inset: The special badge produced for Loughborough Course participants.

Bill Juba commented on the success of the 1948 course which had been designed to make participants *physically and water fit* and not to bring them to a peak of racing fitness. For the first time a Medical Officer, Dr. R.H. Bolton, attended to give talks, to check physical conditions and to compile medical histories. Max Madders's wife, Jane, introduced sun-ray treatment and physio-therapy alongside the *Relax with Max* sessions. By 1949 the ASA had decided that the Loughborough Course should be an annual event with nominees being potential champions between the ages of 14 and 17 years. Their attendance would be regarded as an ASA Scholarship and they would pay no fees. Twenty would come from England, six from Scotland and four from Wales. The ASA would also nominate ten coaches with two more coming from Wales and two from Scotland.

Captain Cummins was in charge of administration with K.B. Martin as Liaison Officer, Lorna Frampton as girls' chaperone and R.H. Brown as boys' warden (from 1950). The Committee decided to purchase an electronic pacing machine to help to improve performances and for learning pace-judgement. Mr. Koskie had designed a metal *passing-out* badge for all partic-ipants. Also Mr. Koskie, being unable to give enough time, handed over the course responsibility to Max Madders but remained himself in an advisory capacity.

Max Madders commented that *'a great field of research awaits investigation in the medical and physical aspects of swimming, and that we ought to follow it up'*. In 1950 he was supported by the ASA in a visit to Japan to study methods of teaching swimming

Dr. N. Bleasdale, ASA Medical Officer, in 1949. He served the Loughborough courses for many years.

in schools and to discover the nature of the competitive swimmers' specialised training. In 1951 Max visited Holland for a similar purpose.

Dr. N. Bleasdale was the new Medical Officer, having already been appointed as Medical Officer for the XIVth Olympic swimming events and for English Universities and Lancashire County Swimming Teams.

Dr. Bleasdale's initial measuring work and observations included *'vital capacity, pulse rate, athletes' foot and blisters'*. He subsequently attempted to relate physical measurements to a common factor and produced a formula:

$$F = \frac{Arm\ Length + Leg\ Length\ (cms)\ x\ Vital\ Capacity\ (litres)}{Body\ Weight\ (kgs)}$$

He then tried to relate his results to individual swimmer's performances to see if there was correlation. His conclusions led him to believe that the best physical development ages were in the 16 to17 year age group and that correlation seemed to be more striking for the boys than the girls. He also found that the best performances at Loughborough were achieved by those swimmers with the highest factor numbers. In 1951 Dr. Bleasdale took all his swimmers to Loughborough Hospital for chest x-ray and subsequently carried out experiments before and after demanding exercise to ascertain statistics on oxygen debt.

All this was pioneering work indeed. Dr. Bleasdale and his team were at the forefront of this sort of thinking and research in the athletic world. His *Swimming Times* articles on a wide variety of medical and physical aspects were to be a source of interest and

enlightenment for years, and were to help to stimulate many swimmers and administrators to think about the body in new ways. In just the first few years his topics included: *Diet, Physiological Aspects of Muscular Exercise, Muscles and Levers, The Ear, Exercises and Circulatory Changes, Nutrition and the Competitive Swimmer* and *The Mechanics of Respiration*.

The Loughborough Course continued to evolve and in 1953 Pat Besford Nievens reflected on its phases of development: the 1947-8 First Phase Years had been mainly for training and selecting swimmers for the 1948 Olympics; the 1949-53 Second Phase had become the two-week Advanced Swimming Training School for 14 to 17 year-old selected swimmers and their coaches.

Austin Rawlinson, President of NCASA in 1954, was very impressed with progress and invented the slogan, *Take The Loughborough Spirit Home With You*. Some of his greatest praise was reserved for the *great co-operation* he had observed between the amateurs and the professionals on the Loughborough courses.

In 1952 Loughborough College was re-organised to become a Teacher Training College with the Physical Education Department as an integral part. The Principal, Mr. Bridgeman, thought that it would no longer be possible to continue with the Summer Course. Negotiations resulted in its being transferred to Easter for 1953 with the added advantage of being able to use the indoor bath for 100 per cent of the time (instead of only four hours a day as previously). In 1952 also there were strong suggestions made to the ASA to produce a new course especially adjusted to the needs of coaches. This was turned down because

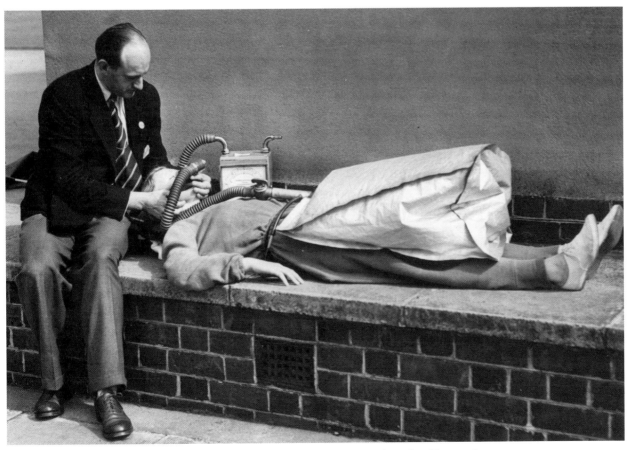

Dr H.N. Bleasdale, medical officer of the ASA, used the Douglas Apparatus to measure maximum breathing capacity.

MATT MANNERISMS

Here are some of the typical sayings of Matt Mann during the course which contain a mixture of useful advice and American idioms.

● Get in the cradle and stay there (balance) . . . Sit in a bucket (back turn) . . . Use that liquid.

● You've got to flip 'em, honey (turns) . . . The Brass (high amateur officials) . . . A rough cookie (tough opponent).

● Put backbone where there is wishbone. Be a backbone swimmer.

● Get to recognise your youngsters' feelings . . . Snazie (smart). Be a killadilla.

● Get up and shoot me a 50 kid. Coaches must always be sticklers about stressing fundamentals.

● If you don't bring back the bacon (victory), don't come back yourselves. . . .

● *We always thought we had to use three-letter words. When you use four you have to have an education to go with it.*

● Now, honey, a time like that only qualifies you to carry their drinking water.

● **When you are tired relax in the water. Don't lie on the side of the bath.**

● You must stay abreast of the times, read your rule book. They don't write it for fun.

● Champions are not ordinary, they give that extra something. . . .

● Watch a 100 yards man, his mouth is way open. He ain't catchin' flies, son. He's after oxygen.

● Every race we have in the book is at top speed. . . . The neck is made to turn the head on.

● **I have a feeling that some youngsters are poison puppies because they get too much air. The important thing is to get rid of it.**

● I think swimmers sometimes get confused from too much advice. . . . The harder you work the better you will like it.

● Never let us get into bickering so that we miss our chances. . . . Get right out there, honey.

● The work will get rougher as we go along—but then water does get rough.

● You ain't got just to beat the next fella, son—you're better'n that—you got to beat the world—and the world's a big place, son!

● What is this peak? If you get a boy up there—there ain't no peak. That's a plateau.

Matt Mann, Swimming Coach at Michigan University, coached at Loughborough in 1954. The Swimming Times extracted some of his favourite sayings.

the ASA considered that the 77 coaches who had passed through Loughborough courses in the previous years could pass their knowledge on to the other coaches within the District orbit, and it was up to the Districts to organise *mini-Loughborough-courses* to disseminate good practice. The Northern District thus used the Derby Bath at Blackpool in 1953 to run such a course for 30 coaches and 60 swimmers. Austin Rawlinson's message was getting through!

Phase Three at Loughborough started in 1954. This time the 40 best Olympic *hopefuls* in the United Kingdom would be chosen. The *District Sharing* selection basis was replaced by *'the best in the land'*. Matt Mann, Michigan University Swimming Coach and the USA Men's Olympic Coach for 1952, was invited to run the course, assisted by Max Madders and Bert Kinnear (the latter for daily exercise routines and group swimming gymnastics). All participants would pay £5 each to defray the additional costs.

At the close of this course Ken Martin, Chairman, said,

> *'British swimming history has been made: your ground work at Loughborough will remain for all time the most outstanding thing which has ever happened to British swimming'.*

These accolades to Matt Mann were echoed in the words of the trainees, who said, *'He makes you feel like work, even if it is Saturday or Sunday'.* Matt's philosophy was one of pressure in training. *'A Champion is one who reacts to pressure'.* He said,

> *'When you say, "I'm tired" I'm going to ask you to go on. How far are you prepared to go? There is a lot of room at the top of the hill. It is crowded at the bottom'.*

He suggested that often the mental approach to competition was deficient, that our coaches were satisfied with standards which did not aim high enough and that if the initial target was the Olympic level, then County, District and National Championships could be taken in one's stride. There was no doubt that with this Loughborough course the ASA's height of ambition had been reached and the Association's efforts in this direction were among the leading examples in the world for this sort of venture.

Matt Mann advises Barbara Kingston.

Bert Kinnear supervises weight-training at Loughborough in 1956.

Spring exercise in the gymnasium in 1955. (Copyright: Studio Margaret, Wisbech)

Coaches from all over the country check their swimmer's times by the pool side at Loughborough in 1962.

A picture-montage of 1958 activities at Loughborough.

Bert Kinnear talks to young hopefuls at a training session.

By 1956 the 10-year plan for the Loughborough Easter Course was concluded but the slogan rang out - *Loughborough Courses must continue.* From 1957 Bert Kinnear took over from Max Madders as Director of Advanced Swimming Training Courses. His theme developed as *Land and Water Conditioning.*

It was proposed by the Education Committee in 1955 to inaugurate an ASA Swimming Coaches' Certificate with a view to eventually building up a National Panel of Coaches. A special committee of H.N. Bleasdale, A.D. Kinnear, K.B. Martin, A. Price and N.W. Sarsfield constructed the syllabus, examination system and the methods of conduct of courses aimed at the introduction of the new certificate. Woodthorpe Bath at Sheffield was the site for the first course in 1955. The staff were Dr. E.H. Kendall, A.D. Kinnear and N.W. Sarsfield. Only two candidates succeeded - Eileen Fenton, famous for her Channel Swim and J. Hardy of Sheffield who tragically died shortly afterwards. The whole organisation was, however, transferred to Loughborough College of Education (the Teacher Training College was renamed in 1963) as part of its Summer School for 1967 with A.D. Kinnear as Tutor. Mr. C.W. Pullan was Secretary of the ASA Coaches' Certificate Committee. The course was rigorous and consisted of strokes; fault recognition and correction; swimming gymnastics and conditioning; and anatomy and physiology. Eventually only those who held the ASA Advanced Teachers' Certificate were accepted as candidates. Between 6 and 10 course members were successful each year for the first few years. By 1964 there were 61 certificated coaches on the panel.

It was then resolved to institute a Club Coaches' Certificate which would enable the holder to coach at club level. This was of elementary standard compared to the Coaches' Certificate. Some coaches who had not quite made the advanced grade were considered for the new award which would certainly benefit affiliated clubs. A *Club Coaches Register* was initiated in 1966. By 1968 additional courses were set up at Crystal Palace and in the Districts. Much of this progress was due to the outstanding efforts of Charles Pullen.

The 1958 Loughborough Course reflected the spirit of innovation which was permeating about every aspect of progress in swimming. There was increased circuit-training and weight-training. The average distance each swimmer achieved each day was 4,000 yards exclusive of practice starts, returns and push-offs. John Atha of Loughborough College of Technology introduced a battery of tests and measurements to record strength, mobility, power, agility, balance, pulse-rate, breath-holding and breath capacity. Also each trainee was filmed at the beginning and end of the course, below and above water and the loops were shown on departure. Kodak supported this part of the work. Each year the ASA acknowledged the gifts received at the course by such firms as Bovril, Peak Frean, Meredith and Drew, Horlicks and Crookes. ITV also publicised the event.

The ASA was becoming interested in Ministry of Education coaching grants paid under the Physical Training and Education Act of 1937. Such grants were received by the All England

John Atha of Loughborough College made many anthropometric measurements in the late 1950s and early 1960s as part of the research into swimming performances.

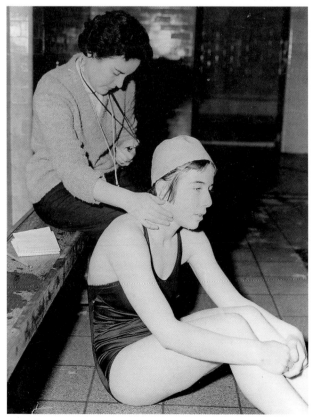

A coach from Dewsbury Swimming Club takes a pulse reading with her protégé during a training break at Loughborough in 1962.

Women's Hockey Association, the AAA, the Amateur Fencing Association and the Lawn Tennis Association. The rule was that coaches' salaries up to £600 per annum could be funded. In 1958, specific details were requested of Government with the aim of funding either a National Technical Officer or District Technical Advisers. Funds were not immediately available but the Ministry hoped to be able to react favourably. In 1959 the grant was agreed and the ASA appointed their first National Technical Officer from January 1960 in the shape of Bert Kinnear. The £1,000 per annum went towards his salary. His main functions were to be: (a) to organise and direct courses for club coaches (ASA Coaches' Certificate examination); (b) to advise clubs on solutions to technical problems; (c) to organise courses for the ASA Teacher's Certificate; and (d) to run courses for school teachers in organised class-teaching of modern stroke techniques. Decisions were made concerning his terms of reference and allowances. The cost to a District for a lecture was determined. Projectors, loops-films, screens and cork-lanes were purchased for his use. During 1960 the NTO visited all Districts giving lectures, coaching and demonstrating.

Bert Kinnear used the *Swimming Times* for his monthly contribution to get his message across, starting with *The Yearly Swimming Training Plan*. He commented on Swimming Club organisation and commended the work done on behalf of youth but he suggested that to make up for a deficiency of adult helpers, the young people of 18 years of age who may have finished in competition, could help with coaching.

A second NTO, Tony Holmyard, was appointed in 1962 and LEAs were invited to apply for lecturing or demonstration services. Also District Honorary Secretaries met with the NTOs to discuss planned visits. In 1963 Helen Elkington was appointed the third NTO and after J.A. Holmyard resigned, H. Hamilton-Smith replaced him. These new staff were the direct result of increased government funding. The NTO's work was demanding not only in the need to satisfy the great number of requests from Districts and LEAs but in the great amount of travelling which went with the job. In 1965 the ASA saw the need for some rationalisation and directed that the work-load should be supervised by an ASA official. This, of course, would also keep the Committee very much in contact with the programme. In 1966 the ASA asked the Department of Education and Science to increase the grant so that there could be six NTOs, one for each District and an extra one to be based at Crystal Palace. Each NTO would be requested to spend at least two-thirds of each year in the District. In spite of the country's economic crisis in 1967 the DES agreed to fund the ASA's extended scheme from January 1968.

It was at this point that Bert Kinnear resigned on a point of principle when he could not agree with the guidelines laid down by the ASA concerning the appointment of new NTOs.

Hamilton E. Bland, J.M. Hogg and R.G. Cayless were appointed. The NTO scheme was now firmly established and in addition to their routine work, these officers were very much involved in such ventures as film-making and the *Learn to Swim* Campaign. Hamilton Bland became specially responsible for Water-Polo. The ASA's Ken Martin and Honorary Treasurer Alf Turner, met the NTOs to discuss their expenditure and their obligations and guidelines were laid down.

The Need for Full-Time Professional Coaches in England

The ASA's imput into the production of coaches in 1970 was to supervise courses mainly at Loughborough College of Education, Crystal Palace and in the Districts for training of ASA Coaches and ASA Club Coaches. Some coaches were interested in coaching for a short-term basis or for just local coaching. These would hope to attain the ASA Club Coaches' Certificate which was of a more elementary standard. Others would be more interested in coaching as a career. For them the full ASA Coaches' Certificate was the aim.

However, at that time there was only one full-time professional coach in the country, Paddy Garrett who coached at Millfield School. Most of the others were teaching in schools or local authorities by day and doing a little coaching in the evenings.

When Hamilton Bland (NTO) won a Winston Churchill Travelling Scholarship to America in 1969 he was more than impressed by witnessing the great number of professional swimming coaches in that country. They all seemed to coach full time and did not spend time teaching learners how to swim. No wonder America produced so many top competitors!

On his return to England Mr. Bland's report to the ASA sparked interest in the initiative of a new scheme here. Norman Sarsfield and Hamilton Bland persuaded the Coventry Baths administration to amalgamate their three swimming clubs and to employ Mr. Bland as a full-time professional coach. Not all of the ASA Committee were in favour of such a venture perhaps because some thought that Coventry might gain unfair advantage. However the Committee, Coventry and the Coventry clubs agreed to pay for this service between them. It proved a phenomenal success and it was not long before the names of Coventry competitors were at the top of results in this country. In 1973 Hamilton Bland withdrew from the need for ASA financial support and branched out on his own as the Coventry Coach.

Other areas followed this example of success and started to employ full-time professional coaches. By 1980 there were around 50 of these operating in England and by 1994 not far short of 200. Most of our successes over the last 15 years are due in the main to this great boost to competitive standards.

Television

The pre-war developments in the field of television had led to a number of Londoners being the first to experience the new medium. The potential influence of television on sporting events was exercising the minds and imaginations of most sports bodies. The fear was that if the public could see events on their screens and on the cinema screens then the event-organisers would suffer financial loss. As the law stood, there was no copyright in a spectacle or in any televising of it. Thus the main governing bodies of sport formed an *Association for the Protection of Copyright in Sport* and the ASA was a founder member. In later years the fears were shown to have been of rather less importance, as the ASA eventually made money out of televised productions.

The extension of television broadcasting stations to areas in Britain outside the London area in the early 1950s revived the

" *This means that engineers visit the bath* " . . .

TV was on its way in 1955.

attention of major sporting bodies to the laws of copyright. The screening of sporting events in people's own homes was uncharted territory to both the BBC and to organisations such as the ASA. There were no copyright agreements, no contracts and no guarantees of any form of financial income. Thus the ASA Committee recommended that, '*Affiliated clubs should support a ban on the televising of sporting events from 1st January 1950 unless satisfactory safeguards are given by the BBC*'. There followed a conference between the Postmaster General (the Minister responsible for broadcasting on radio and television) and the Sports Governing Bodies when the PMG undertook to consult before granting licences for the showing of TV to a paying audience. An independent consultative body to be known as the Sports Television Advisory Committee would be set up with an independent chairman. This organisation would negotiate for an experimental period for the BBC's rights to show around 100 events a year (all sports). All information would also be made available to the STAC to help it to assess the direct and indirect effects of TV sporting events. At the same time as all these negotiations were taking place the Government had set up its own committee under the chairmanship of William Beveridge '*to consider the future of broadcasting in all its forms*'.

The ASA withdrew their proposed ban because they felt that positive action was being taken. Meanwhile the Association was getting its own act together and in 1951 brought out a new law-

'*Affiliated clubs promoting events for T.V. purposes must, at least four weeks beforehand, submit to the Hon. Sec. of the ASA - the programme for scrutiny and approval, together with a licencing fee of three guineas. If satisfactory he shall be authorised to issue a licence*'.

The following year this was amended by the addition of, '*No member of an affiliated Club shall be permitted to take part in any swimming, diving or water polo event that is being televised, unless a licence has been granted by the ASA*'. The loopholes were being closed.

The full impact of television was still to come and even in 1952 the *Swimming Times* leader was able to say, '*Swimming, too long regarded as the Cinderella of British sports, is now receiving greater publicity in the National Press and on the wireless*'. No mention was made of television.

In 1954 the Independent Television Authority had also come into being and in 1955 the ASA resolved to approach both BBC

and ITA to discuss television matters and to work on a programme which had been planned by the Association. Also in 1955 Harold Fern met Peter Dimmock, Head of BBC Outside Broadcasting, in order to make a three-year contract between the ASA and the BBC for televising ASA Championships, International and other events. The contract was approved and signed. To help matters the ASA took up a BBC suggestion to form a Television Advisory Committee with representation from all five Districts. The Honorary Secretary could then more easily resolve the problems for licence applications for events. The BBC contract revealed that half of all television fees would be paid to the relevant District where an event took place. The other half was paid to a pool for annual distribution to the five Districts. To manage all matters connected with the contract the ASA appointed a Television Liaison Officer on £500 annual salary. For the first year this was to be Mr. R. Hodgson.

Some swimmers and divers still seemed to consider that they should receive fees for television appearances and the Southern Counties asked for clarification. The practice was for the ASA to pay for any expenses incurred and then the balance would be paid, half to the Association and half to the individual swimmer's club. Payment to individuals would invalidate amateur status. The ASA looked to FINA to dispel any doubts on this matter and to confirm its own views on '*the protection of the individual*'.

Educational Television was another development of the late 1950s. The ASA Board of Examiners and Publication Committee of 1958 suggested involvement in three types of programme:

(a) Programmes of a technical nature with swimming stars demonstrating strokes.

(b) Programmes introducing swimming to the individual with '*the family unit*' perhaps emphasising the '*mother and child at the bath*' or '*family at the seaside*' approach.

(c) A series on *Swimming Teaching* with N.W. Sarsfield and A. Rawlinson as advisers.

This serious planning would, as ever, help to keep the ASA in the vanguard of programme developments.

The television management were also learning fast, and as the years went on the methods of presentation greatly improved. The public, too, was becoming more perceptive and appreciated improved use of cameras and a stricter form of continuity in programme presentation. John Webb, a BBC commentator and former diver, gave some good advice to those organising swimming events. This advice was particularly directed to those organisers who lacked real planning skills, who had long pauses between races and who perhaps did not always select the most attractive locations. John Webb criticised those who thought a programme could be produced at short notice or who failed to look at carparking, lighting, power and camera siting with balanced judgement.

The great influence of television was increasingly recognised. Beulah Gundling, USA solo synchronised swimming champion, gave her first televised performance at Ilford in 1954. There followed a complete sell-out of tickets at the other nine venues where she appeared on tour.

Televised swimming had much to commend it. It was presented to a huge audience at relatively small cost and no doubt the sport benefited from the resulting publicity and propaganda. *Sportsview*, the popular BBC production which started in 1954, was to be the longest running of all sports programmes and swimming had its share of the screen.

The BBC Audience Research Department made a survey of the interests of 5-20 year-olds of the UK in 1954 and interviewed 3,700 young people. Swimming appeared to come out as the most popular sport:

BBC percentages by age groups interested in swimming in 1954.

Ages (years)	5-7	8-11	12-15	16-20
Boys	27%	42%	62%	51%
Girls	17%	48%	64%	42%

The ASA would have been pleased at these figures in their favour.

The BBC Television contract was re-negotiated in 1962 for a five-year period and covered world rights to televise all events promoted by the ASA and member clubs. Income from this was considerable: £1,175 in 1962, £4,771 in 1963 and £5,000 in 1964. In his report for 1962 Mr. R. Hodgson, TV Liaison Officer, identified four categories of programme:

1. International fixtures: four full Great Britain International contests a year. A problem had developed here. Those continental teams which came to us with expenses paid were now demanding return fixtures in their own countries. This was because their countries had copied the ASA system of becoming sponsored by their television organisation and required international subject matter for their screens. The problem was the demand on the swimmers who now would potentially have double the number of fixtures. This may not have been too difficult in years when Olympics, European and Commonwealth events did not occur but there had to be a limit on a swimmer's imput. Another problem was the omission of water polo and diving events from the television screen. Neither the BBC nor ITV found these sports to be a good subject for the media. If these were part of a *total swimming competition* then there was a better chance that some exposure to the public would occur.

2. District Pool Contests: these special District events were part of the BBC's *Grandstand* programme and were generally successful. As these were part of a general sports programme they had to dovetail in with other sports.

3. Educational programmes: up to then these were screened as part of Children's Television, but rarely.

4. Personal interviews: any financial proceeds had to go to the club via the ASA Committee.

There was always a strong connection between the ASA Education Committee and the work of the TV Liaison Officer. In 1964, for example, this Committee worked alongside ITV in the production of four educational programmes. These were the Butterfly Stroke, Competition Swimming Strokes, Diving for Fun and Looking Forward to Mexico. In that same year the BBC televised nine national and international contests.

In 1965 Mr. Hodgson announced his imminent retirement and Austin Rawlinson was appointed as TV Liaison Officer in his place from the end of 1967. Mr. Hodgson had done a remarkable job since 1956. Another BBC contract was signed in 1967. It was at this period that experimental work was being done in connection with portable closed circuit television. At Coventry College of Education a video-tape recorder and camera, sited in the balcony overlooking the pool, recorded students giving swimming lessons. When the results were played back they were able to appraise their own lessons and to be appraised by their tutors. The early equipment was cumbersome and heavy but from such experiments a new medium gained recognition as a very important teaching tool. The swimming world and other sports would learn the benefits.

For a number of years the ASA Education Committee had lobbied hard to have swimming stroke lessons included in the growing number of *educational programmes*. In the centenary year the BBC made such a series which consisted of ten half-hour programmes, mainly about swimming strokes. Mr. B. Gorton, the Midland NTO, was the technical adviser on behalf of the ASA. It was another success story.

The future into the 1970s and beyond would experience far greater degrees of sophistication in the development of equipment and methods of programme delivery. The ASA throughout the 1950s and 1960s had managed to exploit this medium as a showcase for its wares in ways that press and radio had never been able to do, to increase its income considerably and to extend its main object of '*educating the population in order to produce swimmers and competitive swimmers*'.

Education - 1950s

From its beginnings the ASA had emphasised the *Educative* aspect as possibly its main function. This was a wide field for it included the teaching of the public to swim, teaching competitive swimmers to swim faster, teaching coaches how to coach, teaching local authorities about good practice in bath design. The assessment of swimming teachers has always been a special function in Britain because in other countries this aspect has been controlled by the State. In England the government has surrendered assessment matters to the ASA. The ASA had also concerned itself very much with the *paraphernalia* of education and from early days had greatly encouraged the production of swimming and diving manuals. These publications not only linked the ASA with its widespread public but became a source of income. As the 1950s progressed it became apparent that other media items could help to make the educative aspect more effective, more attractive and more profitable. The 16mm. sound-film projector was becoming a more standard item in schools and colleges and it seemed a positive step to produce the films to go alongside them. Certainly the cheaper film-strip projector became quite a common feature in the classroom in the 1950s. A series of good black-and-white still pictures could, with a good teacher to talk it through, be an excellent stimulus to children who, as yet, had not felt the full impact of television. The underwater-viewing windows at Loughborough College of Education bath proved to be an excellent aid to revealing what was happening below the waterline when producing a teaching film-strip. Coaches were encouraged to be more scientific in their approach to the use of timing and equipment and gradually a whole new industry of technical aids grew up as an adjunct to the sporting world.

The ASA Committee seemed to be responsible for publications initially, but soon a Publications Committee emerged which sometimes was part of the Board of Examiners Committee, e.g. in 1958. By 1959 the Education Committee included the Publications Section. Whichever area it was in, it was obvious that (a) there was enough work involved to justify a separate committee and (b) that there had to be close liaison with the Education, Scientific Advisory and Swimming Committees.

The ASA announced in 1950 that the new edition of *Swimming Instructions* and the *Diving Manual* were selling well, that L.H. Koskie, Max Madders and K.B. Merton were producing the new book *Swimming*, and that *Swimming and Swimming Strokes* was being revised. Also N.W. Sarsfield was preparing *Teaching of Diving* for 1951 publication. The *Swimming Times* in 1953 produced *The Swimmer's Log Book* which generated a great demand. Harry Koskie called it the *'swimmer's barometer'* because if properly used it helped to mea-

Sets of five Swimming Wall Charts, designed and approved by the

A 1956 Swimming Times advertisement for charts which would adorn classroom and clubroom walls.

sure a competitive swimmer's progress. The ASA also published a *Swimmer's Diary* which included a wealth of topical information and hints to complement the sport. Bovril Limited sponsored the ASA Official Wallcharts in 1956. This set of five charts showing the main strokes graced many a school, club and pool wall.

As a result of a general demand in the sporting world and arising out of their work with the Loughborough courses, Dr. N. Bleasdale and Dr. E.H. Kendall, assisted by A. D. Kinnear, published *Anatomy and Physiology* in 1957. It was a great success. K.M.B. Cross was asked to revise his *Modern Public Baths* in the same year.

The *News Chronicle* newspaper, which proved to be a faithful sponsor of sport, worked with the ASA via Harry Koskie in 1952 to produce a black-and-white sound film on *The Crawl Stroke*. This success was followed in later years when the paper was asked to sponsor one film a year for three years - *Back*, *Breast* and *Butterfly*. The Association's 1958 film *Getting Used to Water* was again successful. The loop film was popular with coaches because a short, silent loop could help to teach just one aspect of a stroke. Thus a set of eight loops on the Back Crawl by A.D. Kinnear, together with notes, cost £3.10s. A whole range of loops was developed in the 1950s.

A progressive step was taken in 1956 when Mr. T.E.H. Tanton donated £300 to found the ASA Library. Appeals were made for books, pictures, manuscripts, models, and memorabilia. Since then a sizeable and unique collection has been built up over the

The Swimmer's Diary was more than just a space for recording appointments.

THE YOUNG SWIMMER
The Crawl Stroke

A film produced with the co-operation of the Amateur Swimming Association, under the technical guidance of Harry Koskie, Chief Swimming Adviser to the Association.

All movements are analysed separately and important details become apparent through the use of the slow-motion camera and some remarkable underwater shots.

Running time: 15 minutes

DISTRIBUTORS

To Educational Authorities, Schools and Youth Organisations—
Educational Foundation for Visual Aids,
33, Queen Anne Street, London, W.1.

To Clubs, etc.—
Sound Services Ltd.,
269, Kingston Road, Merton Park, London, S.W.19.

16 mm. (Sound) copies are available for hire (5/6) or outright purchase (£10)

A

NEWS CHRONICLE
COACHING FILM

NEW SWIMMING FILMS

Produced by Boulton-Hawker Films, Ltd., with the co-operation of the National Committee for Visual Aids in Education and Ilford and Essex Education Committees.
(These are the films referred to in " Around and About " in the July issue of THE SWIMMING TIMES.)

LEARNING TO SWIM :
  THE BREAST STROKE (12 mins.)
  THE CRAWL (12 mins.)
  THE BACK CRAWL (9 mins.)
    16 mm. Sound

How the strokes may be taught and learnt. A class of children undergo instruction, from initial confidence exercises, and finally perform the finished stroke, which is also demonstrated in normal and slow motion by experts.

Each film is available for hire at 7/6 one day, 2/6 subsequently, and for purchase at £14, £14 and £10 respectively. Teaching notes are supplied.

BOULTON - HAWKER FILMS LTD.
HADLEIGH - - - SUFFOLK
Have you seen the associated
" LEARNING TO DIVE " films?

A.S.A.
Official Coaching
Loop Films

Technical Advisers
MAX MADDERS   A. D. KINNEAR

COMPLETE SET OF 31 LOOPS £12.10.0 All with full teaching notes	**BREAST STROKE** 8 Loops . . £3.10.0 ELIZABETH CHURCH **FRONT CRAWL** 8 Loops . . £3.10.0 DAPHNE WILKINSON **BACK CRAWL** 8 Loops . . £3.10.0 A. D. KINNEAR **BUTTERFLY** 7 Loops . . £3. 0.0 D. CRIPPS

Produced and Distributed by
Scottish Instructional Films
EAGLESHAM   GLASGOW

A 1952 advertisement for new visual aids.

years. Today the backbone of the library is made up of bound sets of ASA *Handbooks* and *Swimming Times* but there are also many books and magazines, some of antiquity, which provide windows for looking back at swimming in general and the ASA in particular.

It is interesting to delve into the advertisement pages of the *Swimming Times*. They reflect the progress of technical developments, such as timepieces; costume wear and noseclips; publicity for galas and new publications; in addition to a variety of films

whose drink and health products would well be seen to warm up and cheer up the cold swimmer or to promote good health. Bovril, Horlicks, Ovaltine and Crookes Halibut Oil realised the advertising potential as well as often being seen to sponsor swimming developments. Articles by informed innovators also drew attention to such new items as trampolines for diving training, the electro-recorder which *'perhaps would replace judges'* and special new floats as aids for the teaching of swimming. In 1955 Philips Electrical were pleased to announce that they had provided Intraphil infra-red irradiation lamps for the Loughborough Course. Sometimes there were photographs of the Canadian log-rollers who provided a thrilling extra attraction at galas.

In 1955 Captain B.W. Cummins, founder and editor of the *Swimming Times* since 1922, was honoured at a special dinner to celebrate the 33rd birthday of the magazine. The swimming world was there to acknowledge his great contribution to the sport both within the ASA and for his work in developing the *Swimming Times* from a news sheet to the status of monthly publication read in 61 countries. At the age of 75 the Captain had decided that to safeguard the future for the magazine he would form a private company, the Swimming Times Ltd. The speeches at the dinner echoed the sentiment *'that he was the best-loved ambassador in the world of swimming'.*

The ASA's Relationships with the STA and ESSA

Swimming Teachers' Association

This Association had been founded as the National Association of Swimming Instructors in 1932 and Ross Eagle the famous professional coach had much to do with its beginnings. He and others were concerned at the lack of standardisation of methods of instruction throughout the country. The first Chairman, Mr. Unwin, saw the objectives as *'making sure that teachers were properly certificated; helping them to improve their work; and pooling the best ideas, advice and good practice for the benefit of swimming'.* The NASI was founded for professional swimming teachers and instructors and filled an important gap in the overall framework of swimming administration for the country. Members had to pass all-round teaching and swimming examinations before being accepted. In 1948 NASI changed its name to STA because of the implications of the sound of the old title in a war-time world. The STA settled alongside the ASA being fully sympathetic to its aims and work. In the 1950s the STA Diploma was considered to be the equivalent in the teaching world to the RLSS Diploma in status.

In 1950 the National Liaison Committee was set up, consisting of the National Association of Bath Superintendents, the STA and the ASA. The initial aim was to provide a Swimming Charter to ease any friction between clubs, teachers, swimmers and bath authorities for the benefit of all. In 1952 this Committee extended its horizons: (a) to investigate and form a plan for the furtherance of swimming and to ensure young swimmers receive opportunities for training; (b) to urge bath committees to keep open all year; and (c) to effect greater co-operation between the three bodies and to examine ways of eliminating friction. Suggestions were put forward to: (a) limit the number of *serious* clubs per bath; (b) encourage clubs to be representative of a locality; and (c) form efficient links between local schools, social youth clubs and local swimming clubs.

It seems obvious that this liaison committee was a recognition of the necessity to discover common ground where associations could work to further the common aims while smoothing some of the rough edges which existed between them. The ASA was perhaps always very conscious of its leading position in the swimming world as an archetypal governing umbrella but was, at the same time, anxious to co-operate with other institutions which could themselves benefit from the strands of liaison. The overall view of amateurism and the responsibility for the organisation of the country's competitive and recreative aspects of the sport lay firmly with the ASA but the special aspects of the STA and other bodies were to serve to improve the total quality and provision for all swimmers.

English Schools' Swimming Association

ESSA was founded in 1949 with the support of the ASA and with Harold Fern attending the inaugural meeting as an observer. The Constitution was approved at the AGM of 1950, the country being divided into 13 divisions for the purpose of administration. The ASA accepted the ESSA affiliation in 1950. The first ESSA National Championships were held at York Hall, Bethnal Green, in October 1950 and were preceded by Divisional Championships or Time Tests to result in 400 school-children competing in the finals. In 1951 the Championships moved to Blackpool and grew in size.

When the ASA introduced proficiency awards in 1952, ESSA were quick to co-operate and joint ASA/ESSA awards were given to those schools which were affiliated to ESSA. There was no doubt that this schools link via ESSA was very good for both ASA and for the development of swimming in schools. By 1955 150 Schools Districts were affiliated to ESSA whose main functions were listed as: (a) assisting schools willing to build their own teaching bath; (b) working with the ASA to further the proficiency award scheme; (c) running the Schools Team Championships on behalf of the ASA; and (d) running their own Schools National Championships.

The Annual Schoolboys Team Swimming Championship, organised by the ASA, ceased in 1954 and was replaced by the ASA Schoolboy and ASA Schoolgirl Freestyle Team Swimming Championships. ESSA became the joint organisers and took on most of the work. By 1958 the ASA considered that, as ESSA was now so firmly established and in the business of promoting all types of school championships, it was no longer necessary to spend large sums of money on promoting the Schoolboy and Schoolgirl events and consequently withdrew its financial support.

Infantile Paralysis or Poliomyelitis

The 1950's was a time when large numbers of people were affected by infantile paralysis. The disease resulted in many degrees of disablement mainly concerning the use of limbs. Sadly, there was no vaccination available until the end of the 1950s. In the swimming world the problem was highlighted by the sudden death from polio of Nancy Riach, the famous Scottish and British swimmer in 1947 at the European Championships in Monte Carlo. There was much alarm engendered at the time by the suggestion that the infection could be water-borne and initially there was no evidence to the contrary. The 1950 ASA *Report* commented that many baths had closed unjustifiably on the alleged risk of infection. World opinion stated that there would be no risk where water was properly chlorinated. The Director of Water Examination at the Metropolitan Water Board announced,

'There is no evidence of virus ever being distributed in a public water supply in the quantity needed to cause infection or that is capable of surviving in such a quantity in the purification process'.

The ASA advice at the time was that *'large numbers of people should be prohibited from meeting at galas'*.

The Ministry of Health *Report* of 1951 stated,

'At times of unusual incidence of Infantile Paralysis it may be said, generally speaking, that the balance of evidence is in favour of keeping open "properly controlled" baths and swimming pools'.

International experts at home confirmed this attitude.

In 1952 the new ASA Swimming Committee were invited to consider and report on methods of help from remedial classes for patients recovering from polio. The Committee studied the work already done at Halliwick Penguin SC on the teaching of children from Halliwick Cripples School at Southgate, Middlesex.

By 1956 a number of ASA affiliated clubs were doing much work for polio victims as testified by the assisting medical authorities. The need was to *'increase confidence physically and mentally and to help in regaining the use of injured limbs'*. The ASA would furnish guidance to any club wishing to participate in such a scheme.

Prologue to the 1950s

Britain entered the 1950s with the post-war age of austerity still very much in evidence. Petrol rationing did not finish until the end of 1950; housing and school buildings were major problems and labour was scarce; food, consumables and raw materials were in short supply. However, the 1938 Holidays with Pay Act, together with the growth of a post-war leisure boom helped to stimulate masses of folk to take seaside holidays in what seemed to be the long hot summers. Billy Butlin had bought back his holiday camps from army and navy occupation and the camp swimming pool and beaches everywhere became the focus for exercise, relaxation and entertainment. There was ample evidence of the need to swim for exercise and safety purposes. All the country needed were the swimming pools and, where they had existed many were damaged or destroyed by war. There was no chance of pool-building taking priority over housing but the function of the ASA was to keep the problem to the forefront so that, when conditions eased, the Government would be well aware of what they were required to do.

Sports and games administrators' main post-war task was to get everything up and running again. There was little time for real innovation although the ideas may have been there. It was suggested in retrospect that the innovative technology of sport was just not there and that the old-established pre-war patterns were everywhere in evidence. This *implied inertia*, however, was probably a reflection of the austerity and hardship of the period. The ASA and the swimming world were certainly full of new ideas and had already managed the introduction of the Loughborough Course with its built-in emphasis on technical progress in a variety of forms. It was not to be until the latter part of the 1950s that the Government's relaxation on expenditure and building would enable pool-building to start in earnest.

The 1950s

Hector Hughes, KC, MP, started a decade of lobbying by asking questions in Parliament of the then Education Minister George Tomlinson - '*What statistics are kept to show what facilities exist for teaching pupils swimming in state schools?*' '*How many can and cannot swim?*' '*How does this compare with 20 years ago?*' The reply was that no statistics were available but that the Minister was satisfied that LEAs took full advantage of facilities for swimming instruction at public baths and elsewhere. A negative reply was also received when Mr. Hughes asked about how many personnel were lost by drowning in the war. Again, in 1952, Mr Hughes asked the new Minister, Miss Horsbrugh about the use of '*unqualified teachers of swimming*' and about '*the government reduction of education estimates resulting in cutting the amount of swimming instruction in schools*'. The ASA usually had an interested party such as Mr Hughes to lobby internally and, to add weight to this, Harold Fern was always setting up meetings to persuade government about the Association's cause.

In view of the pool shortages the ASA put much pressure on those local authorities which were closing their baths between October and April each year. Many of these authorities wanted to use the bath as a winter dance hall using a false floor, but the ASA asked its five Districts to work on local councillors to stop the practice and to remind election candidates of their duty to use the baths '*as part of a public health service*'. No doubt the councils realised a saving in winter fuel consumption by not having to heat the water for half the year.

The Association did, however, continue to press the point about the need for baths because without these the entire progress of swimming in Britain would be delayed. Throughout the period of austerity the ASA continued to prepare for better times by encouraging local authorities to make plans for the future and to feed them with the best technical advice in order to make those plans. The *Swimming Times* had problems as well. Forty per cent was added to the cost of production in 1952 by increased paper and printing charges but the cost of the publication at nine pence an issue did not increase to one shilling until 1958. Efforts had been made to absorb increased costs by wider circulation. The government's Building Licences system ended in

1954 but loan restrictions continued and the Ministry in 1955 pressed even harder to limit borrowing facilities for public projects. Harold Fern was at this time receiving three bath plans a week for approval on behalf of local authorities. The first public covered bath to be built since the War was at Hornchurch in Essex in 1956. By 1958 Cardiff, High Wycombe and Newport Pagnell were added to the list and local authorities were being encouraged to apply for loan sanctions. An ASA questionnaire of 1958 revealed that, excluding the Southern District, there were 193 *fair-size* towns in England which had no covered swimming-bath. As the 1950s came to an end the picture was rosier. 150 new baths were either at the contemplation or planning stage. Nine of these had been authorised in 1959 for a total cost of about £2 millions. Work on seven open-air pools had been started. Schools were also being encouraged to build.

Another ASA battle, this time with the Customs and Excise Commissioners, also succeeded in 1951 when the tax authority decided to allow exemption from Entertainments Tax on events organised by the ASA and its Districts. It was considered that the institution was '*conducted for philanthropic or charitable purposes*'. Affiliated clubs could also apply for exemption. Harold Fern's tenacity had triumphed and the financial side of galas and championship organisation benefited.

The British Team for the 1950 British Empire and Commonwealth Games in Auckland, New Zealand, left Southampton in December 1949 aboard the *Tamaroa*. The monotony of the 12,600 mile journey was relieved by Bert Kinnear conducting physical exercises and deck walking in rather cramped conditions. A small tank was rigged up on deck but could only be used to practice legwork and turns. The result of the Games was rather disappointing but the experience was beneficial.

The Festival of Britain of 1951 was intended as an official celebration of recovery from the War and of hopes for future reconstruction. In a period of great austerity this was to be a gleam of light at the end of a dark tunnel. The huge Thames-side Festival site was the centrepiece but the Government encouraged nationwide attractions. The ASA decided not to hold any large central functions but to leave it to the Districts to organise their own events as a shopwindow for the expected rush of overseas visitors as well as for the British people, many of whom were eager to be shown any sign of new swimming facilities on the horizon. The widespread organisation of galas and many other events was also a good opportunity to forge good links with local authorities.

It was in 1951 that the ASA's Olympic Games Committee was planning for the 1952 Helsinki Olympics. Trials for swimming, diving and water-polo were held at Blackpool in June 1952 and the selected team would finally train together for three days prior to leaving for the Games. A special treat in July for the team was a visit to Buckingham Palace at the invitation of Her Majesty Queen Elizabeth. Harold Fern could not attend the party or the Games as he fell down a cliff at Swanage and dislocated a shoulder.

The funding of an Olympic swimming team was as ever a problem. £6,000 was needed and only £2,000 had been raised by 1951. In the end the target seemed to be reached but the onus was on the Districts to organise the fundraising via affiliated clubs' efforts. Collecting-cards, seafront events, business donations, raffles, dances and factory collections: all contributed. The performance of our team at Helsinki pleased the ASA Committee because of the indications of *emerging advances* in swimming standards particularly by the juniors. In the swimming events, there were seven finalists and in diving events five finalists. Harry Koskie, the Team Manager, was overjoyed in spite of no gold medals and considered that Britain was back into World class.

The ASA immediately sanctioned a four-year training plan in preparation for Melbourne in 1956 and allocated £5,000 from the Olympic Training Fund to allow the three technical committees to function. The Loughborough Advanced Course, the Dawdon Diving Course and the Districts would combine efforts. Financial consideration was also an early concern and in 1954 all members were urged to contribute sixpence each to the Olympic Training Fund.

In 1954 an English team at the Empire and Commonwealth Games at Vancouver and a British team at the European Swimming Championships at Turin did not particularly shine. The ASA did not have to pay towards the Vancouver event but it cost £1,283 for Turin, an amount which impinged heavily on the Olympic Training Fund.

The 1956 Melbourne Olympics served to show how the Australians had wrested supremacy from the Americans and also how World standards had greatly improved since the previous Games. A.C. Price, the Team Manager, was, however, full of praise for the British team efforts and, of course, Judy Grinham gained the first Gold Medal for 32 years by success in the 100 metres Women's Back Stroke event.

At home some change was taking place in the organisation of the Centralised Championships. In 1950 and 1951 this event was held at Lancaster and in 1952 at Hove. This was to be the last time that the event was organised by a District although the ASA had always been full of praise for the way it had been run. Likewise, the Diving Championships tended to move round to different locations each year. From 1953 the ASA took over the running of the Championships which were to be held at Derby Baths, Blackpool, for the next 11 years. Also the Swimming and Diving events were to be held at the same location at the same time over a six-day period. The ASA later found it necessary to explain that there were good reasons for using Blackpool: (a) because it was the only 55 yards bath in the country; (b) because it provided more accommodation than any other indoor bath both for spectators and competitors; and (c) because Blackpool had adequate housing accommodation for competitors and spec-

tators. No-one could deny these factors or compete against them. A committee was appointed in 1954 to review the annual Championships. The main recommendations were: (a) that minimum qualifying standards were needed (e.g. Silver Medal); (b) that a results board was necessary; (c) improved publicity was essential; (d) more facilities should be provided; and (e) there should be water-polo matches each Saturday.

An important new ASA committee was introduced in 1952: The Swimming Committee . This group of three members would (a) advise the ASA Committee on all matters related to swimming and submit recommendations on methods of improving the standard of swimming; (b) conduct training courses; (c) be responsible for the compilation of a list of international swimming officials; and (d) advise the ASA Committee on the selection of swimmers to represent England in international events. It seemed long overdue that a Swimming Committee should appear when Diving and Water Polo Committees were already in existence and it was very necessary for this group of experts to be able to concentrate on swimming matters and not be sidetracked by the many other aspects of ASA business. Their brief was to be expanded as the years passed.

Another 1950 innovation was to endorse and clarify the functions of the Inter-Country General Purposes Committee. An informal conference of representatives of the ASA, the Scottish ASA and the Welsh ASA was held at Lancaster to explore questions of fixture dates, records, lists of referees, rules, etc. The members also considered relations with FINA and selection problems. A new Constitution was presented as a discussion document. The following year, after another conference in Scotland, the draft was agreed to, and agreement was also reached that *'competitors' expenses should be paid for by the country which selected them'*. The new committee, with a new Constitution, generally met twice a year and played a valuable part in matters connected with British representation. If, for example, Great Britain had a competition fixture with Holland then this committee would organise the entire event.

The Scottish ASA must have been pleased in 1950 to win the Inter-Country Speed Swimming Contest. This annual event between England, Scotland and Wales had existed since 1929 and this was the first time that England had not won. To rub it in, Scotland won again in 1951.

1953 was another opportunity for the ASA to encourage clubs to co-operate with local authorities to run special galas in celebration of the Coronation. The occasion was of extra significance as Her Majesty The Queen saw fit to grant her Patronage to the Association. Later, in 1957 Her Majesty permitted the gift by the ASA of a silver spoon to each of the royal children to mark the excellent progress each had made at swimming. 1952-3 was also specially marked by the investure of the ASA's first lady President, Mrs. A.M. Austin of Beckenham, and by Mrs. K. Whiteside being appointed as the first British woman waterpolo referee. Mrs. Austin was praised for her elegance, calm and dignity. She had been the first President of a County Association and of a District Association, as well as being the only lady to serve on the ASA Committee, the Board of Examiners and the Publications Committee.

The comment had been made in 1952 that *'no longer was swimming the Cinderella of sports in Britain'.* In 1954 Harold Fern was able to confirm the growing public interest in swimming, engendered by the televising of some of the ASA's principal events. A new vista had been opened.

As the decade progressed it became apparent that the ASA's own fortunes were benefiting from the various enterprises which it had initiated and by the good management of the Association's finances. The assets grew steadily from around £6,600 in 1950 to £8,972 in 1955. An astounding leap occurred between the balance sheets of 1955 and 1957 when the assets doubled to £16,745. The accumulation of profits gained from the sale of publications and films, new award schemes, championship meetings, television contracts and increased club affiliations were putting the ASA on a sounder financial footing. The Olympic Training Fund which had become the International Training Fund in 1956 underwent change in 1958 when it was decided to raise income by a new levy on affiliated clubs. This was to replace the collecting box type schemes which had operated until then.

From 1955 Harold Fern's annual reports changed tone to reflect the beginning of the end of austerity and to commend the ASA for the success stories and the more positive results which were emerging. Swimmers' times were much improved and by 1957 a *vintage year* was recorded for the ASA. Many swimming records were broken, record entries for the Championships, growth in ASA Teacher's Certificate success rate, growth in proficiency awards and great demand for publications. These results were followed in 1958 and 1959 by the same glowing reports.

The breaking of seven world records, 66 English and 72 British records in 1958 spoke for itself, as did the winning of all International competitions. The outstanding performance of 1959 was that of Anita Lonsbrough who created a women's world breast-stroke record of 2mins. 50.3secs in Holland.

As the decade came to an end the post-war transformation of the ASA was well consolidated. The new award schemes, new committees, successful lobbying for new pools, development of training courses for coaches, teachers and swimmers and sound financial footing - all contrived to promise that the 1960s would commence from the springboard of success.

Mrs. A.M. Austin - first Lady President of the ASA in 1952.

ASA Award Schemes and Campaigns of the 1950s and 1960s

'Proficiency in Swimming' Awards

Gregory Matveieff, who later became Honorary Treasurer, thought up this scheme after seeing a similar model in Sweden and the ASA Committee launched it in 1951.

Mr. L. Pickering took on the task of organising this new ASA venture in 1952. By the passing of prescribed tests a swimmer could then wear a badge at gold, silver or bronze levels. This national emblem of swimming ability would be a hallmark of achievement for the individual and for the club. The badge was the ASA coat-of-arms in colour with appropriate wording. An enamelled badge was issued, while the costume badge cost 5 shillings extra. All the administration required was an authorised examiner, a proper application form and a registration fee of 5, 10 or 15 shillings. All tests were to be in still water not less than 25 yards long. In some ways this was some recognition for those competitors who did not manage to get in the first three places in a race. This scheme was for the reasonably competent swimmer and not intended for schoolchildren and learners.

In the same year, a second ASA scheme especially for school-children was announced. The successful ones in the tests would also wear a crest in colour.

This *School Swimmer* Award was to be a great incentive for schools to raise their swimming standards, for pupils to wear their badges with pride, and for the ASA's objective of *'Every scholar a*

Gregory Matvieff - President of the ASA in 1964.

swimmer'. Indeed, some schools vied for the highest percentage of pupil swimmers, often over 95 per cent. There is no doubt that the new badge was also excellent publicity for the ASA and parents were keen to see their children succeed.

There were two school categories. The basic award was the *Medal* standard, while the pupils who progressed much higher could attain *Advanced* status. The Medal requirements were:

a. To swim 100 yards crawl or breaststroke.

b. To swim 50 yards back stroke.

c. To swim 25 yards breaststroke or crawl (as alternative to a).

d. A surface dive to pick an object up from 6 feet of water.

e. To dive an English Header from 4 feet.

Initial problems between the ASA and ESSA were sorted out by discussion, the result of which was that schools not affiliated to ESSA would receive the ASA awards, while schools affiliated to ESSA would receive joint ASA/ESSA awards. For the joint award the examiner must be on the ESSA official panel.

The number of awards soared in the early years as did the revenue to the ASA. This extra source of income happily arrived in the 1950s period which still reflected the austere financial conditions of post-war Britain.

In 1959 Lily Cook took over the distribution of awards from Mr. Tackley. She had previously been the Southern Counties breaststroke champion, National Breaststroke champion and the first holder of the 100 yards Women's Butterfly Championship. Lily's work with this scheme was to become

legendary. From her own home in Woodford Green, Essex, she ran labelling, packaging and posting of all awards for a small salary. Her loft became a great storehouse, and a number of part-time women were employed with her to prepare the many sacks of mail for transfer to the local post office. Throughout the 1960s the volume of this work was to multiply out of all proportion to what started as a *'cottage industry'* on behalf of the ASA. The revenue increased correspondingly. Co-operation with ESSA in the administration of schools awards continued.

Table 3.3: 1950s Proficiency Awards and ASA revenue				
1953	ASA Proficiency	563		
	ASA Schools	1,810	(7 months only)	
	ASA/ESSA Joint	549	Total: <u>2,924</u> awards	
1954	ASA Proficiency	502		
	ASA Schools	215	(Adv.) 2,122 (Medal)	
	ASA/ESSA Joint	149	(Adv.) 1,106 (Medal)	
			Total: <u>4,094</u> awards	
1955	(Mr. E.J. Tackley took over from Mr. Pickering)			
1956	ASA Proficiency	134 Gold 207 Silver 309 Bronze		
	ASA Schools	212 (Adv.) 2,216 (Medal)		
	ASA/ESSA Joint	150 (Adv.) 1,522 (Medal)		
		Total:	<u>4,750</u> awards	
		Revenue:	£1,560.18.0d.	
1959	Total: <u>6,122</u> awards	Revenue:	<u>£2,087</u>	

In 1968 swimming awards for handicapped persons were introduced and in just a few months 826 awards were made, together with a new ASA badge of a *'Mountain in the Sea'*.

1. Preliminary Award:-

To swim 10 yards unaided and 20 yards with a buoyancy aid. It was also necessary to achieve 3 out of 5 basic tests.

2. Intermediate Award:-

The distance was to be 25 yards.

To tread water for 30 second.

To achieve 3 out of 5 dive tests.

3. Advanced Award:-

The distance was to be 50 yards by one stroke and 25 yards by another.

Awards were also made for Water Polo and Synchronised Swimming.

Awards for Proficiency in Personal Survival

In 1961 notice was given that the ASA Council was to launch this new scheme which had been devised by the Education Committee. The idea was to devise an award which would be attractive to all swimmers and not just those interested in the competitive side of the sport. At the same time the results should further the aim of the ASA of *swimming to save life in emergency*. It was to be a challenging experience for both teachers and pupils.

Table 3.4:

'Schemes for the Encouragement of Swimming 1970'

	Gold	Silver	Bronze
Proficiency awards	548	969	1,614
Personal Survival awards	31,262	5,7951	114,799

	Stage 1	Stage 2	
ASA/ESSA Joint National award	3,3837	17,326	

	Advanced	Merit	
ASA/ESSA Joint Speed awards	2,822	9,804	

	Advanced	Intermediate	Preliminary
Physically Handicapped	181	251	385

	25 yards	50 yards	100 yards
Incentive Certificates	12,975	9,850	7,700

Norman Sarsfield devised the Survival Awards Scheme and arranged the testing of 5,000 volunteer swimmers at three levels prior to its full acceptance by the ASA. Tony Holmyard (NTO), who had been interested in floatation methods as a recreational activity, was another eager participant in the initiation of this new award. Dickie Underwood was also active in formulating the new assessment procedures.

At the same time Bert Kinnear, together with Dickie Underwood, had been evolving survival swimming techniques at Loughborough College of Education. They worked with their student-teacher-swimmers to develop new survival swimming skills and activities which would, in future, help the schools to process the new ASA awards.

Bert Kinnear, as Chief NTO, was later to be instrumental in disseminating knowledge of the new awards throughout the country and in making sure that Districts and coaches were fully conversant with the requirements of the scheme.

The scheme was launched at Seymour Place Baths in London in April 1962 with many District representatives and other dignitaries entertained by a special demonstration.

The syllabus for each award level involved various degrees of jumping into the water, treading water, undressing in water, climbing out of deep water without assistance and a distance swim. The gold award involved wearing more clothing than for the bronze and silver and a considerable extra amount of swimming prowess. The complexity of the diving required also increased with the award level.

The results were promising. Between April and July 1962 - 381 Gold, 811 Silver and 2,079 Bronze awards were made. A *'Personal Survival'* film was ordered into production at a cost of £450. New costume badges were designed and Lily Cook and her

Lily Cook - 'The lady in charge of award dispatches'.

team were going to be even busier dispatching these from Woodford Green, Essex. In 1963, 46,000 survival awards were made with a profit to the ASA of £3,030.

It seemed that there was room for both the ASA and RLSS to promote such lifesaving schemes. Mr. R. Underwood in 1962 suggested that the ASA's very small share of the 100,000 annual awards made by the two Associations would soon increase, and it did. Even by 1964 - 77,719 ASA awards were made, with an income of £30,647. Bovril Limited had joined in the Education Committee's work by producing a free illustrated leaflet depicting swimming strokes together with material on survival swimming. When Norman Sarsfield became ASA President in 1966 the total awards to date were 232,023 with a profit of £90,822. The significance of this financial income to the ASA was very great and dwarfed the income from the National Championships and Television agreements. The future financial base of the ASA was to be served for years to come from the huge incomes of all the awards schemes.

By 1969, the ASA Centenary Year, a total of 875,000 Survival Awards had been made (125,000 Gold, 250,000 Silver and 50,000 Bronze). As it entered the 1970s the ASA could look back over eight years of what had been one of its great success stories - educationally, socially and financially.

Norman Sarsfield confirmed the ASA's success of stimulating public interest, securing a sound financial base, and improving performances.

A still from the new film 'Survival Swimming'. Bert Kinnear and Richard Underwood are supervising.

ASA 'Learn to Swim' Campaign

In 1960 the ASA helped to launch a *'Learn to Swim'* campaign with the National Association of Bath Superintendents and the STA, the organisation being done by the CCPR. The idea was mainly to help adults learn to swim by group coaching methods. Over 100 classes were started but in some places it was difficult to secure sufficient bath-time. By 1961, 179 courses existed with 3,789 enrolments. The RoSPA joined the scheme in 1962 and enrolments nearly doubled to 6,788. By the mid-sixties it was claimed that up to 25,000 adults had learned to swim in these classes.

Prior to the ASA Centenary celebrations of 1969 a Public Relations Committee was set up mainly to deal with 1969 events but it also revised ideas on the *'Learn to Swim'* campaign. It was decided to concentrate the efforts into a National Swimming Week and to use the Liverpool City Council's successful prototype week as a model. The Districts canvassed the cities within their orbit so that local authorities would co-operate with the project. The August National Week of 1968 was a great success and received good publicity. The Centenary year was obviously an exceptional chance to show off and the Districts made good use of the occasion. The success of the 1969/9 results led to an even bigger effort for 1970. The ASA recognised that it strengthened

links with Bath Managers and others as an outcome of the venture. Liverpool again was the shining example for the event where eight baths were used to give 28,000 lessons and 2,000 people learned to swim. Other successes in the Districts included special newsletters, displays and forums.

The ASA/Coca-Cola Training Scheme - 1967

This revolutionary scheme was originated by the offer of the Coca-Cola Corporation to sponsor to the tune of £15,000 over five years. It was to be hailed as unique to the sporting world. The ASA matched the sponsorship with an equal amount of cash which reflected its own income, mainly from awards schemes. Coca-Cola was to include provision of Olympic kit in addition to new banners and symbols. The firm and the ASA saw the project partly as an extension of the *Dolphin Trophy* scheme which encouraged youngsters in schools to learn to swim. One of the main aspects of this innovation was that it was meant to be a *Winter Training Scheme*. A.D. Kinnear as NTO was to prepare the scheme and budget for approval and to make plans for its implementation. The idea was to discover and train the Olympic stars of the future. Even the ASA were astounded at the initial response. The plan had been to select 1,200 of the best swimmers from their 1,700 clubs and to set up 40 national training centres

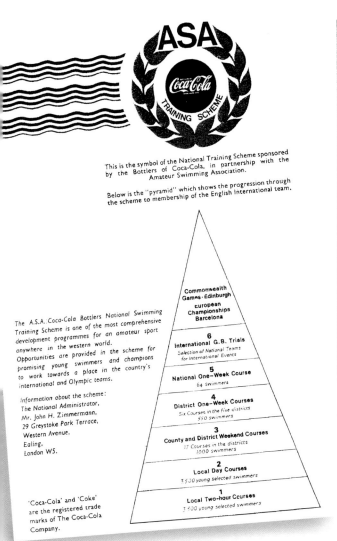

This is the symbol of the National Training Scheme sponsored by the Bottlers of Coca-Cola, in partnership with the Amateur Swimming Association.

Below is the "pyramid" which shows the progression through the scheme to membership of the English International team.

The A.S.A.-Coca-Cola Bottlers National Swimming Training Scheme is one of the most comprehensive development programmes for an amateur sport anywhere in the western world. Opportunities are provided in the scheme for promising young swimmers and champions to work towards a place in the country's international and Olympic teams.

Information about the scheme: The National Administrator, Mr. John H. Zimmermann, 29 Greystoke Park Terrace, Western Avenue, Ealing, London W5.

'Coca-Cola' and 'Coke' are the registered trade marks of The Coca-Cola Company.

The ASA/Coca-Cola pyramid of progression in 1970.

John Zimmermann who organised the Coca-Cola Scheme was ASA President in 1979.

John Zimmermann was put in charge of the project. Each year a money allocation was made to Districts based on the number of clubs involved.

The ASA/ESSA Speed Awards of 1969

In spite of metrication which was to be introduced in 1972 the distances for this new award were specified in yards. Recent timings from schools and clubs were used to establish the initial standard requirements. The new scheme was devised to cater for a national demand for an award which would include elements of speed and versatility. It would also be a good 'building-up' process for youngsters.

There were two awards:-

1. Merit:

    a) swim 150 yards by any stroke(s) within 5 minutes.

    b) the 'mad-minute' during which the swimmer covers two lots of 25 yards by different strokes.

    If one stroke was the crawl it must be under 25 seconds.

    If one stroke was the backstroke it must be under 28 seconds.

    If one stroke was the butterfly it must be under 28.5 seconds.

    If one stroke was the breast it must be under 29.5 seconds.

for them but, in just three months one District alone had set up 26 centres for 1,566 youngsters. Soon there were 3,000 swimmers in five Districts using 80 centres.

All trainees were selected by their coaches for their swimming times and potential. The programme was to be a two-hour training session once a week with a special one-day session twice each winter. With proper selection systems it would be possible for a swimmer to progress from local to District to national courses and thence to the Olympic Training Squad. Some Districts were also running one-week courses for up to 250 swimmers. The ASA organised a one-week residential course for 75 participants at Crystal Palace in the summer of 1968. John Verrier was Course Director and John Zimmermann was Course Organiser. The Districts also organised 16 weekend courses at Crystal Palace for the winter of 1968. The top swimmers would go to the International trials at Crystal Palace. The success of this scheme depended on the hard work of the District NTOs and coaches and on a large number of voluntary amateur helpers, together with ASA administration and joint ASA Coca-Cola finance.

2. Advanced:

   a) swim 400 yards in 10 minutes by any stroke(s) (conforming to ASA laws).

   b) three speed swims of 50 yards each using 3 of 4 accepted strokes.

Table 3.5: Strokes for Boys and Girls

Strokes	Boys	Girls
Breaststroke	53 seconds	54 seconds
Butterfly	51 seconds	54 seconds
Backstroke	52 seconds	53 seconds
Crawl	44 seconds	47 seconds

The Speed Awards proved successful as the 1970 awards table suggests. From a logistics viewpoint it meant more work for Lily Cook, Awards Organiser, and increased ASA income. Another job had been created for that army of ASA-approved volunteer examiners in the Counties and Districts.

Table 3.6: ASA Teacher's Certificate for Swimming, 1950-1970

Passes for 1950-1960		Passes for 1961-1970	
1950	556	1961	541
1951	497	1962	470
1952	358	1963	755
1953	319	1964	651
1954	363	1965	719
1955	409	1966	944
1956	532	1967	1070
1957	501	1968	1329
1958	516	1969	1698
1959	662	1970	1515
1960	572		

Comments:

'1. The 1952 reduction period was due mainly to *theory* examination failures.

2. The 1953/4 reduction was considered to be due to the closing of the post-war Emergency Teacher Training Colleges with less persons thus taking the exam.

3. The revival at the end of the 1960s was due to more Training College students asking to take the exam.

4. In 1954 the total certificates since the examination was inaugurated in 1899 passed the 10,000 mark. The original exam. had been for professional instructors only in order to save the amateur swimming status of professional teachers and show schools and bathing authorities the need to have properly qualified paid teachers. As swim-

ming developed in schools, those teachers working voluntarily needed to be working on lines laid down by the ASA so the certificate was later opened to amateurs and professionals. As the 1950s progressed the certificate became more recognised by local authorities, bath superintendents and professional instructors.

5. In 1954 the Board of Examiners changed the *Elementary Certificate* to the *ASA Teachers Certificate for Swimming*. There was still an Advanced Certificate.

6. Also in 1954 the same examiners recommended that lecturers of teachers of swimming should be able to be paid.

7. In 1957 the syllabus for the certificate was revised and strengthened under the supervision of Mr R.G. Underwood.

8. In 1961 the exam. was deliberately stiffened and numbers fell temporarily.

9. As the 1960s progressed the qualifications were more and more recognised by education authorities as proof of competence when making appointments.

10. The ASA made a point of thanking the large number of volunteers in the Districts who supervised and marked examinations.

Table 3.7: ASA Teacher's Certificate for Diving 1950-70

Passes for 1950-1960		Passes for 1961-1970	
1950	43	1961	24
1951	18	1962	25
1952	20	1963	26
1953	12	1964	37
1954	15	1965	29
1955	18	1966	57
1956	14	1967	24
1957	29	1968	25
1958	27	1969	
1959	20	1970	
1960	22		

ASA Scientific Advisory Committee

Throughout the 1950s the more scientific approach to the teaching and coaching of swimming was developing. Dr. N. Bleasdale at the Loughborough Courses had demonstrated the need for accurate and reliable measurement of an increasing number of physiological aspects. In addition there were a variety of mechanical and electrical innovations whose validity not only needed testing but which perhaps required some refining and then marketing. The ASA needed to be able to say that it supported something such as an automatic timer, provided that it knew that it was right to do so. To crown it all, a National Technical Officer had just been appointed in 1959 and he was to be very involved with science.

This new Committee of six members was set up in 1959 with the aim of scientifically investigating all aspects of aquatic sport and of swimming training. Dr. E. Kendall was appointed Secretary. The brief was to provide answers to specific scientific problems posed by the ASA Committee and, where necessary, to approach University departments, specialist scientists and other bodies for help. John Atha of Loughborough had already worked with Loughborough Courses on a variety of statistical measurements. At Middlesex Hospital Miss J. Jones was carrying out physiological tests on eight selected Southern swimmers. The Committee purchased a variety of measuring equipment. Initial topics for study included physiological implications of training by various methods, somatopying of swimmers, and the mechanics of diving movements. In 1960 this Committee was authorised to undertake the Tank Test programme which was to be carried out at Saunders-Roe Limited for a cost of £248. The tests were to measure frontal resistance due to a variety of body positions and the effect of crawl leg strokes, hand configuration, breaststroke and backstroke. The Hydrodynamic and Wind Tunnel and Aqua Tensometer of Liverpool University were put at the committee's disposal for these experiments.

In 1963 a *Tests and Measurements* course was set up at Loughborough and proved successful. More were needed. John Atha was now in a position to formulate simple tests for use by ASA coaches to measure strength, flexibility and endurance. Other projects to be launched included controlled experiments with vitamin supplements; work on the personality of competitive swimmers; and experiments with a variable-incident starting block. Bert Kinnear was interested in initiating some research into the use of pharmaceutical substances but found it difficult to locate properly qualified persons for the task. He had also designed a periscope for underwater observations and a prototype was to be made. One important result of the Committee's work was the setting up of testing centres in each of the ASA Districts, the equipment to be on loan from the ASA.

The 1968 programme was partly initiated by Harold Fern who requested research into the use of training tanks and the best swimming lanes. Other work was to be based on the effect of water temperature on performance, the value of sports massage and the study of body temperature.

In 1969 the ASA approved of the Committee's recommendation that every affiliated club should have its own doctor, working in an honorary capacity, to advise on medical matters. This must have been a difficult goal to achieve. There was also concern about turbulence in swimming pools in connection with kinetic energy and motion being dissipated by the lane bobbin. It was in this year that the ASA approved the use of automatic timing equipment at the National Championships at Blackpool. The Sub-Committee would then look at further installations proposed at Crystal Palace and elsewhere.

The programme for potential research was enlarged in 1970 when five new topics appeared: the effect of swimming on visual acuity; the effect of swimming on hearing acuity; verrucae; the effect of menstruation on swimming and vice versa; and the best medium in which to swim. The Scientific Advisory Committee forged on with its eleventh year of problem-solving.

Prologue to the 1960s

Looking in retrospect at the ASA as it had evolved up to the 1950s there could be expressions of wonder and amazement at how this large organisation was operated. As it entered the decade which would include its centenary year the Association still had no permanent home. There was no firmly-rooted ASA Office because the administration was run from the private office of Harold Fern in Cannon Street, London, and from his home address in Barnet. His own personal assistant, Gladys Writer, together with a small office staff were the only chief contact points with the outside world. The Council and Committees arranged their meetings in hotels throughout the land, the venues being based on an agreed circulation round the Districts. Very few of the operative administrators or executives received any payment. Expenses were the order of the day and these were strictly scrutinised. The Diary Organiser and TV Liaison Officer received some payment for their efforts. Lily Cook, together with a small army of helpers, organised the daily dispatches of sacks of letters connected with the Awards Schemes. Districts were run without the benefit of central offices. Each District had its own list of official contact addresses published in the *Handbook*. The ASA promotion system from Club to County to District to Committee to Council seemed to work even with the inevitable pressures which resulted for some people. Whatever financial aid could be gleaned from government sources in addition to the internal profits on ventures, events and sponsorship, all helped to pay for the services of the full-time NTOs and the running of special schemes for swimmers to learn and to be competitive. Each year the miracle of the *Handbook* production occurred with remarkable precision. The *Swimming Times*, albeit reflecting a variety of views from varied swimming interests, was in the main, the organ through which to present the ASA's public image. Its editor was a stalwart of the Association.

The amateur aspect was thus run in what seemed to be a remarkably professional way and yet on a comparative shoestring. With all the growth of functions of advice-giving, lobbying, decision-making, administration and technical oversight, surely this great machine would sooner, rather than later have to recognise the need for some changes in order to lubricate the operation of its activities!

Most of what has been described here is only a magnified form of what it had always been like since the early part of the century. Harold Fern's own office was described as of a Victorian nature with its desks and bare boards and with an air of austerity which perhaps belied its ability to generate considerable business for its tenant. The receptionist's job each Monday morning was to make the ink for the week but who would give thought to the volume of business to be generated by its use? From this one room the genius, tenacity and vision of the Honorary Secretary brought him a very good living from the metals market business, organised the ever-expanding affairs of the ASA machine and supervised the work connected with his large numbers of voluntary local government chairmanships.

What would happen when the unique contribution of one man at the heart of the organisation was forced, by reason of age alone, to be replaced? Was there ever to be another Harold Fern and could any other private individual support so much administration and effort from what was virtually a private base?

To those who were near to the power base the questions of the succession, of potential administrative and executive adjustments and even the question of professional administration, were all looming larger. Of course, the arguments would come. There would be those totally opposed to a professional at the top. If the ASA had survived for 100 years as an amateur organisation, why should it change? The army of volunteers at all levels had to be numbered in thousands and were the life blood of the organisation.

There would be those who thought that, without a rigorous analysis of all the internal workings of the ASA, to be followed by equally rigorous action plans, then the organisation could potentially suffer from a form of inertia which it may not even recognise in itself.

This decade was to show that the ASA could rise to the occasion.

The 1960s

The Wolfenden Committee on Sport was set up by the Central Council for Physical Recreation in 1958 to enquire into factors affecting the development of sport in the UK. To help the ASA Committee to collect relevant swimming information, Harold Fern had prepared a memorandum which outlined the principal handicaps to the advancement of swimming in England. This was added to the Association's official reply to a large questionnaire from the Wolfenden Committee. After nearly three years' work the Wolfenden Report emerged in 1960.

The main recommendations to affect the ASA were:

'1. *The need for schools, youth clubs and sporting organisations to close the gaps between themselves for the sake of continuity of interest in the sport.*

2. *The need to establish multi-sports centres wherever appropriate.*

3. *Greater co-operation between specialist clubs, youth services, national sporting bodies, local authorities and local education authorities.*

4. *Sunday games are not improper but only amateur and not professional Sunday sport should be permitted.*

5. *A Sports Development Council with six to ten members should be set up with responsibility to either the Lord President of the Council or the Chancellor of the Exchequer. Each year £5,000,000 of government money would be distributed via the Council to give grants or assistance to national sporting organisations. This would be in addition to sums already granted.'*

The ASA strongly supported the formation of the Sports Development Council. Among other advantages it would introduce extra financial support. It was also aware of the potential discontinuity between the school and youth swimmers and had taken steps, partly through the award schemes and championship events, to improve the situation. The Association had its own

views about Sunday swimming and would not easily give way. The multi-sports centre was, of course, a concept that really took off but not always in sympathy with the ASA's ideas. The leisure pools which emerged as part of the package did not always suit the needs of the competitive swimmers' training programmes although the ASA canvassed hard to put its point of view.

The 1960 Olympics in Rome had resulted in a Gold Medal for Anita Lonsbrough's breast stroke in a world record time of 2mins. 49.5secs. Natalie Steward's 100 metres freestyle (Bronze) and 100 metres backstroke (Silver) added to the success. Elizabeth Ferris got a Bronze in the Women's Springboard Diving. Brian Phelps achieved a Bronze in the Men's Highboard Diving. A.D. Kinnear, as the new National Technical Officer, accompanied the team and coaches to good effect. Austin Rawlinson, the Team Manager, had the highest praise for all concerned. In 1961 he received the MBE for his many services to swimming.

Harold Fern, ageing slightly now, magnanimous and thoughtful as ever, instituted the Harold Fern Award in the same year as he was himself made Life President of FINA. His generous £1,000 donation ensured that the £50 award would be made annually and *'open to an individual (amateur or professional), to clubs or associations who are deemed to have done most to popularise the sport'*. Captain B.W. Cummins, Editor of the *Swimming Times* and past President of the ASA, was the first to receive the award in 1961. He was followed by N.W. Sarsfield in 1962, K.B. Martin 1963, Austin Rawlinson 1964, Cyril Parkin 1965, C.W. Plant 1966, A.C. Price 1967, W.T. Tiver 1968, M. Latimer 1968 and Lucy Heaton in 1970.

Swimming pool construction was proceeding apace but in 1961 the Government imposed a pause on capital expenditure by local authorities and some schemes were delayed. The ASA continued to receive great numbers of requests for information about bath construction and officials were able to confer with the Ministry of Housing and Local Government on these matters. The Ministry of Education was also consulting the Association about school pools.

There was concern that in some areas education authorities were curtailing winter swimming instruction for their schools. The ASA made representations to the Ministry of Education concerning the City of Birmingham's action in closing down winter swimming but nothing could be done inspite of some schools' PTAs offering to pay transport costs. The needs of the swimming world were again in conflict with local authorities' needs to cut costs at times of financial stringency.

A particularly difficult task came to an end in 1961. Three years earlier a special committee consisting of Sir Harold Parker, G.R. Paling and C.P. Parkin had started the work of revising and improving the Laws of the ASA. The suggested changes were studied by the ASA Committee and the representatives of the five District Associations. With this fine tuning the revised Laws were approved by Council and were included in the *Handbook*. Another change initiated by the Association in 1961 was to establish an ASA Charitable Trust. A deed was drawn up which listed the objectives of the ASA together with a detailed account of its functions. Trustees were appointed, and in 1962 the *ASA Swimming and Personal Survival Charitable Trust* was officially

The Harold Fern Trophy.

future (i.e. from 1964). It was acknowledged that the pool would be intended primarily for the use of the ASA and that spectator events would result to the benefit of the Centre finances. It was not clear at the time whether all of the Loughborough Courses were to go or whether it was mainly the intention to inaugurate new courses but the outcomes did crystallise later. The ASA, along with other bodies, was interested in the new semi-automatic and automatic timing devices which were getting beyond the earlier experimental stages. In 1954 Norman Sarsfield had, quite rightly, questioned the problems arising from disagreements between judges and timekeepers. '*Races*', he said, '*were always a matter of personalities and tactics; now they are becoming a cold-blooded mathematical affair*'. He also discussed variations in watches and human reactions leading to errors, but he, along with others, foresaw electrical recording in the future, but with judges still an integral part of the system. There had been many experiments in the 1930s and 1940s. In 1962 London University were experimenting with a four-stop-watch panel with a clock face, a starting pistol to provide an impulse start to the watches and four lane buttons operated by timekeepers. The University of Michigan in 1962 brought out its conclusions which it had worked on for eight years, to find the perfect automatic timing devise based on detailed scientific research. The ASA agreed that this system should be installed at Crystal Palace and that the appropriate Laws would be amended to accommodate this change.

established with a donation of £2,500. The 1963 Trustees' report indicated how they had invested the monies and what interest was received, indicating, of course, that application for recovery of the tax was imminent.

There were many good things to talk about in 1962. The Long Distance Championship was to be revised; Gladys Writer, Mr. Fern's secretary, was presented with a gold watch for faithful service; a second NTO, Tony Holmyard, was appointed with the Government grant to support the post; a *teaching-of-swimming in schools* enquiry was initiated by the ASA; over £3 million was sanctioned by the government to start the building of 18 large swimming pools; the Personal Survival awards scheme was started; three World records, one European, 47 British and 71 English had been broken; a new BBC TV contract was negotiated up to 1966; the TV Liaison Officer's salary was raised from £700 to £1,000; Harold Fern gave a trophy for the new Ladies' National Points Competition. The *Swimmer's Diary*, produced by Harry Brooks, had been a successful venture up to 1962. When he fell ill and the ASA took it over with Mr. Cottle later being appointed as business manager for the project. On top of this, the new Crystal Palace National Recreation Centre was being constructed in London at a cost of £2,000,000 and was attracting the attention of potential users. The Swimming Hall part of the complex would be of Olympic dimensions, with eight lanes and a separate diving pool, and the residential accommodation would facilitate the organisation of courses on a large scale. The country was missing the old Empire Pool at Wembley which was now used for skating, boxing, etc. The CCPR, which was to run the new Centre, held a meeting with the ASA to discuss the practicality of holding the ASA Courses at Crystal Palace in the

---

Amateur Swimming Association

President: A. C. PRICE, Esq.

Hon. Secretary: Alderman H. E. FERN, C.B.E., J.P.

1961
Swimming & Diving
CHAMPIONSHIPS
DERBY BATHS, BLACKPOOL

MONDAY, AUGUST 28th, to
SEPTEMBER 2nd (inclusive)
Two Sessions Daily at 2.15 and 7.30

PRICES OF ADMISSION

BLOCKS A to L (inclusive): —
    Rows A, B, C—
        Single session seats, 6s. 6d.; season tickets, £3 3s.
    Rows D, E, F, G—
        Single session seats, 5s.; season tickets, £2 10s.
    Rows H, J, K—
        Single session seats, 3s. 6d.; season tickets, £1 15s.
BLOCKS M, N, O: Not available for season tickets.
    All seats, single session, 3s. 6d.

All applications for tickets to:—

Hon. BOOKING OFFICER, A.S.A. Championships.
Box 6, Derby Baths, Blackpool.

Season Tickets are available now, but Single Session Tickets cannot be issued prior to July 1st

Two suggestions were made to the ASA Committee concerning extra staffing in 1962. The Education Committee was experiencing a great expansion of its activities and requested the services of a professional organiser and a clerical assistant. The reply was that *'the supply of knowledgeable and dedicated volunteers is not exhausted. If government financial help became available the matter could be reconsidered.'* Likewise, the proposal was made to appoint a Public Relations Officer *'to expand the planned efforts to establish and maintain mutual understanding between the ASA and its public'*. It would have relieved the Honorary Secretary of additional work. The Honorary Treasurer opposed the idea on the grounds of expense and the idea was shelved.

ASA progress was again confirmed by 1963's competition results. Achievements included two World records, 26 British and 34 English. England also won the Six Nations Competition sponsored by the European Eurovision Authority and was defeated in only one out of five of its International fixtures. In the same year a third NTO, Helen Elkington, was appointed and also Mr. H. Hamilton-Smith replaced the second NTO, Mr. T.A. Holmyard, who had resigned. The country was now divided up into three parts for NTO administrative purposes - North and North-East; Midlands and Somerset, Devon and Cornwall and Gloucester; South with Dorset, and Wiltshire. The 1964 Tokyo Olympics were looming ahead and the ASA had to find £3,800 towards swimmers' expenses. Meanwhile, Harold Fern was pleased to see the Government sanction £6 million in loans to build 25 new pools and he reiterated his belief that local clubs should lobby their MPs and local authorities, while the ASA Committee's influence would continue to be brought to bear on the Ministries. Synchronised Swimming was officially recognised by the ASA in 1963 when the *Synchronised Swimming Committee* was set up, partly as a result of a request by FINA. R.H. Brown, P. Jones, G. Rackham and D. Zajac formed the nucleus of this body.

In spite of all this progress, the ASA showed concern at the continued loss of young swimmers to the sport in general and made suggestions to clubs to combat this problem. The remedy seemed to lie with the individual club which, it was inferred, could perhaps hold the attention of its members by providing more social activities, becoming a mixed club, providing more challenging events, encouraging Water Polo and getting parents involved in activities. It is interesting to see the blend of competitive and social factors here. The ASA's wish to help the teenage swimmer did not seem to be reflected in a change of its Law brought about in 1964 when the qualifying age at which Juniors could enter the National Championships was reduced, thus potentially cutting out a number of swimmers who would now have to transfer into Senior events. There was much criticism. However, a more positive side was the introduction of the ASA's Leader's Certificate. This was to encourage the more experienced young club members to undertake coaching, teaching and bath-side work to assist the younger members to learn. It was a way of retaining the interest of the 15 to 21 year-old while at the same time improving a club's coaching facility.

The atmosphere at the 1964 ASA Annual General Meeting was one of calm satisfaction and harmony with *no financial worries and no headaches*. 1963 results had shown a surplus of £17,000 on Personal Survival awards, £5,000 on televised events and £3,000 on the National Championships. In addition, 477 baths

were planned in the country and the Ministry of Housing and Local Government had instructed all local authorities to review their provision for sport and recreation. Various sponsorships were also gratefully accepted. Gillette Limited were to finance a week's special training for the Olympic Team at Crystal Palace, speed swimming suits were to be provided by Dolphex Knitting Mills and also by Janzten Limited. Success bred success.

The 1964 Olympic results were not excellent although Britain had 10 competitors in the finals. The rising world standards, especially those of the USA, were too much, even for our own well-trained swimmers. Back home, the National Championships were held for the first time at Crystal Palace after 11 successive years at Blackpool. Although there were expressions of adulation for this new venue there seemed also an element of propaganda to promote Blackpool as a preference. The difficulties experienced in organising the event at Crystal Palace did not seem to be given a chance to be ironed out and for 1965 the Championships returned to Blackpool. However, the superb facilities offered at the new Recreation Centre were not to be ignored and were gladly reserved for 1965 ASA Courses.

A proposal had been made in 1963 that there should be an Amateur Swimming Association of Great Britain with the objective of bringing the organisation of swimming in England, Scotland and Wales under one heading for administrative purposes. This was rejected and in 1964 another proposal for an Amateur Swimming Federation was considered by all three countries. This, too, was eventually rejected, and as a final suggestion, the ASA asked Scotland and Wales again if they could become Districts within the ASA but another negative reaction resulted. By 1967 the efforts seemed to be exhausted and it was decided to take no further action. There was no doubt that it would be quite a big step for a country to become a District within another country's organisation. On the other hand, there appeared to be a strong need for some improvement in the administration of the many events which were of a *Great Britain* nature or which required an overview of the GB situation.

This machine helped to test 'hit-push' power at Crystal Palace. Dick Champion was the swimmer.

ASA Centralised Swimming and Diving Championships at Crystal Palace in 1964.

1965 began with the *Swimming Times* leader suggesting that, *'For the ASA - Time to Take Stock'*. Someone else suggested that the ASA had outgrown its structure and *'is now marking time'*. Neither of these comments was derogatory. Both sensed the beginnings of a change in the air. Later in the year a full-time salaried Assistant Secretary, Mr. L. Bennett, was appointed with the aid of a Ministry grant. The pressures were being acknowledged and the ASA Committee was to hold an extra two meetings a year (total six) to cope with the expanding volume of business. It was announced that the lease on 64 Cannon Street (Mr. Fern's office) would expire in May 1967. Ideally, it was considered that new premises be sought in London but agents would look elsewhere as well. It was also thought by some that the Association should centralise most of its activities under a General Secretary with a salary, together with other paid staff, but this was not approved. Instead there was approval to increase the grants to the Districts to enable them to cope with the increased work load. Mr. C.W. Plant, Chairman of the ASA Planning Committee and Association Honorary Treasurer, voiced strong views about Mr. Fern's succession. He totally agreed that the increased work be tackled in the field by the devoted voluntary men and women helped by the NTOs instead of employing a new General Secretary. He also cautioned against the Association relying too much on its new-found wealth in the form of profits gained from *Encouragement Schemes*. His rather cautious and defensive approach also warned that television and government income could easily dry up.

Meanwhile business continued as usual. The Council ordered a deputation to be sent to the Government to enquire about provision of public and school swimming facilities. The Government had its own problems, however, and in July put a six-months' embargo on capital expenditure, much to Mr. Fern's annoyance.

Mr. G. Matveieff, ASA Honorary Treasurer for 12 years, died and was replaced by Mr. C.W. Plant. Norman Sarsfield decided to resign as Education Committee Secretary but agreed to stay until May 1966. He was to be invested as ASA President in 1966 and obviously needed breathing space.

The Government's new *Sports Council* was set up in 1965 under the chairmanship of Denis Howell, Minister Responsible for Sport. The Council of 16 distinguished sports administrators and competitors included Ian Black, a very experienced ambassador for swimming. The objectives of the Sports Council were:

> *'To advise the Government on matters related to the development of amateur sport and physical recreation services and to foster co-operation between the statutory and voluntary authorities. It would be concerned with standards, provision, information, co-ordination of resources, training and coaching, expenditures, teams abroad and priorities in developments'.*

Certainly this new body would continue to be a strong force in the sporting affairs of the country and the ASA would do well to work alongside to help to realise its own aspirations.

It was noticeable, therefore, in 1966 that when the ASA Council urged its Committee to send a deputation to the Government, it later delayed this action until there was more certainty about the function of the Regional Sports Councils. It may be that this would be a more proper and effective means through which to channel ASA concerns as it was obviously one of the main reasons for the Sports Council being founded.

One Government announcement to cause understandable concern was that metrication was to become effective in 1972. The implication for bath construction alone was considerable and the ASA consequently revised its advice to local authorities who were making plans so that the future would be metric. The new Leeds Pool to be opened in 1967 was of metric dimensions and planning of metric events was in hand.

The 1966 comments about this being an ASA vintage year were well justified. Signs of success were in every corner: medals at the British Empire and Commonwealth Games and at the European Games; top of the Six Nations Contest; two more World records and 13 English records; District training courses trebled; National Championship success; Synchronised Swimming well under way; 121 Leader's Certificates issued and the huge success of the launch of Age-Group competition. Harold Fern was right when he said that Age-Group competition would have a profound effect on the future of competitive swimming in future. This first year saw 70,000 entries nationwide resulting in 300 finalists at the Blackpool event.

The increase in the new, popular and successful ASA ventures, together with the ever present desire of the Association to expand its influence in all of the many aspects of the swimming world, brought parallel pressures which were sometimes apparent. There were those who felt that the call to increase dependency on an already overstretched but willing voluntary sector of helpers was not the only answer. The Education Committee whose workload, along with others, had magnified greatly in the recent years, stated the concern about its requests for help being denied. The outcome was to be that *'the Committee's plans for expansion had to be shelved and a diminution of the service was to be expected'*. At the same time, the ASA was asking the Government for increased annual finance to fund three more NTOs. There would then be one for each District and one based at Crystal Palace. If it could be funded, it could happen, and it was certainly desirable.

It may be interesting to compare the number of ASA Committees for the years 1957 and 1967 and the number of times each met:

An innovation for 1967 was the formation of an Olympic Training Squad. N.W. Sarsfield (ASA President for 1966) was to take charge, with A.D. Kinnear as coach and Mrs. E. Toms as chaperone. There were worries about the problem of altitude in Mexico for 1968 and a variety of acclimatisation plans were made including the hope of training high up in the French Pyrenees.

The conditions laid down for being included in the new Squad were rigorous, as were the demands to be made upon the participants and their coaches, but being part of this Squad gave stature and identity to the swimmers.

Table 3.8: Comparison of committee meeting in 1957 and 1967

1957	1967
The ASA Committee (4)	The ASA Committee (5)
Water Polo (no meeting)	Water Polo (8)
Diving (2)	Diving (4)
Swimming (1)	Swimming (6)
Swimming Coaches' Certificate (1)	Swimming Coaches' Certificate (4)
Board of Examiners & Publications (3)	Education (3)
Inter-Country General Purposes (3)	Inter-Country General Purposes and Selection (4)
Appeals (1)	Appeals (1)
Special Committee: ASA and ESSA representatives (1)	Synchronised Swimming (3)
	Scientific Advisory (1)
	Age-Group (4)
	ASA Investment/Public Relations (2)
	Special Committees:
	(a) Joint ASA/ESSA (3)
	(b) Increase of number of NTOs (1)
	(c) ASA representatives on Regional Sports Councils (1)

A proposal was made to change conditions of entry to the National Championships. For nearly 100 years the event had been open to the world. In 1965, 20 results had gone to overseas entries. To some it was considered that this was not a true National event and did not show up the top English results. The suggestion was that entry should be confined to those of British Nationality, or *born in Britain* or *lived in England for the last 12 months*. The British Swimming Coaches Association disagreed and considered that external opposition gave the right infusion to our sport. After much discussion the 1967 ASA Council decided to leave the event open to the world entries, but to devise a means of extracting English champions' names rather than allowing a foreign visitor to be able to lay claim to being an English champion.

In 1967 the country was still in the grip of economic crisis but many new pools continued to emerge and the ASA seemed pleased with its links with the new Regional Sports Councils. It also published a book - *Swimming Pools: Notes for the Guidance of Designers* - which found a demand among local authorities.

Success in competition continued. Britain again won the Six Nations Contest, this time at Dortmund. The British team were well beaten by the USA at Crystal Palace but the experience gained outweighed the losses. The visit of the team to the USSR was well received. The match practice would help the Olympic Squad towards optimum performance at Mexico in 1968. All

Awards Schemes were flourishing. Age-Group Swimming and Synchronised Swimming had proved their ability to bring new aspirations to thousands more enthusiasts. Water Polo was seen to be on an upgrade. The new ASA/Coca-Cola National Swimming Scheme, prepared by Mr. Kinnear and labelled *The Winter Training Scheme*, was this year's main innovation. Coca-Cola sponsorship was the key to the thousands of youngsters training under competent coaches nationwide. The ASA Leader's Certificate was also proving a successful venture with 244 being awarded in 1967, twice the number for the previous year. The great amount of activity generated by the Diving Committee seems to belie the underlying problems which existed in this branch of the sport, but any difficulties were not publicly aired. It was simply hoped that differences could be resolved so that full advantage could be taken of the many new diving facilities growing up with the new provincial pools. A committee was formed to investigate alleged grievances in diving administration.

At last the reply came from the Department of Education and Science that financial assistance would be forthcoming to support three additional National Technical Officers from January 1968. Districts and clubs were strongly recommended to take advantage of their expert services. Helen Elkington (NTO) was appointed coach to the British Universities' Sports Team for the Tokyo Student Games of 1967 by permission of the ASA Committee.

It was for many a matter of great frustration and disappointment that A.D. Kinnear, the Chief NTO, resigned on a point of principle as from 31 October 1967. The matter is dealt with elsewhere in this book but it is sufficient here to say that the ASA held firmly to its decision to appoint an NTO who had no teaching qualification. It was this action which Mr. Kinnear could not accept and which led to many letters of protest being sent to the ASA from a variety of sporting organisations.

A variety of items which affected the administration of the ASA occurred in 1967. C.W. Plant, Honorary Treasurer, decided to resign and A.H. Turner from Leeds replaced him. N.W. Sarsfield also resigned as Honorary Secretary of the Education Committee to be replaced by J.M. Noble and A.M. Clarkson started his first year as Administration Officer of the Loughborough Advanced Swimming Training Course. He succeeded Austin Rawlinson who had steadfastly held the post for ten years. The ASA also appointed two new additional Headquarters staff at a total cost of £1,500. A seven-year lease was negotiated on the office accommodation on two floors at 64 Cannon Street, London. The increased space was to be used to accommodate the growing library as well as to provide office room for the slightly increased staffing. At that time it seemed that the ASA Headquarters would not be moved from the capital.

The urgent need for the Association to improve its public image, or at least to present its image to the public, resulted in a Public Relations Committee being set up in 1967 on a permanent basis. The Chairman was W.T. Tiver and the Secretary was E.W. Keighley who had experience in PR matters. E.C. Pope, who already acted as ASA Press Officer, the ASA's honorary officials and representatives from each District, together with Austin Rawlinson, completed the group. The functions of this new committee seemed to expand rapidly. The idea was to launch a

W.T. Tiver, Chairman of the new ASA Public Relations Committee, attended the Devon County Agricultural Show at Exeter in 1968.

National Campaign for 1968, the Olympic Year. Swimming Weeks would be organised throughout the country at holiday resorts, towns and cities and in any place where an exhibition would prove profitable. The press, magazines, radio and television would all play their part. This was the *Age of the Hard Sell* and the ASA realised that it had to actively promote its wares.

A *Learn to Swim Campaign* was also organised for 1968 to coincide with the school holidays from late July to September and needed central and District publicity. A travelling exhibition stand was purchased and the first exhibition was organised at Lewis's Store in Leeds in August 1967. A.H. Turner and Helen Elkington worked with Terry Jackson and Annie Walker to produce a magnificent show of publications, Award Schemes, projection equipment, water polo equipment, costumes and trunks, track suits and badges, Bovril Swimming and Diving Charts and thousands of free leaflets. This was a good example to follow and it was subsequently emulated throughout the country.

The Committee also offered to be involved in the *reception of overseas visitors* and this move was welcomed as a means of providing a recognisable system for catering for the requirements of guests. The *Swimming Times* also took part in the *PR* movement and willingly published a bulletin on behalf of the ASA's Public Relations Committee. This proved of great help to the Districts and for communications in general.

As the 1969 ASA Centenary Celebrations required much thought and planning, the work involved was put to the Public Relations Committee, and so two years before the event much of the spade work was initiated. For this great amount of anticipated activity the ASA allocated £3,600 expenditure in 1967 and 1968.

In September 1968 a Special ASA Council meeting was convened to discuss a proposal that 'the ASA Age Group Championships be introduced in 1969'. This was defeated by 29 votes to 18 making a further proposal that 'the Junior Championships be abolished' unnecessary. The controversy really arose because of the great surge in popularity of Age-Group competition, and partly resulted in the setting up of the Martin Committee in 1970 to look at the whole question of competitive swimming at all ages.

It was in this year that commentators looked at the Association's £100,000 assets as reflecting a *'prosperous ASA'*. Certainly the figure stood well against £2,746 of 1946 and must have given much confidence to those whose work had raised the financial profile via income from Proficiency and Survival Awards, Television rights, National Championships and Educational products.

The number of affiliated clubs now stood at 1,604 and the ASA was able to make grants for the year as follows:

Midlands £1,637   *North* £1,582   *North-East* £1,550

South £1,877   *West* £1,458

[The amount reflected the affiliations.]

A.D. Kinnear, no longer in the ASA but still a recognised voice, asked a number of questions about the future of the Association. He queried whether there was any long-term planning; whether the old definition of *amateur* had any place in the modern world; and he even suggested that the ASA was just *'soldiering on'*. The reply, of course, from C.W. Plant, served to illustrate all the ways in which the ASA was developing swimming and pointed to great expenditures which supported the NTOs and others in providing for the amateur swimmers. There seems no doubt from committee records that there were a number of ways in which the ASA was beginning to look at itself, but there was going to be no quantum leap without a considerable amount of consultation and reflection on future needs.

The Inter-Country and General Purposes Committee in 1968 changed its name to the Great Britain Committee - perhaps a recognition of greater unanimity as well as acknowledging the requirements of the international community for *one body to speak for Britain*.

Britain won the Six Nations Contest yet again but the Mexico Olympic results were a reflection of the difficult altitude condition and of the rising world standards of competitiveness. Set against these rising standards, Norman Sarsfield, the Team Manager, thought it was our best-ever team which included nine finalists and several best performances. Criticism of the National Championships was implied in the failure of many entrants even to reach set standard times and it was resolved to raise the standard entry levels for 1969.

HM The Queen met members of Britain's Mexico Olympics Team at the Centenary Gala at Crystal Palace Recreation Centre in June 1969.

The Centenary Dinner given to members of the ASA Committee by Alderman H.E. Fern CBE on 7 January 1969 at the Great Northern Hotel at King's Cross, London.
Standing left to right: E.C. Pope, Honorary Press Officer; J. Scott-Ormsby, West; M. Rutter, Midland; N.W. Sarsfield, M.C., North-East; E. Warrington, North; J. Bishop, North-East; E.W. Keighley, South; T.H. Cooper, North; J. Jordan, President-Elect; A.C. Price, South; L. Bennett, Assistant Secretary; K.B. Martin, Midland; E.J. Scott, O.B.E., M.C., Past President;
Seated left to right: Miss G.E. Writer, Personal Assistant to Alderman Fern; Alderman H.E. Fern, C.B.E., Honorary Secretary; A. Rawlinson, M.B.E., President; C.W. Plant, Honorary Life President; W.T. Tiver, West.

The ASA had little to complain about in 1968 but the decision of some local authorities to curtail expenditure by stopping school children from swimming really annoyed the Committee. Harold Fern wrote in strong terms to the Districts and to Denis Howell MP to do all they could to prevent the retrograde action but the Government could not act and the local authorities had the backing of their hard-pressed treasurers.

Centenary celebrations of 1969

1969 was a very special year for the ASA. The *centenary* aspect gave an opportunity to look back at one hundred years of effort and of successful development and progress in the many facets of swimming. It was a chance to reflect upon the ways in which the great band of ASA volunteers had made it all possible and how the cause of amateurism had been so strongly defended. Amid the joys of celebrating the good achievements were also the feelings by many that this was the end of an era and that inevitably some elements of change were afoot. Indeed, H.E. Fern's resignation after 50 years at the helm was imminent. Gladys Writer, his secretary, was also retiring. There was still uncertainty about where and how to locate a new ASA Headquarters building. The *Martin* special committee was at work to analyse every aspect of ASA procedures. There was no consensus yet reached about whether a professional secretary should be appointed or whether the top job should remain amateur and no decisions had been taken about the *modus operandi* of the new regime.

The Public Relations Committee had worked hard for two years under W.T. Tiver as Chairman to plan the special events for the Centenary Year. This was launched on 7 January with a television press conference held at the Great Northern Hotel, King's Cross, London. The site was deliberately chosen because on the 7 January 1869 in the German Gymnasium, only a stone's throw away from the Great Northern Hotel, the few swimming clubs had met by gaslight to found the London Swimming Association from which the ASA originated. Austin Rawlinson, as President, supervised the day's celebrations. In the afternoon the ASA Committee met and in the evening Harold Fern entertained the entire Committee at a celebration dinner. On 15 May Her Majesty Queen Elizabeth, Patron of the ASA, attended the Centenary Gala at Crystal Palace with Princess Anne. The 90-minute programme included swimming races, diving, synchronised swimming and a demonstration of personal survival. Britain's Mexico Olympic swimmers were on display in addition to representatives from all of the Districts before an audience of 2,000. The Royal Regiment of Artillery played a selection before Her Majesty arrived. The televised event was a good shopwindow for the ASA. The Association purchased the BBC coloured film of the event for posterity.

The Central Swimming Championships at Blackpool for six days in August were not specific to the festivities but it was special to be a winner in 1969. Entry standards were higher that year. Thirteen titles were won by overseas visitors - around a third of

ASA representative swimmers bear the flag into Westminster Abbey for the Centenary Service in 1969.

a participatory sport for those who did not wish to remain mere spectators in life. Above all, he extolled the virtues of

'that army of voluntary helpers who in their amateur capacity used their energies to found and organise the 1,600 clubs to serve the nation and the nation's youth'.

The new banner was then dedicated on the High Altar and Harold Fern, accompanied by Past Presidents and officials, carried the original minute book to the Dean in a simple but moving ceremony, again at the High Altar. The service concluded with the ringing of the bells of the Abbey Church.

These were the main ceremonies for centenary year but there were many others throughout the land. Other services in churches and cathedrals and other banquets and galas were all organised within the Districts. The BBC televised at least one gala from each District. Many local authorities did not miss the chance to plan their town-centre floral displays around the design of the ASA's badge. The *Swimming Times* organised four national competitions for *A National Poster to Help the Learn to Swim*

Amateur Swimming Association

Centenary Year Banquet

Friday . 3rd October . 1969

GROSVENOR HOUSE . PARK LANE
LONDON W.1

Association & Club Tables Arranged   Tickets £3.3s. 0d.

Early application for reservations to—
A. C. Price, 118 St. Peter's Road, Cowley, Uxbridge, Middlesex

---

A.S.A. CENTENARY YEAR 1869-1969

WESTMINSTER ABBEY

Service of Thanksgiving
to mark the Centenary
of the
Amateur Swimming Association

Saturday 4th October, 1969   .   11.30 a.m.

The Abbey Organ will be played from 11 a.m.
ABBEY CHOIR and TRUMPETERS from
KNELLER HALL MILITARY SCHOOL OF MUSIC

Ticket applications to—
E. W. Keighley, 133 Howarth Road, Abbey Wood, London S.E.2

---

the total. The case for identifying the English champions was not yet really solved.

The Centenary Banquet at Grosvenor House, Park Lane, on 3 October attracted more than 750 representatives of the swimming world. Jack Jordan, the President, read a message from Her Majesty the Queen and Lord Rupert Nevill proposed the toast to the Amateur Swimming Association. Dr. Harold Henning, Honorary Secretary of FINA, spoke of how FINA had started as result of the *'leadership and confidence of the world in British swimming'*. A silver salver inset with the ASA's gold medal was presented by FINA to the Association. Tributes to Alderman Harold Fern were voiced in abundance and he was presented with a cut glass vase. The Rt. Hon. Denis Howell, the Minister for Sport, replied to the toast to the guests by thanking the ASA and praising its campaign to enable every child to swim.

The following day, Saturday 4 October, a Service of Thanksgiving was held at Westminster Abbey. The Lord Mayor of Westminster was received at the West Door by the Dean and Chapter of Westminster and the procession of the Collegiate Body entered the Quire. The flag of the Amateur Swimming Association was borne by a group of Olympic and champion swimmers from St. George's Chapel to the Sacrarium. The trumpeters of Kneller Hall opened the proceedings. The Lord Bishop of London, the Right Reverend Hon. Robert Stopford preached the Sermon, praising the ASA's record of achievement and imaginative leadership. He recognised the value of swimming to save life and to aid the physically handicapped, and he saw the virtues of swimming as

Campaign, A Club Competition for the Number of Personal Survival Awards, A National Photographic Competition and *The Best Club Magazine for the Year*. Three International matches were staged against West Germany, Holland and Yugoslavia, each having the flavour of this special year.

This seat was presented by the ASA to Westminster Abbey grounds as part of the Centenary celebration in 1969.

Many local authorities created floral displays to celebrate the ASA Centenary. This one was at Stoke-on-Trent.

The FINA Medical Conference was held in London partly so that the delegates from 17 nations could be on the spot for the celebrations. Dr. N. Bleasdale, the ASA's own Medical Adviser, organised the conference.

End of the 1960s

With most of the Centenary celebrations completed the matter of H.E. Fern's successor was to concentrate minds. There was no agreement reached at the July Committee meeting and it was decided to hold a Special Meeting in Birmingham on 8 November to make decisions which would change ASA Law 11. The proposal in outline was, that at its annual Council meeting, the ASA should elect Honorary Treasurers, Trustees, Legal Advisers and Medical Adviser, Auditors and Life Presidents but that, 'A Secretary shall be appointed by the ASA Committee on such terms and conditions as they shall determine'. The proposition was defeated and some voiced the opinion that the matter should well be decided by the ASA Committee without the need for calling a special meeting. At the next Committee meeting a proposal that, 'the Secretary should not be appointed by the Council but by the Committee' was debated. No real decision was to be arrived at until 1970.

The Association was still looking out for suitable Headquarters property and in May agreed to purchase 16 St. John's Wood Road, London, NW8, for a maximum of £23,000, but planning permission was refused by the local authority, and the scheme fell through. It seems there was confidence in being able to arrange the sale of the recently negotiated seven-year lease on the Cannon Street premises. Expansion was the order of the day and included the extension of the Swimming Committee from five to eight members to cope with the amount of business and the raising of the salaries of Gladys Writer, Austin Rawlinson as TV Liaison Officer, and Mr. Bennett as the assistant secretary.

Three ASA officials were awarded Winston Churchill Travelling Scholarships. NTOs Helen Elkington and Hamilton Bland, together with J.M. Noble, Education Committee Secretary, would be away for around two months in different parts of the world. It was considered an honour and an opportunity to widen horizons.

The newly-named Great Britain Committee had a revised provisional constitution and a revised national representation in 1969. It was to include the Committee of the ASA with two representatives from each of Scotland and Wales to deal with the greatly increased volume of British business. The arrangement of inter-country matches, verification of records, team selection, referee appointments and representation on FINA and other bodies, all came within the orbit of the new committee. It was the nearest thing to federation that the individual countries would venture. In 1970 it was agreed to try out the new constitution for a period of two years.

The Six Nations Contest was won by Great Britain yet again in centenary year and the BBC presented a handsome trophy for the event. This made five wins out of eight since the event began and was commendable. However, when the results of the European Championships appeared, Britain had little to smile about. The points outcome told it all: East Germany 136; USSR 124; West Germany 117; Great Britain 49. The men were seventh in Europe and were relegated to Division B. They managed one third place,

two fourth places and two sixth places. The women's performance was considered to be the best of their season but still they achieved only one second place, four third places and a second in the medley relay. Youngsters entered the European Junior Championships for the first time and the result was considered a disaster - eight finalists in 20 events, but not one medal. Mrs. Pat Besford in her *inquest* in the *Swimming Times* deliberately set out to criticise and to provoke comment. *'We fail in attitude, coaching, training and leadership and have a collective responsibility;' 'There is not enough organisation and planning at the top level of our competitive swimming;' 'The Martin Committee has not come up with the right answers yet;' 'Coaches are responsible for fitness, competitive attitude and technique'.* Mrs. Besford queried whether all swimmers really trained hard and showed real dedication. Her article provoked a flood of replies but the main criticisms by the writers were against the lack of facilities for training. Norman Sarsfield, the Team Manager, replied on behalf of the Great Britain Committee but he did not disagree with Mrs. Besford. He quoted from his own report on the European Junior Championships - *'Not only were we defeated but the margins of defeat, often by swimmers from so-called "second-class swimming nations" were vast'.* His main diagnosis was that Britain was not tough enough compared with the disciplined Iron Curtain countries. He also believed that coaches tend to overcoach and evaded the real issues of competition and working to the limits. *'Not one of our swimmers was "technically prepared" and almost none possessed the killer instinct'.* Mr. Sarsfield recognised that the 1970 qualifying standards would be higher and he totally agreed with Mrs. Besford about the need for a tougher approach. *'It's no use moaning that the 'strain' of qualifying is always with them. We want swimmers who will take this in their stride.'*

To balance all this critique of the then current state of competitive swimming against the euphoria attached to the centenary year may have seemed a bitter pill, but it subtracted nothing from the multi-sided successes of the ASA, and rather served to indicate that these were aspects of administration and attitude which needed serious consideration.

The growing participation of the Sports Council was felt in 1969. As a new body it was launching a research project into the future needs of sport nationwide. The ASA responded by indicating the type of facilities needed in the larger towns and in less populated rural areas. A pilot scheme for the provision of Sports Bursaries from the Ministry of Sport was discussed jointly by ESSA and the ASA but no conclusions were reached. The largest ASA link with the Sports Council was that of an annual meeting of ASA representatives on Area Sports Councils. This very profitable event was organised by Michael Drinkwater and the outcomes were passed on to local authorities for their guidance when considering facilities. The 1969 discussions involved the use of learner training tanks, metric measurements, pool gradients, safety, sports centres and rural pools. It proved a positive forum for all concerned.

Education - 1960s

If the 1950s had been notable for a considerable output of educational material then the 1960's decade was to build on this foundation and expand the output in many directions. The period was to start with a number of advantages. N.W. Sarsfield, as Education Committee Secretary, worked with enormous enthusiasm and energy to supervise the work of a very skilled and hardworking group. Earlier experience had convinced these members that the visual impact of films, loops, charts, posters and books were vital educational tools to be encouraged in order to disseminate the knowledge of the branches of swimming at college, school and club levels. There were increasing numbers of 16mm. projectors in circulation and more people knew how to use them. To produce a film at Loughborough College baths, with its underwater windows, and thus to be able to show the audience *How it's done* in a classroom situation, brought more than a touch of reality. Silent films for instructional purposes were still being produced in the 1960s. Television too was becoming a learning medium which the ASA wanted to influence even before the development of the video-recorder.

1960 had the advantage of A.D. Kinnear's appointment as National Technical Officer. The influence of this appointment was to be enormous. Clubs and Districts countrywide were encouraged to book his services for lectures and demonstrations and to ask for advice on all manner of details. This method of educating the Districts by expert tuition and by using the most recent state of the art was an ASA innovation of the first order.

Bovril's continued interest and sponsorship of publications was fully exploited by both the ASA and the company. Wallcharts depicting swimming strokes, etc. and free leaflets on a range of topics were professionally designed, approved by the ASA and distributed to a wide audience. At least one classroom or Physical Education corridor in most schools would be profitably decorated with such posters.

The combined efforts of the ASA Education Committee Secretary, committee experts, NTOs and sponsorship were to result in a wide range of products. It may be noted that three long-serving members of that Committee were presented with the Harold Fern Award in three consecutive years, and part of the citation for each was their work for *Education*:

- Norman Sarsfield in 1962 (already 14 years on the Education Committee; he was to serve for 6 more years)

- K.B. Martin in 1963 (when he retired in 1968 he had served for 34 years)

- Austin Rawlinson in 1964 (for work mainly in education).

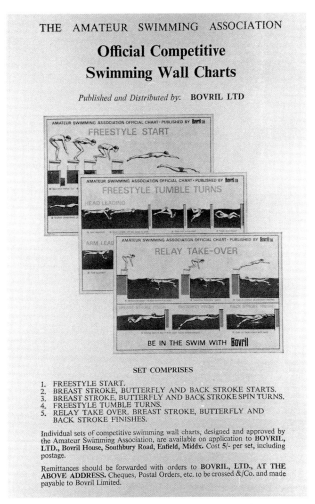

More 'Bovril' charts were issued in 1962.

Table 3.9: Education Achievements and Actions for the 1960s

1960	– More Training College students applied for the Teachers' Certificate of Swimming
	– A new Teachers' Certificate of Swimming syllabus was agreed
	– Revision of books - *Swimming - Know the Game* and *Swimming and Swimming Strokes*
	– NTO was appointed
	– Film - *Record Breakers* supplied by Jantzen Ltd.
1961	– *Learn to Swim* campaign was planned
	– Personal Survival Awards Scheme
	– A.D. Kinnear outlined the need for more films
	– *Advice to Candidates* booklet by R.G. Underwood
	– Course for *Tutors for ASA Teaching Courses* at Dartford College of Physical Education
1962	– Second NTO appointed - Tony Holmyard
	– Some television programmes initiated by NTO
	– New book - *Competitive Swimming*
1963	– Third NTO appointed - Helen Elkington
	– ASA took over administration of *ASA Swimming Diary*. N.W. Sarsfield and Mr. Cottle to manage this work. *Diary* was also a mine of information.
	– Two new films: 1. *Swimming - the Back Crawl* 2. *Survival Swimming* organised by A. Rawlinson, A.D. Kinnear and R. Underwood Also a silent film, *Swimming - the Breast Stroke*, with Anita Lonsbrough
	– Investigation initiated on methods of *Teaching Beginners to Swim* by A.D. Kinnear. This to involve participation of 1,002 school classes across the whole range of schools

A still from 'Learning the Back Crawl' film.

- 3 new booklets - *Swimming to Win*, *Survival Swimming* and *Advice to Organisers and Tutors of Courses*

1964 – 5,000 copies of *Survival Swimming* sold

- Wallchart for Survival Swimming

- TV coverage increasing

- 8,000 *Swimming Diaries* sold

- Refresher Course for full-time teachers of swimming

- *How to Swim and Dive* folders produced by Bovril

- More films planned - *Swimming: the Crawl, Butterfly, Breaststroke* - for completion in 1965

1965 – Bovril leaflets - *Plain Header* and *Survival Swimming* - over 100,000

- Boulton Films now selling many ASA co-produced films overseas

- Horlicks Ltd. provided ASA with copies of Walt Disney film, *I'm No Fool in Water*

- More film teaching loops produced

1966 – New film - *Learn to Dive* - N.W. Sarsfield and G. Rackham as advisors

- New film - *A Swimming Lesson* - A.D. Kinnear and A.H. Cregeen as advisors

1967 – New films:

- (a) *Learning the Dolphin Butterfly* (A.D. Kinnear and J. Sandford)

- (b) *Teaching Beginners Using Artificials Aids* (N.W. Sarsfield and A.D. Kinnear)

- (c) *Beginning Synchronised Swimming* (Helen Elkington and JS. Parkes)

- More NTOs appointed

1968 – J.M. Noble as new Education Committee Secretary after N.W. Sarsfield resigned

- New book, *Teaching of Swimming*

- New films: (a) *Learning Water Polo*
    (b) *Lesson Forms*

- Bovril wallcharts available - *Competitive Swimming*

- Bovril *Competitive Swimming* leaflet planned for 1969

1969 – 2 new Water Polo films

1970 – ASA Library classified and documented

- New booklet - *Advice to Club Organisers*

- New annual meeting of Education Committee with District Education Committee Secretaries

A.D. Kinnear

The ASA's first National Technical Officer of 1960 was a successful Scottish swimmer who had completed his Loughborough College Certificate of Physical Education in 1943. His subsequent experience in the Fleet Air Arm led to him teach survival swimming to the US Navy. In 1947 he was National Backstroke champion and in 1948 reached the Olympic final. He joined the Loughborough Course team in the 1950s and helped Harry Koskie, Max Madders and others in coaching.

When he became NTO he identified three areas which needed attention:

1. Methods and techniques were outdated and needed modernising.

2. There was no systematic training of coaches.

3. There was no method to disperse information about swimming techniques.

Bert Kinnear was also responsible together with Norman Sarsfield of the ASA's Education Committee for introducing change and innovations. Both were well qualified for this, but in rewriting the ASA *Handbook on Swimming*, it was easy to tread on toes when suggesting changes of emphasis, e.g. *'Was the best stroke for beginners the breast or the crawl?'* and *'Was enjoyment to be an important part of the learning process?'*. The Survival Swimming Challenge project was a highly successful scheme developed by Bert Kinnear and by Norman Sarsfield as administrators. Bert's literary input and his work in planning films, loops and aids was enormous. The *Swimming Times* was a vehicle for his countless monthly articles which gave a wide range of advice on the technicalities of swimming, as well as sound suggestions about organisation and procedure. He, perhaps, above all others, was in a position to realise the lack of facilities in so many parts of the country and did much to help clubs to make the most of what was provided. His work with the ASA's Scientific Advisory Committee was at the forefront of research and development connected with the many technical aspects of swimming.

In his capacity as NTO Bert Kinnear took charge of the direction of the Loughborough Courses. His aim, as with that of the ASA, was not only to train coaches but to get the Districts to set up similar courses so that the best information concerning techniques and methods could be cascaded throughout the country. When Crystal Palace became available even more courses were able to make use of the 150 bed facility for up to 160 weekends a year.

Bert Kinnear worked for the ASA for nearly eight years, until 1967, and at the end he resigned on a point of principle. He had always thought that an assistant NTO should have a *teaching* as well as a *swimming* qualification in order to be considered for the part. His reasoning was that when NTOs visited Teacher Training Colleges and developed courses they should be fully conversant with teaching method and practice. The ASA Committee disagreed and an appointment was made against his advice. He resigned immediately, and thus, the first NTO, who had done so much towards the improvement of coaching and towards the dissemination of information (including the production of much of that information), left behind a very different and improved system from that which he had inherited.

Bert Kinnear - Chief National Technical Officer.

Mr. Bert Kinnear afterwards reflected on the ASA as he interpreted it at the time. He saw the ASA system as an example of a ruling oligarchy run by very few personalities. He recognised much good in many of these personalities but wondered whether the power struggles were always a help towards the general progress. On occasions, he identified the Districts as being almost suspicious of his intrusive help although he acknowledged the huge amount of work done by lay people in the Districts, often with little recognition. He was the professional! They were the amateurs!

Bert had little contact with swimming after 1967. ITV asked him to be swimming commentator at the 1968 and 1972 Olympics, at Mexico and Munich, and this he did although he had no further direct contact with the swimmers. He did, however, set up a Swimming Consultancy business organised from his home for a short period.

There is no doubt that most of Bert Kinnear's contemporaries had a high opinion of him. One commented:

> *'He was before his time with ideas and techniques. Many could not cope with his foresight. He was genuine and never raised a voice - a gentle giant'.*

Austin Rawlinson

He became President of the ASA in February 1968 which included within his year of office the hundredth anniversary of the founding of the London Swimming Association from which the ASA sprang. His time in office called for planning the centenary celebrations, a task he relished as one steeped in the history of the ASA, as well as having contributed so much to its progress.

Austin Rawlinson MBE - President of the ASA in 1968.

His own services to the ASA had recognition as early as 1919 when he was one of those receiving a certificate for his services in *promoting high standards of swimming* in demonstrations throughout England during the first world war. His prowess enabled him to become schoolboy champion of Liverpool. The recently introduced back crawl stroke became his strength. He was the under 16s junior champion of the Northern District from 1916 to 1918, and junior freestyle champion in 1917 and 1918. He held the Northern District backstroke championship for seven years (1921-27) and for five years (1922-26) he was backstroke champion of England breaking the record on four occasions. He came fifth of the six finalists in the backstroke event in the Olympic Games held in Paris in 1924.

His enthusiasm for swimming began soon after his birth in Liverpool on 7 November 1902. After his distinguished career as a competitor he served as an official and officer in the Merseyside area and in Lancashire which led to him holding office in various positions in the Northern District of the ASA. His willingness to devote time and organising skills to the service of swimming enabled the ASA to call upon him to work for it nationally. He received the Harold Fern Award for his contributions to swimming. In 1961 his achievements were recognised by the award of the MBE. Perhaps the honour of having his name given to the new swimming pool at Speke in Liverpool gave him particular pleasure. Until that time, in 1965, the city had never named any sports venue after a sports person. For his outstanding services to swimming Ante Lambasa honoured him with the FINA Silver Pin in 1983. In 1987 he was elected an honorary life member of the ASA.

Austin Rawlinson worked hard to encourage swimming, receiving constant support from Edna, his wife. He organised the Yorkshire Bank's Inter-School Swimming Competition from the mid 1970s until 1984. Previously he had made swimming an active interest of colleagues within the police service. He worked closely with Ernest Warrington (also a police officer and later president of the ASA) on many swimming events in the Northern District. Later, Peter Rawlinson followed his father into the police service and in working for swimming, particularly as Vice-chairman of the ASA's National Judicial Tribunal.

The ASA had appointed Austin Rawlinson to undertake many tasks on its behalf. On the international scene he became team manager for both England and Great Britain in 1955 and he managed the British team at the Rome Olympics in 1960. His own pleasure on this occasion was enhanced by knowing that his son John was piloting the aircraft carrying the team to Rome. His demeanour was such that he forged bonds of friendship and respect with team members, not least because he expected them to be disciplined so as to bring credit to swimmers as people who knew how to behave at all times. Between 1966 and 1971 he acted as honorary secretary of the Great Britain Federation.

From the early 1950s the ASA appointed him to various committees the last being Appeals on which he served until 1983. This was a tribute to both to his knowledge of most aspects of swimming and to his personal integrity. The committees included the following: Swimming Coaches Certificate, Advanced Swimming Training, Education, Water Polo Referees, Championships, and, Appeals. His greatest contribution was to the work of the Education Committee where he gave the layman's view and vast practical experience to a body where professional experience was in the majority. Concurrently he attended Council every year. His interest in the ASA continued and he attended the meeting for the 125th anniversary.

One of the important jobs Austin Rawlinson undertook for the ASA was acting as its Television Liaison Officer from 1966 until 1971. He contributed occasional articles to the *Swimming Times* but from November 1979 until 1987 he found time to compile 'News from the North' with lucidity and understanding until District reports ceased to be a regular feature in June 1991.

The Development of Age-Group Swimming in England

Before the Second World War competitive swimming was restricted to Senior (over 16 years on 1 April) and Junior events. This sometimes made it difficult for younger swimmers who often had to compete against those outside of their age groups. The short season from April to September was also a restriction on competition training, but as more baths began to stay open all year some Championships were able to be grouped together to be run by various Associations.

Dickie Brown, amateur Chief Coach to Hull Olympic Swimming Club, learned of the American idea of *Age-Group* or *Top-Ten* events. This innovation meant that swimmers could compete at their own *age-strength*. Mr. Brown publicised the idea in the *Swimming Times* to discover reaction. He also experimented with Age Group Competition within his own club and later in Yorkshire. It could be that Age-Group swimming would help to breed improved national competitors. Carol Bauer of America was floating the idea of age-group ranking for eight to 18 year-olds to replace the novice and junior categories. The great size of the USA precluded the chance for young swimmers to compete against each other directly because of travel problems. A system of *Top-Ten* times to act as a standard was introduced there in conjunction with Beth Kaufmann between 1947 and 1950. In Britain youngsters would be able to compete directly with each other because they did not have the USA's travel problems.

In 1964 Dickie Brown, as an official at the Tokyo Olympics, joined the FINA Age-Group Committee as its Secretary. This Committee worked on the problems of the new grouping, especially concerning itself with the date of birth in relation to entry level. As the idea gained strength in the UK, the ASA permitted the circulation of an Age-Group questionnaire to clubs. The reaction was very positive and various clubs and counties started to experiment.

In 1964 the ASA facilitated the formation of a National Age-Group Committee with representatives from the Districts - Les Ames (Midlands), Fred Moorhouse (North), Ted Vickerman (North-East), Jack Scott Ormsby (West) and Jack Price (South) with Dickie Brown as Secretary.

The competition plan was for one-year groupings for ages 11-14 years. The 11- year-olds would swim 50 metres and the rest 100 metres. Date of birth was to be *The Year of the Competition* and there would be races for boys and girls. The ASA agreed the plan, provided that all entrants had previously competed in District Competitions. Also the five District teams would meet at a central venue for the finals.

By 1964 more Districts and counties had initiated their own Age-Group competitions and many had gained considerable experience and found the event popular and rewarding. All were advised of the need to prepare for the proposed 1966 National Competition and in 1965 about 1,600 swimmers participated in their own county competitions. Meanwhile, Dickie Brown and his team worked hard to sort out the rules and procedures for the big events. The venture was popular with A.D. Kinnear (NTO) who saw it as being a spur to competitive experience for youngsters and as a means of exposing the best young talent for future nurturing. *'The young swimmers could be guided along the road towards the national team in progressive stages.'.* The diving community became interested as well and by 1965 was considering the introduction of an Age-Group Diving Competition. The world was likewise awakening to the benefits of Age-Grouping and early in 1966 FINA gave its blessing to the formation of an International Age-Group Committee.

In 1965 Bert Kinnear commented on the increasingly important part which parents were having to play in the conduct of swimming. Their participation in looking after their children had greatly increased due to the growth of Age-Group swimming and the development of Winter Coaching Schemes. Ethical problems were highlighted as a result. *'Should 9 to 12 year olds be submitted to tough land and water training programmes?'* There were no easy answers but the parent input would colour the discussion.

Dickie Brown of the ASA Committee who did much to popularise Age-Group Swimming and Synchronised Swimming. (Copyright – Hull Daily Mail)

Bert Kinnear identified the parents' job:

a) to be responsible for the child,

b) to transport and look after the child at events,

c) to give encouragement. It was here that problems could arise because on occasions when a coach was not available a parent could step in. The parent in a position of attempting to teach could create a situation fraught with difficulties.

Mr Kinnear's advice was:

'please do not interfere with the real coach's work',

'don't crack the whip too much',

'don't take over'.

'The child is the one that counts'.

These matters represented genuine ASA concern as parents input has always been such a major aspect of organisation and success.

The ASA was fortunate to receive an offer to sponsor the new National Age-Group Competition. This was the first time that an event had been sponsored and it made Harold Fern and the Treasurer happy that the expenses were not to be borne by the

The Polar Bear Trophy presented by Fox's Glacier Mints for the District Winner of Age-Group Competitions.

Association. Fox's Glacier Mints' offer included the presentation of a handsome silver trophy of a polar bear on a mint, £10,000 to support the project over three years and provision of certificates and medals.

As 1966 proceeded many counties reported on the great number of entries for their competitions. Kent had 1,110 and Yorkshire 1,800 while town totals were also high, e.g. Blackpool 270, Liverpool 525 and Birmingham 330. The country's total of under 15-year-olds turned out to be 70,000, all competing for just 400 places in the final. The big event at Derby Bath, Blackpool, surpassed all expectations and was witnessed by around 3,000 proud parents. The *North* versus *South* syndrome gave impetus to the competitive spirit especially as these youngsters would be in good voice.

It was also the beginning of a financial success for the ASA at all levels. Norman Sarsfield, ASA President for that year, commented - *'A flame has been lit that will never be extinguished'*. He also hoped that the scheme would be extended to the 15 to 17 year age groups, especially as so many young people were being lost to the sport at that age. The South were the first winners of the Polar Bear Trophy with 210 points. The North-East had 156, the North 78, Midlands 70 and West 55. The Southern District won many events over the years and when this phase of Age-Group Competition finished, they retained the Trophy.

By 1968 the Age-Group Competition had become so successful that many parents and officials wanted National Age-Group Championships to be held. Dickie Brown and the Committee planned a new scheme in detail and submitted it for scrutiny. A Special Meeting of the ASA Council was called in Manchester in September 1968 to vote on the proposition that, *'The ASA Age-Group Championships be introduced in 1969'*. It was defeated by 29 to 18. If the vote had been successful then the Council would then have voted on whether to abolish the existing ASA Junior Championships. Thus the Junior Championships remained. However, a new series of National Age-Group Competition was started at Blackpool in 1970 when the decision was made to cut

out the District preliminaries and hold all competitions at the one central venue. The age was extended to 15 years.

There were so many aspects of competitive swimming which needed serious consideration that the Special Martin Committee was set up to study the subject. It was the Age-Group explosion which had finally triggered the need for this urgent analysis. When the report emerged in 1970 Ken Martin and his team recommended two main forms of Age-Group events for the future:

1. At National Level in two-year age groups to be held annually at Blackpool in August,

    i.e. 12-13 years   -110 yards

    14-15 years   -110 yards and 220 yards

    16-17 years   -110 yards and 220 yards and 880 yards;

    and

2. Inter-District Age-Group Event in one year groups - 11 years, 12 years, 13 years, 14 years and 15 years - at Coventry Bath in October.

These outcomes were to provide a sound basis for projection into the future.

SEE ENGLANDS FINEST AGE GROUP SWIMMERS AT THEIR BEST

The preliminary rounds of the Fox's Polar Bear Trophy Competition will be held in the following districts—Be there—See our young swimmers battling to get to the Finals Competition at Blackpool.

Midlands District A.S.A.

| August 19th | Central Baths | Coventry | 10.15 a.m., 2.30 and 7.00 p.m. |
| September 2nd | Central Baths | Coventry | 10.15 a.m., 2.30 and 7.00 p.m. |

Information from Mr. L. G. W. Ames, 79, Hinckley Road, Walgrave, Coventry.

Northern District A.S.A.

July 22nd	Austin Rawlinson Baths	Speke	2.00 and 6.30 p.m.
July 29th	The Public Baths	Wigan	2.00 and 6.30 p.m.
August 5th	Wythenshaw Baths	Manchester	6.00 p.m. only.

Information from: Mr. F. Moorhouse, 3, Royland Avenue, Bolton, Lancs.

North Eastern District A.S.A.

August 26th	Armley Baths	Leeds	2.00 and 6.30 p.m.
September 2nd	Leam Lane Baths	Felling	2.00 and 6.30 p.m.
September 9th	Cambridge Road Baths	Huddersfield	2.00 and 6.30 p.m.
September 16th	Yearsley Baths	York	4.30 p.m.

Information from: Mr. E. Vickerman, 10, Plantation Gardens, Wigton Lane, Alwoodley, Leeds 17.

Western District A.S.A.

| September 2nd | Central Baths | Plymouth | 4.30 p.m. |
| September 9th | Central Baths | Plymouth | 4.30 p.m. |

Information from: Mr. J. Scott Ormsby, 5, Queens Park Mansions, Paignton, Devon.

Southern District A.S.A.

| August 19th | Crystal Palace Baths | Upper | 2.00 and 6.15 p.m. |
| August 26th | Crystal Palace Baths | Norwood | 2.00 and 6.15 p.m. |

Information from Mr. J. Price, 82, Church Lane, Cheshunt, Herts.

The Final Competitions will be at Blackpool on October 6th and 7th. Make it a date.

District preliminary rounds for the Age-Group Competitions.

Amateur Swimming Association

NATIONAL AGE GROUP BADGE

CITY OF CHESTER SWIMMING CLUB

AGE GROUP OPEN MEET

Designated to N Counties ASA

on SATURDAY 5th/ SUNDAY 6th MAY 1990

10 years	50yds all strokes + 4 × 25yds IM
11/12	100yds all strokes + 4 × 50yds IM
13/14	100yds all strokes + 4 × 50yds IM
15/over	100yds all strokes + 4 × 50yds IM

AGE GROUP PRIZES TO THE VALUE OF £50/£30/£20

MEDALS TO 1st/2nd/3rd – Pennants to 4th/5th/6th

TOP CLUB PRIZES
1st – £100   2nd – £50.00   3rd – £30.00

☆ AGES AS AT 31/12/90 ☆
☆ POOL IS 25 YARDS ☆
☆ ANTI-WAVE LANES ☆

Entry details apply to:
**Meet Organizer,
Mrs C. Wolfenden,
29 Thackeray Drive,
VICARS CROSS,
Chester**

Amateur Swimming Association

YOUR CLUB MEMBERS WILL BE ENCOURAGED BY OUR AWARD SCHEMES

AGE GROUP AWARDS

BRONZE (CRAWL)   SILVER (BREASTSTROKE)   GOLD (BUTTERFLY)

AMATEUR SWIMMING ASSOCIATION

THE GREEN SHIELD NATIONAL AGE GROUP COMPETITIONS 1977

(under ASA Laws)

INTERNATIONAL POOL, BLACKPOOL
Monday 22nd August to Saturday 27th August
3 Sessions Daily. 10.00 am/2.30pm/7.00pm
2 Sessions only on the Saturday. 10.00am/2 30pm

Session Tickets (unreserved): Adults 50p Children 25p
Coaches' Passes (obtained through Club Secretaries) £4.00
Obtain your tickets in advance. Applications to:
Booking Officer, Box 6, Derby Baths, Warley Road, Blackpool
with stamped addressed envelope. Cheques and POs payable to ASA
Accommodation: List of Hotels and Boarding Houses from **The**
Attractions & Publicity Dept, Town Hall, Blackpool FY1 1LY
Phone 0253 25212

AMATEUR SWIMMING ASSOCIATION

President: Ed Dean Esq

NATIONAL SYNCHRONISED SWIMMING AGE GROUP COMPETITIONS

AT

St. Margarets Baths, Vaughan Way, Leicester

ON

Saturday and Sunday 29th/30th September, 1990

APPROXIMATE TIMES
SATURDAY: Figures: 11.00am and 3.30pm
SUNDAY: Routines: 9.30am and 2.15pm

Entry Fees: Figures and Solo £3 per swimmer
             Duet   £3 per duet
             Team   £5 per team

Entry forms available from the ASA Loughborough
Entries close 31st August
to ASA Loughborough

Spectator entry: £1 per session
NO RESERVED SEATS

A variety of Age Group Competitions were advertised in the Swimming Times in the 1970s to 1990s. Award Badges of the 1970s are displayed. A special National Age Group Badge was awarded in the 1970s for those who qualified for National Competitions.

From 1969 the ASA National Age-Group Committee was subsumed by the ASA Swimming Committee and Dickie Brown continued as Secretary until 1972.

Over the following few years the lengths of swimming for the various ages were adapted as a result of experience. For the first time in 1970 individual and not team entries were accepted for the National event.

From 1974 Green Shield agreed to sponsor Age-Group Swimming and at this time the National Competition moved to the Leeds 50 metre pool where over 3,000 swimmers competed. Esso took over this sponsorship in 1978.

In the mid-seventies the Association was concerned that some youngsters were over-pressured and that if the groups were in two-year sections as recommended in the Martin Report the younger ones would more easily recognise their limitations. The 1976 event catered for the two-year group pattern. The new Championships would be open to the world and only 50 metre pools could accommodate the army of swimmers and live up to its needs. The 1980s saw the inclusion of Diving, Water-Polo and Synchronised Swimming in the Age-Group categories.

In 1989 the ASA completely reviewed the structure of Age-Group Competition. From its beginnings there had grown a huge participation at District, Club and County levels. The National Competition was now a 6-day event with over 4,000 competitors from 12-18 years.

The main recommendations were to revert to the original single year age groupings and to move the 17 to 18 year group to the ASA National Championships. Both of these changes were implemented from 1991.

Throughout those formative years of age-grouping the emphasis on the enjoyment of this branch of swimming has outweighed the potential hazards of physical and mental fatigue to which young swimmers can be subjected. In addition, the impetus given to the sport by so many families who encouraged and supported their offspring, cannot be overestimated.

Entering the 1970s

1970 was to be a year of change resulting mainly from the planning, preparation and reports of 1969 and before.

H.E. Fern retired as Honorary Secretary and in doing so continued to show his satisfaction at the progress made during his 49 years in office. He hoped that the future administration would *'not overlook in this age of competition, that the main objects of the Association are to encourage the teaching of swimming and to press for more and better facilities'*. On the eve of his retirement he was entertained at the Great Northern Hotel, King's Cross, by the President, Past Presidents and colleagues on the Committee. His daughter Eileen was also present as was his principal assistant Gladys Writer. After 17 little speeches of reminiscence he was presented with a silver salver. One of his last acts was to dedicate the ASA garden seat presented to Westminster Abbey to commemorate the centenary year. His great band of volunteers and well-wishers collected nearly £1,000 towards his testimonial and out of part of this he received a colour television set. Alderman Fern did not disappear, however, as he remained on the ASA Committee as a Life President.

The ASA Committee accepted the main outcomes of the Martin Report which had been initiated in 1968. Over the following years this was to have a timely and profound influence on the Association's future although some of its recommendations were put into effect almost immediately. Thus, specialist members were now to be appointed to the Water Polo, Diving, Swimming and Synchronised Swimming Committees in addition to a representative from each District. It was a recognition that the special technical skills were more important than the administrative aspect. Also it was planned that from 1971 individual entries would be accepted for the Age-Group Competition at Blackpool and an Inter-District Age-Group Competition would be held at Coventry Bath.

The Swimming Facilities Committee was brought back into being as a result of the Martin Report to *'maintain the necessary contact with the planners and providers of facilities at local authority level'*. There was felt a need to form Regional Swimming Advisory Groups to work along with the Regional Sports Councils who were the providers on behalf of the Sports Council. It was also thought that changes were imminent in the granting of funds to local authorities and the ASA wanted to be able to advise these authorities on such items as pool provision as matters of priority.

Perhaps the most portentous and unanimous decision made by the ASA Council in 1970 was that of appointing a paid Secretary and it was obvious that it intended to have the *'best possible person'* because it was to offer a salary of *'not less than £3,000 per annum'*. Norman Sarsfield was to be that person and his previous experience and proven administrative ability in a wide variety of positions within the ASA was to serve him well. Much of the work of implementing the proposals of the Martin Report was now in his hands. The beginning of his period of office was, as has been demonstrated, a time of change and in many ways his job was to be the management of change. In 1970, for the first time, the Annual Report was published as a separate document from the *Handbook*. Every section of the sport was separately represented. The year's business meetings were reported as being long and arduous. The secretariat was now wholly professional and it was difficult for those involved to be working in part of the Cannon Street office accommodation with the uncertainty of moving elsewhere hanging over their heads. The impression given was that a body of opinion was in favour of moving to North London. A site for offices was available at Crystal Palace but this was not followed up. However, the ASA did enter into an important agreement together with the Sports Council and Greater London Council to build a 25 metres by 12.5 metres training pool adjacent to the main pool at Crystal Palace. The Association's contribution of £45,000 over a five-year period was in addition to £15,000 towards hostel accommodation. An application was also made to Barnet Council to build just off the A1 at Stirling Corner in a green-belt area. Yet another feeler was put out in the Camden area. Nothing was to come to fruition yet! One innovation was to put all hotel accommodation (and the ASA used a lot of it) out to tender. This was successfully concluded with a consequent saving to the Association. Other points of progress included the clarification of the duties and policies of the National Technical Officers, the rationalisation and standardisation of the procedures for examining ASA officials, and an extension of the activities of

Captain B.W. Cummins, Editor of the Swimming Times and ex-President of the ASA, pictured in 1962.

the Public Relations Committee especially into the Districts' organisations. The administration of Awards was also rationalised by Miss L. Cook continuing to deal with the Proficiency Awards from home and Mrs. L. Mitchell supervising the administration of the teaching Awards at central office.

A very shrewd move was the purchase by the ASA of the share capital of the *Swimming Times*, originally founded by Captain B.W. Cummins, who had nurtured its development for 47 years. Although a new board of directors was appointed to manage the publication in October 1970 it could be officially run by the ASA from January 1971 under the editorship of Kelvin Juba whose late father had been Assistant Editor. The format of the magazine was expected to gradually change but the stated intention was to *'let the Editor be free to represent all aspects of swimming'*. Norman Sarsfield had already begun his bi-monthly *ASA News* pages from the August of 1970. It was in this way that he announced the end of the ASA Centralised Championships in their current form and indicated the future pattern:

G.W. Hawthorne in the Swimming Times gave an interesting look-back over the 35 years of these Championships.

'Since 1935 events had been added, competitor interest had grown, standard times had been tightened and standard entry times imposed. Before 1939 there were 3 races for men and 5 for ladies (3 freestyle, a backstroke and a breaststroke) with a total entry of c.150. In post-war years 3 races for boys and 3 for girls were added with a total entry then of c.240. From 1949 to 1952 freestyle and medley team events for seniors were added. Up to then ten venues had been used. When the event went to Blackpool in 1953 it was to remain there to 1970 apart from one year at Crystal Palace in 1964. In 1953 the 'Butterfly' was added to Senior events and freestyle to Junior events and in that year entries were

620 rising to 719 in 1954. By 1960 this total was 1,400. The 'mile for men' was added in 1961, the two 440 l.Ms in 1963 and in 1964 at Crystal Palace 5 more events were added in celebration. Full use was made of the eight swimming lanes. The 800^x for men was introduced in 1965 and in 1966 the 200^x l.Ms for all four swimming groups. Ladies also took on the 440^x and 880^x freestyle. The extremely high numbers of competitors forced the ASA to introduce the standard entry times which have been adjusted over the years to raise standards'.

The Championships at Leeds for 1971 would be part of the new-style swimming programme as proposed by the Martin Report but the ASA recognised with gratitude the great advances made over the 17 years at Blackpool.

News from the Six Nations Contest was not as good as usual. Britain came third. Eurovision withdrew their future backing for the event probably because of the introduction of the European Swimming Cups. France withdrew and the other countries decided to continue with the *Five Nations Contest* for 1971. The Soviet Union took part in later years. The Commonwealth Games in Edinburgh in July resulted in England coming third out of seven countries and behind Australia and Canada. However, ten new National Records were made and 21 swimmers recorded personal best performances. Mr. A. Clarkson, Team Manager, commented that our competitors had felt that the ASA had not placed sufficient importance upon the Games, and were very conscious of the contrast of the preparation and final training of other competing teams. It was noted that the Omega electronic complex was used for the timing and judging. It was able to time to two decimal points but was able to split and place swimmers performances to three decimal points of a second. Under FINA rules, however, any time of $\frac{5}{100}$ or below reverts back to the next lower tenth, e.g. 58.13 or 58.15 = 58.1 and any time of $\frac{6}{100}$ or above moves upward, e.g. 58.16 or 58.97 = 59.0. Official times were thus given in one decimal point inspite of the improved facility for judging results.

The European Games were held Barcelona in September and Britain was at the bottom of the medals list. Pat Besford commented that our entrants were disappointing. John Verrier, Team Manager, considered that the three weeks of training and acclimatisation were insufficient. He also thought that *'courage failed'* when it dawned on the team that they had not trained as hard or as long as their opponents. *'The will to apply knowledge is missing and we have no reason yet to believe in ourselves'*. Anita Lonsbrough, champion of yesteryear, blamed the whole system for the mediocre performances and itemised her six-point plan to improve the situation. This included:

' (i) the ASA doing more to increase facilities; (ii) universities and colleges to be encouraged to have professional coaches; (iii) local councils to invest in training pools and to provide professional coaches; (iv) top amateur coaches should be paid; (v) coaches should speak the same language; (vi) swimmers must change their attitudes and always aim for a personal best'.

The substance of Miss Lonsbrough's pleas were a reflection of what the ASA and others were actually striving to do through a variety of channels at that period. There is no doubt that the ASA was becoming more confident that the shake-up of the system, due in part to the Martin Report, would in the end provide the outcomes which the competitive side of British swimming badly needed. The successes of the earlier part of the 1960s were being eclipsed not entirely by any failings in the system, but by the high-rise performances of the world's leading swimming countries which were outstripping all previous standards. It had also to be said that there was a contrast between those countries where there was total backing of swimmers and coaches by the whole community, and the countries where training facilities or times of their usage was limited or half-hearted. All the problems were recognised and the solutions were not always straightforward although the *'realisation that a relentless toughness was required'* was on the lips of many.

The ASA had much to be proud of as it entered the 1970's decade. The Association had preserved its amateur status whilst conceding that some aspects of its organisation needed the support of a professional administration. It had realised a financial income which had far surpassed any previously imagined figure and this enabled expenditures for the improvement of its courses. It had evolved new schemes which enhanced the status of the individual swimmer and had developed new systems for competitive participation. Having done all this, it had then looked at its own performance and had recommended the changes necessary for a forward-looking 100 year-old institution.

It was a fitting moment when young Debbie Adams of Bristol became the one millionth winner of the ASA Personal Survival Award in October of 1970. Her bronze and silver awards were won in April at the age of eight but this special gold award was presented with ceremony by the President, Mr. A.W. Keighley. Later, she was to display it on the BBC's *Blue Peter* programme.

The Martin Report of 1970

The entire organisation of the ASA came under scrutiny in 1968 when a Special ASA Council Meeting at Manchester passed a resolution to set up Special Committees to study the *'whole question of competitive swimming at all ages'*. The original purpose of the Manchester meeting had been to discuss the future of Age-Group Competition but it became obvious that this topic could not be viewed in isolation. The final report was published in three parts in 1970/71 and became known unofficially as the Martin Report because of the great responsibilities which had devolved on Ken Martin, the Chairman-Convenor. The Committee was composed of Frank Carter, Alan Clarkson, Thomas Handley, Dr. Philip Penny, Graham Sykes and Kenneth Martin. Working parties were also set up to consider Diving, Water Polo and Synchronised Swimming.

The brief was to canvass the experienced views of those engaged in the sport and in the administration of the sport, of ordinary participants and of those outside the ASA orbit. The *Swimming Times* highlighted the need for opinions and a questionnaire helped to gauge reactions.

The Committee spent time reviewing the current situation concerning competition as it had evolved in post-war times. Within that period the intensity of swimming training, coaching and competition had hugely increased the numbers taking part,

Deborah Jane Adams of Bristol, 8 years old, and recipient of the One-Millionth Survival Award (Gold) in October 1970. (Photographed by Elsa Mayo, Sevenoaks)

especially in the lower age-range. World swimming standards had risen to add to the competitive edge. Improved facilities for travel had stimulated the growth of an *International Contest Circuit*. The advent of television, with the eventual signing by the ASA of a BBC contract, soon changed the *too few international meetings* to *too many international meetings* and often it was the swimmers who suffered as a result of the expectations placed upon them. Televised live swimming events had sharpened the public interest in swimming. More wanted to learn to swim, often with the aim of competing. The potentially critical public eye had also forced organisers to improve the presentation of poolside contests. Disappointingly, water polo and diving received little TV coverage.

The Committee tried to analyse Great Britain's *competitive improvement rate* over the years and concluded that, although various swimmers stood high in the success ratings, *'We have generally not retained parity with the rest of the world and that decline has set in'*. Alongside that statement, however, came the suggestion that *'we have 14 and 15 year olds who would have been among the top six seniors a few years ago'* and *'the success of our women swimmers in international contests was also noted as contrasting with the same of the men's results'*.

The Age-Group Competition structure, inaugurated in 1965/6, was praised for its success in providing competition for large numbers of youngsters. *'Had this, however, happened at the expense of more senior swimmers?' 'Was the swimming calendar to become overloaded with Age-Group events?' 'Are we really drawing new National Team talent from the Age-Group organisation as was intended?'*

K.B. Martin, Chairman of the Martin Report Committee and ex-President of the ASA.

The general competitive environment also came under the spotlight. The resulting opinion was that many of our small clubs were organised in ways which were too traditional and that their activities were little more than an extension of public bathing time. Some clubs were well organised with their own coaches and with a sound administration. Some talented squads work outside the club system with their own coaches and with great measures of self-discipline.

The Committee received critiques from unexpected quarters. One such area was that of the International Team where the decision to impose national training courses at weekends prior to main international fixtures was criticised because individuals were taken away from their own coaches and made to spend too much time travelling in the process.

The ASA were also concerned about the tendencies for some clubs to set up their own training facilities outside the ASA administration. This was a direct reflection of some potential ASA weaknesses which were the very themes on which the Martin Report was concentrating.

Administrative Problems of Competitive Swimming

The greatly increased demand by competitors for coaching courses, for ASA Teacher's Certificate Examinations, for awards, films, publications and advice had pressured the Honorary Secretary and his staff beyond reasonable limits. The same pressures developed for the District Secretaries and Committee Secretaries.

The main ASA Committee was similarly so overloaded with business agendas that the important aspects of planning and policy-making were sometimes sidelined.

Those Committees which in some way were involved in *Competition* were listed as:

- Swimming: Diving: Water Polo: Synchronised Swimming:
- National Age-Group: Loughborough Course: ASA Coaches Certificate:
- Scientific: Coca-Cola: National Championships Management:
- Plus:
- Television Liaison Officer: and, National Technical Officers.

The Martin Committee considered that a much closer co-ordination and amalgamation of functions was necessary for efficient progress. Other concerns were:

a. The need for improved public relations and lines of communication.

b. The need for a full-time paid ASA Secretary with a professional secretariat to cope with the volume and quality of the work.

c. The need to make efforts to get younger people into the administration of sport. Some of the elderly and middle-aged administrators, although of long and valuable experience, were tending to hold on too long at the expense of younger talent.

d. The need for an improved selection of *swimmers* policy and that selection should not be based on just one performance result.

e. The need to provide *Elite* of swimmers with the special training facilities they deserve.

f. The need to retain the ASA Junior Championships mainly because those who perform well at a lower age in National Age-Group competition need the chance to compete with a higher age-group.

g. The need to arrange competitive dates to allow for school examinations and holidays.

h. The need to *think nationally* in all competition planning. This would thus involve the ASA, ESSA. STA and IBBI and press and television making a concerted effort.

* * * * * * *

When all research was concluded the Committee produced their conclusions and recommendations for future practices. This was certainly a thorough analysis and no aspect escaped the probes and comments.

There is no intention to reproduce the fine detail of the Report here. However, we stress the main threads of the discussion and recommendations:

1. The National Programme

(a) A two-part season to be adopted with lay-off periods in December and from late May to early July. (The latter to coincide with school and university exam. period.)

(b) The National Programme must be planned with the major competitions in mind and must be stated two years in advance.

Diary of Events 1970

The following diary of events for this year were compiled by the A.S.A. Public Relations Committee Some of the times are provisional and confirmation will be contained on tickets and literature for each event.

APRIL

4th	Yorkshire County A.S.A. Championships Gala, Armley, Leeds—2 p.m. and 6 p.m.
4th	Northumberland and Durham Counties A.S.A., Championships—Stockton—2 p.m. and 6 p.m.
4th	Surrey County W.P. & S.A. Age Group Competitions—Putney—6.30 p.m.
6th	North Eastern Counties—"A.S.A. Learn to Swim Campaign—1970," Leeds (two baths), Sheffield (two baths), Eston, Middlesbrough, Redcar, Billingham.
10th	North Eastern Counties A.S.A.—Better Swim Conference—Rupert Becket Theatre. University of Leeds—10 a.m. and 5.45 p.m.
10th	Surrey County W.P. & S.A. Championships, Morden Park—7 p.m.
11th	Kent County A.S.A.—Gala, White Oak Bath, Swanley.
11th	Yorkshire County A.S.A. Championships Gala, Doncaster—5.15 p.m.
11th	Sussex County A.S.A.—Junior Time Trials and Selection Gala, Hove—6.30 p.m.
17th	Surrey County W.P. & S.A. Championships, Morden Park—7.15 p.m.
18th	Yorkshire County A.S.A. Championships Gala, Albert Avenue, Hull—2 p.m. and 6 p.m.
18th	Essex County A.S.A. Championships and Age Gr-up Gala, Southend-on-Sea—2.30 p.m. and 7 p.m.
18th	Sussex County A.S.A.—Age Group Competitions, Hove—6.30 p.m.
18th	Northumberland and Durham Counties' A.S.A., Championships, Consett—2 p.m. and 6 p.m.
18th/19th	Six Nations Contest, Holland (Bussum).
24th	Surrey County W.P. & S.A. Age Group Competitions. South Norwood—7 p.m.
24th/25th	Great Britain v. U.S.S.R. Royal Commonwealth Pool. Edinburgh.
24th/26th	Hampshire County A.S.A. Training Course—Crystal Palace.
25th	Surrey County W.P. & S.A. Championships, Epsom—2.30 p.m.
25th	Middlesex County A.S.A. Championships and Age Group Gala, Hornsey Road— 2 p.m. and 6.30 p.m.
25th	Essex County A.S.A. Championships and Age Group Gala, Basildon—7 p.m.
25th	Kent County A.S.A. Gala, Riverside Baths, Erith.
25th	Sussex County A.S.A. Inter-County Match v. Hampshire and Berks., Aquarena. Worthing—6.30 p.m.

MAY

2nd	Hampshire County A.S.A.—Championships Gala, Portsmouth—6.30 p.m.
2nd	Sussex County A.S.A.—Age Group Competitions, Hove—6.30 p.m.
2nd	Surrey County W.P. & S.A. Championships, Epsom—2.15 p.m.
2nd	Middlesex County A.S.A. Championships, Hayes—7 p.m.
2nd	Essex County A.S.A. Championships and Age Group Gala, Southend-on-Sea—2.30 p.m. and 7 p.m.
2nd	North Eastern Counties A.S.A.—Four Counties Contest—Yorkshire v. Lancashire v. Northumberland and Durham v. Warwickshire. at Huddersfield.
4th	Surrey County W.P. & S.A. Championships, Cheam—7 p.m.
9th	Middlesex County A.S.A. Championships Gala, Hornsey Road—2 p.m. and 6.30 p.m.
9th	Essex County A.S.A. Championships and Age Group Gala, Basildon—7 p.m.
9th	Yorkshire County A.S.A. Championships Gala, Spendborough—2 p.m. and 6 p.m.
9th	Kent County A.S.A. Gala, Ladywell.
9th	Hampshire County A.S.A.—Championships Gala, Bournemouth—6.30 p.m.
9th	Midland District A.S.A.—Championships, Leicester.
9th	Sussex County A.S.A.—Age Group Competitions—Grand Finals, Hove—6.30 p.m.
9th	Northumberland and Durham Counties' A.S.A., Championships, Durham—2 p.m. and 6 p.m.
9th	Surrey County W.P. & S.A. Championships, Putney— 6.30 p.m.
15th/16th	International Meet—four swimmers from 12 Countries (Yugoslavia. Czechoslovakia. Spain. Poland. Austria. Switzerland, Holland, Ireland, Sweden, Italy, West Germany and Great Britain), Derby Baths, Blackpool.
15th/16th	Great Britain v. Spain (Under 21) Water Polo, Walsall.
15th	Surrey County W.P. & S.A. Age Group Competitions. South Norwood—7 p.m.
16th	Southern Counties A.S.A.—Championships and Age Group Competitions, Crystal Palace—1.45 p.m. and 6.15 p.m.
16th	Yorkshire County W.P. & S.A. Championships Gala. Huddersfield—2 p.m. and 6 p.m.
19th	Surrey County W.P. & S.A. Championships, Clapham—7.15 p.m.
23rd	Kent County A.S.A. Gala. Eltham.
23rd	Midland District A.S.A.—Championships, Halesowen.
23rd	North Eastern Counties A.S.A.—District Championships Gala, Stockton—2 p.m. and 6 p.m.
23rd	Hampshire County A.S.A. Championships Gala, Southampton—6.30 p.m.
23rd	Middlesex County A.S.A. Championships Gala, York Hall—6.30 p.m.
29th	Surrey County W.P. & S.A. Age Group Competitions, South Norwood—6.30 p.m.
30th	Southern Counties A.S.A.—Championships and Age Group Competitions, Crystal Palace—1.45 p.m. and 6.15 p.m.
30th	North Eastern Counties A.S.A.—District Championships Gala, Felling—2 p.m. and 6 p.m.

A two-month diary for 1970 displays a crowded programme.

(c) ASA should institute its own international meet to fit the LEN calendar.

(d) A pattern of Swimming Leagues should be adopted throughout the country.

(e) The aim of competitive swimming is to achieve highest possible world ranking but other levels of competition also must be catered for.

(f) Open National Championships would encourage foreign competition for our own swimmers.

(g) The Junior Championships should be retained to give 13-14 year-olds chance to compete against slightly older swimmers.

(h) The optimum recommended date for Age-Group championships is the end of August when maximum training has been achieved and before the schools start back.

(i) Open National Championships should still be used as National Trials inspite of foreign entries. They would still provide a useful comparative marker.

(j) The new year's plan would be:

1. Junior and Senior Championships at the end of March to be used also at trials.

2. International fixtures: mid-April to mid-May.

3. Open Championships (no juniors): first week of August - to be used as trial for Olympic and other entries.

4. Age-Group Championships for four days in last week of August.

5. Inter-District Age-Group Competitions in early October.

6. Two-year calendar planned ahead.

7. Other international contests perhaps in September/October.

8. District and County Championships should be made into an integrated programme by proper forward planning.

2. Coaching

In this context *coaching* is for the competitive swimmer and does not include the teaching of swimming.

1. An analysis of the coaching environment revealed the categories of club coach, private squad coach, ASA coaching courses, in-school coaching and the one-to-one coaching situation. There was great demand for coaches but not enough were fully qualified or had the most desired attributes. The country needed better qualified, better organised coaches with more recognition given to perceived success.

2. The *way-forward* was to invest in coaching according to the obvious demand. NTOs should detect potential talent while the ASA and LEAs should fund the training programmes. Younger *budding* coaches would work alongside experienced coaches. Coaching skills and knowledge should be more actively discussed through forums, lecture tours and coaching clinics. Top coaches should be given more international experience and should accompany our teams abroad. Technical information should be circulated by the ASA and Colleges of Physical Education should be receptive to the potential for working with the ASA in providing coaching courses.

3. The Committee stressed the importance of the status of coaches. The many hours of work were not balanced by the financial reward especially compared with coaches overseas. Recognised coaches should also be co-opted to all Swimming Committees to give opinions and to advise. Also the ASA could encourage greater recognition of the BSCA - the largest coaching association.

4. ASA externally-sponsored coaching courses could be County and District organised especially where there was not a strong local club. Also Education Authorities could encourage daytime swimming-teachers to coach competitive swimming in the evenings.

3. Facilities

The Committee recommended the establishment of a Swimming Facilities Committee and of similar committees in each District and County to stimulate new provision, optimise the use of existing facilities and to disseminate technical information. It was acknowledged that the great success of previous publicity concerning facilities was reflected in the fact that more money was being spent on swimming-pool provision than for any other sport or recreation.

Also LEAs were in process of building many new pools as part of their building programmes. ESSA was busy encouraging schools to build their own pools.

In the midst of all this positive activity it was the Committee's brief to analyse the position of the competitive swimmer in relation to the needs of the general public. As pools were public amenities then public swimming was the first priority. Competitive swimming and training could only take place outside general public hours but it was acknowledged that many facilities were under-used, closed on Sundays, closed for winter, or closed when schools were on holiday. The ASA's huge swimming-club structure was often fighting a losing battle in its quest for competitive training time in the pools, although it was obvious that more success had come to clubs which had showed initiative, and which had actively pressed the authorities to give them time and space. When some baths kept open for the swimming club to function between 8 p.m. and 10 p.m., the lateness of the hour did not fit well with the majority age-group of 8-16 years.

The greatest problems faced the specialist needs of diving, water polo and synchronised swimming. Most pools did not accommodate these activities which could only function on a regional basis with participants facing travelling-time as part of their total effort.

The Committee made some constructive suggestions for clubs to improve their use of existing facilities:

1. Several clubs in one area should liaise in planning the total training programme.

2. It could be of advantage for several small clubs to form into one large club.

3. The formation of local squads with coaches could perhaps make better use of facilities.

4. The ASA could make recommendations to the Local Authority when a new pool was being built.

5. NTOs should be used to help plan programmes for clubs.

6. Requests should be made for public pools to be available for training purposes outside normal hours.

The final recommendations are prefaced by the suggestion that,

'If the national prestige of winning Olympic and European honours means anything, then the price to the public should be a small loss of recreational swimming time in order that real competitive training can exist'.

Recommendations in brief:

1. Vigorous ASA campaigns for swimming's special needs.

2. Involve Local Authorities but be prepared to pay for it and hope that local prestige will benefit.

3. Swimmers must accept training facilities in unsocial hours.

4. *Out-of-hours* training sessions need rotas of volunteer responsible supervisors.

5. The ASA should emphasise the *Youth* aspect of facilities provision when making representation for specialist facilities.

6. ASA District, County and Local Associations could profitably liaise with local representatives of the Institute of Baths Management.

7. The ASA Committee should implement recommendations already made in 1969 concerning the setting up of committees and groups to help the provision of facilities.

8. ASA to appoint a National Co-ordinator of *Coaching, Facilities and International Swimming* and to set up a Swimming Functions Committee.

4. Administration

The problems have been outlined early in this chapter. We summarise some of the suggestions which were considered to be necessary to facilitate the smoother running of an overloaded administration.

a. The placing of more responsibility on the technical and standing committees with the main ASA Committee dealing with overriding strategic administration matters only.

b. Standing committees need to be given far more latitude and power to co-opt the right technical personnel to cope with increase of work and to improve the quality of decision-making.

c. The ASA Swimming Committee should be far more active in promoting aspects of competition rather than just dealing with matters referred to it. Co-ordination of thinking and planning should be to the fore.

d. There is a need to adopt some system for close liaison between committees.

e. The increased technical and administrative workload on the Swimming Committee demands the formation of extra specialist technical sub-committees.

f. Instead of all Committees appointing their own secretaries from within, these important appointments should be made by the ASA Council. Each Secretary should also produce an Annual Report.

g. There must be greatly-improved facility for the opinions of coaches to be expressed and considered within the administration of competitive swimming. The BSCA would welcome and facilitate this move. Coaches should also be appointed to technical sub-committees and be nominated to attend international contests. Our senior swimmers should likewise have opportunities to be represented on committees or at least to have the opportunities to express opinions officially. Older, retiring competitive swimmers should be encouraged to use their experience on committees, whether at national, district or local level.

h. A regular pattern of meeting dates for Standing Committees should be drawn up so that outcomes could be presented to the ASA Committees with planned continuity.

i. Team Managers for international teams should have clearly defined job-descriptions. The training of such personnel was also important and the appointments should be made on the basis of suitability and not as a reward for past services.

j. The team structure should be composed of Team Managers, Chief Team and Assistant Coaches; chaperone; masseur and/or physiotherapist or doctor; captain; general utility man.

5. The First Claim Law

ASA Law 53 was in need of clarification so that no ambiguity should exist where a swimmer belonged to two or more clubs within a competition situation. It should not follow that because one club initially taught the swimmer then he/she should automatically swim for that club. Clubs should rid themselves of special rules which smack of restrictive practices and should not in any way poach talent from elsewhere. It should be made easy for all swimmers to join a specialist club (e.g. for diving or water polo) at will. If embargoes on such moves existed then swimmers would be prevented from improving their scope and standards.

6. Presentation of Competitions

A decline in the number of spectators was variously blamed on - *too many heats; too long waiting time for results; poor general presentation; lack of good publicity; and lack of good commentary.*

The Committee analysed these problems and made recommendations to improve programme-planning to the benefit of both spectator and swimmer. It also made suggestions to improve announcers' skills and the presentation of results.

7. Sunday Competitions

The 1920 ASA Council Resolution did not permit Sunday swimming competitions of any kind in England under ASA Laws. By 1970, however, Saturdays were often thought to be overcrowded with galas and the Committee thus canvassed opinions about Sunday swimming. Most people favoured Sunday swimming but the Committee still suggested that, with good planning and management there was no need for this extra day. In taking this step the Committee was considering the views of those who would not agree with Sunday competitions on religious grounds. Such people should not be penalised. Also many swimmers wanted some relaxation.

Thus, in spite of the fact that Sunday training and coaching already existed, the Committee only recommended the change of the 1920 Resolution to suggest that only friendly and privately-arranged competitions could take place.

8. Selection Policy

a. The Committee recommended that selection should be in the hands of a small specialist team.

b. Almost no selection policy is capable of giving universal satisfaction.

c. Selection on one performance at a trial may not produce the optimum result.

However, the Committee still favoured the *death or glory* principle in one trial with a possible *escape clause* for selectors. Thus the first of two and the first two out of three home could be assured of selection, while the second or third places could be at the discretion of selectors based on known recent performance. The selection committee would also take into account the standard of opposition; the order of events so that swimmers do not compete in events close together; the fact that no first strong swimmer has a right to compete in every match (the coach and swimmer need to prepare for specific contests).

9. National Co-ordinator of Coaching, Facilities and International Swimming

The Committee's analysis identified a real need for such an appointment which in many ways had been filled earlier by A.D. Kinnear as the top National Technical Officer. The Sports Council strongly recommended such an appointment as being paramount in furthering *'leadership, direction and co-ordination interests of the ASA competitive structure'*.

A long suggested list of areas of responsibility for such a post was compiled by the Committee. No wonder the members were adamant that it was necessary to find the *right man of the right calibre* to fill the gap. His days would surely be very full.

10. Three additional proposals were made by the Martin Committee:

a. *That the ASA should have its own coach based permanently at Crystal Palace!*

b. *That in the long term the ASA should have its own National College of Aquatic Sport with its own 25 metre pool built centrally where good educational facilities exist and which could become the National Headquarters of the ASA!*

c. *That the ASA should have a National Incentive Scheme of Ranking and a National Registration Scheme for Swimmers!*

Would any of these proposals come to fruition in later years?

Chapter 4

Challenges and Initiatives from 1970 to 1994

Comment by Professor J. M. Cameron, past President Beckenham Swimming Club, 1993.

'Fixtures and events do not just happen. People have to devote time, talent and energy to such achievements; one must offer appreciation to anyone who has contributed in any part to the wellbeing of the Club. It does no-one any harm to reflect on the endeavours and tribulations of one's forebears and to consider the radical changes the Sport has undergone, particularly in recent years.'

Introduction

During the quarter century after 1970 the ASA seized opportunities and responded to a wide range of challenges. Its capability to do so depended on the dedicated and unremitting work of many volunteers. These were certainly not amateurs in the sense of being unskilled or novices; they were dedicated, knowledgeable but unpaid. They participated at all levels: in clubs, county, District and the ASA Council. The work of these people needed effective support so that swimming had the ability to maintain its rightful place alongside other public sports. This need was recognised with the appointment of the first professional secretary in 1970 with the task of heading the administration. The subsequent evolution of the organisation depended on its initiatives to promote and protect swimming. It had to adapt to economic, political, social, scientific and technological changes.

When Harold Fern retired, an era ended. Like many crisp generalisations this statement ignores what continued: the commitments of the ASA to the long established advocacy of swimming as an essential aspect of all children's education, to improving access and facilities for all people to swimming, and to enhancing the performance of the English contribution to British swimming in all its branches of competition with overseas teams. The ASA faced changes and challenges just as in previous years, but the ways of being successful precluded using some of the tried and tested methods from the past. According to those who participated in them these developments were not accepted by the ASA without strenuous debates. The Martin Report of 1970 was an important statement of the ASA's proposals for general and specific reforms.

Since 1970 the context of sporting activities in Britain had altered rapidly, inconsistently, and not always in favour of those promoting sport. Major financial problems arose from the inflations of the middle 1970s and the early 1980s. The role of the state changed markedly with special consequences for the finance and organisation of swimming and its facilities. The code of amateurism waned in international competitions and amongst sporting bodies within the British Isles. Leading performers came to expect that they would have a share of the money which came to businesses that exploited their prowess. The ASA itself had to find new ways of funding its multitude of activities, some of which required entrepreneurial skills not previously found in sports organisations.

Towards new definitions of amateur

Even in the later decades of the twentieth century the vexed question of how to define *amateur* still had life in it. Many of the leading international competitors in swimming at World Championships, the Olympics, and European Games after the Second World War, came from the German Democratic Republic (until 1989 when these teams came from a united Germany). They also came from the Union of Soviet Socialist Republics (until 1989 when each new member of the Commonwealth of Independent States sent its own team) or more recently China. Teams from these nations received very generous financial support from their governments and effectively worked as full-time athletes with access to the full-time services of the finest available coaches and training facilities. These governments supported their sportspeople because victories at international events gave prestige and endorsement to their regimes. The ASA, through its membership of the Amateur Swimming Federation of Great Britain (a member organisation of both LEN and FINA), was obliged to accept assertions of 'amateur' on behalf of competitors from such countries. In these communist states rewards for successful athletes included access to good careers and a privileged life-style. Similarly, in capitalist nations such as the United States of America, wealthy patrons of sports established foundations to finance excellent facilities and highly qualified teachers. They also paid for a comfortable lifestyle for promising sports people at selected universities. Professional careers in later life became possible for many athletes because of the educational programmes which these universities provided for their sports stars.

Some members of the ASA found it hard to reconcile themselves to what had happened in the world outside swimming, either in other sports in the United Kingdom or in swimming and other sports overseas. However, changes in assumptions and attitudes were taking place even in England. For example, in 1977 the *Swimming Times* reported that Ted Blakey, professional chief coach and secretary of the Wells and District Amateur Swimming Club, had become the first professional swimmer elected to serve as Somerset County ASA President. This represented an important step in recognising the contribution which professionals made to swimming. During 1977 the ASA accepted the changes in the definition of *amateur* which FINA had adopted in the previous July and which had the full support of the International Olympic Committee. The first consequence of ASA law changes of 1977 was to recognise that any definition of amateur status applied solely to the activity of swimming. Thus the exclusion of professional players from other sports wishing to enter swimming competitions ceased to apply. This and other innovations gave British swimmers some parity with the freedom of action which swimmers from other nations enjoyed.

Further alteration occurred in 1988 when FINA approved laws relating to expenses and advertising. This led the ASA to abandon any formal expression of what constituted *amateur* in its laws. The criterion adopted by FINA, and thus by the ASA, was *eligibility*. Status, amateur or other, was no longer investigated as long as the person concerned was registered with a swimming club affiliated to the ASA. In the case of international competition, one had to be eligible by nationality to enter.

An illustration of the climate of opinion about financial support for athletes, including swimmers, was shown at the time of the Seoul Olympics in 1988. While some top swimmers undertook preparation for their events, they were without jobs and registered as unemployed. They lived on their social security benefit. Social security rules forbade payments to anyone not available for work in Britain. Thus, for the fortnight when the competitors were in Seoul they received no money. The ASA tried energetically but unsuccessfully to persuade the government to relax the rules because of the financial plight of the these eminent sports people. Britain seemed indifferent to the needs of those who had given up so much to represent it in international competition. However, the eighties were characterised by changes which began to benefit athletes, particularly those who were outstandingly successful.

During the 1980s, the most successful of swimmers in the UK began to seek similar rewards as those earned by athletes in track and field events. Income from sponsorship and other sources would aim to provide a more secure personal future after the period of single minded dedication of time and effort. The new framework of being eligible to compete, enabled the stars of swimming to gain financial returns from their sporting achievements during the time of greatest public interest in their prowess and personalities. The mechanism for achieving this was the Trust Fund. These funds were a legal device whereby any money earned by a swimmer, for example, from endorsing a product or by making a public appearance at an entertainment, could have it paid into a special account. The money in the trust fund could then be used for the benefit of the swimmer in prescribed ways. Such funds were subject to scrutiny in order to avoid corrupt practices.

Thus, for the first time swimmers were able to reap the rewards of their achievements without attracting criticism or indeed exclusion from the ASA. The *show business* aspects of swimming expanded very rapidly from the 1980s onwards.

It is likely that the numbers of swimmers who became world class performers in any period has been small. The vast majority of swimmers, even reaching national championship levels, remained unsalaried and their motivation to swim at their best derived from the pleasure of achievement. In that sense the amateur thrived as much in 1994 as in 1970.

Administration

On the retirement of Harold Fern as Honorary Secretary in 1970, the administration of the ASA underwent a series of changes which were broadly in line with the Martin Report. The most significant was the agreement to create, for the first time, the post of Secretary which was the full-time and salaried. This change had many implications for the ASA's ways of doing business. Norman Sarsfield O.B.E., M.C., who was appointed as Secretary, was keen to see the underlying principles and recommendations of the Martin Report translated into action. This required introducing new methods while ensuring that business continued to be undertaken without loss of efficiency. At a personal level, he had the additional motivation to succeed because there had been opposition to the creation of the office and to his appointment.

One of the first innovations was the creation of a salaried secretariat capable of meeting the current and anticipated demands imposed upon it. These administrative developments needed much more space than that which had served well in the past. The office was moved from Cannon Street, London, to leased space in Acorn House owned by the National Union of Journalists in the Grays Inn Road, London. It was clear from the outset that these offices lacked some of the facilities which the ASA required to fully accommodate the scope of its work.

The Secretary and Alf Turner O.B.E., the Honorary Treasurer, had the task of finding offices which could meet current and expected demands. At first they thought that with Barnet Council they might have a joint venture to the advantage of both: the ASA would have offices adjacent to a proposed high quality modern swimming pool. It proved impossible to make an appropriate arrangement. The ASA then sought premises outside London where prices of suitable property and running costs were lower.

The Secretary and the Honorary Treasurer explored the available possibilities. One of these was in Leicestershire. Ladybird Books Company of Loughborough had built a new factory with offices on a greenfield site and offered their former office block in the town centre for sale. Messrs Sarsfield and Turner liked what they saw: this location in Loughborough had various practical advatages over some other places. First, the building was modern and had space which did not need expensive adaptations. Secondly, the building was less than two miles from Junction 23 on the M1. Thirdly, the main railway line between Sheffield and

Harold Fern performed the opening ceremony of Harold Fern House in March 1973 in the presence of the Mayor and Mayoress of Loughborough, the Chairman of Leicestershire County Council, the Committee of the ASA and their guests.

London served Loughborough with accessible connections to other parts of Great Britain. Fourth, East Midland International Airport provided services with the UK. as well as to other European destinations. Finally, Loughborough University of Technology, and the then separate College of Education had research interests germane to swimming and, at that time, some of best facilities for physical education in Britain.

The ASA moved to Loughborough and, on 23 March 1973, Harold Fern came to open the new offices officially in the building named in his honour Harold Fern House. Initially these premises met the needs of the ASA by providing office accommodation, committee meeting rooms, library, space for the editorial and publishing staff of the *Swimming Times*. There was also scope for new developments such as the early stages of the Institute of Swimming Teachers and Coaches initiative. After such radical changes in office organisation, members of Council and Committee wanted assurance that the evolving administration at Harold Fern House was performing in the most effective way. Thus, in 1978, a management consultancy reviewed the work of the administration. It made only minor recommendations for greater efficiency.

As Council approved further services and initiatives during the 1980s, pressure on space increased at Harold Fern House. Financial services remained at York and some work continued to be undertaken at Croydon. The situation became such that in the early 1990s the Committee began explorations for either extending Harold Fern House or moving elsewhere to enable the administration to have the facilities which a thriving and dynamic organisation required.

Norman Sarsfield, President of the ASA in 1966 and first Secretary from 1970 until 1980.

The first meeting of the Committee at Harold Fern House in 1973.

The professional secretaries - 1970-1994

Norman Sarsfield (Secretary from 1970 until 1981) had a distinguished career before becoming the first paid secretary of the ASA. He had a deep and abiding interest in all aspects of swimming and special concern for the development of diving in England. One of his successes was the creation at Dawdon, Co. Durham, of the finest diving facilities of the period. His professional life as a teacher was combined with an active life in politics in the city of Durham where he worked in the Conservative interest as a councillor, later becoming its mayor. The North Eastern District elected him to serve as one of its two representatives on the ASA Committee. He undertook this task with verve and efficiency. His work for the ASA ranged from writing articles for the *Swimming Times* , accompanying representative teams overseas and arranging matches in England such as the first diving competition with the Soviet Union in 1953. He campaigned for a pool in every school.

ASA progress in the decade after the retirement of Harold Fern owed much to the vision, organising capacity and vigour of Norman Sarsfield. He had good working relationships with the key officers of the Association and his conduct of meetings left little scope for those who had much to say but who did not always make a significant contribution to discussions or debates. This clarity of purpose he shared with Alf Turner, the Honorary Treasurer, and they strove to give the ASA the backing and resources which would enable it to achieve the necessary stable financial basis to further its main policies.

During the *Sarsfield era*, the major innovations were the creation of Harold Fern House as the administrative dynamo of the ASA, the initiation of the ISTC, both in the context of improving standards of performance in international competitions. Some of the initiatives he had taken prior to entering office soon gained momentum, such as, fostering the employment by swimming clubs of professional coaches holding appropriate ASA qualifications. Norman Sarsfield continued to work for swimming and sport after his official retirement in 1981 by serving on the committees of LEN and FINA as well as the British Sports Council.

Harold Hassall (Secretary from 1981 until 1985) succeeded Norman Sarsfield in February 1981 when Council formally accepted his nomination by Committee. His career prior to joining the ASA had included working as a Senior Lecturer in Physical Education and later administering a leisure centre which had its own swimming pool. His practical experience as an administrator was matched by a graduate diploma in management.

Harold Hassall's sporting activities and interests furnished him with a breadth of vision about sport in Britain. He played soccer, having been awarded five international caps for England. Subsequently he became a Football Association staff coach, and was a member of the FIFA coaching panel. He played cricket as a professional and held the MCC qualification as an advanced cricket coach. He had taught dingy sailing for the Sports Council. His catholicity of games qualifications included those of being a tennis coach.

Retirement dinner for Norman Sarsfield was given by the ASA committee on 14 November 1980. Back Row: P. Jones, E.E. Warner, H. Booth, F. Collins, T.H. Cooper, F.W. Latimer. Middle Row: D.R Yeomans, F.G. Thain, J.H. Zimmermann, E. Vickerman, M. Rutter. Front Row (L to R): K.B. Martin, C.W. Tiver, A.H. Turner (Honorary Treasurer), D.F. Scales (President), N.W. Sarsfield (Secretary), J. Wilson, E.W. Keighley.

Harold Hassall, Secretary of the ASA from 1981 to 1985.

His service with the ASA was cut short by illness in 1985, and he decided to retire at the end of August that year. During his period of office the Association had moved further along the major pathways outlined in the Martin Report. In these years sponsorships provided financial backing for the ASA at greater levels than ever before. Pressure on space at Harold Fern House had become more of a problem as the demands for support services continued to grow. One of the major organisational steps taken was the installation of a computer system. This enhanced scope for handling various demanding administrative tasks and permitted the inauguration of the Registration of Swimmers.

David Reeves (Secretary from 1985 until 1994) always described himself as Secretary even though he had responded to the advertisement in the *Swimming Times* of August 1985 where the post was described as '*the Chief Executive Officer of the ASA and Secretary of the Amateur Swimming Federation of Great Britain*'. His term of office began on 1 October 1985. He came to the post with much experience in the world of swimming and service with the ASA. He became involved with administration in his own club, Royal Tunbridge Wells Monson SC and held various offices in the Kent County ASA, becoming its President in 1954. He served on the SCASA District Executive from 1967, being elected the President of the SCASA in 1982. In 1983 he was elected to the ASA Committee.

David Reeves's interests in swimming and water polo were not only as a participant but also as a coach and organiser of courses. He played a leading role in the establishment of the ASA water polo coaches examination system. He was manager for the Great Britain International Water Polo Squad for six years and acted as team manager at European, World and Olympic Games. As an elected staff member of the British Olympic Association he served

swimming at the Commonwealth Games. He rewrote *Know the Game - Water Polo*. He had much experience in negotiations with sponsors and with national bodies such as the Sports Council.

During his period of office, David Reeves played a vital role in a variety of initiatives. The expanding demands of swimming required increasingly rapid responses to new government legislation, advances in technology, international swimming laws and evolving social behaviour. To meet these demands, he inaugurated reviews of the entire work of the ASA and strongly encouraged the concept of the *professional administration sustaining and, sometimes, co-ordinating, the work of the vitally important unpaid volunteers*. Thus the outward signs of reformatting publications reflected the reshaping of the constitution of the ASA and the work of its salaried employees. The success of Masters swimming competitions and of the revitalised awards scheme demonstrated the Association's energy. David Reeves retired from the office in March 1994.

David Sparkes (Chief Executive of the ASA 1994 onwards) became acting Chief Executive in May 1994 and was confirmed in the post later in the same year. The title change had been foreshadowed in the advertisement before the appointment of David Reeves. David Sparkes's career in swimming began when he was a pupil at Bromsgrove Grammar School. After reading for a degree in engineering at Aston University he established his own international business. These activities did not prevent him gaining a wide range of experiences in swimming. He served his own club at Droitwich in various capacities, ranging from lifeguard to various offices of its committee. He represented his club on the Worcestershire County ASA, and became a representative on the MCASA. Later he became a member of the national ASA

David Reeves, Secretary of the ASA, from 1985 to 1994.

David Sparkes, Chief Executive of the ASA, from 1994.

Education Committee and in due course its chair. The Association benefitted from his services on the Facilities Committee and the Coaches Committee. David Sparkes's strong practical experience of coaching had led him to become an active member of the ISTC management body. He was elected honorary secretary of the Midland District in 1990 and representative on the ASA Management Committee from 1990 until 1994. Previously, he had served as a member of the Working Party which had produced the review document *Which Way Forward?* and, later on the newly constituted Management Committee. His involvement in swimming led him to gain a formidable list of ASA qualifications: swimming teacher, advanced swimming teacher, coach and official (referee, timekeeper and judge). His enthusiasm to contribute further to the development of the ASA included making the most of opportunities to further the development of swimming at all levels.

Professionalising the central organisation

By 1970 the ASA already had in place a small number of fulltime paid staff, who, as National Technical Officers undertook the various tasks which Committee and its subcommittees required. These officers had the responsibility of translating advice on best practices given by the ASA technical subcommittees to the Districts and clubs. These officers acted as important conduits for information passing between the ASA and swimmers as well as officials at club, county and District levels.

Some insight into the work of these officers has been provided by Helen Elkington in her description of the hectic life of a Technical Officer during the early 1970s. These officers worked *unsocial* hours and often felt that they had to be available almost round the clock to clubs, swimmers or voluntary officials. There was an almost insatiable demand for their time at weekends and evenings. They arranged advisory sessions, attended competitions and contributed to courses on many aspects of swimming. During the weekdays these officers had reports to write and had to travel by car to widely spread geographical locations throughout the year. The job also required them to keep abreast of changes in water-sports rules, to be aware of relevant developments in sports science and medicine, and to act as a channel of information between clubs and the Association.

The recognition of the undoubted commitment by the paid officers resulted in improvement to standards of swimming. This was eventually matched by the appointment of more officers. In 1975, in keeping with the changing patterns of training, coaching, and specialised knowledge demanded from these NTO's the Association retitled them *National Development Officers.* Each NDO took special responsibility for an aspect of swimming, such as education or the needs of the disabled. In addition the NDOs were based regionally: at Crystal Palace, at headquarters and in the West Midlands. In this way the ASA reached all Districts and maintained communications. These changes did not necessarily make fewer demands, nor make the life of an NDO less hectic than that of the NTOs. However, their specialisation made more efficient use of their skills and allowed for a more direct response to issues as they arose.

The 1970s and 1980s were characterised by the rapid development of office technology. The ASA responded to these opportunities by installing word processors and, eventually computers. These were utilised as a way of reacting efficiently to the increasing demands on time, space and range swimming activities. Like many organisations introducing more sophisticated computerised records, the ASA registered itself under the Data Protection Act of 1985. Thus all persons who are registered with the ASA have the right to access their own information where ever it is held. Some District and clubs have moved towards the use of computerised records and the ASA has provided advice about the appropriate procedures and the safeguards of registering under the Act.

The sophistication and speed of computing facilities have enabled the ASA to inaugurate its National Registration Scheme. This possibilty had been on the agenda for many years. However, until the advent of computers it was not considered a practical possibility. The Scheme was begun in 1986 and became fully functioning in 1987. It recorded details of all swimmers in affiliated clubs. The initiation and maintenance of these records placed a heavy burden on the honorary secretaries of clubs and Districts. However, it enabled the ASA to check that all entrants in competitions were eligible. At the beginning of the Scheme the administration had to record information for over 27,000 people and allocate to each a unique number. To encourage the swift return of information and the payment of the registration fee of £2.00, the Association sent each of the newly registered swimmers a copy of *The Swimmer,* a newsletter giving information about events and activities. By 1989 the number of registered swimmers had grown to over 48,000 and reached just over 50,000 in the early 1990s.

The Martin Report had included many valuable ideas including the importance of reviewing management in order for the ASA to remain effective. In recognition of this a thorough review was undertaken in 1987 initiated by discussion of a paper in the ASA Committee in March 1987. and a report published in December of that year *Which Way Forward?* This was debated by Council in 1988 and formed the basis for the decision to prepare plans for meeting the goals. At the same time the plans were also needed to meet short term requirements without serious departures from its fundamental goals.

The report *Which Way Forward?* was the first thorough assessment of the working of the ASA since the Martin Report. This identified items for immediate action and items where major innovations should be considered. Two steps for immediate action were identified: (1) a requirement that each Technical Committee should submit its budget for the year 1988 for approval at the September 1987 meeting of the Committee; and (2) that a member of the Committee should sit on each Technical Committee so as to provide much closer liaison. For the longer term, a Working Party had the task of preparing a corporate plan so that the Committee could deal with matters of strategy rather than practical details.

The Working Party recommended to Council that the ASA should control its direction by clearly identifying its major corporate activities, by making development plans, and by adopting an appropriate financial strategy. The Working Party wanted the ASA to generate more of its income from its members and from its own resources, rather than from grants and sponsorship, so as to enable it to finance its main objectives.

In assessing the state of the ASA in the later 1980s the document drew attention to both its strengths and weaknesses. In brief, it had strengths by:-

1. being the governing body of the sport in England.

2. operating an envied education structure.

3. enjoying a good public perception of running a clean, healthy sport involving both sexes and all ages throughout society: possessing an excellent safety record: giving access to other water sports; involving high participation for both social and organised events; and being recognised as the agency by which to learn to swim.

4. having a club structure as the focus of most activities.

5. possessing large number of dedicated and multi-talented volunteers.

6. running a professional secretariat working in ASA-owned freehold accommodation.

7. operating a registration scheme giving direct access to participants and financial resources.

8. having the financial basis for future growth.

9. being capable of producing quality coaches.

10. managing an award scheme embracing all ages and abilities with a profit potential for future development.

11. working through ISTC it maintains contacts and liaison with 8,000 teachers and coaches and providing for professional and training needs.

12. possessing ASA Swimming Enterprises Ltd as its marketing vehicle with profit making potential.

13. organising a clearly defined national competitive structure for all disciplines with a focal point for achievement.

The twelve weaknesses were of varying character and were supported by specific examples. In many cases these problems were not difficult to remedy but some had enduring qualities which would take time to address. In brief, these were:

1. slow responses to some challenges caused by lack of authority at the necessary level which is the result of the elaborate committee structure.

2. administrative mechanisms associated with structure of committees resulting in poor communications within the sport.

3. dependence on facilities provided by local authorities and schools.

4. coping with increasing numbers of leisure pools and with privatisation which posed threats in the future.

5. a poor image within the sport.

6. poor cohesion in speaking for the sport to external bodies. The ASA's secretariat was fragmented between Loughborough, York and Croydon, and there were questions about its relationship with the ASFGB;

7. 'The ASA needs to move away from the 'amateur' concept in an organised manner, facilitating greater use of available 'top talent' in encouraging swimmers to remain in the UK and to harness such talent effectively, whilst competing and after'.

8. lack of financial independence giving external agencies potential for undue influence on policies.

9. threats to District and County championships from proliferating of open meets.

10. lack of effective control over swimming and national water polo leagues and a need to give more care to Masters swimming.

11. need to overcome inadequate media coverage of the sport.

12. need for improved support of clubs with advice and assistance with facility provision including Health and Safety matters.

Recommendations for building on strengths and removing or minimising weaknesses were set out in 13 objectives. Some of these were, essentially, that the ASA needed to proceed along lines already in place, as for example, in the operation of ISTC. However, there were organisational changes proposed with the objective of enabling the ASA to develop an administration capable of rapid responses as needs arose. It proposed to make more effective use of the enthusiasm of dedicated volunteers. The Working Party suggested four constitutional changes:

1. **The Council** should retain its present role of determining global policy and control over the affairs of the ASA.

2. **The Executive Committee** should replace the ASA Committee with responsibility for policy making and decision taking.

3. **The Management Committee** should implement policy on a day-to-day basis.

4. **Sub-committees** should carry out agreed programmes and exercise financial control. (These committees were named **Technical Committees** in the formally approved constitution. These were for: Diving, Education, Masters, Medical Advisory, Public Relations, Scientific Advisory, Swimming, Swimming Facilities, Synchronised Swimming, and Water Polo. There were established two sub-committees of Swimming: Swimming Coaches Certificate, and, Swimming Officials Examinations.)

Alan Clarkson, Honorary Treasurer of the ASA from 1986.

The Executive Committee should have powers to delegate specific parts of its responsibilities to appropriate sub-committees. The ISTC, Swimming Times Ltd and Swimming Enterprises Ltd should report to the Executive Committee so that liaison could be continuous and effective.

Council and its Committee authorised soundings of opinions and sought views from throughout the organisation. In the light of these, in 1989, a specially convened Council had before it a set of proposals to translate the necessary constitutional changes into ASA law. These were a combination of the proposals put forward in *Which Way Forward?* and comments and ideas arising from subsequent discussions. Council accepted the proposals which created the means by which the ASA could reform the work of its professional staff, take firmer central control over finances and establish corporate planning.

Council retained its role as the watchdog for the swimmers and clubs who could call to account policy makers and could examine broad strategies. It became the task of the ASA's Executive Committee to identify future strategy and of the Management Committee and the Chief Executive to carry out the operational policies and actions. This structure was functioning by 1994. It was an essential component of efficient administration in a world where the speed of decision-taking had accelerated beyond what had been envisaged even in the early 1980s.

Finances

Ensuring the financial security of sporting organisations has always presented problems. During the period from 1970 to 1994 costs increased and the need for money to support swimming activities grew. The ASA was committed to policies which would keep swimming in the forefront of the sporting life of the nation. This implied not only prudent management of monies available but also close and continuous efforts to match ambitions with available income. Moreover, the ASA's revenues underwent severe pressure from inflation in the 1970s and early 1980s. Between 1970 and 1994 the ASA, like other bodies, had to cope with rapid price increases which followed the oil crises of 1974

and 1975, the further economic and financial problems of 1980 and 1981, and the rise in costs as a result of the declining purchasing power of the pound overseas in the early 1990s. The options for satisfactory funding depended on the skills of the treasurer in persuading the organisation to establish appropriate budgetary controls and to take the necessary steps to improve incomes from a variety of sources, including the creation of new enterprises.

A comparison of the total figures for income and expenditure in 1971 with 1994 hides at least as much as it reveals. In part this is because the basis of keeping accounts changed to meet amendments in UK law and to cover new developments in the larger organisation which it had become in the late 1980s. Compared with 1971 the ASA was involved in a greater range of financial activities. Crude comparisons of sums of money mean little unless we understand that money changed its purchasing power and that some items regarded as necessities by 1990 were unobtainable in 1970.

In 1971 the major sources of revenue came from affiliation fees, fees from candidates for examinations, charges for the associated awards for swimming achievements and from sales of ties, badges and publications. By 1994 the income showed a major shift in its composition. Affiliation fees contributed only a tiny part whereas the most important sources were from the education programme and from sponsorship. Nonetheless the Association gained revenues from its Championship Programme, investments, registration scheme, the joint venture with other sports at Crystal Palace and earnings from commission for administering trust funds and the ASFGB. These important sources of income came from the activities of ASA companies which ran the awards schemes together with sales of publications and various products such as some kinds of swimming clothing and equipment. From the mid 1970s particular emphasis was laid on making successful applications for grants and donations from the government, sports foundations, benefactors and sponsors. A few ventures, such as the ASA Lottery, promised well but in the event could not be sustained for any length of time.

Greenshield sponsored the training of the youth squad at York in 1973.

The Adopta Sport campaign sponsored by Weetabix in 1986 drew on the support of the very prominent swimmers David Wilkie (left), Sharron Davies and Adrian Moorhouse.

One source of income, sponsorship, grew rapidly after the Second World War and especially in the years after 1970. A variety of firms and organisations wanted to gain from their relationship with swimming and the ASA negotiated sponsorship for specific schemes usually tied to an agreement to advertise.

The ASA succeeded in attracting sponsorship for various important aspects of its work. Campaigns such as *Swimfit*, *Swimming for Life*, and *Parent and Baby* enjoyed their long-term successes because of the financial backing from sponsors.

Sponsoring companies had a number of reasons for selecting swimming. First, the sport, thanks to the ASA's effective supervision of competitions and insistence on the efficient management of galas, had the image of having coherence. Secondly, ASA laws ensured that swimming was without the taint of corrupt practice through the use of drugs to enhance performance or corrupt verdicts to sustain record achievements.

Thirdly, ASA concerns covered swimming at all levels of ability and for all age groups. The Association was vigilant in its emphasis on the importance of swimming for physical education and in its contribution to the maintenance of health. Fourth, the ASA gave sponsors access to a very large part of the public. Thus, companies could expect that expenditures from their advertising budgets could be justified to their accountants and shareholders.

Advertising and sponsorship became of increasing importance for the success of many ASA campaigns and competitions throughout the 1970s and 1980s. The beginnings of the decline

Trophies and sponsorship. The Optrex award catches the eye.

in sponsorship can be located in the late 1980s. The specific reasons why companies ceased to sponsor swimming varied from competition from other sports or other activities, alterations of company policies for budgets for advertising or good causes and even going out of business. The Association always appreciated

Adrian Moorhouse promoted ASA swimming awards. Here he presented David Hayton-Hill of Grantham with his certificate. The sponsors had their logo prominently displayed.

119

sponsorship as can be seen in the regular acknowledgement of sponsoring companies in *Annual Reports*.

The list in the *Annual Reports* understated the level of sponsorship for swimming in that it only showed companies and organisations which supported national activities and excluded sponsorships of particular events at District, county or club level. Sponsorship enabled the expansion of many activities although some tensions had to be managed. These were addressed by the Sports Council in *Sport in the Nineties - New Horizons*. Commercial supporters usually wanted rapid returns for themselves, which encouraged them to have short-term market-led goals. Public bodies which provided grants expected greater accountability for funding. The recognition of such pressures made it essential to develop the capability of generating the Association's own income from subscriptions or, increasingly, through its own commercial enterprises.

One of these enterprises was the *Swimming Times* purchased in 1971. The magazine itself now had to sell advertising space in order to meet the costs of publication. Improvements in printing technology raised the expectations of both advertisers and the public for more photographs and, that some of these should be in full-colour. This in turn appealed to advertisers who saw advantages in well-printed colour publicity for their products.

The *Annual Report* of 1975 showed the first grant from the Sports Council in the International Account. This grant enabled the ASA to support preparatory training and to meet some of the expenses of entering international competitions. This money arrived most opportunely since 1975 was the year when inflation reached around 25%. In each year since that date, grants from the Sports Council have enabled swimming activities to be sustained in ways which would have been impossible otherwise. By 1993 the annual support from the Sports Council was a little over £150,000.

In 1979 the *Annual Report* mentioned the support given to 65 swimmers in all disciplines by the Sports Aid Foundation. These grants amounting to £36,295 assisted in meeting the costs of training and helped to remove competitors' anxieties about finance. In every year after 1979 the ASA was in a position to acknowledge the help given by the Foundation.

The Foundation for Sport and the Arts set up in 1991 has become an important supporter of swimming. Its grants were directed towards meeting some of the costs for preparing for major competitions such as the Olympic Games in 1992.

The ASA provided local clubs, county and District associations with advice about campaigning for finance to provide and equip swimming pools. Their opportunities to further these aims grew when the law changed permitting local authorities to licence local lotteries. One of the experiments in fund raising was the ASA Lottery of 1977. The *Annual Report* for 1978 noted that this had not been very successful and changes were introduced to improve its operation. However, the lottery generated even less revenue in 1979. By 1981 it ceased to contribute significantly to the Association's income and was discontinued.

ASA Enterprises was founded as a separate, wholly owned company in May 1982 with a nominal capital of £500. This initiative undoubtedly owed much to the efforts of the Honorary Treasurer, Alfred Turner, in his Presidential year. The purpose of the company was to supply goods and services related to swimming. It sold ASA publications and undertook vigorous promotions of a wide range of personal equipment for swimmers, pool side officials and helpers. In 1989, for example, the company marketed many items of clothing, watches and timers, and other equipment. Among the popular items available in 1994 were scarves, sweatshirts, ASA and GB ties, key fobs, and ASA pin badges. The company also handled the Association's Awards Scheme.

Promoting and protecting swimming

ASA as a pressure group

Lobbying government departments, local authorities and politicians was no new feature of ASA activity, from the late nineteenth century efforts were made to persuade government to include swimming as part of the schools' curriculum. Vigilance on behalf of swimming remained an important aspect of its work between 1970 and 1994. During this time the Association conducted negotiations with the government on:

• the role of swimming in education. (discussed more fully later in this chapter);

• the implications for health and safety legislation for the conduct of galas and training sessions;

• the consequences of changes in taxation law or administrative decisions.

There are many examples which indicate the range of work undertaken. The first draft proposals in 1985 from the Health and Safety Executive seemed to threaten the viability of important swimming activities. Eventually the ASA in collaboration with other interested parties and the Executive agreed to regulations which safeguarded swimmers, teachers, trainers and coaches whilst swimming clubs did not have to pay for very expensive staffing to deal with emergencies. The financial burdens implicit in budgetary proposals of central government and local authorities called for skilful negotiations to remove the heavy costs for swimming as a reult of the applications of Value Added Tax (VAT). The privatisation of leisure services had important implications for the provision of swimming baths, their maintenance and their staffing. In order to make its case to government on this issue, the Association had to pay for the specialised advice of consultants.

During the 1980s Parliament authorised various changes in public finances for both national and local government. Amongst these were obligations on local authorities to provide their services by inviting tenders from any interested suppliers. In most circumstances the lowest bidder was awarded the contract for a specified period of time. The authority stipulated in the contract performance criteria for the quality and quantity of the service to be provided. The consequences for swimming were most evident in the application of the policy to leisure centres.

Many local authorities had built leisure centres during the 1970s which included swimming pools as part of their facilities. The profitability of each of the available activities had strong commercial attractions. The ASA had the task of warning both

Acknowledgements

The Association is grateful for the generous sponsorship of various companies and organisations which is made in a variety of ways as we illustrate here. Our thanks go to:

Speedo Europe Ltd
Official supplier of swimwear and sportswear to International team members.
Swimming squads.
National Age Group Competitions.

A M Multigraphics
Supplier of photocopiers at national events

Chattem (UK) Ltd.
Suppliers of UltraSwim shampoo

Omega Electronics
Official timekeepers to the ASA

Swim Shop
Support of Registration scheme

Travel Alliance
ASA Swimming Calendar

Optrex
World Challenge

Mycil
National Championships
Junior Development Programme

Swimming Enterprises
ASA Inter County Competition

Styrox UK Ltd.
Aquababes · ASA official Parent & Baby Scheme

Southern Water
Learn to Swim Scheme

Anglian Water
Learn to Swim Scheme

Uncle Ben's
Swimming World Cup
Water Polo Teams
Diving Teams

Kia-Ora
Awards Scheme
National Curriculum
Resource Pack

Sports Council
Grants towards the cost of implementing the ASA Development Plan

Sportsmatch
by matching a sponsor's pound with a sportsmatch pound for new projects at grass roots level.

Maxim
Sports supplements

Foundation for sport and the arts
Grant Aid

And many thanks to you

The ASA Committee is mindful and appreciative of the vast amount of voluntary help and expertise given to the Association to assist in the running of a major national sport. The Association wishes to place on record its thanks to each and every one:

In International Competition - the team staff, technical officials, coaches, medical staff and physiotherapists:

In National and International events at home - the organisers, management committees and officials:

In Education - the teachers, coaches, tutors and all who help at the Residential Schools and on courses:

Local Authorities and Leisure Service Divisions - who provide facilities and administrative help for ASA events:

In Administration - officers, members of technical committees and all who sit on a multitude of working parties:

Last but by no means least, to everyone who assists in any way at Club, County or District level.

Acknowledgements of sponsors of national activities became a regular feature of the Annual Report. This summary showed aspects of support in 1994.

national and local government of the threat this posed to swimming sports. First, it was essential to ensure that teaching children to swim would be possible where schools did not have their own pools. Second, it was necessary to provide conditions in local swimming pools where high standards for training and for coaching promising competitors could be achieved.

Promoting swimming

Finding ways of attracting people to learn to swim had a continuing place in the activities of the ASA. The *Annual Reports* recorded efforts to alert and to encourage the public. Exhibitions were organised by the Public Relations Committee in collaboration with a wide variety of bodies, including the Duke of Edinburgh's award scheme, National Water Safety Conference, and the International Boat Show. During 1971 the ASA was associated with the Royal National Lifeboat Institution's sponsored swim. During the years between 1971 and 1994 successive campaigns were developed, often in association with sponsors. However, the emphasis increased on the *Parent and Baby* group and in making swimming accessible in all schools as part of the physical education curriculum.

Co-operation with the RLSS remained one of the hall marks of the history of the ASA. For example, in 1974 the Association launched *Learn to Save a Life in 1974.* The virtue of being able to save a life, including the swimmer's own, has been continually emphasised since the late nineteenth century. Examples of the campaigns to encourage non swimmers to learn included:

1   In 1972 the National Water Safety Committee of the Royal Society for the Prevention of Accidents (RoSPA) jointly with the ASA organised a national *Learn to Swim* campaign.

2   Each year the Public Relations Committee produced promotion materials with the objective on encouraging members of the public to learn to swim.

A new dynamism coincided with the launch of the *Swimfit* campaign aimed at improving the general health of all age-groups in the population. Derek Stubbs, who became Director of Swimming in 1986, was responsible for the inauguration of the *Swimfit* campaign which began in 1989. Its purposes were to point out to the general public the benefits of swimming as exercise for good health, and to raise money through the enjoyment of swimming for both the ASA Education Fund and for a national charity. The campaign depended on the co-operation of local authorities, leisure centres and swimming clubs to make facilities readily available. One of the important developments was the involvement of General Practitioners who referred patients to undertake swimming in order to improve their fitness. The first area to adopt this scheme was Dorset.

During the 1990s the ASA formulated its first quadrennial development plan so that tactics fitted into strategy. The day-to-day decisions had to conform to workable longer term policies. Although polices had to allow for some flexibility in detail the overall aims need to be well understood. Thus achieving financial strength remained essential and to this end the ASA sought support from its own awards scheme, sponsors, and from its *Swimfit* campaigns. The prestige associated with international competition could also be used by the association to enhance the interest

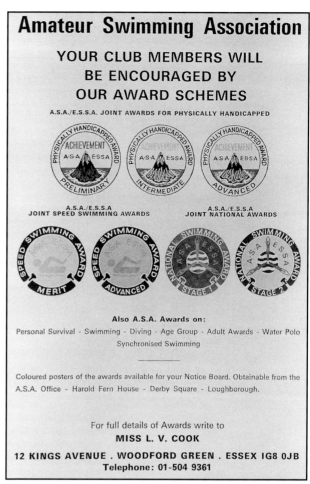

Above and right: Badges available in 1978 for Awards available from the ASA.

in less glamorous swimming activities. With the same end in view, the 1993 ASA accounts show that it had become a formal shareholder in Crystal Palace Sports and Leisure Ltd., the company which owned and managed the large sports facility based in south London.

Awards scheme

The ASA Distribution Centre at Redditch, established in October 1991 inherited an impressive legacy from Lily Cook. She retired in September 1991 having completed 32 years service with the ASA. During her career Lily Cook had organised the despatch of 15,450,768 badges and nearly 650,000 certificates from her base in Woodford Green, Essex. The new Centre operated as part of ASA Enterprises under the management of Hamilton Bland. His credentials included swimming for Loughborough Colleges teams in the 1960s, serving as a National Technical Officer, being the first salaried swimming coach at Coventry in the 1970s, and commentating on swimming for the BBC over many years. His expertise and advice on building swimming pools was continually put to good effect. His task in 1991 was to manage the rapidly expanding ASA Enterprises, by creating modern facilities, and by training a dedicated staff to utilise the latest computerised distribution methods for the dispatch of awards. Such an operation offered the ASA the advantages of increasing its regular disposable income from the fees earned.

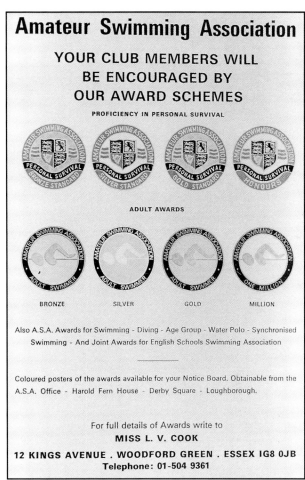

Hamilton Bland beside the Swimming Awards Scheme display mounted for the ASA Council in 1993.

The ASA encouraged swimming for all ages as the mother and baby scheme demonstrated. Above: in 1980 the Dairy Milk logo of the sponsors, Cadbury, was prominent on floats used by babies for gaining confidence. Bottom: Peaudouce became the sponsors in 1988.

Swimming for various age groups

The ASA education programme included efforts to foster familiarity with water amongst very young children. From the early 1970s there had been a scheme to encourage swimming for the *Under Fives*. Such activities required support at pools all over the country and appropriate training for instructors. The success of this initiative depended every year on adequate finance.

There is no question that sponsorship had a crucial role in making the parent and baby scheme possible. During the 1970s and part of the 1980s Savlon provided this support. In 1981 Savlon also helped to promote a seminar on *Parent and Baby* at the Crystal Palace National Swimming Centre, chaired by Dr Bleasdale. This was extended by encouraging the under fives with the *Savlon Water Baby Award Scheme*. The programme continued during the 1980s with growing annual participation until Savlon ended its support in 1986. Peaudouce took up the initiative and introduced the *'Water baby of the Year'* competition in 1987. In 1991 Styrox UK Ltd became the sponsors of the ASA's Parent and Baby scheme with the title of *Aquababes*.

During the 1970s the National Age Group competition also attracted sponsorship. In 1978, for example, the ESSO company supported what had become the Association's largest competition which was held at Coventry.

Masters Swimming was developed in the United States of America and spread to Europe during the 1970s. The term described competitive swimming for people more than twenty five years of age and included men and women. Until its introduction, many swimmers had ceased to involve themselves in the sport they had once enjoyed, possibly because they no longer saw themselves as strong competitors once they had reached their early twenties. As a consequence there had been a serious loss of experienced and committed practitioners. It was from the older people that clubs looked to recruit their dedicated officials and helpers. In England, the Association approved the establishment of its first Masters competitions in 1981.

Events of 100 metres were arranged in each stroke and an individual medley for men in the age groups younger than 45 years and for women younger than 39 years. For older men and women the distance was reduced to 50 metres. In addition, there was a 400 metres race open to all groups with winners declared from each age-group. The masters programme offered an opportunity for enthusiastic swimmers to compete in their own age groups with every likelihood of achieving success.

The costume manufacturers, Arena, sponsored the Master Swimmers programme. On the dais were Bobbie McGregor, David Wilkie and Colin Cunningham.

In 1984 Gresham Life sponsored the London Masters Open Swim Meet. Mr and Mrs Cherriman received a portable television set from Nigel Peck, Wimbledon Branch manager, watched by John Gordon, coach and hon. secretary of the Spencer Swim team who promoted the match.

In 1985 the Sun Life Assurance company presented a cheque to Harold Hassall to sponsor the National and District Masters events in England.

Table 4.1: Age Grouping for Masters Competitions

Men	Women
25 - 29	25 - 29
30 - 34	30 - 35
35 - 39	35 - 39
40 - 44	40 - 49
45 - 49	50 -59
50 - 54	60 and older
55 - 59	
60 and older	

Masters swimmers gave support to their clubs and in turn received the rewards of companionship as well as competition. Some high performers received support from their clubs to enable them to compete in international events. The first World Masters Championships were held in Japan in 1986 and in 1987 the first European Masters Championships took place.

Swimming events

The role of the ASA as law-maker and umbrella organisation in promoting swimming events was well established before 1970. From 1970 to 1994 this traditional function continued with increasing numbers of events crowding the calendar which aimed to accommodate all the activities of clubs, counties, and Districts. The role of the ASA was to try to resolve conflicts of timetable interests and, in particular, to protect high level performers and

to balance their competitive swimming between national and international competitions. Such behind-the-scenes activities demanded the talents of diplomats and negotiators of a high order from ASA officials.

Promotional officers

In 1992 Paul Bush became the ASA's Director of Swimming. His remit demanded breadth of support for swimming sports since it included water polo, diving, synchronised swimming as well as competitive racing. Unlike his predecessor, Derek Stubbs, his portfolio covered the discipline of long distance swimming. One of his first tasks was to integrate the pro-grammes for national and international events into a coherent calendar. This was published in 1994 ready for the year 1995. Its purpose was to enable swimmers to plan their training and coaching to the best effect. Thus the calendar defined periods outside the competition structure so that the needs of athletes to recuperate and train were recognised.

Making the best of these and other initiatives depended on the liaison of the five Regional Development Officers with the Districts and their member clubs. The RDOs, all women, were first appointed in 1993. Their work was coordinated and sup-ported by the National Development Manager. To ensure the effective implementation of policies, the ASA management con-tributed directly to the work of the Technical Committees which oversaw the swimming disciplines.

Regional Development Officers appointed during 1993. Their tasks reflected the policies of the ASA for which the titles NTO or NDO were no longer appropriate. Left to right: Lynn Hogarth, Pippa Jones, Viv Firman, Nora O'Brien and Jane Gorst.

Paul Bush, Director of Swimming from 1993 to 1996.

Alan Donlan, Honorary Secretary of the ASA's Education Committee from 1973 and Secretary of the Swimming Times Company.

In 1982 Duncan Goodhew met a penguin with some young learners as part of the Penguin Learn to Swim scheme.

Education

The ASA maintained a strong concern that swimming should form part of physical education for all. When, in 1973, Harold Fern House was opened officially, the President of the ASA reported that just over half of the population could swim. Improving the participation of people in swimming had to remain a priority. ASA publications encouraged the teaching of beginners of all ages. Thus the *Swimming Times* during the years between 1970 and 1994 carried articles about teaching innovations for beginners and arguments about which styles were appropriate for the novice in the pool. However, it was lobbying concerning the creation of the National Curriculum during the later 1980s that gave the best hope for ensuring that swimming was adopted by all schools. The ASA worked closely with the RLSS and ESSA in securing these aims. The culmination of these efforts came with the requirement that all schools following the National Curriculum had to teach swimming as a compulsory subject from 1 August 1994.

A *'pool for every school'* was the dream expressed frequently during the 1960s and in the early 1970s. There is no record of the extent to which the dream was realised, although many school pools were built. The economic climate during the early 1970s turned much more gloomy: massive rises in oil prices in 1973 and in 1974 had severe consequences for the national economy and hence governments had to review their priorities of essential pub-

Joanne Atkinson was one of the champions in the ESSA competition of 1975.

The Penguin Learn to Swim scheme, was sponsored by Associated Biscuits Company which made presentations to the Shipcote Swimming Pool Class in Gateshead. (Copyright: Gateshead Metropolitan Borough)

lic expenditure. The national balance of payments had deficits which increased rapidly as inflation mounted. Although pool building for schools almost ceased, the interest in swimming amongst the young was still promoted as vigorously as possible.

The ASA developed its educational activities in several ways. The main policy-making body was the Education Committee which oversaw major innovations. This committee worked closely with ESSA, and communicated with many clubs and swimming teachers and coaches through the *Swimming Times*. Some contact was made through the Technical and Development Officers who had regular contacts with Districts, counties and individual clubs. The Association had invaluable direct contacts with all *swimming schools* through its awards schemes. In addition the possibilities of lobbying the government or local authorities were never ignored.

The ASA carried out its advocacy of swimming education in national forums first in the Central Council for Physical Recreation, and in the Sports Council and subsequently also in the National Council for Physical Education. The patient affirmations of the role of swimming had their fruits, in the provision of funding and by ensuring that the government and its advisers could not ignore the importance of swimming in physical education.

When the firm decision had been made to include swimming as a compulsory subject in schools, the ASA's Education Department prepared a resource pack to provide the necessary support. This pack was launched at the Savoy in London on 1

June 1993, just over a year before the National Curriculum became compulsory. Duncan Goodhew, the Olympic Gold Medalist, gave the project his strong endorsement. This was undoubtedly a triumph after more than a century of campaigning. It marked the inauguration of closer contacts between the ASA and schools throughout the country. The ASA had achieved another first in being the first sport's governing body to have provided a comprehensive teaching programme for schools.

In many respects the importance of the ASA in education lay in its sustained efforts to improve the quality of the swimming knowledge and techniques. The Association stands out in the history of all sports organisations for its evolution and scale of education programmes. This culminated in September 1994 with the inauguration of the National Vocational Qualifications for swimming which had received recognition by the Department for Education. It was a demonstration of the quality of the ASA system which had coherence, thoroughness and competence, giving it unique status amongst British sports. To reach this position the ASA had been prepared to invest in people. It had recognised the importance of blending the services which professional specialists and organisation can provide to support its very large number of volunteer teachers and coaches.

The Martin Report of 1970 had stressed the importance of education. This gave pointers about how the ASA should proceed and resulted in the formation of ISTC whose main purpose was to keep coaches and teachers abreast of current knowledge once they had completed their formal qualifications.

The development of swimming for the disabled had an interesting history. Society had ignored the plight of those of the disabled who were interested in sport. Swimming had formed a part of the treatment for some injuries and disabilities but within the confines of special baths at spas or in hospitals. These medical uses of water were well established. There was no expectation that the disabled could enjoy exercise in a sporting context with all the attractive social life associated with such activities. The development of this type of swimming had to await the later years of the 1960s when the demands of the disabled were highlighted in many spheres of life. The general public, the governing bodies of sports, and the providers of sports facilities were then ready to give support.

Disabled swimmers had received some support from member clubs which had organised swimming for children but usually in the context of a wholly separate activity. The first substantial support from the ASA, together with ESSA, came in 1967 when they established a joint awards scheme for the physically handicapped. Awareness of changes in the provision for the disabled led to the appointment in 1975 of Mrs S. Dobie as the ASA's Senior National Development Officer for the Disabled. This initiative was made possible by central government grants to pay the salary. It coincided with the reshaping of the Association's work in the Districts by redefinition of the task of Technical Officers as Development Officers. Essentially this broadened the scope of the work by laying a greater emphasis on innovations and promoting best practice. One of the early demands on Mrs Dobie was to encourage and assist with the *Olympiad for the Disabled* in 1976. Miss S.R. Green took over in 1979 and she continued in office until 1982. She had the opportunity of contributing to the

Swimming as part of life. In 1973 Mrs Ada Osbourne, then 82 years of age, swam 70 lengths (a mile) in a sponsored swim on behalf of the Gravesend Swimming Club. She qualified as a swimming teacher twenty years before and taught many hundreds of people to swim.

Anglian Water sponsored the Learn to Swim Scheme. Mark Foster (extreme left of front row), 'the world's fastest man in water', gave his support at a lesson

publicity which focused on the United Nations designated Year of the Disabled in 1981. In 1979 the ASA had introduced its pilot scheme for awards to those who qualified as teachers of swimming to the disabled. In the *Swimming Times* of 1979 Sara Green wrote an appeal for volunteers under the ISTC logo, *'Helping the Disabled'*. The Association had no suitable applicant for the post when she resigned in 1982. The post remained vacant until the appointment of Paul Barber as National Development Officer for the Disabled for 1985 and for 1986, after which the ASA reorganised its development work.

ESSA had been reformed with a new constitutional framework in 1950. Its continuing link with the ASA was much valued. The development of the ASA's efforts to ensure that every child became a swimmer depended for its effectiveness in gaining support from the Department of Education and Science (by 1994 known as the Department for Education) and from local education authorities and especially from the schools. Among the important aspects of the ASA and ESSA collaboration was that of securing sponsorship for the award schemes for children learning to swim, and for their progression to achieve good performances. Saving life, skills in diving, synchronised swimming and racing formed diverse parts of the programme.

The ASA sought to publicise ways of organising school swimming clubs and how these could be linked with local clubs. The importance of coaching for the more advanced pupils received impetus from the National Coaching Foundation and there is evi-

The boys of Highgate Junior School were presented with the Dolphin Trophy, sponsored by Coca Cola Company, by Colin Cunningham (right) who accompanied Barbara Mahony.

Wessex Water became sponsors of the Bournemouth Dolphins in 1990. The adults (from left to right) were Ian Gordon, chairman of the Dolphins, David Reeves, secretary of the ASA, John Eastwood, water resources manager of Wessex Water, and Terry Denison, chief coach of the Great Britain Swimming Team. (Copyright: John Beasley, Bournemouth)

dence that the levels of competitive performances improved. The Youth Sport Trust and National Youth Sports Development Council made possible the establishment of four activities designed to encourage swimming:

1. *Top Play* for imparting skills to the 4-9 years age group.

2. *Water Sports* for teaching water polo and synchro.

3. *Champion Coaching* for the 4-16 age group.

4. *Top Club* for establishing better club structures.

The ASA's campaign for a *pool for every school* did not have priority amongst many local authorities nor independent schools. Nonetheless a number of schools in the independent sector saw the opportunities which sporting prowess offered to them and to those pupils who were athletically gifted. Such developments were not made at the expense of academic performance but formed part of an educational outlook which distinguished them from many other institutions. Millfield School in Somerset adopted the policy of seeking sporting excellence, including swimming, and these ideas were developed rapidly so that by the early 1970s the reputation of the school was nation-wide. Similarly, Kelly College in Devonshire appointed a professional coach and vied with Millfield as a swimming school. Both schools offered special courses for promising swimmers outside of regu-

lar school terms and made good use of their outstanding facilities and expertise. Their advertisements appeared in the *Swimming Times* and their example was followed by other schools including Sedbergh College in 1979.

Universities were relatively slow to develop swimming prior to the 1970s. Many teacher training colleges made little of their swimming facilities and expertise until after 1970. Even then, there were no significant numbers of scholarships or other awards to enable promising swimmers to develop their potential. Instead, some of the leading swimmers chose to move to the United States to take advantage of the much more congenial atmosphere for both education and swimming training.

John Lawton was appointed as the ASA's Director of Education in 1991, charged with giving effect to ideas and to initiatives which had long formed part of the agenda of the Association. He had been an adviser to the Leicestershire Education Authority and was well placed to advance the cause of the ASA in schools. John Lawton made an important contribution to the negotiations which ensured that swimming became compulsory within the National School Curriculum and to the Final Report of the Physical Education Working Group of 1991 which set out the requirements in the Key Stages 1 to 3.

Coaching and training

Coaching and training swimmers in competitive swimming underwent many changes. The consequences of some of these can be seen in the improved times of leading athletes in all levels of swimming during the quarter century after 1970.

The coaches and trainers received systematic instruction and explanation of concepts derived from physiology, nutrition, psychology, medicine. They also learned how to apply such information to assist individual swimmers and teams in order to make the most of their abilities.

The use of knowledge on a systematic, scientific basis received strong support from amongst coaches and trainers of leading competitive nations. English practices were influenced by the findings of sports scientists in Britain and overseas. Particular attention was paid to the methods adopted in north America. The *Swimming Times* carried many reports from English coaches who had visited Canada and the United States of America. For example, the Institute of Swimming Teachers and Coaches (ISTC) drew attention to the successes of Doc Councilman, one of the

John Lawton, Director of Education from 1992.

leading swimming experts, whose ideas received much coverage in the *Swimming Times* as well as in publications which originated in the USA. By the later 1970s the impressive performances of the East German swimmers in international matches merited study. The market in ideas became truly international although the use of drugs to enhance swimmers' performances came to overshadow the once totally unsullied reputation of competitive swimming at the highest levels.

Whilst there was a decline in the prejudice against the applications of the findings of the biological, medical and social sciences in the sporting world, these changes occurred unevenly. Thus, it was only in the late 1980s that officially appointed psychologists contributed to the motivation of British swimmers in major competitions. As in many spheres in the wider society, the numbers of women occupying positions as top coaches or in other offices in swimming remained small. Social and legal awareness of harassment, both racial and sexual, grew during the 1980s and 1990s. One aspect of this problem had been met traditionally by appointing chaperones to accompany female competitors. Nonetheless, the potential for harassment existed because of the power vested in coaches who had a crucial influence in the selection of swimmers to enter the highest levels of competition.

High flyers in swimming, as in some branches of athletics, looked overseas for sustained training and coaching. The principal destination for such development was the USA where scholarships and facilities at some colleges and universities had no counterpart in Great Britain. These contacts influenced the ASA in its policy of seeking to ensure that similar expertise and opportunities were developed in Great Britain. This was one of the rea-

The first National Curriculum Resource Pack, prepared by the ASA, was delivered in 1994 to Doris Law, teacher at the Virginia Primary School in London by the Olympic swimmers Adrian Moorhouse and Sharron Davies.

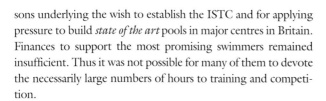

Judy Grinham autographed her display in the Hall of Fame at Fort Lauderdale in Florida, USA, in 1981. Beside her stands Buck Dawson, Executive Director of the Hall of Fame.

The Trustee Savings Bank supported swimming in 1989 and Zara Long had just won the 200 metres individual medley.

sons underlying the wish to establish the ISTC and for applying pressure to build *state of the art* pools in major centres in Britain. Finances to support the most promising swimmers remained insufficient. Thus it was not possible for many of them to devote the necessarily large numbers of hours to training and competition.

One perpetual problem facing all swimmers who wanted pool time for training, was access. This was true for all levels of competitors. The difficulties were recognised and aired repeatedly in ASA meetings. Some improvements in the situation were possible by changes in administrative arrangements at baths, but usually the times made available were *unsocial hours*, that is very early in mornings and in late evenings. Such provisions curtailed training and coaching.

Less conspicuous, but playing its part in the methods available to teachers, trainers and coaches was the introduction of technological innovations. The popularisation of personal computers during the later 1980s made record keeping easier, with possibilities for making rapid use of information about swimmers. In the early 1970s cinematographic or television films were used for demonstrating the techniques of top performers, but it was unusual to record training sessions for coaching individuals. During the later 1980s inexpensive video equipment made possible almost instant feed-back.

Institute of Swimming Teachers and Coaches (ISTC)

The development of the Institute of Swimming Teachers and Coaches was proposed in 1975 by the Association's Assistant Secretary, Brian Relf. Its purpose was to provide '*a comprehensive "after sales" service to ASA qualified teachers and coaches*'. Many of the people who had achieved official qualifications wanted to keep up to date in order to remain effective. The rapid increase in knowledge about the sport demanded more of teachers and coaches than in the past. Such demands had increased further within the recent past. The ISTC was yet another development which had been foreshadowed in the Martin Report. When it was established in 1975 K.B. Martin himself, became chairman of the new institute.

The particular needs of swimming teachers were attracting a great deal of attention during the 1970s. An alternative body, which could be seen as a rival to ISTC had been established in 1976. This was the Swimming Teachers Association (STA) which had reconstructed itself as a corporate association in 1976. The STA offered qualifications to learners, teachers and coaches and competed with the powerful ASA. Shortly before the formation of ISTC the ASA had abortive discussions with the STA about the development of a partnership to represent professionally all swim-

The pressure to raise funds for international competition reached its climax for the Olympics. Lorraine Banks was helped by the Weetabix Adoptasport Scheme for the Seoul Games of 1988.

Young children under instruction from a member of ISTC in 1985 where enjoyment and learning went hand in hand.

Brian Relf, Secretary of ISTC from its formation in 1975.

The ISTC logo, introduced in 1977.

ming teachers, and with the ASA in control of syllabuses and awards. Once established the two organisations went their separate ways.

The British Swimming Coaches Association (BSCA) remained in being and continued to act as a body meeting the professional interests of its members. ISTC enjoyed cordial relations with the BSCA. The latter supported the British Association of National Coaches (BANC), an umbrella organisation, whose aim was to ensure that the needs of coaches in all sports had a voice in discussions and in offering advice to national bodies concerned with sport. In 1990 the BANC became the British Institute of Sports Coaches.

It was decided at the foundation of the ISTC that its Management Committee should have representatives of each of the Sports Council's English regions and from Ireland, Scotland and Wales. Contact with the members was through regional committees which organised meetings and seminars for in-service training, and acted as a channel to pass members' views to the Management Committee. Initially the ASA provided the necessary support using facilities in Harold Fern House until ISTC was able to establish of its own organisation. The ASA agreed that ISTC should be represented on its National Technical Committees because this provided a good means of taking account of the views of ordinary members. Subsequently the ASA Districts included ISTC representatives on their Technical Committees.

By 1977 the ISTC had grown to a membership of 5000 and Brian Relf moved from the post of the Association's Assistant Secretary to the full-time job of Secretary to the Institute. The demands on the organisation increased as did its membership. In 1979 the Royal Life Saving Society's teachers and coaches became eligible for ISTC membership. The work expanded so that in 1983 ISTC moved from Harold Fern House to Lantern House in Loughborough. In 1984 the Institute became a limited company with J.H. Zimmermann as Chairman and Brian Relf as Secretary. After ten years the expansion of the work of the ISTC forced another move, this time to Dawson House in Loughborough.

ISTC initiatives in the education and training of teachers and coaches have taken many forms including those developed to serve the needs of large minorities of swimmers having particular problems. For example, in 1982 the Asthma Swim Group movement, with sponsorship from Fisons, began its work. By 1994 the group had become financially self supporting with a membership of over 300 groups. ISTC also had an increasing international

Ken Martin received a Silver Salver from the ASA as a token of thanks for his many services during half a century. The committee he led produced the 1970 reports 1970 which defined much of the course followed by the ASA until Which Way Forward?

influence as a result of its expertise. It participated in expanding swimming education in Egypt, India, Nigeria, Turkey and the West Indies.

Undoubtedly the most significant innovation of the early 1990s was ISTC's deep involvement with the ASA in formulating education policies in a joint working party. Its report formed the basis for National Vocational Qualifications for teachers and coaches of swimming.

Communications with members took place not only through programmes of meetings and classes but in the columns of the *Swimming Times*. By 1983 the *Swimming Times* lacked space to meet all the needs of the ISTC and so the newsletter *SWIM* was launched. This included technical information and notices of meetings in Regions and Districts. When the *Swimming Times* radically changed its format in 1988 the journal was able to offer ISTC sufficient space to cover all its activities and so *SWIM* was discontinued.

Among the initiatives which involved the Institute was the pressure brought to bear on the ASA and the RLSS to improve the proposals for swimming pool safety made by the Health and Safety Executive (HSE) in 1985. The draft regulations for health and safety proposed restrictions on access to swimming baths which would have reduced sharply the time available to clubs. This arose because the costs for staffing requirements at baths could not have been met on a regular basis by many clubs. After two years of consultations about the practicalities, the final guidelines were published in 1988. These had taken into account many of the recommendations from the ISTC and ASA. Broadly, the concerns of the HSE were also those of RoSPA, RLSS and ASA.

In 1994 the ISTC had a membership of more than 12000 from within the British Isles and from overseas. Members benefited not only from their access to knowledge and techniques but, in Britain, from insurance to cover public liability and personal accident. Members also had access to a wealth of legal, technical and medical advice, essential for the responsible conduct of teaching, training and coaching work. ISTC raised funds to make a number of grants for assisting with research projects relevant to the interests of teachers and coaches. The organisation even offered discount and pension schemes to its membership.

Performance standards, 1970 to 1994

Although much had been learned and applied by those involved in international competitions, improvements were still being sought in the early 1970s. In the *Swimming Times* of August 1973 the then recently appointed GB Coach for Women, Maurice Sly, wrote about the situation as he saw it and what needed to be done. Many swimmers, according to his report, had attitudes towards the training programme best described as indifferent or hostile. Swimmers were said to be unfit on arrival for the course and believed that warming-up swims were totally unnecessary. *'It was generally characteristic for swimmers to completely dissociate the actual swimming regardless of pace with starting, turns and finishing'*. He listed other shortcomings including a great reluctance of most to take part in any mobility exercises before a swim. In summary it was the lack of self-discipline which seemed to be at the root of lack-lustre performances. There can be little doubt that improvements in the performances of out-

Margaret Kelly in action. She represented Great Britain in European Championships, Commonwealth Games, three Olympiads, and World Championships.

Training at swimming clubs became of ever greater importance for top performance. At Beckenham a well-equipped gymnasium was available to members who included such stars as Margaret Kelly.

Table 4.2: Comparison of Men's and Women's performances in National Competitions in 1971 and 1993.

	Men			Women	
	1971	1993		1971	1993
Free style					
100m	0:55.10	0:50.55	100m	1:02.20	0:56.54
200m	2:02.00	1:50.84	200m	2:13.90	2:02.59
400m	4:18.50	3.55.46	400m	4:44.60	4:16.04
Back stroke					
100m	1:02.60	0:55.92	100m	1:10.70	1:03.90
200m	2:15.70	2:01.90	200m	2:30.70	2:14.86
Breast stroke					
100m	1:09.80	1:02.16	100m	1:18.80	1:11.55
200m	2:33.70	2:11.56	200m	2:51.20	2:33.18
Butterfly stroke					
100m	0:58.40	0:55.67	100m	1:10.00	1:03.27
200m	2:10.10	2:02.11	200m	2:37.20	2:17.05
Individual Medley					
200m	2:19.50	2:03.77	200m	2:33.90	2:19.03
400m	4:58.10	4:27.28	400m	5:26.90	4:53.28

standing competitive swimmers between 1970 and 1994 owed much to the ASA's insistence on better coaching and training and to the responses of individual swimmers to this provision. The high performance of the very top competitors came as a result of the general development of swimming skills, of attitudes and from the application of relevant knowledge.

Records of British national competitions in the two years 1971 and 1993 give an impression of the differing standards attained.

The speeds of winners shows major improvements for both men and women. In many events women swam faster in 1993 than the best of the men in 1971. This convergence of performances probably was the outcome of better training, coaching and the motivation of the athletes themselves. This improvement demonstrates the inaccuracy of Maurice Sly's comment in 1973 when he wrote that international comparisons supported his harsh view that '*we are, at present, a second-rate swimming nation and are not likely to improve*'. The improvements owed much to the ASA and its ISTC initiatives.

Medicine and swimming training

The ASA appointed its first medical adviser, Dr Noel Bleasedale, after the Second World War, in 1950, and this represented the recognition, shared with a number of sports organisations of what a good medical adviser might contribute to the enhancement of

the sport. This contribution was not only to the welfare of injured sports people but to the application of scientific advances for the improvement of athletic performance. Effective use and development of knowledge required research into sporting activities. In addition it no longer seemed appropriate to rely on coaches who may have first aid knowledge but no deeper understanding of anatomy, physiology and nutrition. By 1970 the ASA had received much valuable advice from Dr Noel Bleasdale who worked almost until the end of his life on behalf of the Association. In 1964 he had been a founder member, and then Honorary Secretary of the ASA Scientific Committee, a post he held from 1968 until 1985 when he retired. Sadly, he died only a few months later. As the first medical adviser, Dr Bleasedale had made a particularly important contribution to all aspects of the relationship of medicine and swimming and his contributions benefited swimmer at all levels.

When the ASA revised its Swimming Challenge and Personal Survival awards in 1985 the opportunity was taken to ensure that the new conditions took account of recent physiological discoveries relating to the way body heat loss occurred in cool or cold water. The new test alerted participants to the necessity of keeping the body warm for as long as possible during prolonged exposure. Among the innovations was advice on techniques which could minimise the onset of hypothermia and death.

One of the consequences of the development of sports science and medicine was the acceptance by the ASA, and the ASFGB, that the support for international teams ought to include members with specific medical knowledge. The first competitions to benefit from this were those held in 1976. The British competitors at the Montreal Olympiad had Dr Douglas McIntyre as their assistant manager and Tony Power as their physiotherapist. There was never any suggestion that coaches who had attended earlier competitions ignored medical issues. It was more a recognition of changing circumstances and the need to offer British teams a level of specialist support comparable to that provided for other leading international competitors.

The recognition of the needs of competitors in stressful international events led to a reappraisal of the support given to their athletes by leading swimming nations. As a consequence, the British swimmers at the 1992 Olympic Games at Barcelona had four medical staff in attendance: a doctor, two physiotherapists and a psychologist. The selection of a psychologist was the result of much research undertaken in the United States, and elsewhere, concerning the importance of fostering the *'will to win'* . There was a need for competitors to be able cope with the very great public attention which leading sports people could experience as a part of the intense competition where national prestige was perceived to be at stake.

Ideas about the relationship of nutrition to athletic performance had had a comparatively short history. In their book *Swimming* published in 1890, Sinclair and Henry summarised the opinions of contemporaries and themselves. They suggested no specific diet, only that it was unwise to eat a *'hearty meal'* before entering the water. Montague Holbein, writing in 1903 in his book also called *Swimming*, claimed that his regime for training himself as a swimmer was to abstain from tobacco and to drink alcohol seldom. Otherwise, almost every Victorian book about swimming ignored the subject of nutrition. There was some comment about the best way of reviving swimmers after their exertions, and there were advertisements for *drinks as food*. One of the earliest in a swimming publication was placed by the Bovril company in the 1890s.

Awareness of nutritional issues amongst the general public was not very great, to judge from the swimming books and magazines available during the first half of the twentieth century. There were some theories about diets, food, drinks and meal composition. However, the arguments for most of them depended on premises whose validity depended solely on vigorous assertion. What was supposed to happen to the body, as a result of consuming the foods and drink recommended, was explained in terms of beliefs. Basic research about the composition of nutrients, and how the human body made use of them, lagged far behind the claims of publicists and advertisers.

Austin Rawlinson recalled the dietary regime followed by himself and his fellow British swimmers at the Paris Olympics in 1924. In essence he ate what he assumed would give him energy, stamina and strength. This approach rested on commonly held attitudes that meals should comprise a wide range of foodstuffs. Meat, in particular, had prestige in such diets. Austin Rawlinson also recollected that achievements of athletes, and others, who ate meat and meat products in quantity and of good quality, were claimed to be self-evident justification for such regimes.

Advances in the sciences of biochemistry, microbiology and physiology in the half century since 1945 brought about many changes in medical education. Innovations entered the practice of medicine more rapidly than in any previous period. Since about 1970 the relationship of nutrition and health became of increasing interest to the general public. The press carried many articles and advertisements for dietary systems associated with fitness and beauty. The government took steps during the 1980s to provide accurate information about diet. It became clear that some of proprietary schemes could be dangerous to the public and that some made unverified claims. The UK's National Advisory Committee on Nutrition Education (NACNE) produced its first comprehensive Report in 1983. This rested on a range of studies of the relationship of diet to various illnesses related to obesity, the heart and circulation, and diabetes. Such findings were reiterated in a further report published in 1993.

In essence the diet for healthy living stressed the necessity of a balanced intake of foods and drink. Many people ate too much fat, sugar and meat and too little bread, pasta, fresh fruit and vegetables and fish. The dietary changes advocated in the studies suggested that people should choose to eat for healthy living. Many choices of food and drink contained the necessary vitamins, trace elements and fibre essential for the body to function effectively. People with differing life styles on account of age. gender, or activities, needed to ensure that they had enough each day to keep well. Those who followed athletic activities were recommended to select plenty of carbohydrates to produce energy, and to limit intakes of fat and protein to the quantities appropriate for maintaining the mind and body in good condition.

The ASA's medical advisers and others directly concerned with the well-being of swimmers wrote in the *Swimming Times* about nutrition. Medical advisers also contributed to training programmes for swimmers, coaches and teachers and did much to alter their eating and drinking habits. Regular articles reinforced the spread of the information about good nutrition and its close relationship to maintaining health and performance for readers at all levels of achievement. In January, 1967, S. Leon Walkden wrote on 'Eat, Drink and be First' and, in the February issue of the *Swimming Times* , Dr Bleasdale discussed 'Iron deficiency in athletes'. In 1970 Norman Sarsfield's 'Nutrition for Swimmers' was on the same page as a special reader's offer for Nutrament, a proprietary food. An article by M.H. Arnold entitled 'Endurance and Nutrition' was accompanied by an advertisement from Dectrosol (glucose tablets) since glucose was argued to be as a rapid provider of energy to athletes. As early as 1975 Keith Bagnall wrote in the *Swimming Times* about the purposes of food especially for athletes and swimmers, under the well-chosen title of 'We are what we eat'. His generalisations rested on the then consensus of researchers. Later in the same year the *Swimming Times* reproduced Dorothy MacDonnell's advice on balanced diets and what particular needs active youngsters had in 'Feeding your Family Athlete', which had appeared first in *Sports and Fitness Instructor*. In an interview, *'Chat with a Champion'* in January 1976, Katy Archer, a competitor and a synchronised swimmer, said *'I don't like steak very much'*. She was not only uttering a personal preference but was adding to the increased awareness that for highly demanding sports, it was essential to have food which made energy available rapidly.

Soon after the 1983 NACNE report the *Swimming Times* had a series of articles, in 1984 and 1985, by John Whetton on

'Nutrition for Swimming'. This series stressed the importance of eating a diet to supply not only energy but to sustain the different functions of the body in order to perform efficiently in competition. ISTC section in August 1986 embodied such concepts in 'Supplements in Sports Nutrition'. Awareness among swimmers of dietary issues prompted a research programme outlined in ISTC section of the magazine for January 1987: 'Nutrition and Sports Performance - A Factual Report'. Direct advice on swimming nutrition had coverage in replies to readers' letters about dietary questions ranging from the feeding appropriate for a young competitor in training, and on the great day of competition to the suitability of a vegetarian diet.

As late as October 1986 Maurice Sly commented in the *Swimming Times* that many Olympic competitors seemed reluctant to accept and follow the advice of experts. Some justification for this view was evident in the Barcelona Olympics when some competitors did less well than anticipated, possibly because of being de-hydrated in the heat.

Swimming as an exercise to maintain health for people of all ages received continued support in the period under discussion. Understanding health rather than illness became of greater consequence for the government, the medical professionals and educationalists. Evidence about the efficient and effective performance of bodies grew as a result of the studies about nutrition, the causes of illnesses and the factors contributing to *good quality of life*.

Some of the initiatives for studying health and exercise arose from the increasing length of life which became evident during the last quarter of the twentieth century. All the richer nations have had similar experiences and the enjoyment of longer life has included recognising the need to sustain health, both physical and mental. Swimming sought to reach the ageing population by its *Swim-fit* campaigns and by promoting the Masters' programmes. Even without competitive events the attendance censuses for leisure centres showed that many of the elderly enjoyed swimming as a recreation. Their numbers increased to the extent that they formed the largest group of swimming pool users. There were growing numbers of elderly people who had greater leisure time, some of it enforced or chosen by early retirement from full-time work. The exercise of swimming itself attracted some people who found other activities too demanding on their bodies or even too expensive. Swimming had social advantages: it might be either companionable or solo at the whim of the swimmer.

The attractions of swimming were often said to include the safety as well as the healthiness of the sport. The Association of British Insurers in 1995 published data showing the number of injuries sustained by participants. Swimming came at the bottom of this table of twelve major sporting activities. It indicated that for every 1000 participants only 8 swimmers sustained injury whereas Rugby headed the list of sports with 145.

Although swimming remained free from severe injuries, diving and water polo both presented problems for competitors from time to time. Most athletes could suffer from great exertion to muscles and tendons subjected to continuous stress. An article in the *Swimming Times* in 1982 drew attention to the issues of sports medicine in relation to the injuries of swimmers. During the 1980s much thought was given to the special treatment needed for sports injuries as distinct from other types of injury. This often aroused controversy. Although some of the debates owed much to the hidden arguments about the allocation of resources within the National Health Service, there were concerns that those involved in sport might have privileged treatment compared with the requirements of other patients.

Since 1970 many advances in medical knowledge had importance in educating the public about contracting certain diseases in swimming pools and how to cope with some illness and injuries. Advances in understanding how diseases were transmitted, what kinds of exercise harm damaged bodies, and how some physical conditions could be managed, have each led to significant changes of practice. Transmission of illness has been, for many decades, a source of anxiety for people meeting and sharing facilities. For example, as early as 1967 the *Swimming Times* printed a letter about the treatment of verrucae suggesting that prevention required simple hygiene procedures by all pool users. Such advice was reiterated in 1982. More serious was the emergence in the early 1980s of anxieties about the transmission of AIDS. Again, the advice was that transmission of the disease was not possible providing the basic care rules about hygiene and bleeding wounds in the waters of pools were followed.

Swimming as an exercise for asthmatics became of interest to the *Swimming Times* during the 1980s, a period when various athletes who suffered from the condition, performed outstandingly well, as for example, the distance runner, Steve Ovett. In 1982, Peter Stringer, of the pharmaceutical division of Fisons, in 'Swimming for Asthmatics', advocated that asthmatic children should learn to swim at the age of 4 or 5 years as part of their education and that this exercise provided valuable techniques in combating some aspects of the illness. In the following year ISTC and Fisons organised a seminar at Leicester to demonstrate and answer some of the questions relevant to encouraging asthmatics to swim. By 1990 anxieties still arose amongst asthmatics about the use of inhalers and the attitude of the ASA towards competitors. In the *Swimming Times* the advice usually given by medical advisers was repeated with the caution that, if an inhaler contained isoprenalin, efforts should be made to find an alternative because this substance was a banned drug within competitive sport.

Uses and abuses of drugs

Victorian swimmers received little advice about uses and abuses of drugs other than in the context of attitudes found in society in general. Thus, evangelical teachings condemned any drug taking which diminished the responsibility of the individual for his behaviour. Evangelicals supported the temperance movement which conducted campaigns against alcohol consumption. There was also an associated hostility to the consumption of tobacco or any other drugs which modified perception. The idea that drugs could improve athletic performance was not discussed. It was not until 1920 that legislation made a specific range of substances illegal.

Ever more sophisticated analysis of chemicals with medicinal properties took place during the middle and later years of the twentieth century. The significance of some of the discoveries became apparent when it was found that some drugs, which relieved pain or improved nervous and muscular responses, could be used by athletes to enhance their performance. Such a development became apparent during the 1960s when steroids became available to those who wanted to increase muscle power. Such developments as part of training regimes gave physical advantages to competitors. Their capability increased beyond the innate limits imposed by their own bodies. The long term effects of these drugs were either ignored or minimised for the short-term advantage of a good athletic performance. There was little doubt that the use of drugs gave unfair advantage to competitors. The ASA carried out its first drug tests on competitiors at Darlington in 1981. The suspected cynical abuse of these materials to enhance performance by some countries created a climate in which drug testing became part of national and international competition.

In 1984 the Olympic movement took the important decision to ban the use of drugs to enhance performance in all events. This decision raised the problems of monitoring athletes so that any cheating could be detected and minimised. The ASA and FINA adopted similar laws relating to drug use for the first time in 1984. The evidence suggests that swimming might have suffered less than athletics from abuse. However, there remains the possibility that the records achieved in some international competitions owed much to the use of drugs.

Publicity

By the middle of the twentieth century all major sports found that publicity was essential to maintain or increase public awareness and support. By the 1970s swimming already had an image of being clean and active. It was recognised as important to maintain this image and to gain public interest as often as possible.

The Association's Public Relations Committee had commissioned various books and pamphlets, and by 1970, its publicity and display materials were available through the Districts for exhibitions, displays, conferences, fetes and other events. By 1971 the ASA publications included: *The Teaching of Swimming*; H.N. Bleasdale and E.H. Kendall, *Anatomy and Physiology for Swimming Coaches;* N.W. Sarsfield, *Diving Instruction;* as well as a range of items about organising swimming clubs, swimming galas, swimming pools, the rules of swimming sports, and forms and certificates for club use. There were also guides on the various disciplines such as diving, synchro and water polo and there were pamphlets on drugs in sport and AIDS. The *Swimmers Diary* contained information vital to all club officials and others closely involved in the running of swimming. The ASA also approved some publications from sources other than its own, most notably in the 1990s, films, film loops and video-cassettes produced for hire from D.S. Information Systems.

Swimming Times

The ASA purchased the *Swimming Times* in 1970. Once the magazine became a publication of the Association magazine it was intended to continue the traditions of reporting the activities of the five Districts, the achievements of competitors in national and international events, and the main decisions of the ASA Council with various articles intended to inform, to instruct or to entertain readers. The development of the magazine, for which

The ASA joined with Butlins to promote swimming and offered a range of activities to the purposeful holiday-maker.

*Logo of the Swimming Times used
from 1956 until 1970.*

the ASA had paid £9000, depended upon increasing the circulation. This necessitiated being responsive to a diverse readership whose concerns ranged from seeing their own achievements recorded, to wanting to learn more about swimming without the need for searching in specialised libraries or journals.

The magazine was in competition with other popular sports publications. These were often more general in their coverage and were adopting layouts using more photographs and colour printing in order to attract readers. Advertisers too wanted to reach as large a market as possible with eyecatching advertisements. In the context of this competition the *Swimming Times*

was stimulated to keep up-to-date with printing and presentation techniques.

Captain Cummins had introduced colour for covers much earlier, using coloured card for cover and a contrasting coloured ink, but there were few illustrations in colour until the 1960s. In the 1970 issues there were a few full-colour covers for some summer numbers but these were financed by Speedo, the costume maker. However, the body of the magazine remained in black and white including advertisements. Under the new ownership Kelvin Juba became editor in January 1971. By 1972 there were some colourful innovations for some of the headings. Making more of pictures was difficult because these cost money both for the methods of printing and for the costs of photographers. Some efforts to divert readers in 1972 included a regular feature called *'Bird's Eye View'* using the photographs taken by Tony Duffy. These were pin-ups of female swimmers with captions such as *'And now .... for something completely different .....'*. From January 1973 that particular feature disappeared and in February of that year Richard Brown became editor. He was able to increase the range of reporting in response to the growth of more activities such as Age Groups and Masters. Beside writing a substantial part of each issue, chasing contributors and dealing with printers, the editor was himself the photographer at many of the events. One of his innovations was to number the pages of each month's issue separately, instead of sequentially through the annual volume.

David Wilkie took part in the Kellogg's Breakfast Swims in 1988 and this encouraged young people to participate in the sport.

Richard Brown edited the Swimming Times until 1987. His period of office spanned major developments both in the financing and the format of the magazine. In his first four years rapid inflation curtailed dreams of expansion or of any significant innovations of layout. The task was to maintain the magazine as the voice of swimming. This was how Cummins had conceived the magazine and the editorial notice in each issue acknowledged the debt to him as the 1923 founder. However, as the ASA broadened its basis of finance and activities the magazine faced challenges and seized new opportunities. One of the indicators of its success was that of increases of circulation. The Audit Bureau of Circulations showed the average sale of issues in 1971 numbered 8240. The comparable figure for 1995 was 18,000.

When the ASA established the ISTC it needed a means of reaching these members on a regular basis. The *Swimming Times* incorporated a regular section devoted to the interests of members of the Institute and gained in circulation thereby. In April 1976 the first chairman of ISTC, K.B. Martin, contributed the first article under the heading of 'Institute of Swimming Teachers and Coaches'. It was more than a year before its logo adorned its leading page. The section increased in size and contributions ranged from reports on organisational matters and notices of meetings, to series on major topics of importance, such as teaching babies to swim and evaluations of particular coaching techniques.

The *Swimming Times* always gave reports on sponsorship deals. For example, in 1976 the Yorkshire Bank provided funds to double the number of swimmers in the National Swim Squad. The bank itself benefited from a full page advertisement on the page facing the appropriate news item.

In 1987 Richard Brown persuaded the *Swimming Times* management that the A5 size page format ought to be replaced by the larger A4. The advantages from a technical standpoint were considerable and gave more scope for varied page layouts, better displays of photographs and other graphic illustrations. The subsequent format no longer fitted into an overcoat pocket so easily, which was the original aim, but the magazine's visual impact was greatly improved.

When 'Dickie' Brown relinquished the post of editor in April 1987 he was succeeded, as acting editor, by Alexander T.G. Cave, who had worked for some years as assistant editor. In 1988 Douglas Pyecroft became editor but he was succeeded by Karren Glendenning who served until the summer of 1994. On her arrival ISTC formally reincorporated its magazine *Swim* within the *Swimming Times*. This had the advantage of broadening the readership still more. Peter Hassall was appointed editor in 1994.

Other regular publications

In 1970 the *Annual Accounts* ceased to form part of the *Handbook* and became a separate distinctive publication. In 1988 the format of the accounts was changed to correspond with the changed financial organisation of the ASA and in 1989 and in subsequent years the *Annual Report* and the *Financial Statement* were published separately.

The larger part of the *Handbook* always contained the separate handbooks for each of the five Districts as edited by their own

The Directors of the Board of Swimming Times in 1973:
Seated left to right: Richard Brown (Editor), Alf Turner (Chairman) and Norman Sarsfield (Secretary). Standing: left, Ernest Keighley and right, Ernest Warrington.

honorary secretaries. For many years each District Handbook was printed in its own locality and had its own ethos as befitted the federal nature of the ASA. The information covered in the *Handbooks* included lists of officials, records of achievements at all levels and the laws of the ASA. The *Handbook* carried advertisements for competitions and schemes and events. The first advertisements from outside the ASA began in 1988 when the TSB, as official sponsor, took a full page in the ASA section. In 1992 the *Handbook* underwent a total revision which changed its format from the Octavo, as used from earliest years, to A5 pages with full colour photographs forming part of the cover and with each section having appropriate illustrations.

ASA and external media

Well before 1971 the ASA had recognised the need to co-operate with the media, newspapers and sports magazines, film newsreels, television and radio. Its successes in the next 25 years depended on what news gatherers believed to have value in capturing the attention of their audiences. There were considerable changes over the period. Technology and fashion took their toll.

Cinema newsreels were discontinued in favour of the immediacy of television coverage. Newspaper reports on sporting events had to take into account the pervasiveness and immediacy of both radio and television. Many sports pages in national newspapers devoted relatively little space to reporting events and recording results. Instead they sought to attract readers with speculations about forthcoming events or information and controversies about sports personalities. In this respect the swimming world held fewer attractions, largely because of the youthfulness of many of the participants. In contrast local radio gave scope for fuller reporting events such as galas. Local newspapers carried reports and features about local or regional sporting achievements, much as they had done in the past. Such coverage often depended on the established contacts between clubs and the newspaper or local radio station.

National coverage of swimming, particularly on television, diminished during the years after 1970 when programme makers seemed increasingly to emphasise the achievements of individual 'personalities' whose successes led to expectations of gold or silver medals in international competitions. Nonetheless the ASA *Annual Reports* recorded for many years its pleasure in the co-operation which it had received, particularly from the BBC. However, there was a decrease in the exposure of gala events, even of such visually attractive activities as synchronised swimming or diving. National competitions or achievements became less com-monly reported in the sports news. Such neglect from the broadcast media produced vigorous comment from within the ASA. However the sports editors had a wide choice of sports and seemed to give priority to events which were easier to cover.

The sensitivity of the Association was shown when the BBC programme *Sportsview* organised a poll of viewers, covering all sports, which awarded the BBC Team Trophy to the men swimmers. In the individual awards David Wilkie was ranked third in 1976. The *Swimming Times* commented:

'........ *many swimming fans still feel that had swimming been more exposed to television this year, there could have been a change in voting*'.

A year earlier David Wilkie had been voted Sportsman of the Year by the British Sportswriters Association. The relative neglect of swimming during the following decade prompted the *Swimming Times* in July 1987 to carry a note by David Reeves:

'*A recent survey of major sponsors of sports events televised by ITV and Channel 4 during 1986 produced a very interesting "top 10" - Snooker 394 hours; Soccer 261; Tennis 188; Athletics 131; Bowls 112; Darts 54; Motor Racing 42; Ice Skating 40; Rugby Union 39 and Cycling 27. Swimming was too far down the list to warrant a mention but I am quite certain that total coverage including BBC was less*

Duncan Goodhew, Olympic Gold Medallist in 1980, winner of the 100 metres Breaststroke. (Copyright: Tony Duffy, All Sport)

than 10 hours. I am equally certain that we will do little better in 1987 but it really does make you wonder what, undoubtedly the most popular participation sport, has to do to obtain media coverage? Any repeatable ideas would be welcome'.

In the same issue, John Holden was writing in the ISTC section on 'Take Advantage of your Local Radio Station', where he outlined the way to obtain air time and how to create interesting listening.

It is ironic that it could well be that swimmers lacked interest because they behaved themselves. There were few scandals of unsporting responses to results or out-of-pool misdemeanours. Swimming provided few stories for headlines about shocks or unhappy personal relationships. As a consequence they appeared to have received less coverage than other sports with which they competed.

ASA and international relations

The ASA had played important roles in the creation and success of international swimming. It had been a founder member of FINA (Fédération International de Natation Amateur), the world authority which regulated swimming sports, and of LEN (League Européenne de Natation) which was responsible for Europe-wide swimming competitions. The role of FINA grew during the twentieth century and its rules for competitive swimming sometimes reflected ASA policy. In turn the ASA adopted FINA legislation even though this might not have always been entirely to its taste. LEN supervised the conduct of swimming competitions. Although it did not seek to avoid the rules of FINA, it was ready to supplement them as appropriate.

FINA succeeded because it took the responsibility for the practical arrangements for international competitions and negotiated agreements on them on a worldwide basis. It regulated important activities such as timing, taking into account advances of technology. Other regulations referred to the appropriate characteristics of costumes. It was also involved in establishing the duties of referees, and officials, and established guidelines for monitoring, policing and coping with evidence of drug taking. Negotiations with differing national political regimes were undertaken in order to agree on the meaning of the term *amateur*. In all respects FINA had regard to the general rules of the International Olympic Committee.

ASA officers and members held senior offices in these international bodies between 1970 and 1994. For example, Norman Sarsfield was the first Briton to be appointed Honorary Secretary of LEN in 1974 and, in the same year, Miss J. Brayshaw became the first Honorary Secretary of the LEN Synchronised Swimming Committee. In 1993 the *Annual Report* recorded that British representatives sat on three of the FINA technical committees and five of those of LEN.

The ASA abided by the laws of FINA and accepted whatever decisions were made about international competitions or the rights of competitors. South African participation was not allowed in English swimming during the international boycott of apartheid. British swimmers took part in the Moscow Olympics

even when the USA sought to undermine them. The ASA tried to limit the effects of political issues on what it regarded as sporting events. Such a stance was capable of being misunderstood by friends and by enemies - 'he who is not for us is against us'. In the old amateur tradition, sport was believed by many members of the ASA to serve the ideal of encouraging understanding and friendships between individuals.

Within the United Kingdom the Association was represented on the British Olympic Committee through the Amateur Swimming Federation of Great Britain (ASFGB). The national organisations of swimming in Wales, Scotland and England had formed the ASFGB, whose major function was to select representative teams for Great Britain in Olympic and World competitions.

Relationships with the Scottish ASA and the Welsh ASA occasionally presented some problems. Suggestions had been made from time to time for a reformed *ASA for Great Britain*. Negotiations proceeded between England, Wales and Scotland and affiliation received strong support in 1972. However, at the ASA Council the proposal for a merger was lost when Alf Turner pointed to the financial implications. Scotland and Wales, having few capital resources to bring into the union, would have access to the accumulated funds of the English ASA. Moreover, government help for swimming in England came through the Sports Council which involved competitive bidding against other sports, whereas in Scotland and Wales the support came from the funds available to the Scottish Office and the Welsh Office. This proposed development raised not only financial and administrative questions but aroused feelings touching the national sensibilities of each country.

Swimming in the 1990s

By the beginning of the 1990s the administrative and organisational changes which had been had been debated during the preparation of the Martin Report were put into place after Council had accepted another report entitled *The Way Forward?* All provided a comprehensive framework for planning.

The newly established system of decision making combined with efficent use of paid and voluntary workers made possible the preparation of the first of the ASA's quadrennial plans.

The first of these plans was designed to cover the years 1993 to 1996 inclusive. The Plan covered both broad strategy, which incorporated the overall aims of the ASA, and tactics for achieving specific objectives in particular areas of the Association's work. The first part of the document analysed the contemporary situation or 'where we are now'. There was then a section relating to staffing and premises. The main part of the Plan focussed on a series of programmes which covered virtualy all aspects of the Association, both administrative and swimming disciplines. Included were discussions of membership, marketing and public relations, swimming for fitness, and performance for excellence in swimming, synchronised swimming, water polo, diving, BLDSA, and development projects. More general issues of the development of education and coaching and the training of officers were also subjects of the Plan.

Many of the issues covered in the Plan did not lend themselves to once-and-for-all solutions. Rather they represented the identification and clarification of tasks which were at the heart of the Association's fundamental purposes and so were likely to remain on its agenda. The discussions in this and other chapters have attempted to give an account of the successes and set backs in tackling them. Some parts of the Plan are so far advanced that it is possible to make predictions about outcomes, for example, the likelihood of improved office accommodation, and better computing facilities. In addition the organisation of schools' swimming through the Youth Sport Trust and the National Youth Sports Development Council is well under way. Links between the ASA, FINA and LEN are well established and continue to guide rule making. In all areas of its work the ASA stands ready to ensure the place of swimming amongst other sports. The preliminary work has already started on the Quadrennial Development Plan for 1997 to 2000.

Relationships with other sporting organisations remained important in the 1990s. The ASA has links with its Scottish and Welsh counterparts through the ASFGB. In September 1994 the ASFGB published the results of a workshop: *Great Britain Swimming - Development of Structure and Organisation*. This set out the case for much closer relationships of the Scottish, Welsh and English ASAs and looked forward to producing agreements which would enhance all aspects of swimming in Great Britain in the coming years. The links between these organisations and their coordinations under the auspices of the ASFGB has been fostered by such powerful bodies as the Sports Council, the British Olympic Committee, LEN and FINA, each of which has wanted to liaise with an organisation capable of representing British swimming.

Chapter 5 :

The Provision of Swimming Pool Accommodation and Facilities

The first objective of the ASA is:

'To promote the teaching and practice of swimming, diving, synchronised swimming and water polo, and stimulate public opinion in favour of providing proper accommodation and facilities for them.'

Introduction

The ASA was always bound to have an interest in the provision of baths and equipment because these were the media through which the sport was operated. From its beginning the Association was implicated through its affiliated clubs which used a variety of swimming locations - covered or open bath, lake, sea, estuary or river. As it made the rules to govern amateurism, competitions, galas, awards, costume and education across the sport as a whole, so it followed that it would show concern for the expansion of the bath building, for improved water quality, and for the co-existence of both competition and recreation.

There were baths long before the advent of the ASA in 1869 but there was no central body of knowledge about them, in spite of the fact that many were well designed and well built in their day. The ASA always had to put competitive swimming to the forefront of its priorities. It had to inform the various authorities

147

that there was more to the use of a pool than recreation. The clear aims were to educate non-swimmers, to encourage those who could swim to improve through competition and to select for training those who showed promise. Thus there developed a body of *good ASA practice* in bath design to match the objectives. Dimensions and depth, spectator space, diving facilities, pre-cleansing and water purity were also valid ideals. The National Association of Bath Superintendents and the Institute of Bath Managers were, of course, able to share the concerns of the ASA although their terms of reference were somewhat different.

The use of bath space and time for competitive swimming and training has always been in need of protection, especially when threatened by winter bath closing. Many local authorities have been reluctant over the years to lose the revenue from public swimming time to the needs of competitive swimmers.

The whole history of the ASA is peppered with lobbying government, advising and persuading local authorities and producing standard publications to illustrate the point. It was, however, not at all a one-sided affair, because the government often found it necessary to dwell on the virtues of physical fitness, of being able to swim to save life, and of being able to compete successfully.

The Early Days

Although the ASA was not founded until 1869 it is relevant to look at the developments in England prior to that date in order to puts its aspirations in context.

In ancient history it is sufficient to say that the Romans introduced organised bathing in Britain in the first century AD. The fall of their Empire was marked also by the gradual disappearance of their fine bath systems which had been a main feature of their civilisation. It was not to be until the nineteenth century that efforts were made to develop purpose-built swimming baths for public as well as private use. In the eighteenth century there had been a great interest in sea-bathing around our coast. This would lead to a need for places where people could learn to swim in the quieter waters of an enclosed pool.

In the early nineteenth century almost all existing baths were privately owned and exclusive to those who could afford them. Birmingham, as an example, had a number of well-appointed baths often lined with marble and some supplied with constant spring water.

The Industrial Revolution had changed the whole way of living for the masses of folk who crowded the new factory towns and cities. It was difficult for the poor to escape from their cramped, smoke-filled, insanitary conditions. There was the constant threat of disease such as cholera resulting from the unavoidable lack of cleanliness which was a feature of home and workplace. In this industrial society where most work was dirty, the clothes and body needed hot water which in most homes was not available in any quantity. The great reformers of the time had in mind to improve the health and sanitary conditions of the industrial population and to raise standards of education. Swimming and washing supplied the images of cleanliness and would help at the same time to provide a fitter, cleaner, school population. Reformers in Liverpool persuaded the Town Council to build St. George's Bath close to the Pier Head in 1828. This sea-water bath was leased to an operator because the Corporation had no legal powers to run it. It was also in Liverpool that the first public washhouses in Britain were erected in 1842. The work of Lord Shaftesbury and other reformers led to the construction of public baths near to London Docks and at Euston Square in the same period.

These free public baths at Derby were presented to the town in 1873 by Michael Bass MP. The industrial scene nearby is obvious. These baths, one for men and one for boys, were refilled every week with filtered water. On Tuesdays and Fridays ladies and girls used the facility. The baths were closed in 1936.

A washhouse facility in a large town c.1900.

In some towns the initiative of commercial entrepreneurs was responsible for some of the early baths. In the 1840s Mr. J.P. Clarke, a cotton-reel manufacturer of Leicester, used surplus hot water from his factory to feed his private swimming pool which had been constructed nearby. The Town Council agreed in 1847 to pay him £100 annually in return for opening the bath to the public, and by 1869 the Local Board of Health took over the bath for an annual rent of £500. Leicester did not in fact have a municipally owned bath until 1881. Mr. Clarke had set a good example.

Many Public Schools by the mid-nineteenth century had provided a swimming facility. Harrow had an open-air bath by 1811 and its title of *Duck Puddle* resulted from the need to regularly clean the mud from it. Eton boys used the Thames side where a special bank had been constructed for the purpose. Rugby had a heated pool and Uppingham a covered pool in the 1880s.

The first Baths and Washhouses Act of 1846 was a landmark in legislation. The Act gave a borough or parish ample powers to provide *Public Baths and Washhouses*. The term *bath* here means a single cleansing bath or slipper bath and not a swimming bath. At least two-thirds of all baths erected had to be of the cheapest class – thus catering mainly for the poor. A fixed maximum charge for a warm bath was two-pence at the lowest class and included the provision of a clean towel. The washhouse had facilities for women to do their own laundry work.

Many towns and cities took advantage of the 1846 Act and later amendments and a period of bath accommodation building ensued. By 1854 there were 11 bath and washhouse facilities in London, 3 in Liverpool and 24 in other towns.

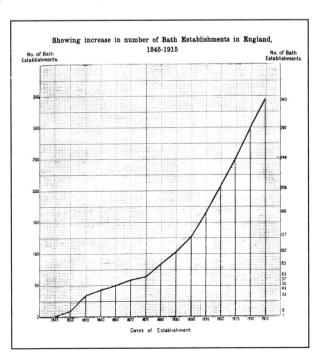

149

Boys at Eton College, Buckinghamshire, swam at the side of the River Thames with a specially constructed facility early in the 19th century.

Harrow Public Baths. 'Duck Puddle' or 'Ducker' was originated as early as 1811.

Neither Oxford nor Cambridge owned a swimming bath. Cambridge created this 'bathing place' at Grantchester depicted here in 1912.

During the 1890s Ravensbourne Swimming Club made use of Westminster Swimming Baths (Top) in Great Smith Street but sometimes used St. George's Baths (Below) in Buckingham Palace Road. Gas lighting is suspended over both areas.

This 'slipper' bath was an example of a private bath in a public establishment. These were used by all classes of the community and were part of the swimming-bath-laundry-slipper bath complex found in most large towns and cities up to the 1950s. This was at Lower Dartmouth Street Cottage Baths in Birmingham.

It was obviously both convenient and economic to house swimming baths and slipper baths under the same roof. Thus in 1878 an Amending Act empowered local authorities to provide covered swimming baths in addition to the baths and wash-houses. From November to March these could be used as gymnasia or for recreation and were thus closed for swimming in winter. An 1899 Act allowed music and dancing on the premises.

It became a matter of municipal pride in many towns to build grander and more imposing structures to house the swimming baths, slipper baths and washhouses. As a result some of the wealthier towns produced some very fine buildings after the 1880s. Bristol, Cheltenham, Exeter, Manchester and Southampton were good examples. Some firms such as Cadburys of Bourneville commissioned their own baths for their workforces in the same period.

The 1878 Act was followed by a steady growth in swimming pool facilities in Britain's towns and large numbers of school-children were admitted to swim either free or for a very small sum. The young people tended to form clubs but often had difficulty in securing bath time in the crowded evening programmes.

Bath administration was very different in those days. Boys and girls swam in different sessions, as did men and women. Often there were separate baths for men and women, the baths for the

Extracts from Swimming Notes and Swimmi[ng] Record of 1870s and 1880s

THE PADDINGTON PUBLIC BATHS AND WASHHOUSES.

A

Our edition of March 21, it will be remembered, contained a very brief allusion to the above establishment, which is situated in Queen's-road, Bayswater. Thinking it highly essential that the swimming world should be made acquainted with the formation of such establishments, we hasten to place before our readers the subjoined information :—The 1st and 2nd class swimming private, and ladies swimming baths, ar entered from the Queen's-road; the approac to the 3rd class swimming bath and wash houses being from Douglas-place. The 1 class swimming bath has occupied more a tention than the others, and stands in the centr of the site. It holds 100,000 gallons of wat is 90 feet long by 40 feet wide, and measur 5 feet 6 inches at the deepest end. T bath is lined with white glazed tiles for t sides, and glazed white bricks set on ed for the bottom, the cost of the latter be £16 a thousand. The dressing boxes amo to 50 in number. At the building's will be found the 2nd and 3rd class sw ming baths, which are 70 feet long by eet wide, and contain dressing boxes for bathers. The ladies swimming bath is feet long by 36 feet wide, and possesse dressing boxes. Each bath is lighted f the roof, the glass being free from co and of foreign manufacture. The eleva of the Queen's-road front is said to be in Italian style, and the materials empl are white Suffolk bricks with Portland dressings. Mr. Thos. Elkington, of Gol lane, undertook the contract for £22

BATHS ON THE SERPENTINE.

B

When Sir Thos. Chambers drew attention in the House the other day, to the limited area allowed to bathers in the Serpentine, he pointed out (remarks the *Globe*) one of the most remarkable deficiencies of London—the want of good bathing accommodation. Our public baths are not only few and far between, but too small to accommo date the numbers who use them. Where th population requires them most they are not to b found. The St. Martin's and Holborn Baths ar the best we possess, but there the prices for ad mission are unreasonably high, quite beyond th means of hundreds who would gladly use them they could afford to do so. We have no sati factory swimming baths, and the result is th public are offended by the spectacles presented them in the parks, while many lives are lost ever year in the river and canals. Mr. Ayrton ve characteristically commented on the question substituting an anecdote for an answer. Af confessing the deficiency, he informed the Hou that a lady who had long resided in the met polis offered to provide large baths at her o expense, but just as the contract was being m she unfortunately died without leaving powers to fulfil her intentions, and the scheme through. Whether Mr. Ayrton's anecdote create an anxiety to imitate the benevolence illustrates, is probably quite as doubtful as whe its talented narrator will ever learn to giv definite answer to a straightforward quest This bathing accommodation question is an portant one : it has been too long disregarded, when Mr. Ayrton promised that it should rec " full consideration," we trust for once he m what he said.

THE LONDON SWIMMING CLUB.
ESTABLISHED 1859.
—
FLOATING SWIMMING BATHS FOR
THE THAMES.

The hon. sec. has much pleasure in informing swimmers generally that the "Floating Swimming Baths Company, Limited," will erect their first Bath at Charing-cross, in the recess of the Embankment, now occupied by a landing stage, with access by the ordinary steps, and will be 180 feet long by 31 feet wide, and it is expected that the Bath will be ready for bathing purposes early in the ensuing summer. The second Bath will be erected at Pimlico, close to St. George's-square, and near the Pimlico Pier, of the following dimensions: 260 feet long by 47 feet wide. Special advantages will be given to shareholders, therefore, those who wish to become Shareholders are invited to apply at the offices of the Company, 3 Queen-square, Westminster.—Advt.

THE FLOATING BATHS.

These establishments are being rapidly progressed with, and will, ere long, be available for the public's general use. The following gentlemen comprise the directors, &c., viz.: Admiral George Elliott, M.P. (chairman), the Honourable Henry Noel, Arthur Iago, Esq., Cecil John Shepherd, Esq., Colonel the Hon. William Feilding, and Walter John Turner, Esq., late 3rd Dragoon Guards. Bankers, Messrs. Hallett and Co. Solicitors, Messrs. Combe and Wainwright. Engineers, Messrs. Whittaker and Perrett. Auditors, Messrs. C. F. Kemp, Ford, and Co. Secretary, John George Elliott (hon. sec. of the London Swimming Club). A very sensible and elaborate prospectus has been issued, wherein is stated that the water will be filtered, continually changed, and regulated in temperature according to the season of the year. The various sites will be, firstly, the river close to Charing Cross Station, in the position now occupied by one of the landing stages at Hungerford-bridge, and secondly, near the Thames, off the embankment, near the Pimlico Pier. The charge for admission will be sixpence, and if desirable bathing accommodation will be provided for ladies with every privacy and convenience. Season tickets will be granted to shareholders at a reduced rates, in conjunction with many other advantages. In order to encourge swimming, handicaps and other species of natation will be instituted for prizes. &c. The dimensions of the baths will be as follows: Charing Cross, 180 feet by 31 feet; Pimlico, 260 feet by 47 feet. The water area for the former being 135 feet by 25 feet, and the latter 200 feet by 40 feet. The estimated cost of the establishments is under £30,000. It is confidently expected that the first bath at Charing Cross will be opened by the end of June.

FLOATING SWIMMING BATH, Northumberland Avenue, Charing-cross.—PROF. C. WHYTE, SEN. (five miles ex-champion), begs to announce that his Nineteenth Annual Entertainment will take place at the above bath on TUESDAY, SEPTEMBER 30th, when the following valuable prizes will be competed for: 90 yards race for boys under 15 years of age; first prize, a silver medal, presented by Mr. R. Humphries, jeweller, 52, Seymour-place, Bryanstone-square; second, a silver medal, presented by Mr. W. Holmes, medallist, 129, Cloudesley-road, Islington. 90 yards race for boys under 17 years of age; first prize, a gold centre medal, presented by Mons. Louis, photographer, 326, Euston-road; second, a silver medal, presented by Mr. Williams, Serpentine Boat House. 90 yards race for novices who have not won an open race: first prize, a gold centre medal, presented by R. G. and W. Rogers, "Queen's" Dining Rooms, Bayswater; second, a silver medal, presented by Prof. C. Whyte, senr., Paddington Baths; third, a silver medal presented by Mr. G. S. Ibbs, hon. sec., North London Club. 90 yards handicap, open to all amateurs; first (annual) prize, a massive cup, presented by W. Whiteley Esq., the Universal Provider, Westbourne Grove; second (annual), a pair of field glasses, presented by Mr. J. Webster, optician, 4, Porchester-road; third, gold centre medal, presented by Mr. Walter Buckeridge, builder, Leinster-street, Bayswater; fourth, a silver medal, presented by Mr. R. W. Galloway, Wheatsheaf, Haverstack Hill. Plate diving competition: first (annual) prize, a handsome tankard, presented by Mr. W. Hollett, the Redan, Westbourne Grove; second a valuable meerschaum pipe, presented by Mr. J. Stone, tobacconist, Praed-street. W. Beckwith (champion of the world) Professor Charles Whyte and son in their unrivalled display, including undressing in the water, and the sensational Monte Cristo sack feat. Handicapper starter, and judge, Mr H. J. Hackett. Entrance fee to each race 1s. Entries to close on Saturday, to Prof. C. Whyte, at the Paddington Baths, Queen's-road, Bayswater. Admission 1s., reserved, 2s. Doors open at 6.30, commence at 7 sharp.—ADVT.

• • • • • • • • • • •

SALE BY AUCTION OF THE FLOATING BATHS.

Last Friday the Floating Bath, moored to the Thames Embankment at Charing-cross, was put up to auction at the Mart, Token-house-yard, by direction of Vice-Chancellor Bacon, the sale being necessitated by the winding-up of the company by whom it was built. The auctioneer said it had been in existence for the last ten years, had cost nearly £18,000, and that the average gross receipts had been £1,902 per annum. It was subject to rates and taxes to the amount of £60 per annum. The first bid was £500, and the highest £1,600. The property was then withdrawn, the Court of Chancery having fixed a reserve price considerably over that sum.

SILVERTOWN, NORTH WOOLWICH.

PUBLIC BATHS AND DISPENSARY,
Market Place, Silvertown.

OPEN DAILY.

—

DR. BRENNAN
RESIDENT SURGEON

THE South Kensington Crystal Swimming Bath and School for Swimming, open to Ladies Monday, Wednesday, and Fridays, from 9 till 3, throughout the year. Proprietor, F. Cavill, Champion of the South of England, and Superintendent of the National Swimming Association. This bath has a continual flow, at all hours, of pure spring water, being the only one in England possessing such a luxury. It is open all the year round, and the water regulated at a temperature of from 80 to 85 deg. Terms: 2 Guineas per annum, 1 Guinea per Quarter, 1s. per Bath. F. C. is open to make arrangements with first-class clubs and families at a great reduction. Address 30, Fulham-road, one minute's walk from the South Kensington Station and Museum.

Description of Paddington's facilities in 1873.
The Serpentine: the need for far more bathing accommodation in London (1873).
Floating swimming baths proposal for Charing Cross and Pimlico in 1873.

D *Floating swimming bath progress with development - 1873.*
E *An event at the floating swimming bath in 1884.*
F *The baths are auctioned in 1884.*
G *This advertisement of 1885 links 'health' to 'swimming'.*
H *South Kensington Ladies Baths used spring water (1873).*

latter usually being smaller. When men and women used the same pool at different times, the women's hours allowance was often shorter. The explanations given at the time in the Carnegie Report of 1918 included such reasons as:

'Women's dressing accommodation being more elaborate; hair and nap from costumes fouling the bath; women being too tired to swim after a hard days work in the factory; earning less money than men; and lastly, that womens free time is less free and home claims and duties tend to make them give up swimming at an early age.'

The strict Victorian rule against mixed bathing was partly relaxed around 1914 in some areas, but not until the Public Health Act of 1925 was there any real progress towards it. Harold Fern, as Secretary of the SCASA, was a great campaigner for mixed bathing. Even then boys and girls could only enter a bath with mother or father. There were very stern rules about males leaving the bath on one side and women on the other.

There were also first- and second-class baths. Sometimes a bath could be charged at first-class price on the day it was newly filled and later in the week, as the water deteriorated, the same bath would revert to second class. First class could also imply better dressing-boxes, more towels, and the exclusion of *'dirty rough children'*. If there were two baths filled and emptied at different times then the first- and second- class status would be arranged according to the quality of the contents of each bath. The *fill-and-empty principle* of keeping reasonably clean water was in operation prior to the introduction of the filtration plant system. Austin Rawlinson of Liverpool experienced the fill-and-empty method as a young man. The River Dee would fill up the bath at

---

BOROUGH OF BIRMINGHAM.
PUBLIC BATHS AND WASH-HOUSES.

NOTICE is hereby given, that the BATHS and WASH-HOUSES, situated in Kent-street, Bromsgrove-street, will be OPENED to the Public for BATHING and WASHING, THIS PRESENT MONDAY, May 12.

The Baths will be open daily until the 1st of October next, at Six o'clock in the morning until Nine o'clock at night; and from the 1st day of October to the 1st of April, at Seven o'clock in the morning to Eight o'clock at night, Sundays excepted.

During the same periods the Baths will be opened on Sundays, from Six to Nine in the morning.

The Wash-houses will be open daily, Sundays excepted, from Seven o'clock in the morning to Eight o'clock at night.

The charges for the use of the Baths are—

FIRST CLASS.	d.
Private Warm Bath, each person	6
Warm Plunging Bath	6
Private Cold Bath	3

Two Children, not above eight years old, to be allowed to use the same Bath-room at the same charge as one Adult person.

SECOND CLASS.	d.
Private Warm Bath, each person	3
Private Cold Bath	1

Two Children, not above eight years old, to be allowed to use the same Bath-room at the same charge as one Adult person.

	d.
PUBLIC SWIMMING BATH, with use of Dressing-room	3
Ditto, without use of Dressing-room	2

FOR THE USE OF THE WASH-HOUSES.

	d.
For the first hour	1
For every half hour after the first hour	1

By order of the Council,
S. BRAY, Town Clerk.

20, Temple-street, May 12, 1851.

Outdoor swimming baths were built in increasing numbers from the turn of the century. This men's open air bath at Kings Meadow, Reading, was a good example.

The open-air swimming bath for women and girls at Kings Meadow, Reading.

Boys bathing in an indoor pool in Birmingham at the end of the 19th century.

SWIMMING BATHS v. THIEVES

Metropolitan swimmers are not alone just now with the light-fingered gentry. On Monday morning, I had occasion to travel down to the Potteries, and am in the habit of calling at a certain bath down there. Always having some time to wait for my train to take me to my journey's end it being very early, I, as usual, strolled into the manager's house. There I found, to my surprise, a poor woman (the manager's sister) almost heart-broken. Her brother had gone to Manchester to see his child and wife, who are in ill-health, and had left a noted swimmer and runner to assist in keeping matters straight. But the fellow quickly made off with the cash box containing about £8 or £9, of which there was about £1 6s. in coppers. Whether it was too heavy for him to carry or not I don't know, but the box and coppers were found in a field. I now see in a certain bath in Lancashire a notice as follows: "Beware of pick-pockets." I don't know if there has been much stolen of late, but it is a common thing for the lads to rob each other of their boots and clothes, and now and then there are a few shillings missing.
POMPOUSE.

I HAVE no wish to interfere with the means whereby a man obtains his living, but I strongly recommend a close watch being kept upon portable property taken into swimming baths. The organised gangs I alluded to last year have had a profitable season with a very slight diminution in their ranks.

NOTICE TO FEMALE BATH ATTENDANTS.—WANTED for the season by the Portsmouth Club, a FEMALE ATTENDANT, able to swim and instruct ; hours 10 to 4, 2 on Saturdays. No Sunday work ; 15s. per week. Extras : Towels 1d., costumes 2d. Send full particulars with copy testimonials, to H. Fisk, (hon. sec.), Victoria-road, Southsea. [ADVT.]

Some newspaper extracts from 1884.

West Kirby at the beginning of the week. Some mud deposits inevitably came in with it and when the pool became browner at the end of the week the deposits had to be cleaned out as well.

A first-class bath could cost up to sixpence while second class usually cost twopence. Special concessions would reduce the latter to one penny. It was suggested that *'if you could see the bottom of the deep end, then the second class pool should still not be emptied'*. On some days an extra attendant was put on to watch the deep end *'to make sure all who dived in came up again'*.

It was interesting to see how the winter use of baths developed, especially as the ASA would in later years become concerned with this matter. The off-season uses included skating-rink, rifle-range, badminton courts, concerts, dances and cinematograph shows. A strong removable floor was essential. The economics of the situation did not permit winter heating of the water for *just a few enthusiasts*.

Many open-air pools were constructed across the country often in public parks. These were cheaper to build and maintain and were often able to fulfil the functions of recreative and teaching pool at the same time. Some were built next to rivers to make use of the water supply. At the beginning of the twentieth century many clubs, most of which became affiliated to the ASA, attached themselves to a particular bath and paid a lump sum fee for the privilege. In 1913 Islington Baths had 100 attached clubs; Manchester, 134 men's and 30 ladies' clubs; and Liverpool, 75 men's and 63 ladies' clubs.

In 1911 the Old Kent Road Swimming Pool, London, was arranged as a hall with a wooden floor covering the swimming area.

Swimming Times advertisements of the early 1930s highlighted the developments for improving water quality.

The sanitation of swimming baths was of paramount concern at the beginning of the twentieth century. Dirt and mud were taken into pools because of lack of rules and lack of education. Excretion from skin and other parts of the body were the result of bad, ill-informed habits. Human hair and costume fluff and dye played their part in contamination. It was recognised that a smooth clean-able bath lining, pre-washing facilities, good toilets, surface over-flow, use of bathing caps and education against spitting, would all help to ameliorate the problem. However, proper filtration of the water was to result in great improvements. A new filter installation would cost between £800 and £1,300, a lot of money in those days. To that would be added the fuel costs, but in many cases a large saving could be made by not having to continually purchase new water. The introduction of filters occurred mainly from the 1920s to the early 1930s, and it was helped along by a Ministry of Health Report of 1925 which recommended greater water purification. The first Liverpool bath to be filtered was in 1909. At the beginning of each season the plunge baths would be filled with fresh water and then tons of salt were added. At the end of summer the baths were emptied, having been continuously filtered.

Another important development in the promotion of bath cleanliness after 1910 was the use of shower-baths instead of cleansing-baths for cleaning the body prior to entering the pool.

Not only was the system cheaper and more efficient, but the immediate removal of dirt meant that others would not be affected by it. It was considered to be especially important to learn good bath habits at a young age.

The development of the provision of *Swimming for Schools* occupied the minds of many administrators at the turn of the century. By that time swimming was recognised as an optional part of Physical Education and in most large towns there was swimming instruction for children in school hours. In Birmingham, as early as 1885, the Town Council Baths Committee and the School Board sold books of one penny and half-penny tickets to schools, for admission to either the first- or second-class baths by the children, with their teachers. Free passes for *out-of-school* use were issued to pupils who could swim one length of a thirty yard bath. A few education authorities had built school baths. Liverpool was to the forefront with 17, but Leeds, Bristol, Bradford, Nottingham and others had their own schemes. Instruction took place, however, mainly in public baths. The SCASA in 1912 published *Public Baths and Bathing Places* in order to give good advice about bath construction for those who needed to study good practice. An ASA booklet in 1919 gave advice about *School Swimming Baths.* This was perhaps the first ASA booklet to use the professional advice of outside experts.

The 'Turn-Over' Filter Company made claims for its success in 1933.

Westminster Public Baths were opened in 1931. This grand architectural facade reflected the pride of the City Council in its new development.

Into the twentieth century

In 1914 there was a joint deputation of the ASA and the National Union of Teachers to the Board of Education to urge the provision of small teaching baths to be provided alongside public baths or at schools. This body also urged education committees to provide swimming instruction for children. The deputation resulted in some success, namely that: (a) time taken by swimming may be counted as physical exercise; and (b) that land drills for swimming and life-saving can be taught in *physical-exercise* time. The ASA, as an educating institution, was always eager to stimulate the progress of school swimming. After the First World War the Association actively promoted the teaching of swimming to schoolchildren by paying some of its own newly-qualified professional swimming teachers to teach children in the London area. The prominence given to this venture was indicated by the fact that the funding was diverted from ASA competitive swimming accounts for the purpose.

The ASA's interest in baths may be gauged from the fact that each year from the turn of the century around 50 pages of its annual *Handbook* were devoted to the printing of a long list of *Baths and Bathing Places*. The details for each included dimensions, depth, prices, whether used by ladies, which class and whether it was open air, covered, lake, river or sea.

Harold Fern's presence was felt in his early days as ASA Secretary when in 1922 the Association complained that the terms of the 1878 Baths and Washhouses Act was being breached by some local authorities, which were closing their baths for more than five months of the year. This was the beginning of a long battle. Winter closure was never looked on favourably by the ASA and the danger was that some municipal corporations were planning to bring in private bills to extend the legal period of closure to seven months instead of five. These bodies also sought powers to increase admission charges.

These difficult post-war years posed many problems for government, but in 1922 a plan to build more baths emerged. This would not only provide relief work for the unemployed but would give favourable government grants of 50 per cent of the interest on loans and sinking-fund charges on money borrowed by local authorities. It was not to be a reality until nearer 1930.

The statistics are interesting and Harold Fern published them:

Old Scheme - £12,000 borrowed with interest over 30 years would need a total payment back of £23,635.

New Scheme - The Government would find all the interest for the first seven years and 50 per cent of the interest for the next 8 years, making a total interest of £6,025, i.e. equal to only half of the cost of the original system. Total payment back would be £18,015.

Capital was still not easy to come by but some new baths were completed from 1930 onwards. After 1931 the bank rate was very low and therefore money was cheap to borrow.

The first-class bath at Westminster was 100 feet by 35 feet and up to 10 feet deep. It was lined with Sicilian white marble interspersed with Swedish green marble lines.

The second-class bath was 60 feet by 30 feet and lined with white glazed tiles. It was used mainly by children and non-swimmers.

Newcastle Swimming Bath was opened in 1928 and was illuminated by electricity. The bath-side changing accommodation is completed by curtaining. There appears to be a spectator gallery at the top level.

The 1930s

Harold Fern commented in the *Swimming Times* in 1932:

> *'We have got to bring home to the public and make them realise that swimming baths are not a luxury but a definite part of a good public health service.'*

He also berated the lack of facilities for mixed bathing and suggested that swimming time allocated to girls and women was quite inadequate. The ASA saw itself as a *clearing-house* for all information related to publicising the needs of the swimming world. Ministry of Health inspectors were therefore directing local authorities to seek ASA advice on pool developments.

The ASA was pleased to note that by 1928 its affiliated club list totalled 1,505, having climbed back to more than its pre-war figure of 1,468.

In 1930 Kenneth and Alfred Cross, bath architects, produced a book which had been commissioned by the ASA. *Modern Public Baths and Washhouses* was an authoritative work and sold in large numbers to local authorities and to many people who had any part to play in bath design, building and administration. Apart from surveying past developments, the authors gave advice on siting, layout, first- and second-class bath requirements, planning, hygiene and school baths. This was the standard work. The book's comments on hygiene were topical. These advocated chemical treatment (chlorine) for purity, filtration for clarity and aeration for sparkle and detailed how to achieve each. Water chlorination was gradually being introduced to cleanse water and

make it safe. There were to be many problems attached to its use, not least of which was making sure that correct quantities were added. The need to rid the water of a potential multitude of bacteria was paramount and doubtless outweighed the irritation of smarting eyes. Special attention had to be paid to the requirements of the Ministry of Health circular of 1929 which advised constant monitoring of bath water quality. As the 1930s progressed so other ideas appeared which could be aids to improving water. The use of ultra-violet rays was discussed as a means of destroying bacteria. The use of silver as a purifying agent was another consideration. In 1936 the Dutch invented a biological purification system which would use the natural enemies of bacteria to destroy them as part of the water recycling process. Ozone was, at that time, considered to be a health-giving agent. In 1937 Croydon's huge, open air pool, 200 feet x 100 feet, with dressing accommodation for 1,000 bathers, advertised that *'Purification is effected by ozone'*. Ozone was well known as a sterilising agent and as a very powerful oxidising agent. Thus it had a decomposing quality which in later years was discovered to be harmful because of the rapid rate at which it oxidises in living creatures including in human body.

Throughout the 1930s the ASA continued to be overwhelmed by the volume of enquiries about bath construction. Great numbers of new baths were built particularly in the mid- and late-1930s. No wonder a *Swimming Times* article was headed, 'Baths, Baths and Still More Baths'. New open air seaside baths attracted more people to the resorts. Some seaside pools were covered and Brighton built the world's largest sea-water, covered pool.

SWIM YOUR WAY
.. TO HEALTH ..

at the

County Borough of Croydon

Ozone Bathing Pool

(Opposite the Aerodrome)

PURLEY WAY BATHING POOL.

DISPLAYS AND CHAMPIONSHIPS FOR 1937.

No extra Charge is made for these Events.   *Swimming continues before and after the event.*

Date.	Event.	Time.	Date.	Event.	Time.
21st June to 27th June.	CANADIAN LOG ROLLER W. C. R. Bradborn.	Twice daily.	Thursday 22nd July.	SOUTHERN COUNTIES CHAMPIONSHIPS. Men's High Diving.	7.30 for 7.45
Thursday 1st July.	INTER COUNTIES DIVING CHAMPIONSHIP Surrey, Middlesex and Essex Ladies' High Men's Spring	7.30 for 7.45	Thursday 5th August	PETE DESJARDINS MISS MARIAN MANSFIELD Olympic Champion and America's Most Beautiful Girl Diver.	7.30 for 7.45
Thursday 8th July.	SOUTHERN COUNTIES' CHAMPIONSHIPS Ladies' High Diving Men's 100 Yards	7.30 for 7 45	Thursday 2nd Sept.	INTER-COUNTY DIVING CHAMPIONSHIP. Surrey, Middlesex and Essex. Men's High. Ladies' Spring.	7.30 for 7.45
Thursday 15th July.	COUNTY WATER POLO CHAMPIONSHIP of ENGLAND Surrey v. Essex	7.30 for 7.45			

Under A.S.A. Laws, under the auspices of The Surrey County Water Polo and Swimming Association and the Croydon Municipal Officers' Swimming Club.

The pool is designed in the form of a cross, being [2]00 feet long by 100 feet on its major axis. It is [p]rovided with water chutes and super diving [b]oards with a 15 feet diving pit. It is a famous [r]esort for athletes of all Nationalities and has [d]ressing accommodation for over 1,000 bathers. [T]here are two large sun bathing beaches with [w]aving palms and five acres of laid out gardens [a]nd shrubberies for sun bathing, lazing or reading [o]n the deck and arm chairs which are provided free. [T]he pool water is constantly filtered, heated and [a]erated, being completely changed every four and [a] half hours and has a capacity of approximately [2]50,000 gallons. THE PURIFICATION IS EFFECTED [B]Y OZONE AND IS THE MOST UP-TO-DATE METHOD [I]N EXISTENCE.

Ozone

Of late years Ozone has been coming to the fore [a]nd Croydon, bearing in mind its famous motto, [d]ecided to lead the way in its application to LARGE [s]wimming baths. Although Ozone has been known [s]ince 1785 it was not till 1840 that Schönbein [r]ecognised it as a peculiar gas and named it OZONE. [(]Greek OZO.)

ONE OF THE SUNBATHING BEACHES.

ONE OF THE CHUTES ON A BUSY DAY.

Croydon 'Ozone' Pool of 1937 was a great attraction. These extracts from the pool booklet show the variety of activities available. In later years ozone was discredited because of its oxidising properties.

This Pool has been designated by many as the ELECTRIC POOL. The reason is not far to seek, in fact it is electric in more senses than one. HERE ARE FIVE OF THEM.

(1) *Sterilising is by Electrified air (OZONE) Nature's natural steriliser which imparts the sparkle of Southern seas.*

(2) *A 6,600 volt electric boiler maintains that equitable temperature which many doctors declare should be regulated according to the day whether it be humid or dry.*

(3) *Under-water floodlighting which gives that delightful sensation of swimming in the clear sparkling water of the coral strewn Southern seas.*

(4) *Colour floodlit cascades with delightful colour change Lily standards.*

(5) *Thousands of twinkling lights scattered over the flower beds and shrubberies, the pool itself being surrounded with octagonal column lights and lily standards.*

A staff of courteous attendants is ever willing to oblige, with a corps of fully qualified lifesavers to advise or instruct and watch over your safety.

INTERNATIONAL TEN METRE HIGH DIVING BOARD.

Our Motto : Sanitate Crescamus (By Health We Progress)

Swimming brings into full action not only heart, lungs and muscles, but also that great organ the skin, whose eliminative, heat regulating and other more subtle functions we are just beginning to understand. It should also be borne in mind that the beneficial effect to the body of contact with water is immensely increased by the added effect of sunshine and the open air.

Ozone

Of late years Ozone has been coming to the fore and Croydon, bearing in mind its famous motto, decided to lead the way in its application to LARGE swimming baths. Although Ozone has been known since 1785 it was not till 1840 that Schönbein recognised it as a peculiar gas and named it OZONE. (*Greek OZO.*)

What is Ozone ?

Chemically it is O_3, each molecule of Ozone is made up of three atoms, two atoms only go to make up the molecule of Oxygen, it is the third atom that does the work.

As a sterilising agent its properties are well known and indeed it is one of the most powerful oxydising agents known, most people will at once recognise it at the pool by that pleasant smell they remember so well from their visits to the coast, with the sea dashing on the rocks and beaches and the wind whipping the spray to a light foam.

We have in effect brought the sea to you.

Many roadhouses were developed around London in the 1930s. It was a 'day out' to drive to one of these pools in the countryside. Most were not far from main roads. This one was at Bagshot in Surrey.

The new Uxbridge Bathing Pool or Lido was opened in 1935 and is a good example of the structures which were built in many parts of England at the time. It was 220 feet long by 72 feet wide. There was a deep water area of 90 feet by 75 feet where water polo could be played whilst not interrupting leisure swimming. Swimming instruction was available. Admission was 6 d. for adults and 3 d. for children. Spectators paid 4 d. In just one week in July 1936 the pool had 9000 bathers and 1066 spectators and took £203.

The pier pools, such as that at Clacton-on-Sea, drew great crowds. Public park baths catered for those at home. Towns, clubs, schools, colleges, private establishments and the new roadhouses in the countryside all sported their new and often exciting structures. The use of reinforced concrete enabled designers to embellish many pools with attractive shapes including arched diving platforms and interesting façades. A brochure by the Cement and Concrete Association gave technical details necessary for the use of the product. When the money was available the new pools had the most recent editions of filtration and chlorination. One of the first modern pools to be built with underwater viewing windows was at the Loughborough College in 1936. This was one of the reasons why the pool was to be the scene of so many ASA post-war courses. The potential for filming and viewing below water-level was obvious.

The lido pool became the pride of many city suburbs. The name had derived from a beach resort near Venice. These were very large open-air pools usually on the edge of densely populated areas. The sunwarmed pools were magnets for city dwellers who could hop on to a bus or arrive by car. When the sun was out thousands of folk took to the waters. The lidos were not heated and therefore were only used in summer. A temperature of only 49° F. (just over 9° Celsius) was often acceptable at the time. Most lidos were privately owned and flourished until the late 1950s when many owners decided to sell. Local authorities would not or could not afford to convert them to heated water and these centres of 'lazy and idyllic days' disappeared one by one and the sites were redeveloped. Many thousands of people had learned to swim or to improve their performances at these lidos and the ASA had taken a keen interest not only in pool construction but also in the quality of instruction.

Loughborough College indoor bath was built in the late 1930s with inspection windows below water level.

The Empire Pool at Wembley - a huge structure of concrete and glass. The large spectator accommodation ensured its international reputation.

The Wembley Pool in action for the 1948 Olympics.

The Wonder Pool had many facilities.

Perhaps the pride and joy for the country was the new Empire Pool at Wembley which was started in 1933 as part of a great recreation complex. It was to cost around £100,000 and was to be built of concrete and glass on a nine acre estate development. The pool building would cover two acres and be 420 feet long with a roof span of 240 feet. The bath itself was to be 200 feet by 60 feet and up to 16 feet deep. Diving stages at 1, 3, 5 and 10 metres and a full-size water polo pitch were part of the design. Underwater illumination, wave-making machinery, and room for a buffet, and dancing were all indications of what was fashionable at the time. Seating accommodation for between 8,000 and 10,000 spectators ensured that this great showpiece would cater for international events with ease. Wembley was host to the Empire Games in 1934, the ASA National Championships in 1936 and the European Championships in 1938. It was a great boost to the status of swimming in Britain. For the public it was a place to swim. In 1935 in one day 7,000 people used the pool. That was a real test of hygiene.

Harold Fern in 1934 was asked to lecture to the NABS on 'problems of mutual interest' which he summarised as: (a) overdosing of chlorine; (b) the need for better pre-swimming cleansing facilities; (c) winter opening of baths; and (d) water heating. Of the latter, he suggested, that *'if aeration filtration and chemical treatment are in place - why not water heating'*. The *heated pool* factor was receiving much attention. Stonehaven had recorded attendance figures increased by 90 per cent for adults and 70 per cent for juveniles after the installation of a gas heating system. Conversely, Cambridge still had no bath at all in 1936, just an enclosure and changing shed up river.

Some things seemed to be a continuous fight. In 1936 a Bill was introduced to Parliament to consolidate all Public Health Acts since 1875 but the main object of some local authorities was to extend the permitted period of bath closure from five to seven months a year. The ASA advised clubs and Districts to petition urban district councils and their local MPs. They succeeded in ensuring that the result was that the period of closure was fixed at six instead of seven months. A 1938 Ministry of Health report sided with the ASA and suggested that covered pools should be kept open all year and that additional halls should be built for other recreational purposes.

The Government's interest in supporting pool building was reflected in the amounts of loan sanctions granted from 1933 onwards as the country's financial situation eased:

Table 5.1: Annual Government Loan Sanctions 1933-39

1933-4	–	£312,237
1934-5	–	£638,058
1935-6	–	£1,160,242
1936-7	–	£790,975
1938-9	–	£1,003,754

The Board of Education in 1936 agreed to sanction grants for building school swimming pools. The Government also set up the National Fitness Council in 1938 with £1 million a year to be spent on sporting facilities. Some of this money would come under the ASA's advisory jurisdiction. With these loans and grants available the ASA must have thought that some of its prayers had been answered.

Kenneth Cross's ASA book, *Modern Public Baths*, was in such great demand that in 1938 he revised it for re-issue. Things had changed since 1930. There was no longer a separate admission entrance for men and women. He made great efforts to show which functions were now mandatory, and to suggest improvements in design, cleanliness and the wider range of heating options available. There is no doubt that the ASA's effort to inform architects and local authorities was reaping rewards, and was helping to raise the level of the Association's public image.

With the approach of the Second World War it may be seen that a number of social and technical changes had together influenced the growth, management, use and development of the *world of the swimming bath*. Since the First World War the great strides achieved in pool design and building methods and also in making water *safe to swim in*, had given the public the confidence to use the product, and had opened up new horizons of entertainment and competition. The change of emphasis away from the slipper bath and cleansing the body had moved on. The public could, in most regions, find new facilities for recreation which had for most people, become a feature of modern living. When the public went to the seaside or to a roadhouse or a Lido then the swimming bath was a focal point. The *travelling public* was also a relatively new innovation. The car, bus and train had facilitated access to vast numbers of bathing locations, especially for the seaside holiday crowds.

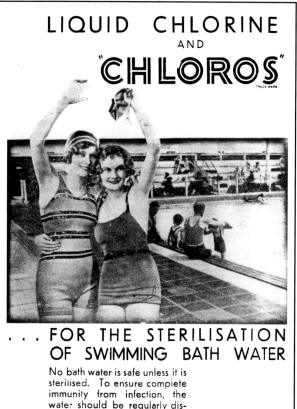

LIQUID CHLORINE
AND
"CHLOROS"
TRADE MARK

... FOR THE STERILISATION
OF SWIMMING BATH WATER

No bath water is safe unless it is sterilised. To ensure complete immunity from infection, the water should be regularly disinfected with Chlorine.
Chlorine may be applied at very low cost, either alone as Liquid Chlorine or in conjunction with Ammonia, or it may be conveniently used as a solution in the form of "Chloros."

Ask the nearest I.C.I. Sales Office for further particulars and literature.

"Chloros" is a registered Trade Mark, the property of I.C.I. (General Chemicals) Ltd.

IMPERIAL CHEMICAL INDUSTRIES LIMITED
at Belfast, Birmingham, Bradford, Bristol, Dublin, Glasgow, Leicester, Liverpool, London
Manchester, Newcastle-on-Tyne

A Swimming Times advertisement for 1934.

This huge growth in entertainment, enjoyment and recreation was, for the ASA, part of a success story, and provided a fertile ground for sowing the seeds of the *need to be able to swim, the need for safety* and the *need to encourage fitness*. At the same time the ASA had to protect its special interest in the development of competition and to make sure, as far as it could, that bath-time facilities were set aside for the purpose. The use of pools for educational purposes and club use was part of this thrust. The growth of affiliated clubs from 624 in 1904 to around 1,900 in 1939 was an indication of the need for the Association to continually advise these clubs on how to protect their interests. The Association also had an increasing interest in the use of baths for competition and galas and realised the propaganda importance that such activities presented to the public at large. The continual pressure exerted by the ASA to keep baths open throughout the year was beginning to have effect and this was due in part to increased usage and the increase in the number of heated pools. In 1939, Paul Herbert, General Manager of the Empire Pool, suggested that the ASA was wrong not to accept winter closing because it was not economical - a suggestion he withdrew after a storm of protest. Mr. Herbert did, however, forecast the introduction of *multiple use buildings* for the future. The leisure centre was under discussion even in 1939. The *teaching bath for every town* was another pre-war slogan which reflected both the pressure on existing facilities and the need to develop a parallel educational facility.

The 1930s had seen the introduction of commercial ventures connected with pool activities. The bath-side gramophone for the playing of music and Jabez Wolfe's aquatic earplugs were two examples. The introduction of automatic ticket machines and improved clothes storage equipment were symptomatic of modern innovations.

The invention of the swimagraph by W.H. Downing was a forerunner of the development of pool-side equipment to aid the swimmer and the coach. The swimmer wore a belt attached to a

Splashes

A Useful Poster.

EVERY user of a swimming bath likes to see the water clear and colourless. Local authorities, by installing the most up-to-date filtration plant and passing the whole of the water through filters about three times daily, do much to achieve this happy result, but every bather can contribute his or her share to maintaining the wholesomeness of the water by always having a good wash after undressing. The swimmer, too, will be far healthier by thus removing perspiration and dust from the body. A sponge down with soap and water should be a compulsory preliminary, and many Pool Managers are taking advantage of the posters issued by the Health and Cleanliness Council and exhibiting them in their pools, in order to remind bathers of this desirable routine.

Our illustration is a facsimile of the double crown poster.

A GOOD WASH
before using the swimming bath

HELPS EVERYONE TO BE
HEALTHIER

HEALTH & CLEANLINESS COUNCIL

How the bather could contribute to cleanliness - 1938.

line connected to an instrument on the bath side. The crawl stroke actions were recorded on a revolving drum thus producing graphs which could be analysed. The instrument was named the *Swimmer's X-Ray*. Such brave experiments in the field of technology were to encourage others as swimming became subjected to increased scientific study. In the same way, the use of the camera was to presage, in a simple way, the wide variety of visual recording and analysis which would be available in later years.

When the War came in September 1939 all bath-building ceased. Many of the nation's baths were ordered to be closed and to be used for the essential purposes of war. The end of the War was to record the destruction of many swimming facilities and to raise the need, yet again, for a period of construction.

Post Second World War

There was to be no new pool construction or repair in England for several years. The main need of the nation was for housing and industrial reconstruction. These were times of austerity and were to continue as such well into the 1950s. The 1947 February winter freeze-up meant that coal would not be moved from collieries to the baths. This caused hundreds of baths throughout Britain to be closed for many weeks. Birmingham's dilemma, as an example, was enshrined in verse:

'Twenty modern swimming baths!
For women and for men.
Half closed for the winter,
Then there were ten.

Ten modern swimming baths!
We said, "We're doing fine";
But another closed for dancing,
Then there were nine.

Nine modern swimming baths!
We said, "Please don't take more";
But five were closed through lack of coal,
Then there were four.

Four modern swimming baths!
To serve the whole of Brum.
Now they've closed the blinking lot!
And we are left with none.'

The ASA accepted all these post-war problems and concentrated its energies, on other areas of development and on making sure that those in power would back the building of facilities when this became possible. The 1948 Olympic Games at Wembley Empire Pool was a boost to post-war swimming. This was followed by the unavoidable 1949 closure of that facility which was

BLACKPOOL'S
SUPER OPEN-AIR SWIMMING STADIUM
SOUTH PROMENADE

The first combined ASA Championships was held at Blackpool's South Shore Bathing Pool in 1935. This open air venue had accommodation for 5000 spectators and a championship course of 100 metres. The depth varied from 1 foot 9 inches to 15 feet.

The Centralised National Swimming Championships in progress at Derby in 1949.

In 1953 the National Championships were held at Derby Baths at Blackpool (not to be confused with the 1949 location). This was the only 55 yard bath in the country. The relative increase in seating accommodation is apparent. The event was to be located here for 11 consecutive years.

168

a great blow. The 1951 Festival of Britain, designed to boost Britain's morale after the long War, was celebrated by special ASA galas, and a display was put on at the Marshal Street Baths in London.

In 1949 a special conference was organised to bring together the ASA, the NABS and the STA for the sake of identifying and discussing ways of co-operating on swimming matters. These Associations each had its own functions and did not always agree on matters of principle, but the general goals were the same.

Pool-side inventions were still arriving. During the Second World War, in 1941, a *swimometer* had been devised. This machine was to measure the effort expended by a swimmer who was attached to the pool side by a spring-loaded belt. The coach voiced instructions to his pupil down a speaking tube. In 1949 a cumbersome-looking machine was made for the purpose of racing-timing. This art or science had a long way to go. This particular piece of machinery was said to record dead heats, give immediate results to ⅟₄₀ of a second and show placings by illuminated figures. Without such early work we would not have today's electronic masterpieces. In the same year a mechanical pacing machine was devised for use by Max Madders at the ASA's Loughborough Advanced Training Course. Professor Austin of Birmingham University and H.A. MacDonald had worked on the machine which consisted of 24 lights placed at one yard intervals along the bath side. The setting of the speed of each light coming on one after another would be controlled by the coach. Swimmers would have to pace themselves against the lights. Another machine by Frank Plumpton appeared in 1952. By 1955 the trampette was in fashion. This small version of a trampoline was developed as a bath-side aid or for land practice especially for divers.

By 1952 the ASA was beginning to voice its concern at lack of movement towards bath building, but little could be done. The abolition of the need for building licences in 1954 was a step in the right direction. It was noted that by 1955 West Germany had built 48 new baths since the War and Britain none. The ASA was receiving three local authority plans a week for approval and comments. The first bath in England since the War was opened at Hornchurch in Essex in 1956, but by 1958 there were still only four new pools against Germany's 300.

In 1955 ESSA was doing for schools what the ASA was doing in general, i.e. encouraging the building of baths. Frank Rudge, Head of Mount Pleasant School at Harrow, organised the building by voluntary labour of a 50 feet x 15 feet teaching bath costing a total of £400. This was to be a model for others to follow and by 1959 250 more school pools were built on the same pattern. *"A pool for every school"* was the slogan.

In 1958 a Ministry of Health and Local Government circular indicated hopes of higher public sector investment and encouraged local authorities to apply for loans. Meanwhile, the ASA had identified 103 fair-sized towns in England which had no covered bath of any sort. The slightly-eased restrictions meant that in 1959 the ASA were advising 150 local authorities on the planning of a new facility and nine schemes were authorised costing £2 million in loans. In addition, five bomb-damaged pools were being repaired. In 1960 the Association stated that: *'There is no sign of any departure from conventional pre-war type of buildings. There is a need for a simpler design and a cheaper form of construction.'* A special committee was set up to study the problem. Construction continued and in 1962 18 pools were planned, with an expenditure of £3 million. In 1963 25 pools were planned at a total cost of £6 million.

Other pool building developments were occurring. Fibreglass was being widely used as a new stable material able to cope with the elements and capable of being formed to any shape. Huge fibreglass pools were moved on the backs of lorries to be inserted

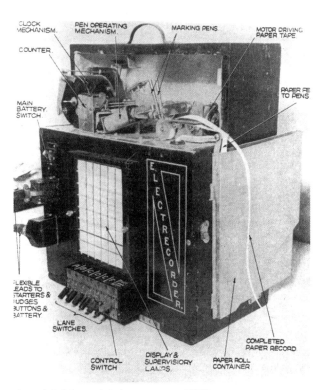

Mechanical pacing machine used by Max Madders at the Loughborough Advanced Training Course in 1949.

An early judging and timing apparatus of 1950.

Parents contributed to this pool for the under 11s at St. Peter's Church School, Farnborough, Hampshire, in 1965.

A school pool at Hatfield School, Hertfordshire, which was constructed and paid for by the Parent-Teacher Association in 1956.

A school outdoor pool built at Wareham County Modern School in 1956.

into holes dug in private gardens, and also for schools and other institutions. One reinforced pool was erected indoors in an old school kitchen. Polythene, part of the new plastics industry, was used to line pool excavations of all sizes - *'a pool in a plastic bag'*, as it was described. A.D. Kinnear, the ASA's new National Technical Officer, in 1960 was astonished to be invited to inspect a teaching pool erected in a school classroom. This was enterprise indeed. Other innovations were: in the 1964 Millfield School's inflatable pool cover which was kept aloft with the aid of a small mechanical air pump, and in 1965 a pool built at Gloucester for physiotherapeutic purposes to assist children from wheel chairs to enter the water safely. Innovation was in evidence all around. In 1960 the Swimming Pool Construction Association was formed and the Swimming Pool Supplies Directory was circulated. The Wolfenden Committee Report of 1960 was about to have an influence on sporting developments in Britain. It recommended the expansion of public facilities and the establishment of multi-

This 'bath in a classroom' at Craven Park Primary School in London was constructed in 1962.

sports centres with more swimming baths. Out of this report the Sports Development Council was to be born and monies would be distributed to regional centres.

The Crystal Palace Sports Centre - or National Recreation Centre - was planned in 1960 and opened in 1964 by the Duke of Edinburgh. This 55 yard pool was of a uniform 6 feet 9 inches depth all over. There was a 16 feet diving pool and a teaching pool 2 feet 9 inches deep. Seating was available for 1,706 in addition to some temporary seating. The observation windows afforded facilities for underwater viewing. A hostel with 129 student flats had been built with a grant of £100,000 from the King George VI Foundation. This project was to provide prestige facilities for training top coaches and sportsmen and sportswomen and was run by the CCPR.

While Crystal Palace was being built in 1963 Liverpool was declared a Development Area by the Government. £600,000 was to be spent to relieve unemployment. The previous year Liverpool Education Committee had built a new school pool for £25,000 in six months at Quarry Bank. With this scheme as proof of success, a further nine pools, 55 feet by 24 feet, were built from government money for £20,000 each and three junior pools were built for £20,000 each. In addition, 12 more pools were rehabilitated with filtration and chlorination plants at £7,000 each. Other areas of the country followed the pattern. Austin Rawlinson, who was fast becoming the elder statesman of English swimming, had a new bath in Liverpool named after him in 1965.

The building of school baths was gaining momentum in the mid-1960s and costs were tending to drop with the increased numbers. An indoor bath 50 feet by 25 feet could now be built for around £20,000. By 1964 an ESSA study revealed that there were 3,500 school baths in existence, most of these having been provided with Parent-Teacher Association help. The ASA Awards Schemes, especially those linked with ESSA, must have received great impetus from the ability of so many school children to learn and improve in their own facilities.

A fibreglass pool delivery in 1958. Some were 24 feet in length.

British international, Malcolm Tucker, a pupil at Millfield School in 1964, trained in the all-weather plastic dome-covered pool. The dome of inflated nylon was kept inflated by a motor-driven fan. The tent cost £1,500.

Two of Britain's top performers in the 1960s, Linda Ludgrove and Brian Phelps, stood in Crystal Pool as it neared completion in 1965.

The new Crystal Palace Pool in action.

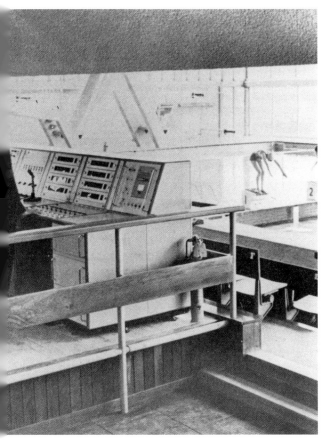

A.D. Kinnear, NTO, advised the building of 25 metre baths as part of looking to the future. He also praised the increasing use of the many bath training aids such as kicking-boards, floats, training clocks, nose-clips, and caps. In particular was he impressed with the recently invented transmitter from coach on land to pupil in the water. He was not so happy with pacing machines but found that the new bleeper hearing aid device was very useful. This could be pre-set as a pacer to the coaches' requirements.

As NTO, Mr Kinnear extolled the virtues of the Scientific Advisory Committee and stated that much of his work was increasingly connected with *measuring and testing* in line with modern scientific coaching methods. He was also planning a number of new courses at the new Crystal Palace Centre.

Bath development in the latter part of the 1960s was in a transition period. In 1966 the ASA made a decision to go metric on pool sizes in anticipation of government action for 1972. The new Leeds Pool opened in 1963 was exactly of metric proportions, being the first 50 metre pool. It was obvious that facilities for International events were now going to be part of the English scene. The new Coventry Bath was a prestige development of 1966. Costing £1,500,000 it was 165 feet long and had six lanes. The seating accommodated 1,174 spectators. Additional facilities included a diving recess, a second bath for school or club work, and a learner pool. A new electronic timing system had been tried and accepted by the ASA for the 1966 Blackpool National Championships. Others would follow. There were, however, other changes to come. Denis Howell, Minister for Sports and

This large 'Electronic Swim Timing Assembly', installed at the Crystal Palace baths in 1964, reflected the increased level of sophistication permitted by electronic developments.

Austin Rawlinson, Olympic finalist of 1924 and indefatigable worker for the ASA at all levels, had a new swimming bath named after him in Liverpool in 1965.

Recreation, announced a large funding award towards the building of Basingstoke Multi-Sports Centre. The multi-sports centre was now a serious proposition. In 1967 A.D. Kinnear discussed the merits of competitive swimming and 'Irregular Shaped Pools.' The West Midlands Sports Council had suggested that: 'The traditional shape of bath is rectangular which is necessary for competitive swimming, but this only interests a minority group of swimmers.' This statement was, of course, worthy of the pages of detailed analysis which Mr. Kinnear devoted to it. It had to be realised that if the needs of recreational swimming took over entirely from the consideration afforded to competitive swimming, then much of what the ASA stood for could be lost.

A temporary threat to school swimming occurred in 1968 when the Government's request to local authorities to cut expenditure resulted in some authorities stopping or partly stopping school swimming by stopping the transport of children to the baths. The ASA, of course, complained bitterly. In the following year the ASA urged the DES to include a swimming pool in the plans for all new comprehensive schools. In the same year the Sports Council were attempting to measure the needs of Sport in terms of facilities and money required. The ASA suggested that 33.3 metre pools should be for swimming and teaching purposes only.

In 1970 the ASA pointed out to the new Sports Council that Britain still had no pool complex capable of staging Olympic, World or European Championships. The Association also reported on its research into the financial viability of building training pools alongside conventional pools. It was considered that this would be a most cost-effective way of using public money. These training pools, or *training tanks* as they had been labelled, were thought by ESSA and the Sports Council to be a proposed substitute for a learner pool and that learners would possibly lose out on the deal. The Sports Council's costings also suggested that the training pool would be more expensive to construct. The ASA replied that the new pools could be for dual usage (training and learning) and that such a proposition would reserve main pools for more recreative use.

The Martin Report of 1970 had analysed the current and future facilities needs in detail and the outcomes are considered in Chapter 3. One of its first recommendations was the setting up of an ASA Facilities Committee.

The 1970's decade was a period of change when the ASA was to be continually alert to the needs for adjustment, research, discussion and liaison. The Association's views as an institution concerned with teaching, educating, coaching and competitiveness needed to be heard in forums concerned with innovation. Part of the concern was to implement as far as possible the recommendations of the Martin Report but there were other considerations.

Throughout the 1970s the re-organisation of Local Government in England was to result in the emergence of *Leisure Services Departments* as an integral part of local authority functions. The concept was that 'sport is associated with leisure'. The Sports Council sponsored family recreation. The Minister of Sport became the Minister for Sports and Recreation. There was the need to encourage participant-recreation; to cater for youth; and to use the increased free time profitably. The local aspect provided a special point of view to which the ASA had to relate.

Part of the 50 metre Leeds Pool which was opened in 1963. The recessed diving area was a special feature. (Copyright: Alan Towse)

In 1971 government financial policy changes meant that direct loans no longer existed. Instead, the determination of capital works expenditure was to be administered locally in the regions. For the ASA this would add weight to the policy of strong liaison with local authorities and especially the new Regional Sports Councils. In 1972 the Swimming Facilities Committee published a pamphlet entitled *Swimming Facilities - Suggestions for Local Authorities*. This Committee also raised the alarm: '*Provision of new pools does not mean more opportunities for training or coaching*'. Administrators tended to be more interested in the recreational aspect.

The 1972 Sports Council Report, *The Optimum Use of Swimming Facilities*, appeared. This caused the ASA to announce to affiliated clubs that they should ensure that allotted water time in baths was purposefully used and that any new club should not duplicate the activity of existing local clubs. It also confirmed that *affiliation* does not convey with it the right for sole use of public pools. In order to gain more facilities a plea was made to make more extensive use of school pools for evening classes and other activities at off-peak times. Meanwhile there was a boom in the building of new seaside pools in the mid-1970s. An innovation was the use of Butlin's Minehead Centre for special teaching weeks when 2,000 school children a week were supervised by ASA coaches.

The Science Advisory and Facilities Committees were busy as usual at this time. Hamilton Bland was researching the use of deck-level pools, while the merits of anti-turbulence lanes, adjustable angle starting boards, portable PA systems, moveable floors, adjustable booms, diving safety, timing devices and water

purification - all came under scrutiny. There was also further study of pool covers with the aim of fuel conservation in mind. In a reassessment of deep water areas, the ASA recommended that there should be at least one full size water polo area for each region, and a water polo pitch for each sub-region.

In 1974 Norman Sarsfield praised the new pool complex at Altrincham (Cheshire). The ASA had commissioned Rex Savidge, a pool architect, to do a feasibility study on the building of a larger than usual learner training pool adjacent to the normal swimming pool. Thus in one hall is the public pool, 25 metres by 10 metres., and in a separate hall a learner pool, 20 metres by 7.5 metres up to 0.9 metre deep, together with a toddlers' splash pool. The new building at Altrincham was made according to the above specification and with comparatively little extra cost above that of previous layouts.

A new teaching and training pool was also built at Crystal Palace and an ASA NTO was assigned full-time to the Centre. The facility was to be used for coaching and as a warm-up pool for competitors.

1979 was Britain's '*Winter of Discontent*'. The country, having endured some years of difficult economic climate, was to go into recession. Restraints on public spending affected building progress and many school pools were closed down. Pool temperatures were lowered and hire costs were raised. When things were to improve, however, the discussions and debates about the new leisure centres would multiply. The problems of urban renewal and pool replacement were, perhaps, part of that same concern.

The Altrincham Pool Complex in Cheshire. This toddlers splash pool is close to the learner pool. The public pool is in a separate adjacent hall.

1973 SHORT COURSE SWIMMING CHAMPIONSHIPS

(Under ASA Laws)

MARCH 29, 30 and 31, 1973
at the
PITTVILLE POOLS TOMMY TAYLOR'S LANE
CHELTENHAM

Sponsored by the **British Bottlers of Coca Cola**
and
Speedo (Europe) Ltd.

All seats are bookable - **50p** per session
Children half price
£2.50 for session tickets for 8 sessions
Daily tickets - Thursday and Saturday (3 sessions) **£1**
Friday (2 sessions) **70p**

Tickets obtainable from: **ASA Championships Booking Office,
Pittville Pools, Tommy Taylor's Lane, Cheltenham, Gloucs.**
(Telephone Cheltenham 28764)   Please enclose SAE

Cheltenham's new Pittville Pool was opened in May 1971 by Queen Elizabeth, the Queen Mother. It had a very impressive six-lane pool 33⅓ metres long and a separate diving pit.

There was accommodation for up to 600 spectators. The 1973 ASA Short-Course Swimming Championships were hosted there by the Western Counties. 59 records were broken at the event.

Since 1971 the main pool has been used also by the Cheltenham Swimming and Water Polo Cub.

The teams currently train there up to three times a week and use it for their home matches.

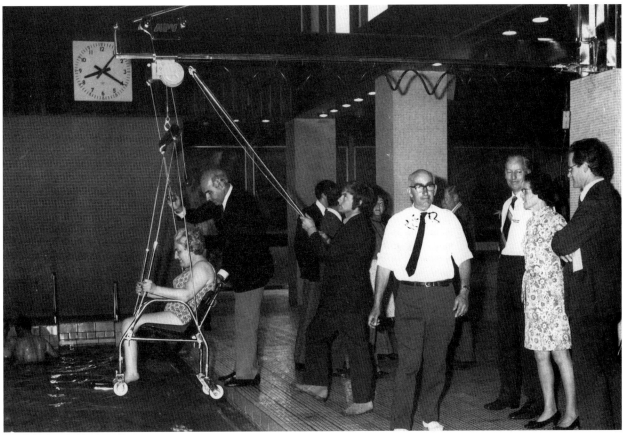

New developments in technology enabled the disabled to enjoy a swim in the 1980s.

In the early1970s a number of these moveable stainless steel bulkheads were installed in swimming pools. Hamilton Bland was involved in this development at Cumbernauld in Scotland. Cost at that time was c.£25,000 per installation. It enabled existing pools of 33⅓ yards or 33.3 metres to be adjusted to 25 metres for competition purposes.

Hamilton Bland demonstrated pool covers at his Swimming Pool Equipment Centre in 1982.

Mr. Alf Turner, OBE, AIB, (Hon. Treasurer of the ASA) presents a cheque for the purchase of a pool cover to Mr. D.J. Roberts, Chairman of 'Swim Torquay'. The ease of operation is adequately demonstrated. The President of the ASA, Mrs Stella Margetts, a stalwart of the Western District, looked on. (Copyright: Herald Express and Weekender Publications of Torquay)

In 1987 Ken Martin had a new pool named after him in Nottingham - an honour well deserved. Opened also in 1981 was the world's first permanent *Swimming Pool and Swimming-Pool Equipment Centre* at Leek Wootton in Warwickshire. This brainchild of Hamilton Bland was well supported by the ASA. In his position as NTO, coach and BBC commentator, his entrepreneurial talent was the springboard for this new venture where 20 companies exhibited under one roof. Here was a display which could be viewed by local authorities, architects and all those involved in pool developments. One of these companies, Omega, celebrated 50 years of the timing of world swimming events in 1982. It had been involved since the Los Angeles Olympic Games of 1932, although the first non-manual timing system was operated by Omega at the 1956 Melbourne Olympics. Technical developments had forged ahead over the 50 years and the expensive timing equipment was usually to be seen only in the most prestigious pools. Many clubs were aiming to raise money to install the OSM5 system together with an electronic scoreboard.

The main concern of the mid-1980s was that of leisure pool design: some ASA-affiliated clubs were dissatisfied with the proposed designs and the Association responded by forwarding a *'package preferred'* to local authorities.

In 1986 an ASA Conference - *Changing Design of Pools* - was organised at London's Barbican Centre. Hamilton Bland, as facilities expert, spoke on behalf of the ASA:

> *'There is no satisfactory compromise, either practical or financial, when considering the design of a free-form leisure pool. Research shows that very few leisure pools incorporating a 25m. straight actually staged swimming galas at any level although some training was done in them. The most successful leisure pools do not try to compromise competition and educational use with recreational use; separate water areas have been provided with great success in other areas. There are 2,500 swimming pools including 157 outdoor pools in the UK and hence controlled by local government. There are also 6,000 school pools, 300 public/preparatory school and college pools and 1,000 hotel and institutional pools. There are only 39 leisure pools. Most pools need refurbishment and local authorities then consider putting in flumes and water-slides to make them more attractive.'*

David Butler of the Sports Council's Technical Unit for Sport spoke on *The Leisurised Conventional Pool*. He confirmed the growth of slides and flumes in all kinds of pool and that in many areas leisure pool features were being superimposed on conventional pools to provide a completely new image. Some of these changes would adversely affect the use of pools for competition. He suggested that the ASA, Sports Council and IBRM should form a panel of experts to advise and develop a strategy. In fact such a committee comprising the ASA, IBRM, RLSS and the Sports Council representatives was set up in 1988.

In 1987 the Sports Council was considering the conversion of the Crystal Palace Pool to an ice-rink. The commercial pressure was great but opposition pressure was brought to bear and instead it was decided to invest £5 million in refurbishment.

Hamilton Bland in 1988 became the official ASA Facilities Consultant and spoke to architects about the leisure pool problems:

Extracts: *'(a) The first leisure pool was built at Bletchley in 1974. Since then 61 have appeared and eight more in the private sector. In spite of this there has been no in-depth study.*

(b) Swimming is the most expensive recreation or sport and needs the most expensive buildings. The ASA is the fifth largest sports governing body in the country with 1,700 clubs and the third highest club membership (300,000+).

(c) In 1978 - 1,073 public pools in England. In 1988 - 1,500 public pools.

(d) Leisure pools construction:

> *1974-79 - 17*
> *1980-86 - 20*
> *1987-88 - 24*
> *Perhaps 100 by 1992.*

(e) No one knows the effect these pools are having on the teaching of swimming, clubs or on the fitness of swimmers.

This Leisure Pool at Sunderland's Crowtree Leisure Centre was opened by Prince Charles in May 1978. Date palms, wave machine and irregular pool outline were typical features of leisure pools. Slides and flumes were also introduced. The ASA was concerned about competition swimming space.

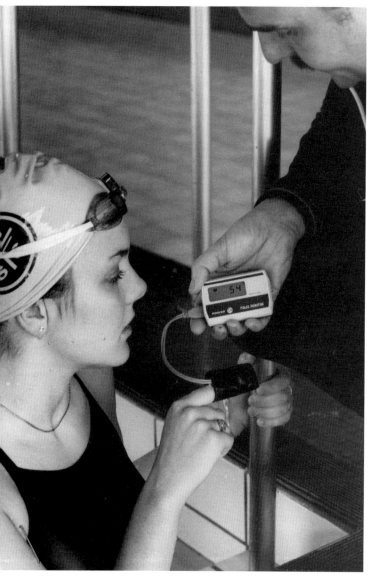

Taking the pulse! Easy-to-use bathside instrumentation benefitted both coaches and swimmers in recent years.

(f)   *In 1974 the Sports Council looked at the development of leisure pools and had commented on:*

(1) the high middle class usage;

(2) the part played by the car;

(3) the large catchment areas; and

(4) the attraction of such innovations as the wave machine.

There were no answers about the effect on the teaching of swimming.

[The Sports Council have now (in 1988) commenced such a study.]'

Hamilton Bland then confirmed the ASA belief that leisure pools should be complementary to conventional pools.

He provided a checklist for the purpose of analysing the needs of a local population in swimming terms. This included an analysis of existing facilities and user groups within an area, establishing the physical bath requirements for each user, estimating user figures and considering the effect of a new facility on existing provision.

A new threat to swimming loomed in 1988 with the Sports Minister's announcement that 'local authority pools would all be subject to *Compulsory Competitive Tendering or "Privatisation" by 1993'*. This would mean that all aspects of local authority-administered sport and leisure facilities would have to be put out to tender. David Reeves, ASA Secretary, reacted strongly. He supported the idea of *value for money* but many parts of the proposals would be against the swimmer's interest. Hamilton Bland was asked to oppose the proposals. The strategy was not to oppose competitive tendering but to try to protect three areas of importance: charges for admission and group hire; opening hours and programming; the use of facilities by minority groups such as *Water Polo, Synchronised Swimming* and the *Handicapped*. Early indications were that local authorities would, perhaps, retain some discretionary powers. The petitioning of the Government was the advice of some MPs. In 1988 David Reeves and David Sparkes both voiced the concern about clubs being put at the mercy of financial operators intent on achieving financial targets. In 1990 Hamilton Bland advised clubs to canvas their local leisure services committees to ascertain that club nights and training times would be fully protected and the ASA brought out a policy document for *Local Authorities to Safeguard the Use of Facilities by Swimming Clubs*. A variety of specimen questions were prepared: *'What happens to pool hire charges? When will clubs be allowed to hire pools? Will clubs be allowed to teach swimming? Will lifeguards be required on club nights? Who will provide pool equipment?'*

These were worrying times for the ASA when a number of its main assets and achievements were being subjected to stress and strain.

As the ASA entered the 1990s its concern for developing soundly researched facilities and equipment continued to improve the lot of the swimmer. At some pools, such as Plymouth, Gloucester and Leicester, booms were developed to reduce pools temporarily to 25 metres in length. Water treatment research continued and consequently in some places chlorinisation methods were phased out. Lactate testing helped coaches to understand more about the onset of cramp. The scare about the onset of the AIDS disease being spread in swimming pools was soon dispelled. Research was initiated to improve acoustics in pools and a study was made of changing-room requirements. The TSB backed an ASA initiative in 1988 to promote health and safety in pools and new sets of guidelines were produced.

In 1990 David Reeves emphasised the need for 50 metre subregional pools to be developed in England. These need not be so sophisticated as the prestige pool and would need no great spectator areas. The strategy would be for a final figure of ten 50 metre pools for international and national events and 20 more modest sub-regional pools. This was a very ambitious target.

In 1991 the 50 metre Ponds Forge Pool opened in Sheffield. Hamilton Bland acted as the senior consultant to the architects Faulkner Browns of Newcastle on Tyne. He was responsible for the layout, design and grouping of the 50 metre and diving pools.

Two views of the 50m. Ponds Forge Pool in Sheffield which was opened in1991. (Copyright of both images: Alan Towse)

The ASA had acted in an advisory capacity to both client and architect at the planning stage. Built at a cost of £52.8 million it would accommodate the needs of the World and European top swimmers. A National Conference of 73 local authorities and many architects was held there to display this new showcase.

In 1993 the 50 metre Stockport Pool was opened as a good example of a Regional facility and Hamilton Bland had acted as consultant to Stockport Metropolitan Borough Council. As Facilities Consultant for the ASA he was now receiving well over 200 enquiries each year from local authorities and other interested parties.

The ASA's part in the development of the world of the swimming pool had come a long way since 1869. The striving for basic conditions and cleanliness of the early days had given way to the pursuit of technical excellence in every aspect of the sport. The achievements are legendary.

The 50 metre Stockport Pool opened in 1993. (Copyright: Alan Towse)

Chapter 6 :

Costumes and Personal Equipment

JEUX OLYMPIQUES DE 1924 _ NATATION
ÉQUIPE DE GRANDE BRETAGNE

Comment in *Breaking the Ice*, 1964.

'....... *another contribution to swimming development is the matter of costumes and the disappearance of Victorian prudery. Modern costumes and trunks present minimum resistance and incidentally are less likely to cause offence than the complicated absurdities of the last century which, when wet, were often objectionable and certainly uncomfortable.*'

Introduction

Nude bathing is not an innovation of the twentieth century and the evidence suggests that from the earliest times most people swam unclothed. Parsons Pleasure at Oxford was a celebrated riverside bathing place where males of all ages and status, even fellows of colleges as well as their students, swam naked. Almost all early drawings of swimmers show them without clothes. The concern about the wearing of swimming costumes seems to have been a product of the nineteenth century. It is during this period that challenges to the tradition of nude bathing began to appear, particularly if the venue lay adjacent to public rights of way where both sexes passed. Many reports of affronts to taste and dignity of passers-by were published in local newspapers in all parts of Great Britain. For example, on 9 June 1837 *The Loughborough Telegraph* carried such a news item about the indecency of male nude bathing in the River Soar.

Expressions of what is meant by decent have depended upon arguments between, on the one hand, the judiciary and law enforcement agencies, and on the other hand, those leaders of changes in social conduct and fashion. Real or imagined obscene gestures and antics or circumstances which challenged the mores of polite society always attracted the attention of the state law

'Ladies Bathing', from Sinclair and Henry's 'Swimming' of 1893, shows costumes and caps. On the left an instructor in street costume holds a rope attached to the harness. The presence of the ship suggests that the modesty screen had limitations.

enforcement agencies. Indelicate or gross behaviour was assumed to be more likely when swimmers wore no costume. The outward form of decorum was synonymous with being dressed in a costume. It seems likely that in informal settings swimmers might include amongst their number, people who had scant regard for authority. Such persons enjoyed the prospect of shocking the conventionally minded. Targets for attack were those people who had arrogated to themselves the right to judge and laid claim to being morally impeccable.

Support for the covering of bodies came from people with a variety of motives. Nakedness or near nudity offended some people because it was thought to arouse lust or vicious desires. Such opinions were found in the writings and speeches of evangelicals but were shared by other groups in society. Shyness of exposure of the body to the gaze of others made costumes seem desirable protection. Yet others did not wish to offend anyone's susceptibilities. We possess neither evidence about how widespread these values were in society, nor what part fashion played in altering attitudes to enable politicians and others to claim to know what public opinion was. All we have are published editorial views in the press and the records of organisations which discussed the making of legislation or tested legal opinion in court cases. We have access to the reactions which were reported in letters to members of Parliament, at public meetings or other places where views were aired as, for example, at ASA Council.

Until the early nineteenth century both sexes swam naked. It seems to have been customary for the sexes to have chosen separate venues. Proprieties required avoiding each other in such places. Covering the body became increasingly common to avoid

peeping toms. Expectations changed during the nineteenth century as a consequence of the increasing concern about decency and respectability. However, books about swimming produced during the first part of the century usually showed men and boys unclothed. By the end of the century it would be impossible to find a contemporary publication with an illustration of a swimmer without a costume.

⁎⁎

WHEN are promoters of entertainments to which ladies are admitted going to insist on competitors wearing strict University costume. Under such circumstances it is impossible to be too circumspect, in fact a greater necessity exists for properly and effectually clothing the body and extremities to the knee than is enforced at athletic meetings. I am not a bashful man, but really the disregard paid to attire generally at swimming entertainments is becoming a serious question, and if an improvement is not soon effected, and due consideration paid to deportment just before starting for a race, ladies will be conspicuous by their absence.

———

NOTTINGHAM CLUB.

Next Tuesday the members hold an entertainment at the Sneinton Baths in costume. The programme includes a two lengths handicap, novices handicap, ornamental swimming, tub tournament, four-in-hand chariot race, Siamese twins race, long dive, and polo match between the Nottingham and Birmingham Leander Clubs.

For much of the nineteenth century men swam naked but in later years this custom declined. Insistence on costume became widespread. In 1884 it still made news as in the case of the Nottingham SC.

MISS AGNES BECKWITH.

No. 2.—Feb 23, 1884.]   [Price, One Penny.

Bathing beauty was used to promote 'Notes'. Later in the year it became 'Swimming Notes'. Agnes Beckwith swam professionally with her father and brother at many galas in the London area.

Many earlier descriptions or representations of swimming costumes survive having had women as their subject. Sea bathing for women in the middle years of the nineteenth century required wearing garments which, in later reports, were said to be all enveloping. Even then women so clad were shielded from prying eyes or casual glances from passers-by through the judicious use of a bathing machine and canvas hoods. Such garb probably limited swimming and might have been hazardous for anyone attempting to swim more than a few strokes.

Slightly more suitable was the costume illustrated in Ralph Thomas' *Swimming* as '*the old fashioned bathing gown*'. The girl waded ashore wearing a long sleeved dress with skirts covering the ankles. It is probable that she wore drawers or knickerbockers too. It is said that the skirts were usually hitched up under water so that a woman could make the leg movements in swimming. The artist seems to have sketched a rather cumbersome bathing cap.

The costume reproduced in Thomas's study came from Harry Gurr's *Swimming* and it was said to have been worn in the mid 1860s at Biarritz in France. It is not clear how the bowler hat was secured to the lady's head in the water. Her sculpted tunic top had a tight belt at the waist and it covered a voluminous dress with sleeves to the elbows. The outfit was completed with boots. If such attire was more than a fantasy of the publisher's artist, there can be little surprise that many women chose not to swim - or even to bathe in the sea.

By the middle of the nineteenth century upper and middle class women had become encumbered with very bulky clothing as a result of the dictates of fashion and taste. Its consequences were to restrict the normal workings of internal organs and to ensure a burden of about 6 kilogrammes of garments. These usually included six full petticoats, whale bone corsets and tight lacing to produce a shaped figure. Not all women, so dressed, welcomed the tediousness of dressing nor the restrictions it placed on normal movements. Challenges to this orthodoxy came from several quarters but undoubtedly the most effective publicist for dress reform was Mrs Amelia Bloomer, an American Quaker, who campaigned for women's rights in the United States and visited the British Isles to support colleagues of the same persuasion. Adopting '*Bloomers*', a form of pantaloons, in place of skirts not only made cycling feasible for women, but it indicated that there were numbers of women who wanted to lead more active lives. This included a desire to swim in appropriately designed costumes fit for the task.

By the end of the nineteenth century '*a modern costume*' illustrated in *Swimming* showed the bather was about to enter a bathing machine wearing knickerbockers to the knees and a short sleeved tunic belted at the waist. Such a modern costume had its rivals including the one approved by the ASA for ladies in the 1890s.

Men adopted swimming costumes regularly only after the middle of the nineteenth century, coinciding with the formation of the ASA. The pressure to wear costumes became increasingly the norm during the 1860s. Swimming bath proprietors, particularly local authorities, required such dress and even offered them for use, usually at no charge. The progress of the custom amongst men of wearing costumes was sufficiently recent for a report in *The Swimmer* of May 1886 to state:

'*Polytechnic. The swimming bath of the Polytechnic Institute, Regent-street (London), was crowded to excess last Monday when an entertainment, as opening ceremony for the season took place. As costume was worn by all competitors, a large number of ladies availed themselves of the opportunity to witness the racing and appeared to take very great interest in the proceedings. In addition to the subjoined racing, Professor Oakes, the instructor gave an exhibition of ornamental swimming, and the programme also included a Water Polo Match and an Aquatic Derby*'.

the old fashioned bathing gown

lady's bathing costume f~
(s.s.)

a modern costume   a more modern costu~

Thomas, in 1904, described this mid nineteenth century costume as 'the old fashioned bathing gown'. It impeded movement in water as much as the costume shown by Gurr in 1860s. By about 1900 costumes had become less cumbersome. Thomas called one 'a modern costume' and another 'more modern costume' which resembled the style authorised by the ASA.

One of the last baths to oblige men to be dressed was the Endell Street baths in London in the later 1890s when, at first, swimmers were charged one penny for the hire of a costume. This was soon discontinued.

ASA and the regulation of swimming costumes

Private organisations such as the ASA presented themselves as respectable: they were reluctant to offend the established order in any way. For many years since its foundation the membership of the Association included people who shared the values of those who objected to nakedness in public places. Dress provided an immediate advertisement of probity and respect for legality. The significance of the ASA being above reproach became of immediate concern when swimming galas were open to spectators of both sexes. The advent of mixed swimming gave further impetus to the scrutiny of costume as an adjunct of propriety.

The ASA adopted the approach taken by its predecessor bodies in legislating about dress and equipment. It regarded laws for costumes as a necessity because *respectability* and *decency* were unchallengable watchwords during the Victorian era and afterwards. Concerns about balancing fashion, efficiency and accept-able dress have continued until the present time. The history of costumes has reflected both the attitudes of the legislators to fashion and the needs of swimmers, particularly when the fabrics available for making costumes have undergone many technical developments. Laws about personal equipment (such as caps, ear plugs, goggles and nose clips) had their rationale in the desire of national and, later, international bodies, to ensure that competition was fair. Again technological innovations made possible the creation new kinds of equipment as well as changes in the social and physical environment in which swimming took place.

Laws about costume and personal equipment formed part of its assertion of authority over swimming activities. This aspect of the Association's work had its counterparts amongst other major sporting bodies where uniformity of dress was becoming accepted as symbolic of being a member of the group which followed a common code of behaviour. Examples of such dress requirements amongst competitors included those in amateur athletics, those cricketers accepting the jurisdiction of Marylebone Cricket Club, and at the end of the nineteenth century, all club members of the Lawn Tennis Association. Standardisation was argued by Cummins, editor of the *Swimming Times*, writing in 1928 to have been one of the

Old styles fascinated readers of Swimming Times. 'What we wore - a few years ago!' is the title here. This writer of 1933 did not date the garments. These resembled those worn between 1880 and 1900.

motives for the original costume law of the ASA with the intention of making all swimmers equal.

The first formal legislation of the ASA about costume was introduced in 1890. It specified dress as follows:

Regulations for university costume, which must be observed in all costume races

1. Only black, red, or dark-blue costumes, shall be worn.

2. Drawers shall be worn underneath the costume.

3. Trimmings may be used ad lib.

4. The shoulder-straps of costumes shall not be less than two inches wide.

5. All costumes shall be buttoned on the shoulder, and the armhole shall be cut no lower than three inches from the armpit.

6. In the front the costume shall reach not lower than five inches below the pit of the neck.

7. At the back the costume shall be cut straight from the top of the shoulder to the top of the shoulder.

8. The costume shall extend no less than four and a half inches from the crutch downwards, and shall be cut in a straight line round the circumference of the leg.

N.B. - It is recommended that manufacturers make their costumes in accordance with the above regulations'.

Subsequently, the ASA amended its regulations to include women when, in 1899, they entered competitions under ASA laws. Although ladies' costumes had similar specifications to men's there was a requirement that the ladies should have '*a shaped arm at least three inches long shall be inserted*' and by 1904 the law stated that ladies costume '*shall be cut straight round the neck*'. There were alterations to meet various changes of taste and fashion. In 1901 the ASA law restricted colour choice even more by the deletion of red from the permitted list.

In 1909 the costume law was revised to define some aspects of dress design more explicitly. Drawers under the costume '*must be of a triangular pattern, with a minimum width of two and a half inches at the fork; they must meet on each hip, and must not be less than 3 inches on each side when fastened*'. The other change was to redraft the requirement about the legs to read: '*In the leg portion the costume shall extend to within three inches of the knee, and shall be cut in a straight line round the circumference of each leg*'.

The men who constituted the Committee of the ASA directed their serious attention to the increasing numbers of women competitors by inserting a new dress requirement. In 1909 the Law 122 had a special clause (i) which said:

'Ladies' Races in Public. - At all meetings where both sexes are admitted, lady competitors over 14 years of age must wear on leaving the dressing room, a long coat or bath gown before entering and immediately after leaving the water'.

These requirements remained unchanged until 1931.

In a discussion of costumes suitable for lady divers in 1915 a commentator referred to the value of stockings. Amongst the advantages it was said that '*the rougher stockings deaden the splash*'.

At the Olympic Games held in Amsterdam in 1928 British ladies, according to the ASA Law, wore bath gowns over their costumes. The British Olympic badge decorated the left arm.

One of the disadvantages of stockings was that they '*tend to make the wearer slip*'. The author came to the conclusion that stockings were aesthetically displeasing and had few practical merits.

In 1931 the ASA simplified the wording and length of the law. The debate about the alterations to costume had begun several years before. Many foreign swimming competitors at the Olympic Games in 1928 had worn costumes much less restrictive than the style favoured by the ASA. Particular criticisms included the chaffing caused by sleeves and tight cutting of material under the arms. Progress through the water was slowed or made difficult by the costume skirts. Other points included the view that the lack of colour gave a drab image to swimmers and swimming. The editor of *The Swimming Times*, Captain Cummins, wrote in 1928 that the requirement: '*compels ladies to wear more in the swimming bath than they do at a dance*'. However, a journalist, *Water Rat* of the *Birmingham Sports Argus*, feared that ladies swimming races '*will look like a lot of jockeys lined up for a horse race with their different coloured shirts*'. He wrote in 1930 that the races will develop into a '*glorified mannequin parade*'. Such prejudice, without evidence, may have captured some support but the new law was passed unanimously by the ASA Council.

Captain Cummins commented in 1930 on two newspaper articles. First was 'Girls Who Arouse Dangerous Passions', which stated:

'*Many young men have been sexually aroused either by taking part in mixed bathing or, more particularly, by attending some bathing pool or being at some similar place and watching a number of women in bathing costumes*'.

Cummins observed:

'*Young men of the type he refers to can get cheap sensations on many places other than the swimming bath, and further, this criticism seems out of place in a publication of a periodical which publishes photographs of men in the nude (except for a fig leaf), and girls in bathing costumes, etc*'.

The second item, 'Hands Off' was a contribution in *The Leader* praising the University style of costumes for girls of that time and comparing them to the Mrs Grundy styles of 1900. Cummins merely remarked: '*After all we must either be 'pessimists' or 'optimists*'. *Honi soit qui mal y pense* ('*Disgrace be to him who evil thinks*').

The ASA *Handbook* of 1931 set out the revised law as follows:

'*Competitors' Costumes. Competitors in events held under ASA laws before audiences of both sexes shall wear swimming costumes and drawers or slips, except that, other than in diving events, drawers or slips may be dispensed with when the costume worn is of the skirt variety. In the case of female competitors over 14 years of age, a long coat or bath gown must be worn before entering and after leaving the water.*

Costumes. These must conform to the following specifications:-

(a) *The material shall be cotton, silk, wool, or any combination of such materials providing the texture is non-transparent.*

(b) *Cotton or silk costumes must be black or dark blue in*

In 1929 Messrs J. Crofts organised a mannequin parade of Bathing Belles for a ball at the Skegness Casino for the local swimming club. Not all this 'beach apparel' would have satisfied ASA law.

THE "JACK HATFIELD"

SWIMMING COSTUMES

as worn by himself in all his successes; also by all the
World's Champions. None genuine without Jack Hatfield's
photograph attached to the neck of the costume. Supplied to
all the British Olympic Teams.

Gent.'s	...	...	..	...	...	2/11
Ladies' (without Sleeves)	..	...	...	2/11
Ladies' (with Short Sleeves)	..	...	...	3,6
Light Silk Racing Costumes	...	...	...	21/-
Racing Slips to wear under the Costume	per pair	1/6

JACK HATFIELD

Wholesale & Retail Sports Outfitter,

6-8, Newton St., MIDDLESBOROUGH.

Official Outfitter to the British Olympic Swimming Team

Jack Hatfield had represented his country in international swimming competitions and was ASA national champion in the 220 yards free style in 1912, 1913, 1922 and 1925. As a sports outfitter his endorsement of swimming garments in 1928 was a valuable business asset.

colour, but bindings of club colours may be used. Wool costumes may be of any colour or combination of colours, provided that such colours do not make the costume appear transparent.

(c) Costumes shall be one-piece, devoid of open work, and reach within three and a half inches of the base of the neck, back and front. All fastenings shall be on the shoulder, and the arm hole cut not lower than three inches from the arm pit. In the leg portion, the costume shall extend two inches from the inner leg seam, and shall be cut in a straight line round the circumference of each leg.

Note. - Manufacturers are advised to submit to the Association samples of costumes, and if these are approved, they will be permitted to advertise them as approved ASA costumes'.

The significance of the Note lay in the desire of the ASA to assert its authority, its wish to protect competitors from buying 'illegal' garments. Perhaps it intended to send a warning to Mr Eyles, owner of the Jantzen Company, whose costumes were worn by some competitors at the Blackpool ASA Olympic trials of 1928. These did not conform to the, then current, Association law.

Outside of competitive swimming there was considerable variation in the design and materials used for costumes. When the *Swimming Times* introduced its ladies' page in 1936 an early article described how to make a brassiere style swimming top from handkerchiefs and a button. Thus the home dressmaker had the opportunity of making the modish two piece costume. Of course, this fashionable costume departed from the austere law of the ASA.

Some further recognition of fashion and the prevalent attitudes to dress resulted in a much briefer statement of the law relating to swimming costumes in 1939. The new regulations read:

'Competitors in events held under ASA laws before audiences of both sexes shall wear:

MALES: Either:- (a) swimming costumes with drawers or slips underneath; or (b) swimming trunks with drawers or slips underneath providing the wearing of trunks is sanctioned by the bath authority concerned.

LADIES: Swimming costumes of one piece, devoid of open work excepting at the back. Fastenings, if any, shall be on the shoulders.

The texture of all swimming costumes and trunks shall be non-transparent'.

In the *Handbook* for 1948 there was a reminder that stewards at events had the duty to enforce strictly the law, which had remained unchanged since 1939.

The ASA Council was anxious to encourage swimming in England, particularly since the Olympic Games were to be held in London in that year. Council petitioned the government in 1948 to allow more rubber swimming caps and woollen costumes to be placed on the home market. Shortages of these garments arose from the post war rationing of clothing which was intended to release manufacturing production of all kinds for export. The Second World War had left amongst its legacies massive overseas debt which the nation needed to reduce. Special provision was made for those selected for the British Olympic Team. The *Swimming Times* announced in July 1948 that the British Olympic Association was supplying each competitor with a uniform whilst:

In 1934 Myers, the Bradford manufacturers, advertised costumes and beach suits in the Swimming Times.

Left—Miss Ruby Keeler, the Warner Bros. famous film star, in her new Jantzen Costume.

Right — Warner Bros. favourite film star, Miss Lorena Layson, in her new Jantzen Costume.

During the 1930s the Swimming Times ran a series on fashion 'for our lady readers' and in 1933 Gabrielle de la Mare used these to illustrate 'what we wear to win'.

'Messrs Jantzen's Knitting Mills Ltd are generously providing specially woven and made silk costumes/trunks for swimmers and Lastex costumes/trunks for divers and water polo players; Messrs North's Rubber Company, Ltd., are making a gift of caps for ladies and Mr Church (father of one of the competitors) white shoes of uniform pattern for the ladies'.

At this time the clothing did not carry the makers' names in visible places. This would have been contrary to tradition and not in accord with the amateur ethos.

During the decades following the Second World War there had been many changes in materials, design of fashions, and the swimmers' requirements. New materials were usually accepted but

---

The Swimming Times.
July——1936.

Ladies' Page
by
"PEARL"

FASHION

This youthful frock is just the thing for sports, for swimming galas, for holidays, for the garden and for the river—for all sorts of pleasant fresh-air days and "going places." Its special claims to smartness are the new round neckline and amusing round pockets to match. Make it up in white, with coloured buttons, belt and stitchings; slip a gay coloured hanky into your pocket, and you've a frock of real personality.

The newest sports-and-fresh-air frock, with a smart round neck and amusing rounded pockets to match. Buttons and belt are in contrasting colour. For 36 inch bust: 35/6 inch material, 3¼ yards. Bust sizes 32 to 40 inches.

Pattern (1/-, post free) from Weldons Ltd., 30/32. Southampton Street, Strand, W.C.

97793.

FOR SUN BATHING AND SEA BATHING!

You can tan without burning and bathe without shivering if you use 'Bronzola.' It is a perfect Skin Food, made specially for the famous Jersey Swimming Club, whose members are noted for their lovely sun-tanned skins. They also use 'Bronzola' for long distance swims, because it keeps out the cold and makes swimming easier.

This nourishing skin protection is only obtainable from the Jersey Swimming Club, Jersey, C.I., and they will send you a large jar on receipt of a P.O. for 1/- or you can have the double size, price 1/6.

Whatever you do, don't fail to include 'Bronzola' in your summer holiday outfit; it is essential for acquiring a beautiful even tan.

The Swimming Times.
July——1936.

Made from a Handkerchief!

This well-fitting brassiere costs less than 6d. to make and is extremely simple to do. You will only require 1 handkerchief, 1 yard ribbon, ¼ yard elastic (½-in.), 1 button.

The size of the handkerchief depends upon your bust measurement. For 34-in. and 36-in. busts, an 11 inch square is best; for 38-in. and 40-in. busts, a 13 inch square is most suitable.

Making.

Cut handkerchief in half, diagonally, see Diagram 1. Hem bottom of each triangle. Put in darts as shown in Diagram 2. Stitch elastic to point A, attach button to point B. Cut ribbon in half and attach one piece to point C and the other to point D. Loop the other ends round elastic and pin into place. Try on the brassiere and adjust straps and elastic accordingly. Finish sewing the straps. Make a small ribbon loop on the elastic for fastening and your garment is complete!

ARE YOU A BAD SAILOR?

If you take an "1870" Tablet before going on board you will not be sea-sick during the trip. I know, because I am one of the world's worst sailors, yet "1870" Tablets keep me as fit as a fiddle whilst tossing about on the high seas! This sea-sickness cure is absolutely harmless and has no after-effect.

I can tell you where to buy these tablets if you write to me enclosing a stamped addressed envelope for the reply.

"Pearl,"
c/o. "Swimming Times,"
4, Waddon Park Avenue, Croydon.

Mark your envelope "1870" in the top left hand corner.

During the later 1930s the Swimming Times ran a regular feature: 'Ladies' Page' by Pearl whose tip for July 1936 was for a costume 'Made from a Handkerchief'. Undoubtedly this was daring advice when two piece costumes were still novel and would not have satisfied ASA law.

prizewinners of 19...

A.S.A. approved and all
carry off the trophies
sleek classics are i
to fit, knitted for co
knitted for
'**Racer**', the trim dr
trunks, are s
designed to gi
athletic con
action. The
in smoot
point, fe
quick
inside sup
30" to 42"
Same style i
pure wool, fron
and in crimp nylor
'**Y' Back Sw**
for women an
in wool from 2
petit point fron
Women's
crimped nylor

• Matching
swimcaps
rubber.
DIVING C
design, 5/
DIVING B
de-luxe m

Jantzen — best-fitting, best-looking

Jantzen, a major manufacturer of swimming garments, won design prizes in 1958. During the 1950s styles evolved and, by 1958, ASA laws allowed discrete logos and trims.

costumes in synchronised swimming and racing. The specifications read:

*'**Costumes.** A competitor in any event under A.S.A. laws held in the presence of both sexes shall wear:-*

Male. A swimming costume or trunks, providing the wearing of trunks is permitted by the bath authority.

Female. Costumes of one piece devoid of open work except at the back. The front extension for the legs shall not be less than 5.0 centimetres from the crotch and may be cut in a curved line extending upwards and backward around the circumference of the thigh; the highest point of this curved line shall not be less than 10.2 centimetres below the crest of the hip bone (ileum).

The costume shall be cut no more than 11.5 centimetres from the sternal notch in front and not more than 5.0 centimetres below the crease (axilliary fold) of the arm in front.

If any type of fastener is used it may be placed on the shoulder strap or extending between the two shoulder straps at a functional (suitable) position in the region of the shoulder blades (scapulae).

occasionally the ASA committee had to advise on costumes which new technology or ingenuity made possible. For example, in 1953, the Committee ruled that unsinkable swimwear was not in accord with ASA laws. During this period there was a sharp divergence between the designs of costumes for sun bathing and swimming. Sunbathing costumes became briefer - daring, according to the press commentators - so that by the early 1960s in some Mediterranean resorts topless bathing for women had become permissible. By the 1980s tolerance of nudity had extended to some public beaches in Britain. The priorities of swimmers were different. They did not want an all over tan but they required garments which were comfortable to wear and provided the lowest possible drag in the water in order not to lose speed. Costume designers took advantage of the newer textiles which became available after 1945. Figure supporting garments for men and women became available in many colours and styles. These paid some attention to fashion but met the needs of swimmers. Some swimmers wanted to dress ever more in line with sunbathing taste and this caused debates between those who favoured tradition and those who wanted freedom of choice. The debates culminated in 1987 with the attempts of FINA to define the characteristics of an acceptable costume.

The 1987 FINA regulations on costume were accepted by the ASA at its 1987 Council in the context of FINA's comments about the concern, world wide, about the wearing of scantier

Bukta used the latest materials in the 1960s such as bri-nylon, a knitted fabric. It enabled garments to hug the figure and might have reduced drag through the water. The Olympic Games of 1960 inspired their 'Roma 60' which conformed to ASA laws, a further selling point.

The texture of the costumes and trunks shall be non-transparent.

Note: The measurements as given are approximate. The object is to debar immodest costumes'.

The comment of the *Swimming Times* report on the acceptance of these specifications was that referees would only check a costume if it seemed to be immodest. Such minute specifications raised questions about the methods needed for their enforcement and the meaning of immodest.

In the ASA costume laws for following year the law was renumbered 116. In 1989 the ASA law was renumbered and rewritten entirely to accord with further changes by FINA. Again it was accepted that the referee had the power to decide what was acceptable. The new law 121 stipulated:

'121.1 The costumes of all competitors shall be in good moral taste and suitable for the individual sports discipline.

121.2 All costumes shall be non-transparent.

121.3 The referee of a competition has the authority to exclude any competitor whose costume does not comply with this rule'.

No further changes had been made by 1995.

Technology and Fabrics

In the nineteenth century makers of swimming costumes used the fabrics currently available. These included cotton, silk and woollens. Amongst the latter the most popular were flannel and serge because these had a density which prevented garments becoming transparent when they were immersed in water. Silk seems to have been reserved for bathing caps for ladies and for the more expensive decorative costumes.

Although ASA authorised change in styles between 1890 and the 1920s, costumes at affordable prices were mainly made from knitted woollen materials. More expensive garments were available in silk. Many costumes, unless carefully designed in an appropriate fabric, altered their shape when wet. Thus, a demure garment, once immersed, revealed many contours of the wearer's body. Even the officially approved costumes made from specified materials were not always as unrevealing as designers intended.

At the Olympic Games of 1924 in Paris, Austin Rawlinson recalled that he, with the rest of the British team, wore silk costumes. Hatfields of Middlesborough supplied them. Jack Hatfield, son of the founder of the firm, had been an outstanding swimmer and a national champion no less than 38 times. He understood the finer points for making comfortable and practical garments, given the constraints of the laws of the ASA and, later, FINA regulations.

The emergence of cheap man-made fibres made relatively little impact on costume manufacturing before the Second World War. The production of rayon (artificial silk) seems to have been used only to a limited extent in the 1930s. However, by 1939 the ASA laws no longer specified the materials to be used, a tacit recognition of the advances in technology. After the Second World War ended in 1945, major changes in fabrics became commercially feasible and were promoted as fashionable. One of the first of the new man-made fibres to attract costume designers was nylon but by the 1950s other polymers came on the market. The processes of making these gave scope for developing garments which looked attractive at the same time as satisfying the requirements of swimming's ruling body. Sparing the embarrassment of swimmers and spectators was an important criteria. It was hoped to prevent officials having to enforce the regulations.

Among the subtle external influences was the promotion of sunbathing. The expectations among customers that garments served the dual purposes of sunbathing and swimming. Thus, for women the two piece costume of pants and brassiere top gradually diminished in their coverage to become the bikini which was sold extensively by the 1960s. Trunks with leg coverings for males were replaced by briefer pants. In the early 1990s the known dangers of prolonged exposure of the skin to harmful radiation did not have an immediate impact for design.

In 1962 the ASA authorised Dr George Eaves, chairman of its Scientific Advisory Committee, to undertake research on the problems of drag in swimming costumes. Such an investigation of the nature of the fabrics and their positioning on the swimmer's body had become necessary because of the importance of small differences in timing in speed competitions. Swimmers hoped to improve their results. The outcome of this work did not receive any publicity in ASA sources but seems to have informed swimmers in their choice of costume.

Ironically, in the *Swimming Times* during the ASA's centenary year, 1969, there appeared an article: '100 years of swimming costumes - the ultimate is with us now'. The authors, Mavis and Derrick Plume, argued that the ultimate was nakedness! However, they also argued that in due course a one piece garment, made of an as yet unknown material, weighing only 7 centigrams, would become available by the year 2069. In the quarter century after 1969 further developments, rather more mundane than those predicted by the Plume's, occurred which took advantage of fabrics knitted from new fibres. By the 1980s Lycra and other fibres allowed costumes to become lighter in weight and with characteristics which reduced drag as water passed over the fabrics. The processes of experiment and designs continued. It was announced in 1994 that Teflon treated fabrics had moved from the laboratory into clothing production. Two swimwear companies (Adidas and Triumph) produced garments in the new fabric. This process added to the water repellent qualities of the materials whilst permitting them to 'breathe'. It was claimed that these costumes would give some advantage to swimmers who are high speed performers because of the very low drag quality. Such assistance to the highest performing athletes might make the difference in timing of a fraction of a second, crucial in these sports.

One of the most spectacular changes in official ASA costumes was the use of colour once the laws restricting the range were removed. New materials and dyestuffs made possible the manufacture of colour-fast prints in many hues. Some changes were made in the 1930s with a more open policy after 1970. Even ASA representative teams came to wear much more colourful costumes. Perhaps the advent of colour television for British viewers in 1968 gave impetus to the provision of visually attractive garments which appealed to the fashion-conscious.

Costume Manufacturing

Making costumes at home or by bespoke tailoring undoubtedly took place but large-scale output required factory methods and appropriate marketing. Knitted fabrics had been produced in the East Midlands long before the growth in demand for swimming costumes and these were readily adapted as the need arose. By the early twentieth century the firm of Jarvis and Company of Leicester was taking advantage of the owner's swimming achievements to advertise costumes associated with his name in trade papers such as *The Sports Trader*.

Changes in the relationship of costume manufacturers to the ASA became manifest after the Second World War. Ever wary of the potential danger to the amateur status of the ASA's swimmers, manufacturers initially restricted themselves to taking advertising space in the *Swimming Times* and to offering costumes for purchase which conformed to ASA law. By the 1970s these advertisers were continuing to take prime spaces in what had become the Association's publication, and were also providing some costumes free of charge. Manufacturers were permitted to sponsor the official costumes in international events. For example, in 1973 Speedo provided the clothing for the Commonwealth games and in 1984 the Arena company made them for the British Olympic team. From the 1970s manufacturers also sponsored the events themselves.

By 1989 sponsorship was well established and the ASA moved to follow FINA regulations about the display of manufacturers' names on costumes. The Association insisted that there should be

Badges indicating club, team membership, or achievements were an important accessory for many swimmers. In 1960 Franklin's advertised the adornments permitted by ASA law.

no other promotion than the manufacturer's trade mark '*not exceeding 16 sq cm in area*'. However hats '*may carry two advertisements, including that of the manufacturer which might be no more than 16 sq cm in area*'. One of the two advertisements could be for a sponsor other than the manufacturer.

It seems likely that the relatively modest cost of costumes designed for competitive sport assisted in making swimming widely accessible to most classes in society. Swimming clubs

Costume parade at a London trade show in 1984 promoting Speedo designs.

Relaxation of the strict codes by 1980 permitted J. Wilmott to wear her team badge on her cap with the trade mark of Arena.

affiliated to the ASA had laws which specified the cut of garments, but not what additional embellishments clubs might wish to see on members' costumes.

Generally, bathing caps were worn by women more frequently than men. There was no ASA requirement that this should be the case but such head covering had the practical advantage of keeping hair out of the swimmers' eyes. Cap design for women in the later nineteenth century resembled cooks soft hats except that they were made of various fabrics, including pure silk. Such relatively voluminous hats were needed because the majority of ladies wore their hair long. Close fitting skullcaps became more common during the 1920s when fashionable young women often had their hair close-cropped. Many bathing caps were made from rubber to help to preserve hair styles and prevent the action of salt water or treated pool waters from damaging the hair or reacting with the chemicals used in its styling. In the years immediately following the Second World War rubber continued to be used, but the rapid changes in polymer chemistry made possible other water-proof materials for bathing caps which increased the range of styles and colours.

Personal Equipment

Aids for swimming have taken many forms since they became prevalent in the middle of the nineteenth century. Publications after about 1850 include many advertisements and articles about devices to help learners or to assist experienced swimmers. They usually focussed on ways improving buoyancy, promoting speed or adding to confidence in the water.

Sinclair and Henry, in their book, *Swimming* of the 1890s provided illustrations of water-wings, hand enlargers and flippers for the feet. They commented that some of the devices then on the market owed more to theory than to practical validation. Nonetheless a few of the less complex devices seemed to have foreshadowed some of the aids for learners which became available in the later twentieth century. For example there were hand paddles for additional thrust through the water, floats to provide buoyancy and flippers for speed.

During the twentieth century attempts to control the quality of water in pools generated additional problems. Hygiene was maintained by filtering and using chemical disinfectants such as chlorine. As a consequence infections of the ears and irritants in the eyes became hazards for some swimmers. Various types of goggles have been part of the swimming scene for more than half

Left and above: Norths produced swimming caps during the mid twentieth century. During the Second World War rubber became scarce and shortages continued after the war. This notice in May 1947 was later followed by prestige advertisements saying that limited quantities of their quality products were available. The price of 6 shillings 11 pence (about 35p) was relatively expensive.

O' Flanagan's, makers and wholesalers of goggles, advertised such items regularly in the long distance swimming season during the 1940s and 1950s.

a century. Increasing concerns about the safety of equipment culminated in the publication in 1979 of regulations covering the design and manufacture of goggles. Most goggles kept chlorinated water out of sensitive eyes and, some of those which had come on to the market, were made of materials which were easily damaged. They could themselves cause injuries, for example, when made of glass which chipped easily and created splinters. Coping with water in the ears taxed the ingenuity of various designers and manufacturers. There was a wide range of ear plugs on the market. Some were designed to ease the pressure in the ear which could sometimes be damaging for divers. The ASA laws set out in 1987 did not go so far as to recommend particular designs but merely specified that: '*Goggles, nose clips and ear plugs may be worn, except in Diving and Water Polo*'.

Overall costumes and personal equipment remained an ongoing matter of concern for the ASA. In relation to costume the initial responsibility of the Association could be seen as an attempt to guarantee the decency and respectability of all members. Only later did it moved towards regulating costume in terms of swimming efficiency and speed. It is also possible to trace a move away from closely prescribed costumes towards greater relaxation and greater choice of colour and style. In addition the Association has developed yet further its definitions of amateur in the acceptance of sponsorship and gifts to swimmers from manufacturers as well as the sponsorship of events.

Ear plugs were used by swimmers and divers from Victorian times. These had significance for swimmers and divers who were vulnerable to infections.

From earlier times floats were popular as swimming aids and continued in use as shown in the examples from 1970 and the 1980s.

EASISWIM HAND PADDLES

Something New for the Holidays!

The Easiswim Hand Paddles are not a novelty, but a proven aid to both the swimmer and the non-swimmer.

Made from a substance much lighter and even more buoyant than Cork. They give confidence to the novice and their large area provides the experienced swimmer an astonishing increase of speed.

The Easiswim Paddles are made in six popular colours and can be obtained from your local sports dealer, stores, etc.

Price **2/6**

Manufacturers :—

K. C. MORGAN
77 WATLING STREET, LONDON, E.C.4

Easiswim hand paddles took a full page advertisement in 1934.

20 out of 21 World Records broken at Munich Olympics by swimmers in Speedo

If you are after Olympic Golds then you need Speedo! Speedo Jetstream Swimsuits are designed to help you perform like the champions - just look at the Munich Olympic Medal count – 26 Gold, 23 Silver, 22 Bronze medallists all raced to success in Speedo Jetstream.

With Speedo Jetstream - the shape, the pattern, fit and stitching - all are meticulously designed for speed through water. Speedo's nylon material is so fine its no more than a second skin. Olympic medals have proved Speedo to be the world's leader in swimwear - it works for Champions and it can work for you.

Speedo has the largest range, in designs, colours and sizes - for men, women and children - see your Speedo stockist or write for his address to:-

Speedo (Europe) Ltd.
Sales Office:- Ascot Road, Nottingham, NG8 5AJ Tel: 0602-292341
London Office:- 4, Warwick Street, W1R 5WA Tel: 01-734 3449

Speedo Swim Goggles by Protector 75p each

1972

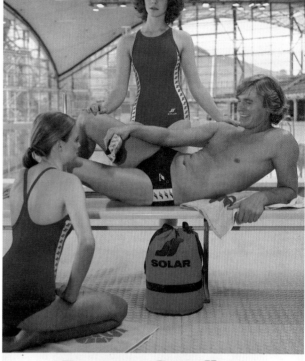

Duncan Goodhew Collection

SOLAR

1982

1986

1993

Between 1970 and 1994 swimwear styles reflected fashions, costume laws and the availability of new materials. These examples illustrate changes during this period.

Chapter 7

Diving

RUNNING HEADER

Comment by A. Sinclair and W. Henry in 1894.

Comment by A. Sinclair and W. Henry in 1894.

'The daring nature of the feats performed by modern divers are in themselves incentives to ordinary swimmers, and the general ambition of a beginner to become an expert diver. The whole secret of diving is in the possession of plenty of pluck and self-confidence. A man need not be a good swimmer to become an expert diver; there are many indeed, who can dive well but swim little......... The swimmer will fearlessly dive from a height, enter the water gracefully, and emerge therefrom ready for another dive immediately.'

Introduction

By the early nineteenth century there were many accounts of diving as a part of the world of work. Working under water was necessary for those harvesting pearl bearing oysters or for undertaking some tasks such as ship repair at sea. There was also the work of retrieving objects from the sea bed or the bottoms of pools or rivers. There were strict limitations on the depth to which workers could go and the length of time they could remain under water until the inventions of diving bells, pressurised suits, and wet suits. The history of diving as an employment, and of the technical developments which made it less dangerous, are outside the scope of this book.

The diving which is the focus of this chapter was not clearly defined until the beginning of the twentieth century. During the nineteenth century the term was ambiguous and attracted heated arguments about definitions. By the early nineteenth century *diving* had the meaning of swimming under water, often to depths, but included nothing about how the water was to be entered by the swimmer. The *plunge* was the distinctive term used to describe the way of springing or jumping into the water. The term also implied travel through or under water, but it did not imply any swimming action. People still continued to take plunges as in the past in order to see how far it was possible to move through the water from a land base but without making swimming strokes. However, plunging did not become a recognised event for international competitions. By the start of the twentieth

Above: Charles Peterson Mauritzi is in a graceful Swallow Dive at Highgate in the early twentieth century.

Below: J. Melville Clark is in the mid turn of a dive at Highgate.

century, it had become common to use the terms *diving* and *plunging* interchangeably, but the sport of springing or jumping into water *'so as to penetrate to some depth and then swimming'* soon came to have the exclusive designation of *diving*.

This type of diving became part of the entertainment at galas as well as less formal swimming events. The fancy and trick swimming performances included diving by such professors as Beckwith during the later years of the nineteenth century, and were described in reports of swimming club spectaculars arranged as galas or annual celebrations. The opportunities for spectators to see smoking underwater took place in juxtaposition with dives from stands which involved somersaults in the air and showy turns in the water. Dives from Tower Bridge into the River Thames or from high platforms into barrels at circuses and funfairs drew crowds, and gained both publicity and payments for the exponents of such showmanship.

A more serious consideration in fostering diving was the campaign by the RLSS to ensure that those who swam to save people in danger of drowning, had the proper techniques. Even so, William Henry, the driving force of the Life Saving Society (later Royal) and a prominent member of the ASA, wrote in *Pearson's Magazine* in 1900 about 'Diving as a fine art'. He illustrated his argument with the aid of the latest available technology, i.e. photographs. Creating the sport of diving required several conditions to be satisfied: places with sufficient depths of water, pleasure in achievement, acceptance of what constituted styles of diving, and agreed procedures in competition.

Finding appropriate locations for diving varied across the country. In many inland places it was necessary to build baths with sufficient depths to make the sport feasible. This limitation provided one of the sources of conflict between divers and other swimmers who regarded the increased costs of such depths in bath construction as inimical to their interests. Moreover, divers' needs in the use of baths conflicted with the time and space available for other swimmers.

Generating popular support for diving became a matter of growing importance during the last quarter of the nineteenth century and remained an important consideration during the twentieth century. This led to demonstrations of diving for the general public wherever possible. The beauty and the utility of skilful diving received great emphasis. Whilst some people appreciated the finer points, crowds often craved spectacular feats.

Diving in England was not an insular activity. The international connections of some of the leading divers allowed new ideas to flourish and to cross frontiers, no matter where they originated. In 1898 Otto Hageborge and Charles F. Mauritzi came to London to demonstrate *fancy diving*, which was being developed in Sweden. This took place at the Life Saving Society gala held at Highgate Pond, London. Mauritzi was a prominent exponent of gymnastics and undoubtedly made contact with members of the Life Saving Society who had visited Sweden that year. During their tour they saved someone from drowning, and for this the King of Sweden awarded them a medal. William Henry ensured that these activities gained maximum publicity.

The sport of diving had made its claim for recognition by the end of the nineteenth century. Crowds came to watch but participation depended upon facilities and opportunities to learn and practice techniques. These requirements were limited to the London area and to a few major urban centres elsewhere in the British Isles.

Organising diving and developing the laws of the sport under the ADA

Events focused on diving seem to have begun during the 1880s. The earliest United Kingdom diving championship took place in Scotland in 1889. This championship required competitors to dive from the side of the bath, about six feet above the water, and to make a surface dive. The first Plunge Dive Championship took place in 1893 under the laws of the ASA which had defined plunging and it remained listed in the *Handbook* until 1992. The first High Diving Championship took place in 1895 at Highgate Pond with the title of the National Graceful Diving Competition. The dives included standing and running dives from 15 feet and 30 feet. The rules of this competition remained unaltered until 1961. The event of 1895 attracted a small number of entrants despite being open to allcomers from anywhere in the world.

Diving received its international accolade as a sport in 1904 when the Olympic Games held events for men, but women divers had to wait until 1912, when a more limited programme was included for them.

The establishment of diving as an amateur sport depended on overcoming obstacles about what constituted diving, and how to compare and assess styles of performers. Within the swimming world some hostile critics regarded diving as *gymnastics with water* and did not wish to accept that distinctions between performers could be made with any consistency. Later synchronised swimming, which was dismissed somewhat scathingly as *ballet in the water*, had to overcome similar opposition. Nonetheless British exponents and enthusiasts continued to make efforts to encourage and organise diving as a competitive sport.

The success of championships and competitions necessitated some agreement on the criteria of what could be expected of performers. Thus it became imperative to have a recognised authority for making laws, to provide accurate definitions of styles, and to regulate the eligibility of participants.

These tasks fell to the Amateur Diving Association rather than to the ASA. Indeed in 1904 Thomas, in writing a history of swimming, noted that the ASA did not recognise for record purposes either diving or remaining under water. This did not prevent leading divers from taking steps to improve the standing and the quality of their sport. The Amateur Diving Association (ADA) was formed in 1901. Leading members of the diving fraternity regarded the ASA as the one sporting body whose principles of organisation might serve as a model for themselves and they accepted the term *'amateur'* to have the same meaning as the ASA. The ADA stated in 1903 that:

> '*This Association has been founded for promoting the sport of artistic diving - an art which the Swedes have brought to perfection, but which has been much neglected in this country - and for the purpose of representing the needs of divers to the various county and borough councils and others having charge of swimming baths and open-air bathing places*'.

The ADA published a statement of constitution and laws listing its founders, affiliations and member clubs as at 20 June 1903. However, the statement made plain that the ADA was formally established in 1901.

The ADA elected as its first President, the Earl of Mansfield on whose Kenwood estate the Highgate Pool was located. For many years the earl continued to make the pool available for the sport during the summertime. The four Vice-Presidents were Guy M. Campbell, Sir Claude Champion de Crespigny, O.A. Howell and Lord Rosemead. Sir Claude was elected President in 1906 and remained in that office until 1926. His wide-ranging career had included service in both the Royal Navy, the army and journalism and he received awards for exploits from the Ballooning Society, the Royal Aero Club and the Royal Humane Society. The first committee comprised twelve men, most of whom were at that time very active in diving competitions. Some also had strong connections with the ASA through their swimming clubs. The committee members and their swimming club memberships were: D.F. Cooke, R.L. Ede, H.E. Fern (all listed as members of Holloway Unite! SC), G.W. Glassborow (Surrey Commercial Docks SC), O. Groenings (Queen's Westminster Volunteers SC), Otto Hageborg (Swedish Society member and devoted demonstrator of diving), William Henry (Honorary Secretary of the Life Saving Society and committee member of the ASA), Charles Mauritzi (compatriot of Hageborg), S. Monks (Amateur SC and President of the London Water Polo League for 1902), F. O'Rourke, R.T. Serrano (Trident SC), A.Shinner (Polytechnic SC). W.E. Webb, a champion gymnast and mountaineer became the first Honorary Treasurer. L.W. Balck was elected Honorary Secretary with J.S. Featherstonehaugh as Assistant Honorary Secretary. Almost all these founder members of the ADA belonged to London based diving clubs. They arranged affiliation agreements with the ASA and The Life Saving Society and had the patronage of the Bath Club of London. The significance of the latter arrangement lay in the informal political and social connections afforded to the ADA including those with royalty. The Bath Club had a ladies section where members could learn swimming, diving and life saving.

Sidney Monks claimed that he initiated the ADA in 1901. When discussing diving with a group of enthusiasts he gave a half-crown (2s 6d) to W.E. Webb as the most likely person present to act as Treasurer of the newly invented Association. Then Webb and Monks set about persuading others to take the major necessary offices. Monks claimed that the body at first conceived of itself as a diving club rather than a body to regulate the sport.

Membership of the ADA was open to individual members and to affiliated clubs. The representatives of clubs had to be qualified as individual members. The number of member clubs by mid 1903 totalled 29, of which only one was for women, the Victoria Ladies SC. Only three clubs had joined the ADA from outside of London and the counties of Kent, Surrey, Middlesex and Essex: these were the swimming clubs of Bedford, King's Lynn, and Swindon. The number of clubs affiliated to the ADA grew to 48 by March 1904 though only few of the new clubs were from outside the south east of England.

The ADA published eight rules for the conduct of business by its committee. The London focus of the ADA was reiterated in the small print at the bottom of page 9 of the 1903 membership

The Amateur Diving Association published its annual Handbook. These extracts from 1903 show the relative simplicity of both the organisation and the sport in the early years of the twentieth century.

- THE -
Amateur Diving Association.

Affiliated to the Amateur Swimming Association, and under the Patronage of the Life Saving Society, and of the Bath Club.

FOUNDED 1901.

President.
The Rt. Hon. The Earl of Mansfield.

Vice-Presidents.
Lord ROSMEAD.
Sir CLAUDE CH. de CRESPIGNY, Bart.
GUY M. CAMPBELL, Esq., F.R.G.S.
O. A. HOWELL, Esq., Otter S.C.

Committee.
D. F. COOKE,
R. L. EDE,
R. E. FIRN, Holloway United S.C.
G. W. GLASSBOROW, Surrey Com. Docks.
O. GROENINGS, Qu. West. Vol. S.C.
OTTO HAGBORG, M.A., Swedish Society.
W. HENRY, Hon. Sec. L.S.S., and A.S.A.
CHAS. P. MAURITZI, Streatch Society.
R. MONKS, Amateur S.C.
R. T. SERRANO, Trident S.C.
F. SHINNER, Polytechnic.
F. O'ROURKE,

Hon. Treasurer.   W. E. WEBB.

Hon. Secretary.
L. W. BALCK,
15 Boscastle Road, Dartmouth Park, N.W.

Asst. Hon. Sec.
J. S. FEATHERSTONEHAUGH, Vandals S.C.
37 Claremont Road, Highgate, N.

Official Medal Engravers,
Messrs. COWLES & SONS, 24 Bedford Street, Strand.

Clubs Affiliated.

Amateur S.C.
Barking S.C.
Beckenham Baths S.C.
Beckenham S.C.
Bedford S.C.
Belle Sauvage S.C.
Brentford S.C.
Clarence S.C.
City & Whitechapel Schools S.A.
Goldsmiths' Institute S.C.
Holloway United S.C.
Ilford S.C.
King's Lynn S.C.
Kingston S.C.
London & India Docks S.C.
Nautilus S.C.
Otter S.C.
Polytechnic S.C.
Queen's Westminster Vol. S.C
Romford Town S.C.
South Eastern Postal S.C.
Southwark (late St. Saviour's S.C.)
Surrey Commercial Docks S.C.
Swindon A.S.C.
Tottenham House S.C.
Trident S.C.
Union Castle S.C.
Vandals S.C.
Victoria Ladies' S.C.

Up to June 20th, 1903.

THIS Association has been founded for promoting the sport of Artistic Diving—an art which the Swedes have brought to perfection, but which has been much neglected in this country—and for the purpose of representing the needs of divers to the various County and Borough Councils and others having charge of swimming baths and open-air bathing places.

Besides the Officers, the Executive, and Committee, the Association is composed of (1) Individual Members, (2) Affiliated Clubs.

Individual Members have the advantage of the company of expert divers with whom to practice, and from whom they may learn. As they become expert they **will be invited to join in the public displays of the Association.**

Affiliated Clubs are represented by a Delegate, and should any such Club desire to approach the Committee on any subject affecting its interests, their delegate may attend to put their views before the Committee. Notice of such application must be given to the Hon. Sec. three days before any advertised Committee meeting. Club delegates, if elected on the Committee, must qualify as individual members before sitting (see rule 3, Rules).

Standing Committee Meeting without notice on last Tuesday in the month at Holborn Baths, Bloomsbury, at 7.30 p.m.

Silver and Bronze Medals are offered for competition to all Clubs affiliated. Special arrangements for Ladies' Clubs.

The Association arranges Competitions for Clubs affiliated, and will give assistance to such Clubs by instructing members and judging when required, and will furnish teams of Expert Divers to take part in displays, and assist in any way thought desirable.

NOTES.

The Medals awarded by the Amateur Diving Association are struck from a die which is the exclusive property, and a fine example of the die sinker's art.

Members are requested to wear the **Club Badge (Price 2 6)** on all suitable occasions.

The Hon. Sec. will be glad to receive from members notices referring to the Association or any cuttings of interest to divers.

All Notices appear in the "Club Notices" of the "Referee"

ORNAMENTAL DIVING is the art of entering the water in a graceful manner.

The ideal diving-board should be about 2½ ins. thick and 2 feet broad, projecting outward at least 2 feet over the water, and for running dives as convenient, covered with coconut matting, and should have a white band, 3 ins. wide, painted on its upper and lower side, 18 ins. from its outward extremity. This outward extremity is called the "take-off."

The Association Standard for a Plain Dive.

The start should be made immediately, and squarely, not slantwise; it should be powerful, with an upward and outward spring, with the body, limbs and feet forming themselves into a graceful, unbroken line before entering the water.

A break, or angular bending at the hips, is a serious fault.

Before entering the water the hands must be extended above the head, spread laterally, with the forefingers touching; the legs in their whole length must be kept straight together, and on no account must they "throw over," nor must the vertical position be exceeded.

As little splash should be made as possible.

The surface must be reached as quickly as possible.

The practice of placing the palms of the hands together in diving is to be strongly condemned, as it carries the diver dangerously deep, and prevents him from rising to the surface quickly and gracefully. In running and fancy dives, the position is a matter of taste of the Competitor, and in all dives grace and boldness will be considered.

In a competition any diver shouting or posturing to the public shall be disqualified. No communication to the public shall be made by voice or gesture by the competitor.

A Competition for Plain and Ornamental Diving will take place at the Highgate Bathing Pond, on Saturday, July 25. Three good Prizes are offered.

Entrance Fee for Members of the A.D.A. 1/-, of affiliated Clubs 2/-.

Entries close on previous day.

NOTE.—The Diver is under the eye of the judge the moment he steps into the "take-off."

All notices appear in "Club Notices" of the "Referee."

ON JUDGING COMPETITIONS.

The practice of stationing two or three judges in a group to register a personal opinion is open to serious objections. An otherwise capable and honourable man can scarcely help being influenced by his companion judges, to the detriment of his own independent opinion of the merits of the candidates.

The Association appoints three Judges (who shall draw amongst themselves to decide who shall be Referee) in different positions apart from each other, to award marks (7 maximum) to each competitor for each dive. **They must not communicate with each other during the Competition.** The mark sheets are then handed to the Referee, who will add the points allowed by each judge to each Competitor, and announce the winners. The Referee will also judge for points, but his award will only be referred to in case of a tie. Should the Referee's points make it a tie the competitors must dive again.

RULES.

1.—That the name of the Association be "The Amateur Diving Association," and shall be conducted in accordance with the laws of the Amateur Swimming Association, and be affiliated to the Southern Counties' Amateur Swimming Association, and the Life Saving Society.

2.—That the objects of this Association are: To encourage the art of high and ornamental diving, and to combine the various swimming clubs and individual members for their mutual benefit in the promotion of this art.

3.—That the managing body of this Association shall consist of a President, Vice-Presidents, a Treasurer, a Secretary or Secretaries, and Ten Members (with power to add to their number, to be elected by ballot at the Annual General Meeting, which shall be held in March of each year. The Executive to meet as may be required. The Secretary to give six days' notice to each member of such meeting.

4.—All competing members of the Association must be amateurs, as defined by the Amateur Swimming Association, and must be proposed, seconded, and duly elected by the Committee.

5.—That the Annual Subscription to the Association shall be: For individual members, **2s.** and for the affiliation of Clubs (which must be already affiliated to the A.S.A.) **5s.**; for Honorary Members, **10s.** Fees payable in advance on April 1st.

6.—The Executive shall have entire control of the Association, and shall have power to expel any member whose conduct shall, in their opinion, be injurious to the character and interest of the Association.

7.—That no Rule shall be altered or rescinded, nor a new Rule made, except at the Annual General Meeting, or a meeting specially called for the purpose (for either of which meetings seven days' notice must be given to each member), and then only by a two-thirds majority of those present.

8.—That the Executive have power to deal with any subject not provided for in these Rules.

NOTE.—All Association notices and Committee meetings will be forwarded for insertion to the **"Referee."**

From June 1st to September 1st, members will meet for practice at Highgate Pond on Saturdays, 4 to 5.30. (A.S.A. costume must be worn, and the remainder of the year at Holborn Bath, Bloomsbury, W.C., on Tuesdays, 7.30 to 8.30 p.m.

RESULTS & COMING EVENTS.

A.D.A. Competition. Highgate Pond, 1902
1 G. M. Clark.
2 J. S. Featherstonehaugh
3 R. L. Ede.

A.D.A. Competition No. 1.
Holborn Baths, May 27th, 1903. Open to all members.
1 J. S. Featherstonehaugh.
2 M. Clark.
3 R. L. Ede.

A.D.A. Competition No. 2.
Holborn Baths, May 27th, 1903. Open to members who have never won a prize (diving).
1 H. Goodworth.
2 R. Applebee.
3 E. Lopresti.

June 20th.—Display at Highgate Pond, 4.30 p.m.
July 11th.—Life Saving Society's Gala, Highgate Pond.
July 18th.—Final of Inter-affiliated Clubs' Competition for a Silver Medal. Highgate Pond, 4 p.m.
July 24th.—Entries close for A.D.A. Members' Competition, Highgate Pond.
Sat. Aug. 25.—A.D.A. Members' Competition, Highgate Pond, 4.30 p.m., 3 good prizes.

Height of Running Board at Highgate Pond, 14ft. 6in. and 2ft. 6in.; at Holborn Bath, 14ft. 9in.

card where there is a note about the location of diving practices: in summer at Highgate Pool and in winter at Holborn Baths. The sole written requirement about costumes stated that divers were expected to wear the ASA approved costumes, although this requirement only appeared in parenthesis in a footnote. Individual members were encouraged to wear the club badge, which cost 2s 6d (12.5p), on all suitable occasions.

The exploits of women divers received much less attention than those of men. In 1903 the ADA offered silver and bronze medals for competitions between '*all clubs affiliated* ' with a note saying '*Special Arrangements for Ladies Clubs*'. This statement reflected awareness of the growing participation of women in all swimming sports as indicated in chapter 2. In 1911 the ADA offered a challenge cup, the *Ladies' Ede Cup*, donated by R.L. Ede who had previously donated a cup for male competitors. Sidney Monks, writing in 1915, contrasted the positive ADA support for womens diving with '*our governing body of swimming (which) does not encourage diving amongst women or girls*'. The Ladies' Diving Association (LDA) had come into being in 1908 with Lady

Constance Stewart Richardson as its President and Miss Gustafsson as the first Honorary Secretary. Several of the Honorary Vice-Presidents were members of the ladies section of the Bath Club. The idea of the LDA was promoted by Madam Vautier who served as Treasurer from 1908 until 1915. Its membership was drawn only from London clubs. The organisation included a separate section for professional divers who had their own distinctive competitions under the auspices of the LDA. The LDA invited ADA judges to adjudicate in the finals of the ladies' diving championships. Monks reported that each season the increasing number of entrants showed '*the extension of diving amongst the ladies*'. The LDA did not feature in any of the reports in the *Swimming Times* so that its full history remains incomplete.

In 1903 the ADA issued its basic definition: '*Ornamental diving is the art of entering the water in a graceful manner*'. Then it advised on what ideal facilities should comprise:

> '*The ideal diving board should be about two and a half inches thick and two feet broad, projecting outward at least two feet over the water, and for running dives as long as convenient, covered with coconut matting, and should have a white band, three inches wide, painted on its upper and lower side, eighteen inches from its outward extremity. This outward extremity is called the "take-off"*'.

At its inception the ADA did not present precise definitions of what constituted the specific attributes of the Dives for which judges would award maximum points. The Association Standard of the Plain Dive was preceded by the simple statement:

> '*The moment the diver steps into the 'take-off' he is said to be in position. A dive commences at the moment the diver takes his position, and finishes when he has completely disappeared in the water*'.

On the Plain Dive, information is given in considerable detail:

> '*The start should be made immediately, and squarely, not slantwise; it should be powerful, with an upward and outward spring, the body limbs and feet forming themselves into a graceful unbroken line. A break, or angular bending at the hips, is a serious fault.*
>
> *Before entering the water the hands must be extended above the head, spread laterally, with the forefingers touching; the legs in their whole length must be kept straight together, and on no account must they "throw over", nor must the vertical position be exceeded.*
>
> *As little splash should be made as possible.*
>
> *The surface must be reached as quickly as possible.*
>
> *The practice of placing the palms of the hands together in diving is to be strongly condemned, as it carries the diver dangerously deep, and prevents him from rising to the surface quickly and gracefully. In running and fancy dives, the position is at the taste of the competitor, and in all dives grace and boldness will be considered.*
>
> *In a competition any diver shouting or posturing to the public shall be disqualified. No communication by voice or gesture may be made by the competitor*'.

Isabella Mary White (Belle White) was born 1 September 1894 and was Ladies High Diving Champion in England from the beginning of the contest in 1924 until 1929. She had won the bronze medal for high diving at the Stockholm Olympics in 1912, the first of such events for ladies. She was a member of the British Olympic Diving Team in 1920 when she took fourth place. In 1924 she had sixth place, and in 1928 was unplaced. She represented England and Great Britain in many international diving matches.

Such detail was no doubt the basis of criteria for judging competitions. In addition the conduct of the judges themselves was prescribed so that fairness was seen to be the basis of verdicts on the performance:

'The practice of standing two or three judges in a group to register a personal opinion is open to serious objections. An otherwise capable and honourable man can scarcely help being influenced by his companion judges, to the detriment of his own independent opinion of the merits of the candidates.

The Association appoints three judges (who shall draw amongst themselves to decide who shall be referee) in different positions apart from each other, to award marks (7 maximum for each competitor) for each dive. They must not communicate with each other during the competition. The mark sheets are then handed to the referee, who will add the points allowed by each judge to each competitor, and announce the winner or winners. The referee will also judge for points, but his award will only be referred to in case of a tie. Should the referees' points make it a tie the competitors must dive again.

NOTE.- The diver is under the eye of the judge the moment he steps into the "take-off".'

Sidney Monks stated that these unspecific guidelines had been written by the first Honorary Secretary of the ADA and soon needed clarification.

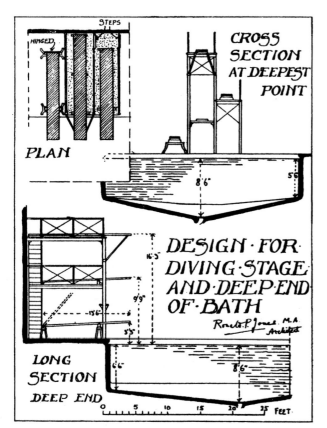

Diving was taken into account when the ASA published 'Swimming by Champions of the World' in 1915. It advised on diving and the need for purpose built facilities. Ronald Jones, the architect and enthusiastic diver, set out the requirements in this sketch plan.

Divers wanted to have the opportunities of showing greater skills and variety in their sport. In 1903 some fancy or ornamental dives were introduced as part of the ADA competitions. A Springboard event was included in the Olympic Games of 1904 but High Diving first formed part of the programme in 1906 for the Supplementary Olympics at Athens. Such rapid recognition of the sport of diving in the international arena made it imperative to produce agreed scoring methods. William Henry devised the first classification system of dives for judging purposes for the Olympic Games held in London in 1908. This table of values made ten points available for each dive. It formed a tariff (scoring system) for later competitions in England and overseas, although it necessarily had to be revised to take account of new dives and the experience of judges in using it.

Excitement about diving grew with the rapid introduction of *Fancy Diving* which owed much to techniques associated with gymnastics. Their elaboration had increased to such an extent that in 1915 the ADA listed and described 21 dives, which had formed part of International and Olympic Competitions. This listing was deliberately limited. Among the excluded dives was the *'English Header'* known in the USA as the *'Swan'* and in continental Europe as the *'Swallow'*. It did not survive because it required techniques which were too difficult to control. However, a new version of the swallow or header became compulsory in the men's and women's Olympic competitions in 1932.

In 1914 the ADA began to publish its own *Handbook* which was compiled by Ralph Errington, the Honorary Secretary. That edition included a list of 38 different dives embracing all that were used in the Olympic Games. Some of these were illustrated by photographs supplied by William Henry. Amongst the contributions was the design for the ideal divers' bath drawn by Ronald Jones who was both an architect and a keen diver.

One of the aims of the ADA was to obtain improved or new facilities for divers. The Highgate Pool provided the summer venue for many of the outdoor competitions and, thanks to the financial help of Ronald Jones and F. Geoghegan, the ADA had a stage with running diving boards at the heights of 3, 10, 11, 20 and 33 feet. It was opened in July 1914 by Grand Duke Michael of Russia. At the pool the ADA possessed dressing accommodation for ladies and for gentlemen. In contrast, local authority swimming baths left much to be desired. The London County Council had strong reservations about the safety of the 33 foot diving board, for which it gave a temporary licence. This was despite its use for the National Graceful Diving Championship and for the Olympic Games without any mishaps. At the Holborn Baths, the venue of the baths-based diving championships, the highest board was 13 feet 6 inches, since the crucial feature was a sufficient depth of water for safe diving, which limited the height of diving boards.

The apparatus used and recommended by the ADA in 1915 rested on the experience of the Olympiads of 1908 and 1912. The height and type of boards were:

Spring Board at 1 metre (approximately 3 feet)
Spring Board at 3 metres (approximately 10 feet)
Firm Board at 5 metres (approximately 16 feet)
Firm Board at 10 metres (approximately 33 feet)

Ayer's advertisement from 1933.

national competitions owed much to the superior facilities of fully equipped baths. The competitors had the support of trainers and coaches who constantly evolved techniques to improve performances. Such progress also depended on the availability of adequate finances to pay professional assistants and to provide scholarships at the appropriate universities for the more promising young divers. Although there was some reduction of funding after the Wall Street Crash of 1929 (which marked the start of major economic depression), the generous support for sport in the USA had revived by the middle 1930s. The contrast with the British experience was reflected in the relatively few divers who could compete at world class and the limited facilities existing in the entire country.

In 1930 an ADA article on diving in the *Swimming Times* discussed the importance of dry land training. The anonymous author commented on the successes of the German Olympic teams prior to the outbreak of war. He argued that this prowess owed much to the training the team undertook in a country which was the home of gymnastics. Similarly the use of the dry land apparatus invented by their coach, Ernst Brandsten, was said to have contributed to the American diving dominance in the Games of 1920, 1924 and 1928.

The resources available for diving in England increased in quality between 1919 and the outbreak of the Second World War. The surge in provision for swimming and diving took place during the 1930s. The location of the best diving places acted as a powerful determinant of where the sport could be developed to high standards. The most prestigious venue became the Empire Pool at

The minimum depths of water for each height respectively should be 7 feet 6 inches, 8 feet 6 inches, 10 feet and 12 feet. The ADA advised that all boards should be at least 14 feet in length and project at least 2 feet over the water, more if the bottom shelved. This indication of the use springboards appears to contradict Hobden, writing in 1936 on *The Art of Springboard Diving*, who asserts that the first springboard did not appeared in Britain until 1923. The springboards he described were fixed both at the landward end and at the fulcrum so that their flexibility was limited to the properties of the piece of timber used.

The First World War reduced the scope of ADA activities, although it did not adopt the explicitly low key policy of the ASA. Nonetheless, in reality the ADA could not advance the sport before 1919. During the war the sport was only active as and when divers had opportunities to demonstrate their skills at galas to entertain the armed services, the wounded or local people.

The Inter-war years

After the end of the First World War the revitalisation of all sports took time. The general history of the ASA showed that the losses of people and of momentum in the war years left a legacy which was difficult to overcome. The only way forward appeared to be in confident leadership which had an awareness of advances in other countries. The successes of the swimmers and divers from the United States of America between 1919 and 1939 in inter-

Diving from Clacton Pier drew the spectators to watch Professor Webb's High Dive. Professionals earned part of their living from showmanship.

In 1929 A.E. Dickin (Polytechnic SC) won the National Graceful Diving Championship and the English Plain Diving Championship.

During this time Britain selected men's and women's teams for the diving events of the Olympic Games. The Olympic movement first accepted a women's diving event in 1912, which was Plain Diving from the high board. In that contest the British diver, Miss Belle White, gained third place. The women's Springboard Diving event was introduced at the 1920 Olympiad.

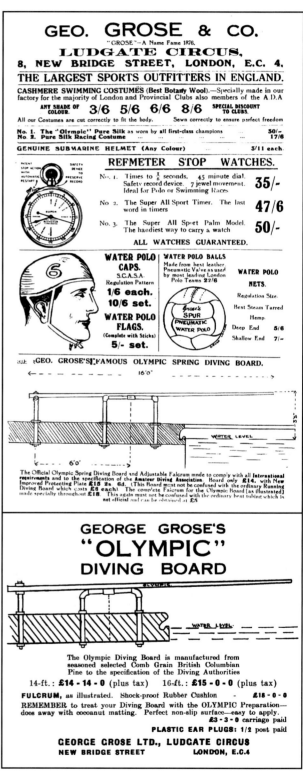

George Grose's supplied many kinds of diving, swimming and other water sports equipment. We can compare their advertisement of 1932 with that of 1946. Their Olympic diving board was in British terms - state of the art. In 1946 purchase tax was levied on many items and the rate depended on the Budget presented in April of each year.

Wembley which was opened in time for the Empire Games (now known as the Commonwealth Games) held in 1934. There were 98 other pools with approved diving facilities of which 67 were outdoor and usable only for a limited summer season. There were 25 pools with fixed boards but only Wembley had fixed boards at 5 and 10 metres. Fixed boards at 10 metres were available at 18 venues of which most were at seaside pools. As the table shows the facilities available were often much less than at Wembley:

Table 7.1: Indoor Pools with Springboards in 1934

5	–	1 metre only
10	–	1 metre and 3 metres
2	–	3 metres only

In 1933 the Borough of Henley-on-Thames created their new swimming baths in the River Thames. It provided the most modern diving frame, as used at Wembley Olympic Pool. However, they economised by not having the correct springboards. In 1940 when the Wembley Pool was not in use, their springboards were brought to Henley by Ronald Jones in attempt to improve the swimming facilities. These were used by school classes of evacuees from London as well as by the locals. No other Thames-side local authority had followed this example by the outbreak of war in 1939.

However, the first events of Plain and Fancy diving from the high-board for women took place at the 1928 Games.

By 1932 the programme of high diving events required men to offer 8 dives of which the 4 compulsory dives were 1 Plain Dive and 3 specified Fancy dives, and women to offer 3 Plain dives and 1 Fancy dive.

The popularisation of diving had remained a vital aspect of the aims of the ADA. After 1918, it undertook various promotional events at galas wherever feasible, supplying teams to demonstrate the variety of diving. This publicity was assisted by tours of divers with both skill and panache such as the American champion, Aileen Riggin, during 1930. In 1931 *The Morning Post* (later merged with *The Daily Telegraph*) held a dinner for the ADA to welcome the American champion, Pete Desjardins, to England. He had gained maximum possible points from the judges for one of his dives at the 1928 Olympic Games where he had won both the Highboard and Springboard events. Pete Desjardins and Harold 'Dutch' Smith, the American Olympic champion of 1932, attracted large crowds to their demonstrations and so contributed to the upsurge of interest amongst youngsters in the early 1930s.

Not all the effort to make the most of diving as an entertainment depended upon international celebrities. In 1930 the Highgate Diving Club held what was '*probably the first all diving gala by a diving club*'. During the programme, spectators saw almost all of the 112 dives appearing in the ADA tariff and '*several unknown and involuntary ones*'. This same club formed a team who called themselves the Four Lucratics. They claimed, in their advertisement in 1934, to be '*the finest diving team in Europe*'. They offered to perform at any aquatic sports. A professional calling himself Dare Devil Peggy advertised for custom in 1934.

The ADA, like the LDA, had regarded the work of professional coaches as of great value. In 1930 this point was emphasised in an official statement published in the *Swimming Times* which proposed an ADA validation test for coaches. This required a written examination on the theory and practice of diving together with a demonstration of teaching pupils. The regulations not only implied that the coach wishing to take the examination, could practice what was taught; but also that he or she would bring some pupils, who had already achieved the ADA badge, for a practical demonstration. This requirement failed to take into account the expense for candidates from outside London so that it was dropped from the final scheme. In 1931 the ADA ran a scheme to improve coaching but only at several London baths.

The ADA *Handbook* of 1930 included descriptions of perfect dives based upon those provided by FINA. The ADA accounts were brief and in some cases were acknowledged to be incomplete but these were the reference points used by some judges in

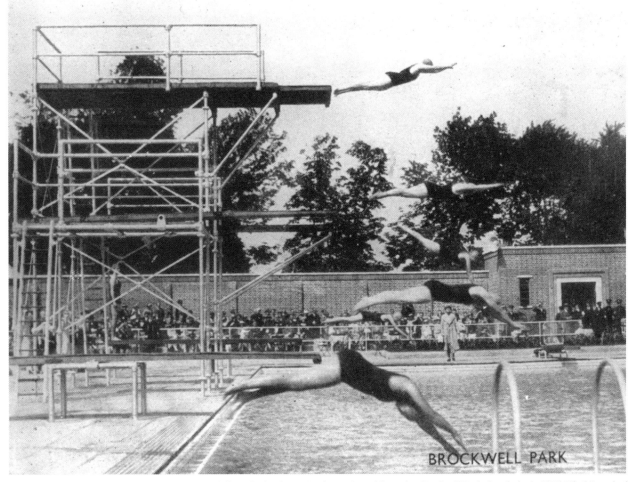

A diving demonstration team from the Mary Datchellor School took part in the opening of the pool at Brockwell Park, Lambeth, in 1935. The Mayor had the duty of throwing one member of the team into the water. Music accompanied a display of ornamental swimming by the same team.

diving events. In an article on 'Judging Diving' written by the ADA for the *Swimming Times* the shortcomings of some judges were exposed and formed the basis for arguments in favour of their systematic training.

ASA and ADA

As indicated in the early part of this chapter, the ASA and the ADA had worked in close cooperation. For example, the ASA law on plunging, which was made in the 1890s, was accepted within the ADA and the ASA did not include diving in its laws. Prizes for plunging were included in the awards made under the auspices of the ASA. Both Associations followed the FINA rules for swimming and diving and the ASA *Handbook* recorded in full the FINA rules of 1914 for Spring Board and High Board Diving. During the 1920s the ADA supported the ASA in promoting diving. The ASA Certificate for Proficiency in Diving, introduced in March 1926, was developed in close co-operation with ADA.

When the ASA began to develop competitive diving in the 1920s, ADA gave the ASA the prize for the Ladies' Plain Diving Championship as a '*tangible evidence of good will*'.

Despite the undoubted successful efforts to improve the quality of diving and the enthusiasm for the sport in England the leaders of the ADA came to the conclusion that their Association should cease to remain independent. Several of the principal officers and active members of the ADA had been founder members or early recruits. It was said that there were problems in finding people from the next generation to take office. A review of the role of the ADA was recognised as being essential. Accordingly, a special general meeting was called at the St Bride's Institute on 26 November 1935. Resolutions were carried which wound up the ADA as from 31 December 1935 and transferred its functions to the ASA. The resolution was subject to the formal agreement of the ASA Council at its March 1936 annual general meeting. Council was able to have a full account of the issues because one of the founder members of the ADA was at that time the

During the 1930s and 1940s diving provided entertainment as well as competitive events at galas. In 1934, for example, The Finest Team of Europe earned money from its performances for the High Gate Diving Club of London. By contrast, in the same year was the professional promotion by Dare Devil Peggy. In 1946, Weston-super-Mare celebrated the end of the war with displays by the Greatest Aquatic Stars. American influences on Britain by 1947 included the Aquacade which event organisers could provide by hiring The Aquabats. Trampolines were a novelty and as yet not much used for training.

Honorary Secretary of the Association. Council agreed to the transfer of functions.

In retrospect it is clear that the ADA acted as a very effective pressure group in its members' interest. By 1935 the ADA had achieved some notable successes in securing recognition for diving as a sport in its own right, in the development of the sport and interest amongst the public. Its weaknesses as an Association had been its inability to acquire the financial resources on a sufficient scale to be able to support and enhance diving activities nationwide. Moreover, the heavy emphasis on the London area, from its inception in 1901, had continued to undermine links with the provinces. The ADA never became for diving what the ASA had become in the general world of swimming.

The ASA and diving

A new era in diving began in 1936. Council agreed to become the authority for diving and accepted two diving championship trophies from the ADA and, from 1937, decided to award the

National Graceful Diving Championship trophy. The ASA Committee decided to appoint an advisory committee of five people together with the honorary officers. This first committee comprised: R.G. Jordan (chairman and Honorary President of the ASA), T.M. Yeaden (Honorary Treasurer), H.E. Fern (Honorary Secretary), G. Melville Clark (formerly ADA), R.A. Colwill, C.S. Kerin, G. Matveieff (formerly ADA). Clark and Matveieff had represented their country in international diving competitions. The ASA used all diving expertise available to it. For example, Gordon Melville Clark represented the ASA on the International Diving Committee.

In its preamble to a report on its first year of work in relation to diving the ASA admitted: '... *until recent years the ASA itself (or its District Associations) has done very little directly to encourage diving beyond promoting a championship or two*'. It noted the achievements of the ADA but emphasised the geographical concentration of diving in the Southern District. The ASA decided that diving should be arranged on lines similar to its other specialised activities. Thus, it empowered the Committee to appoint officials for championships, to compile a list of diving judges, to deal with the Teacher's Certificate for Diving, and to advise the Committee on the selection of divers for international competitions. Simultaneously, it recommended Districts to appoint

This imposing steel diving stage at Plymouth stood in front of the impressive fortifications whose pathways gave vantage points for spectators. It was erected in the period between the two world wars. The running boards were at 12 feet, 16 feet 3 inches, 22 feet, and 32 feet six inches at three quarters of full tide.

Diving Committees with the intention of promoting the sport wherever possible.

The ASA started the process of giving more emphasis to diving in 1936 by arranging to publish its own *Manual on Diving* in the following year. The Teaching Certificate scheme began very modestly in 1935 but more interest was shown in every year until the outbreak of the Second World War in 1939. At the time of the administrative changeover the ADA had work in progress on three films. These became available in 1936: *The Amateur Diving Association Instructional Film* which showed how to undertake the Plain dive; *Land Training for Diving*, and *Diving*. The latter starred several international competitors demonstrating a variety of Fancy dives.

The Second World War disrupted diving as all other swimming disciplines. Following the end of the war in 1945 low priority was given to the release of resources for diving or other swimming. Although the ASA had made some progress during the later 1930s in giving diving a higher profile nationally, it suffered severe checks attributable to the war and its aftermath. The post-war revival began with tours of teams which displayed diving at

The first Diving Manual issued by the ASA was published in 1937. The latest coaching techniques of 1955 together with advice concerning the revised diving laws appeared in the 1955 edition of Swimming and Diving.

galas throughout the country. Lack of available facilities remained a continuing brake to progress. Nonetheless where the facilities existed excellent divers acquitted themselves well in national competitions. In 1948 the Olympic Games were held in London and preparatory training for them took place at the pool of the Henleaze SC in Bristol. This location was also used by the ASA for training the water polo team. Despite these innovations in Olympic training, the British challengers in diving earned no gold, silver or bronze awards. This outcome was very disappointing but contributed to a new positive development. The first regular diving coaching course in England, the Middlesex Diving Training Scheme, was held in 1951, organised by Pat Besford, the *Daily Telegraph* sports journalist.

Facilities and training

Without improved facilities diving in England was confined to the areas where it existed before 1939. Even where there had been developments, as at Henleaze Pool, these often had unusual characteristics. For example, Norman Sarsfield recollected divers emerging from the waters of Henleaze pool shaking small fish and other creatures from their costumes! In a lecture about *'General Physical Conditioning'*, given at the Summer Training School for Diving at Henleaze in 1950, he drew particular attention to the problems of temperatures at open air facilities. Significant changes depended upon building appropriate baths with tanks or depths to accommodate diving.

The first post war innovation was the creation of the Dawdon Colliery Pool in 1948. This was the outcome of the transformation of a pit pond used for cooling purposes and as a reservoir for the colliery engines. Although it was out of doors, the waters usually reached a temperature of about 72° Fahrenheit throughout the year. With the permission of the National Coal Board Dawdon SC had erected in 1948 a firm board at 5 metres and in 1949 inaugurated springboards at 1 metre and 3 metres. These facilities were augmented in 1951 with further springboards at 3 metres and 1 metre together with a sand pit. Miners changing and

H. E. FERN.

NATIONAL SWIMMING
AND
DIVING CHAMPIONSHIPS
(Under A.S.A. Laws)

AT THE BATHING POOL
St. Leonards-on-Sea, Sussex
General Manager : Major HAROLD PYCOCK, M.B.E.

JULY 23rd–26th, 1947

SOUVENIR BROCHURE

THE EVENT OF THE YEAR ★ ★ ★

National Swimming and Diving Championships

(Under the direction of S.C.A.S.A. and under A.S.A. Laws)

at the

Bathing Pool, St. Leonards-on-Sea, Sussex

General Manager : A. H. PYCOCK, M.B.E.

Wednesday, 23rd to Saturday, 26th JULY, 1947

Seven Sessions :   Each accommodating 7.000 spectators.

Numbered and reserved seats, 5/- and 2/6
Standing, 1/6
Season tickets for reserved seats, 30/- and 15/-

Children under 14 half rates at all prices.

Tickets obtainable from the Box Office at the Bathing Pool. Postal applications **must** be accompanied by remittance.

Swimmers: Arrange your holidays to support your sport, and enjoy the health-giving facilities of this popular South Coast Resort, noted for its sunshine and beautiful surroundings.

All enquiries for accommodation and general guidance to A. K. Vint, Public Relations Officer, Borough of Hastings, Verulam Buildings, Hastings, Sussex. In view of the anticipated demands of holiday visitors, Mr. Vint advises competitors and spectators to make immediate enquiries, mentioning " National Swimming Championships."

Harold Fern's copy of the programme for the 1947 ASA's National Swimming and Diving Championships. The promotional advertisement had a distinctive tone. This four day event in 1947 ended on Saturday with a diving display and a water polo match. Neither were part of the ASA Championships. On the other days a water polo match took place to entertain holiday makers.

Training squad at Dawdon in the early 1950s. Norman Sarsfield in on the right end of the second row from the front.

Liz Ferris of Mermaid SC in training, used the sandpit at Dawdon in 1957. She was ASA champion (1957) for 1 metre Springboard, 3 metres Springboard (1960), and the Plain (1959 and 1960), and won the bronze medal for the Springboard in the 1960 Rome Olympics.

washing facilities were made available to swimmers and divers. Furthermore, a natural bank provided accommodation for as many as 4000 spectators. Norman Sarsfield recalled visiting timber merchants in the area to look for the right kind of wood for diving boards. The materials for the diving frame came from recycling parts of old mine cages. Improvisation and collaboration with the National Coal Board had made possible a nationally significant diving pool. The first national ASA diving school at Dawdon took place in July 1951.

The government relaxed and removed restrictions on the use of building materials only during the 1950s. Although this explained the slowness in erecting new diving facilities, it frustrated the divers who hoped to see their sport taken up nationally. Continued inadequate provision limited the opportunities for improved training that was so important in developing competitors for national and international events.

After the Helsinki Olympics in 1952 the ASA agreed to continue the Dawdon school for the next four years in order to prepare for the Melbourne Olympics. The Association also decided to invite two American coaches to come to assist. Improving coaching and training was the purpose of the Annual Schools held first at Henleaze and then at Dawdon. Regular contributions by Norman Sarsfield, then the honorary administrator for diving, appeared in the *Swimming Times* and in 1953 he produced the book *Diving Instruction*, for the ASA. In 1954 he drew attention to the new trampette, a gymnastic apparatus which combined some of the characteristics of a trampoline with those of a springboard. George Rackham undertook pioneering research to advance understanding of the mechanics of diving. He collaborated with Wally Orner. They used Brian Phelps, the international diving champion, as their guinea pig in applying the principles of physics to discovering how diving techniques worked. This innovative study was incorporated in the book *Diving* by George Rackham, first published in 1959, and which is still regarded as the standard text for learning to dive.

By 1955 there was a proposal that diving coaches should form an Association for the purpose of discussing common problems arising from their experiences. In 1964 the British Diving Coaches Association produced a newsletter about both ASA and STA qualifications and diving personalities. It also drew attention to the help available from George Rackham, one of the ASA's National Technical Officers whose multifarious responsibilities included diving. The British Diving Coaches Association did not remain active. One explanation may have been that coaches could not survive as professionals on an income solely derived from diving. John Wardley noted that:

'coaches for diving were either professional swimming coaches and teachers or had a normal day-time job. Similarly divers had "normal lives", went to school or worked, and trained in the evenings and weekends at pools in public time.'

The British Diving Coaches Association re-emerged in 1989, after a lapse of 28 years.

Individual coaches nonetheless made their ideas known through the Diving Committee, the *Swimming Times* and their own publications. In 1963 George Rackham advocated that diving skills should form an integral part of the programme of

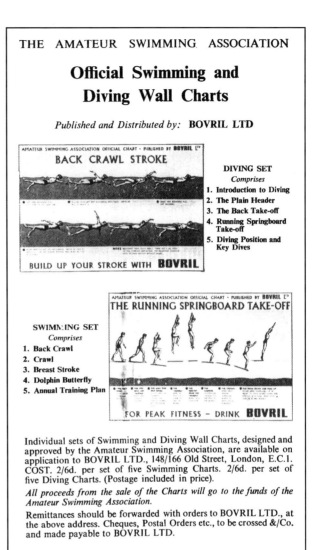

THE AMATEUR SWIMMING ASSOCIATION

Official Swimming and Diving Wall Charts

Published and Distributed by: **BOVRIL LTD**

DIVING SET
Comprises
1. **Introduction to Diving**
2. **The Plain Header**
3. **The Back Take-off**
4. **Running Springboard Take-off**
5. **Diving Position and Key Dives**

SWIMMING SET
Comprises
1. **Back Crawl**
2. **Crawl**
3. **Breast Stroke**
4. **Dolphin Butterfly**
5. **Annual Training Plan**

Individual sets of Swimming and Diving Wall Charts, designed and approved by the Amateur Swimming Association, are available on application to BOVRIL LTD., 148/166 Old Street, London, E.C.1. COST. 2/6d. per set of five Swimming Charts. 2/6d. per set of five Diving Charts. (Postage included in price).

All proceeds from the sale of the Charts will go to the funds of the Amateur Swimming Association.

Remittances should be forwarded with orders to BOVRIL LTD., at the above address. Cheques, Postal Orders etc., to be crossed &/Co. and made payable to BOVRIL LTD.

Diving promotion received support as part of the 1962 ASA's education programme.

learning to swim. He drew attention to the inadequate preparation of many young competitors for events which began with a dive from the pool side. At the more advanced level of diving, Dick Kimble, Olympic Diving Coach (USA), advocated the use of the '*save*' in diving. The role of good coaching was emphasised in a *Swimming Times* review in 1968. It pointed out the influences of Wally Orner, John Wardley and George Rackham on the notable successes of Brian Phelps and Liz Ferris in winning bronze medals at the Rome Olympics. In 1969 John Wardley's analysis of the 1968 Olympics served to underline the inadequacy of some of Britain's coaching. It was decided to study and adopt the methods currently used in the USA, the most successful diving nation. The ASA supported the development of coaching by funding the attendance of John Wardley and Steve Still at the Summer Diving School of Indiana University run by Hobee Billingsley, the top USA coach of the 1960s. In October 1969 the ASA announced the inauguration of its Advanced Teachers Certificate in Diving. Early in 1970 the Association issued its thoroughly revised *Rules for Diving* which incorporated all the up-to-date FINA changes. Sales were undoubtedly boosted by the fact that all who wished to take the Advanced Teachers Certificate had to use the *Rules* in their qualification.

THE AMATEUR SWIMMING ASSOCIATION

in conjunction with

THE CENTRAL COUNCIL OF PHYSICAL RECREATION

present

SWIMMING AND DIVING COURSES

at

DARTFORD COLLEGE OF PHYSICAL EDUCATION, KENT

Saturday, 3rd August, to Saturday, 10th August, 1963

These courses will be under the direction of Mr. N. W. Sarsfield, M.C., Honorary Secretary, A.S.A. Education Committee and Chairman of the A.S.A. Diving Committee, assisted by Mrs. E. M. Starling, member of the A.S.A. Education Committee, Mr. J. A. Holmyard, A.S.A. National Technical Officer, Mr. G. W. Rackham, S.T.A., and visiting lecturers including Mr. W. Orner, member of the A.S.A. Diving Committee.

Course No. 83 SWIMMING   FEE : £12 10s. 0d.

For men and women not under 17 years of age:

There will be two sections:

A—for those with little or no experience, and
B—for swimmers of reasonable standard who wish to take the the A.S.A. proficiency and/or personal survival tests.

Applicants should state on their forms for which section they are applying.

Course No. 84 SWIMMING (TUTORS)   Fee : £12 10s. 0d

For tutors of courses for the A.S.A. Teachers' Certificate (including training college lecturers and organisers of physical education):

Particular attention will be given to the requirements of the new syllabuses for the A.S.A. Teachers' Certificates and modern developments in swimming.

Course No. 85 DIVING   FEE : £12 10s. 0d.

For men and women not under 21 years of age:

The Course is intended for those who possess the A.S.A. Teachers' Certificate for Diving who wish to qualify as A.S.A. Diving Coaches. This is the first course to be held for this qualification (examination fee, 1 guinea).

Dartford College stands in its own grounds and offers excellent facilities —covered swimming bath, hard lawn tennis courts, extensive playing fields, gymnasium, etc., with a golf course adjoining. Accommodation is mainly in single rooms, but some students may be asked to share. Courses in other activities will be taking place during the same period and all students combine for social activities.

Applicants requiring financial assistance for Courses Nos. 84 and 85 are advised to apply for help to their local education authority.

All enquiries should be accompanied by a 3d. stamp and addressed to The General Secretary, the C.C.P.R., 6 Bedford Square, London, W.C.1.

Swimming and Diving

AMATEUR SWIMMING ASSOCIATION SUMMER SCHOOL

at the Crystal Palace National Sports Centre

Director: D. G. P. Smith, member of A.S.A. Education Committee.
Deputy Director: Mrs. W. Duane, A.S.A. Advanced Teachers' Certificate.

CLUB COACHES' CERTIFICATE

Course No. 197C Crystal Palace—July 25th-August 8th (Two weeks) £35 0s.
A two week course for men and women over twenty-one years of age who hold the A.S.A. Teachers' Certificate and wish to study for the Club Coaches' Certificate. The course will include both theoretical and practical work and the examination for the certificate may be taken.
Under the direction of Miss H. J. Elkington, A.S.A. National Technical Officer, and J. Terry, A.S.A. Coach.

ADVANCED TEACHERS' CERTIFICATE

Course No. 198C Crystal Palace—July 25th-August 1st £17 10s.
For men and women over eighteen years of age who hold the A.S.A. Teachers' Certificate and who wish to qualify for the A.S.A. Advanced Teachers' Certificate. The theoretical part of the examination may be taken, but not the practical.
Under the direction of G. W. J. Corlett, A.S.A. Coach.

TEACHERS' CERTIFICATE

Course No. 199C Crystal Palace—July 25th-August 1st £17 10s.
Course No. 200C Crystal Palace—August 1st-8th £17 10s.
Under the direction of G. W. J. Corlett, A.S.A. Coach.

For men and women over eighteen years of age who wish to qualify for the A.S.A. Teachers Certificate. The theoretical part of the examination may be taken, but not the practical.
Under the direction of J. A. Holmyard, A.S.A. Coach.

DIVING TEACHERS' CERTIFICATE

Course No. 201C Crystal Palace—July 25th-August 1st £17 10s.
For men and women over eighteen years of age who wish to coach or teach diving. The course will cover the syllabus of the A.S.A. Diving Teachers' Certificate and will give a wide background of modern diving techniques and coaching. This certificate is essential to candidates for the Coaches' Award. The examination may be taken.
Under the direction of A. Wade, A.S.A. Diving Coach.

SYNCHRONISED SWIMMING COACHES

Course No. 202C Crystal Palace—July 25th-August 1st £17 10s.
For men and women over seventeen years of age who wish to teach or coach synchronised swimming. The syllabus will include films and practical work covering individual instruction and coaching, class teaching for schools and clubs, and preparation for competitive work.
Under the direction of G. Rackham, member of A.S.A. Synchronised Committee, and Mrs. D. Rackham.

SWIMMING LEADERS' CERTIFICATE

Course No. 203C Crystal Palace—July 25th-August 1st £17 10s.
Course No. 204C Crystal Palace—August 1st-8th £17 10s.
For men and women over fifteen years of age who wish to obtain basic knowledge of the teaching and coaching of swimming. The course will be based on the syllabus of the Swimming Leaders' Certificate. It will however go much wider than this syllabus and range over the teaching and coaching of most branches of swimming. The examination may be taken.
Both courses under the direction of B. Newman, A.S.A. Advanced Teachers' Certificate.

RECREATIVE SWIMMERS

Course No. 205C Crystal Palace—July 25th-August 1st £17 10s.
Course No. 206C Crystal Palace—August 1st-8th £17 10s.
For men and women over seventeen years of age. There will be two sections for:
(i) those with little or no experience who wish to learn to swim
(ii) swimmers of reasonable standard who wish to take the A.S.A. proficiency and/or personal survival tests and enjoy swimming as a recreation. Please state which section you wish to attend.

Both courses under the direction of Mrs. W. Priddy, A.S.A. Advanced Teachers' Certificate.
Note: The fees stated above include full board and accommodation. Non-residents will be accepted at a fee of £9 10s.; meals may be purchased at the centre restaurant.

Applications should be made to the C.C.P.R., Dept. B, 26 Park Crescent, London, WIN 4AJ. Telephone 01-580 6822/9.

Diving formed an essential part of the regular Summer Schools organised by the ASA. The changing scope appears in the advertisements for 1963 and 1970.

The Olympic Squad at Dawdon in 1956.

The ISTC included diving within its activities. Among its regular publications were contributions by Jennifer Gray, a National Development Officer, on *Teaching the Back Dive* in 1978, and *Progressions for Teaching the Reverse Dive* in 1983.

Diving followed, perhaps somewhat belatedly the lead of swimming in helping competitors to reach their highest level of performance. As well as better coaching and training, many leading British divers during the 1970s and 1980s owed much to their attendances at Colleges and Universities in the USA. The most outstanding during these decades was the Olympic medallist, Chris Snode, who after retirement from competition in 1989, founded the Diving Institute at Crystal Palace.

The ASA purchased two aluminium springboards from the USA. In 1953 Highgate Diving Club made their own aluminium diving board having decided that they could not afford to import one. Their board was used with ASA permission for the 1 metre championships held at the club venue in the same year. The ASA Committee in 1957 noted that the quality of timber used for diving springboards had been declining. One answer lay in using new materials. During the 1950s Wally Orner had founded a pool equipment company which developed glass fibre laminated wood springboards. These proved to be cheaper than the imported aluminium boards from the USA and were widely used. The ASA bought a Duraflex Springboard, used it first in 1960, and subsequently it was available according to the requirements of the international programme. Nonetheless it was only in May 1968 that the appropriate fulcrum fittings, which enabled the full potential of this equipment to be realised, became available in Great Britain. In 1964 the National Diving Championships, held for the first time at the Crystal Place, had the use of purpose built facilities for diving, a major improvement for the English competitors. This new location replaced the Derby Baths in Blackpool and was able to accommodate the growth in the number of events of the ASA's National Championships.

Filmed records of performances enabled coaches to show their charges how they had dived and then to advise on improvements where appropriate. John Wardley began using ciné equipment, first 16 mm. and later 8 mm., for this purpose during the 1950s. His lead was followed by Wally Orner. In 1967 Dennis Borton reported an early example in Britain of the use of a television camera and video tape for training Helen Koppell in Leicester. In 1969, she won the ASA Centenary Springboard Diving Championship.

The Diving Committee noted in 1975 that technological advance had made the bubble machine available at the Crystal Palace. This equipment enabled divers to improve their technique without the fear of painful injury arising from an awkward entry into the water. The machine generated large quantities of air bubbles which cushioned their entry. Al Williams had used the first *bubble machine* in Great Britain at the Hillingdon Diving School at Hayes Pool, Middlesex. He had created the necessary bubbles by using high pressure motor tyre inflation equipment. However, such equipment was still lacking in many other places more than a decade later. In their Report of 1988 the Diving Committee drew attention to the need to improve the availability of dry land training of divers by making available physical education equipment, including trampolines. Interestingly the use of trampolines had been advocated by Tommy Mather, the British Empire

Margaret Austen of Iselworth Penguins, diving at Dawdon. She was ASA champion for 1 metre springboard (1961), for Highboard (1962) and for Plain (1962).

Amateur Swimming Association

President: A. C. PRICE, Esq.
Hon. Secretary: Alderman H. E. FERN, C.B.E., J.P.

1961
Swimming & Diving
CHAMPIONSHIPS
DERBY BATHS, BLACKPOOL

MONDAY, AUGUST 28th, to
SEPTEMBER 2nd (inclusive)
Two Sessions Daily at 2.15 and 7.30

PRICES OF ADMISSION

BLOCKS A to L (inclusive):—
  Rows A, B, C—
    Single session seats, 6s. 6d.; season tickets, £3 3s.
  Rows D, E, F, G—
    Single session seats, 5s.; season tickets, £2 10s.
  Rows H, J, K—
    Single session seats, 3s. 6d.; season tickets, £1 15s.
BLOCKS M, N, O: Not available for season tickets.
  All seats, single session, 3s. 6d.

All applications for tickets to:—

Hon. BOOKING OFFICER, A.S.A. Championships,
Box 6, Derby Baths, Blackpool.

Season Tickets are available now, but Single Session Tickets cannot be issued prior to July 1st

Advertising the Championships took a different tone in 1961.

217

Diving Champion of 1934, in a series of articles in the *Swimming Times* during the early 1950s.

Health and safety

Issues of health and safety became more explicit and the focus of specific comment just after the Second World War. An indication of the range of potential problems was given by Dr Bleasdale, the ASA's medical adviser, writing about some diving injuries in the *Swimming Times* of 1952. For example, sinus and ear infections could arise from diving with an active cold in the head, or hitting the water could cause spinal injuries of varying degrees of severity. Awkward impact with the water could produce injuries to the skeleton from which arthritis might develop in later life. The consequences of falling into water might induce blast damage to some tissues. Formidable as these injuries appear, Dr Bleasdale concluded that the risks of damage from diving were in fact low, providing divers followed training procedures advocated by qualified coaches. As always, the diving area in a pool should be of adequate depth and properly supervised in order to minimise accidents. Many of these points about care in swimming baths were reiterated by George Rackham on behalf of the British Diving Coaches Association in 1964. The ISTC restated the importance of good practice in publications such as Joanne Moles' *Diving and the Back* published in 1988 and Keith Sachs and Philip Penny's guidance on practical ways of minimising risks of neck injuries for ISTC in 1991. The potential for injury was particualrly high if certain diving styles were used in badly designed pools. Problems were highlighted in 1989 by Harry Hitchin's *Swimming Times* article 'The Male Macho Diving

Lacy-Hulbert of Croydon produced a 'safety-net' for divers in collaboration with the National Coach, Al Williams. This involved using an air compressor to generate sufficient bubbles to reduce the density of the water so that if a diver entered the water incorrectly the risk of injury was greatly reduced.

Liz Ferris of Mermaid training with the trampette under the direction of her coach, John Wardley.

Syndrome'. In 1990 David Reeves set out ASA advice about the responsibilities of organisers in relation to safety in diving and restated the position in a further article in the *Swimming Times* three years later.

Diving and the Martin Report

Part Two of *The Report and Recommendations of the ASA Special Committee on Competitive Swimming* was published in 1970 and dealt with diving. Kenneth Martin chaired the working party whose members were coaches and divers of international standing. Their conclusions took into account verbal evidence from witnesses and written submissions. Many of their findings had been debated piecemeal in previous years, but the report brought these together and fitted them into the overview of all the work of the ASA. There were 37 recommendations in all, with detailed arguments set out to justify them.

The working party addressed a wide range of issues associated with diving: its programme of events, competition, coaching, training and teaching, judges and judging, facilities, administration, selection policy, qualifying standards in examinations, courses, awards and incentives. It also recommended that improved standards in national and international competitions could be achieved only by adopting the best practices from overseas.

In proposing a national programme of events it was suggested that the annual diving calendar should incorporate periods without competitions in December and from late May until early July. This structure had the purpose of accommodating the range of international competitions as well as making adequate time available for training and coaching at the major levels. Districts and Counties were advised to follow a similar plan in composing their calendars.

Improving the quality of diving required action at all levels of competition. It was recommended that the ASA should extend or increase the degrees of difficulty in the boys and girls Highboard and Springboard championships. This would bring these events into line with European standards for junior competition.

This theme of improvement underpinned recommendations for the National Age Group Competition, for District and for County Championships and competitions. To this end, consideration should be given to Inter-District competitions and to inviting a leading American coach to *'give inspiration to our leading divers and their coaches and to conduct clinics in various centres'*. The Diving Committee was requested to consult with leading coaches and former international divers so as to set

> *'realistic qualifying standards for our national competitions with progressively increasing standards, bearing in mind the major competitions we hope to enter in the next four to six year period'.*

Consistent with efforts to improve qualifying standards, the working party wanted the basis of the selection and training of judges to ensure uniformity and consistency. It noted:

> *'The education of judges has not been generally explored except in a perfunctory manner. Judges need education and*

practical experience throughout their judging career to be kept abreast of development of new dives and techniques'.

Specific steps were suggested to the ASA and the Districts as to how to obtain what was needed. These included clinics where dives would be demonstrated and coaches, divers and judges could exchange views so as to raise the standards of judging. Concurrently the ASA was advised to review thoroughly its judges examinations and to set a national standard.

In concert with the efforts to raise standards, the crucial importance of coaching and teaching demanded efforts to increase the numbers of coaches and teachers and to improve their opportunities to learn. Moreover, the ASA needed to advance the cause of diving in schools by encouraging interest amongst physical education specialists. Although the ASA had appointed a National Technical Officer with special responsibility for diving, his base in the Southern District made it essential for non-diving NTOs elsewhere to have some *'in-service'* training in the fundamentals of teaching and coaching processes.

On issues relating to organisation and administration, the Martin Report made a series of suggestions compatible with its main findings. It wanted the ASA to revise membership of the Diving Committee to include specialists having knowledge of diving and to have a secretary, who could, where appropriate, receive some payment. The overall strategy was to meet the basic needs of diving, which like other disciplines, required improved or new facilities in many locations. To meet these needs it was suggested that there should be new publications for beginners, for diving coaches, and for those establishing new clubs. Increasing the popularity of the sport would lend more weight to the case for more public expenditure on facilities. Concurrently spectators ought to receive more assistance in appreciating the finer points of diving.

In reviewing the potential for diving, the working party had asked itself about standards of diving in Britain between 1945 and 1970 and made comparisons with British performances in international competitions: *'our standards, rarely in the gold medal class, have not kept pace with those of other countries'*. Since this section of the report dealt with the special problems of diving, it made the strong point that diving had suffered from the absence of facilities in many parts of the country. Even where facilities existed the pressures on using swimming pools often severely limited access and in some cases the equipment remained unused.

The Diving Committee, 1966 to 1994

In 1966 the Diving Committee reviewed its work and analysed what was necessary to encourage the sport. In many respects this action foreshadowed recommendations of the Martin Report in 1970. The Diving Committee had suggested that there was inadequate support for diving both within the ASA and elsewhere in the sporting life of Britain. It proposed the appointment of an NTO, whose sole task would be to promote and encourage diving. It also recommended the revival of the British Diving Coaches Association and improved collaboration with the Welsh and Scottish ASAs, ESSA, and the Institute of Bath Managers. Concurrently, the diving committee proposed: to inaugurate Age-Group diving; to promote inter-town and inter-district competitions; to revise the ASA proficiency tests; to seek ways of improving diving facilities throughout the country; to publicise diving through television and sponsorship arrangements; and, to invigorate the education programme. The Diving Committee recommended producing visual aids for competitors and officials and also *Notes of Guidance* for international events. It was suggested that there should be a nominated international squad with appropriate training and trials for major competitions. The Committee agreed to meet quarterly and expected individual members to be prepared to oversee specific items of business

In 1978 the ASA Diving Committee reported that its work had required the creation of various working parties to produce a thorough review of every aspect of diving. Examples cited were:

'(i)   *The entire structure of Championships has been revised to create more interest, meet current demand, and rationalise the diving calendar in line with FINA requirements.*

(ii)   *The Diving Teachers syllabus has been discussed at length and is being streamlined to bring it in line with other disciplines.*

(iii)   *The Diving Judges examination has been rewritten and is now operating from and through the ASA office.*

(iv)   *The National Senior Training Squad has been revised, particularly with regard to training schedules and will operate with effect from 1979'.*

The Diving Committee in 1980 stated that the implementation of most recommendations would take effect in 1981. These included taking account of the FINA law changes which defined the degrees of difficulty in both compulsory and optional dives.

During the 1980s the Diving Committee strove to improve the accessibility of the sport and to claim full backing from the ASA for making more facilities available at the National Swimming Centre at Crystal Palace. It included the formation of a Diving Institute. It was especially important for any scheme to develop the place of British diving in international competitions. Training for such competitions needed to be underpinned by more teachers and coaches in every District. By 1985, the ASA had evolved an awards structure for diving teachers and coaches. At the same time the training of judges received attention and their qualifying examination was changed to include a more complete appreciation of techniques and skills of performers. An indication of the financial pressures is provided by the fact that the National Training Squads scheme for divers based in each District ended because of lack of funding.

During the early 1990s the Diving Committee had working parties developing qualifications relevant to the National Curriculum for Physical Education in schools and for the National Vocational Qualification in the same area. The latter was of great importance in revising and improving the Diving Teachers' Certificates.

Tina Fage (Jersey SC) taking part in the All England Age Group Championships in 1977.

By the early 1990s the position of diving within the ASA had become contentious. The *Development Plan* for 1993 to 1996, published in 1992, recognised some of the problems which included the *'preoccupation throughout the sport with the elite and inevitably the base of the pyramid suffers'*. The Diving Committee suggested that more resources should be devoted to the foundations of the sport and it recognised that, at the top, the élite was sufficiently small so that not all the high grade facilities were properly utilised. Many active divers who were not members of the Diving Committee, wanted a more representative and proactive Committee. At the Council of 1993 these arguments about the role and value of the sport led the ASA to accept that diving *'is facing a crisis'* and to suspend the existing powers and constitution of the Diving Committee. The Diving Committee was reconstituted. Immediately the new Diving Committee established a working party to review the administration and organisation of the sport. Strong feelings persisted concerning the support diving was receiving from the ASA, with some divers believing that they had less than their due. Its findings were endorsed overwhelmingly by a National Diving Conference.

Diving continued to be a focus and debate and development. In 1994 the ASA of England and divers from other parts of Great Britain negotiated a partnership agreement. The membership of the new body, the Great Britain Diving Federation, included recently or currently active divers aware of and interested in the challenges facing their sport.

Changes in diving styles

The full story of the development of diving styles is yet to be written. There is information incidentally in accounts of the organisation of diving and in the *notes for the guidance* of judges in making their assessments. Comparing the styles of diving from 1901 to 1951 Ronald Jones, first President of the Highgate Diving Club of London and a veteran diver, wrote in the *Swimming Times* of 1953:

> '.............diving reached its perfect development about 1930-35, the period of C.D. Tomalin, Freddie Hodges and Betty Slade, and has since been gradually declining into virtuosity, particularly since the end of the war. The main cause of this is obviously the development of the twist, which has led to too many complicated movements being crowded into the available time. As a work of art a dive should be, in architectural jargon, 'symmetrical on each side of its axis', but the twist breaks this symmetry and often requires awkward and ugly contortions. As late as 1935, the last Handbook of the ADA .... describes only a few simple "screw" dives and the twist had not begun to intrude into somersault dives'.

Nonetheless diving styles underwent many developments during the 1940s and the early 1950s, particularly in the United States where more than 40 were added to the repertoire. The ASA itself had little taste for adding to the tariff of difficult dives and it opposed innovations for 1952. It had supported the FINA agreement of 1948 that no new dives would be accepted until the meeting in 1956. The ASA case rested on the point that many of the innovations were dangerous, even life threatening. However, the International Diving Committee wanted some changes

before 1952 in clarification of some of the rules. Between 1952 and the early 1970s FINA made technical changes in diving rules from time to time. For example, in 1968 there were alterations to allow for the effects of high winds during outdoor competitions. During the 1970s, 1980s and 1990s the ASA accepted various additions and changes to the range of dives permitted and to the tariff for scoring approved by FINA. In general these increased the levels of difficulty for the top competitors.

Competitive diving

From time to time the ASA received trophies for diving competitions. These often commemorated people who had given much to the sport and were prestigious awards for high performers. The awards established during the time of the ADA, some of which became ASA awards after 1935, disappeared from use during the Second World War when competitions were suspended. Thus, although championships continued after 1945, many of the cups and trophies were no longer awarded. All the awards made in the 1990s had their origins after 1945. These were:

- The *G. Melville Clark National Memorial Trophy* for men's clubs, instituted in 1951. G. Melville Clark had been an international diver and subsequently an officer of the ADA and then the ASA.

- The *Belle White National Memorial Trophy* for ladies' clubs began in 1974. It commemorated the achievements of the high diver who won the ASA national award from 1925 until 1929, and who represented her country in many international competitions before and after the First World War.

- In 1954 the *Swimming Times* gave *The George Hearn Cup* to be presented annually to the diver *'who is best for the year in the opinion of the ASA Diving Committee'*.

- The *Dawdon Trophy* first awarded in 1973 to the club or clubs achieving the highest points score in competitions for Age Group diving.

- The *Norma Thomas National Memorial Trophy*, instituted in 1985 awarded for the junior diver adjudged to be the best in the year by the ASA Diving Committee.

The levels of success for British divers in the post war years varied. At the British Empire Games in 1958, 9 of the 12 medals for diving came to English competitors. These improved achievements had their counterparts during the same year in the European Games when Brian Phelps won the Highboard final and other English competitors were also in the finals.

Judgements made in diving competitions were often a topic for debate. Pat Besford, the sports journalist, criticised judges of international diving competitions in *World Sports* and her article was reprinted in the *Swimming Times* in February 1963. She drew attention to the possibilities of unfair assessments of aesthetic performances in cases where decisions were made by some judges for reasons of national prestige or to make political points. This article was one of the first to stress the pressures which threatened to undermine the values which were the basis of the Olympic Games and other international competitions. The points made by Pat Besford in relation to diving were applied with equal validity to other sporting activities dependent on artistic interpretation. After the Tokyo Olympics in 1964 further accusations of biased judging were made and, although FINA conducted an enquiry, it still maintained the need for seven judges in diving, with the scores of the highest and lowest eliminated from totals. Some British divers favoured the removal from consideration of the two highest and two lowest scores. However, the selection of judges and the possibility of political pressure in making their assessments remained problems.

The international performances of British divers rarely brought the highest awards during the thirty years between the Tokyo Olympics and 1994. Many explanations of this lack of the highest achievements have been proffered. Amongst the issues discussed have been the lack of resources of all kinds, from club level upwards, to provide the opportunities for training and coaching so vital in developing competitive sports. For example, in 1994 the first International Synchronised Diving Competitions were held. Although the Great Britain team did well in the European Competition it was not prominent in these events in either the Commonwealth Games or the World Championships.

This overview of diving shows that it flourished where the basic facilities existed. Their geographical distribution influences assess to practice, coaching and training. The work of the ADA and ASA until 1935 and the ASA after that year to persuade those who owned or controlled baths and pools to spend the necessary money for sufficient deep water for diving, had but limited success. Moreover, many top performing divers had to train at unsocial hours and were obliged to travel long distances in order to sustain or improve their skills. The grace and beauty of diving, recognised over a century ago, possessed powerful attractions for performers and provided thrills for the spectators, even if diving as an activity has not always been supported by the appropriate resources and facilities.

Brian Phelps (left) and John Candler of Highgate DC in happy mood in August 1964 at the Olympic Nationals before the selection of the British team for the Tokyo Games.

Diving had its lighter side:
1939 - the Dancing Master;
1954 - Let the Board do the work;
1955 - How about it Ref.?;
1961 - carpeted diving board.

Seaside Diving Stages

Open-air seaside pool of the 1930's to post-war times boasted some interesting concrete diving stages. The divers' performances were both exciting and breath-taking and certainly proved a great attraction for the large crowds.

Scarborough South Bay Pool – 1948.

Weston-super-Mare's International Diving Stage – 1950

Minehead Swimming Pool – 1939.

Chapter 8:

The Development of Synchronised Swimming

Comment by A. Sinclair and W. Henry in 1894.

Discussing 'Scientific Swimming'

'It is not necessary for an amateur to learn scientific swimming but the ability to do almost anything in the water brings with it an increased pleasure in bathing and swimming, not attained by merely being able to cover a certain distance in a given time.'

'Synchronised Swimming is a sport requiring overall body strength and agility, grace, split-second timing, musical interpretation and a bit of the dramatic. It is a unique sport in which power, strength, and technical skill are displayed in an artistically choreographed routine. The competitive rules and the way of judging are similar to its counterparts, figure skating and gymnastics.'

'A gymnast performing underwater... A 400 metre freestyle event in swimming with little opportunity to breathe... The figures, leaps, and spins of a figure skater performed in an unstable medium... The water polo player's ability to emerge above the surface of the water with power and strength with an added touch of elegance... A dancer's artistic flair with choreography, musical expressions, and audience contact... Add grace and fluidity and multiply by two, three or eight individuals synchronising each part of every movement and...'

The above descriptions from an ASA handout are the end products of what the American Katherine Curtis had originally devised in the 1920s. The results of her efforts were displayed at the Chicago World Fair by the *Modern Mermaids* in 1934.

To understand the part which the ASA played in the development of synchronised swimming in England we should look at the beginnings.

Before 1890 *Scientific and Ornamental Swimming* was performed mainly by men. Girls were introduced into professional displays at Blackpool prior to 1900. Professor Beckwith and his daughter Agnes attracted large audiences at their gala performances across the country. Amateurs also joined in this swimming display medium early in the twentieth century and performed in gala shows at St. George's Baths, London, and at the other swimming clubs. Some people called this activity *'trick swimming'*. In the publication *Swimming* of 1894 Sinclair and Henry suggested a variety of pool performances including the *torpedo, propeller, the washing-tub,* and *smoking underwater.* Ralph Thomas in 1904 preferred the words

> *'Fancy swimming to cover all varieties of feats performed in the water, to the exclusion of the term ornamental, which is not objectionable, and the word scientific, which is. There is plenty of art, skill and practice required for fancy swimming, but no science.'*

He also refers back to 1816 when Frost had called this activity - *'sportive or playful swimming'.*

In the 1920s, *Floatation Teams* were organised in some North American and continental European countries and the idea spread to England. The Beckenham Ladies Club, the Polytechnic Ladies and Lewisham Ladies were all early starters in the art of floatation and gradually increased their repertoire of patterns. Changes in swimming patterns were notified by whistles, and music was gradually introduced to enhance the performances. Technical progress in sound reproduction was matched by improved lighting systems, powered by electricity, instead of the earlier gas lamps. Thus, ornamental swimming was encouraged

Why Not Swim to Music?
That Wonderful COLUMBIA PORTABLE, Better Still *!*

Sounds Fine in the Baths or Open Air!

The **NEW Columbia PORTABLE**

£4 . 15s.

THE New 1929 Columbia Portable Model £4.15s. challenges comparison with any other portable gramophone AT ANY PRICE. The fullest test will show it to be far and away superior in Tone and Value. It is beyond question the finest portable gramophone yet made. Enormous production alone has rendered such a reduced price possible. British throughout in every component part, its workmanship is of the highest possible standard, and its reproduction of records is amazing in its beauty and volume. You are invited to hear and test it at any Columbia dealer.

Model No. 112a
Like an attaché case when closed, and fitted with nickelled Carrier to take Eight 10-inch Records in perfect security. Constructed in selected hardwood, covered black morocco-grain cloth. Length 16¾-ins., width 11¾-ins., height 6½-ins. Spring cover cup for needles. Hinged winding-crank that folds into the cabinet. Powerful British single-spring motor to play 10-inch and 12-inch records. Latest Columbia No. 9 Soundbox .. **£4.15s.**

Columbia Portable "Junior" No. 109a
A "Junior" model Columbia Portable that represents another amazing standard in Value — no other portable gramophone offering such tone or quality at anything like this price. Shape! like an attaché case and fitted with Carrier to take Eight 10-inch Records in safety ... **£3.10s.**

Illustrated List post free from Columbia, 102-108, Clerkenwell Road, London, E.C 1

This portable record-player advertisement of the 1920s and 1930s was linked to the growth of poolside entertainment, galas and ornamental swimming.

to become an entertainment and gave impetus to bath constructors to provide spectator seating accommodation and this in turn would result in increased financial income. The musical background encouraged story-themes or pageant displays to emerge and costume was able to reflect the theme. As more floatation teams developed competition between them was initiated.

England's first water pageant was organised at the Marshall Street Baths in London in 1936 as part of the first Women's League of Health and Beauty Swimming Gala. Maimie Willis of the USA organised the event. The theme was *The Evolution of Swimming Throughout the Ages* and depicted all forms of water-life from primitive times via *cave girl* to *the girl of the future.*

The *Swimming Times* in 1936 started a series of articles on figure floating and included diagrams of patterns and a number of suggestions for introductory exercises. There was comment that *'most, if not all, women can float naturally, but men are not so favourably gifted, for hardly fifty percent can do so even under most favourable conditions.'* This magazine also had a section for *The Young Swimmers League* or *Sea Lions* and this age group too was encouraged to participate in floatation swimming.

THE GRANDEST BATHS IN ENGLAND.

THE MARBLE BATHS, Junction-road.—Proprietor, E. H. Blunt, Esq.—These new and elegant Baths will be OPENED With a GRAND ENTERTAINMENT of

FAST and ORNAMENTAL SWIMMING,

By the members of the North London Swimming Club, assisted by prominent amateur and professional swimmers, on TUESDAY, APRIL 14, 1885. Doors open at 7 30, commence at 8 o'clock.

Under the patronage of SIR JOHN BENNETT. F.R.A.S.

During the evening the following well-known amateurs will appear :—
G. BELL, Amateur Champion of Great Britain ; G. BETTINSON, Ex-100 Yards Amateur Champion ;
T. H. CLARKE, Ex-Amateur Plunging Champion ;
E. C. DANELS, Ex-Mile Amateur Champion ; J. S. MOORE, Ex-100 Yards Amateur Champion ;
W. HENRY, winner of the Clayton £50 Silver Cup ; W. COLE,
D. AINSWORTH, Ex-Half-Mile Amateur Champion ;
Ex-100 Yards Amateur Champion ; A. F. BETTINSON.
F. MOSES, A. E. FRANCE, F. J. WALTERS,
A. J. GIFFORD, G. COLE, B. FITZHENRY,
G. S. IBBS, G. DUNMORE, T. FILMER, C. A. ITTER.
H. R. SHEVILL, G. YOUNG, W. CURTICE,
Also the following talented Professionals :—
Mrs. NELLIE EASTON, Swimming Mistress of these Baths ;
Miss BROWN, Miss CRANWELL,
CHARLES WHYTE, Sen. and Jun. ; THOMAS W. BRAY, Superintendent and Swimming Master of these Baths.
All swimmers will be dressed in appropriate costume. Ladies are especially invited.
ADMISSION 2s., 2s. 6d., and 3s.
The following Friday a meeting will be held to celebrate the inaugural night of the New Marble Swimming Club. Advt.

Ornamental Swimming was used in this 1885 bath-opening ceremony as the main attraction of the evening.

Polytechnic Ladies' Swimming Club demonstrate Figure Floating in 1934.

Swimming's theatrical aspect in the 1940s did much to publicise the graceful art.

A 1941 wartime article by Will Edwards in the *Swimming Times* seemed to mention *synchronised swimming* for the first time. The ASA had, over the years, advised those who organised galas to engage added attractions to increase the interest for spectators. Thus a water-polo match or diving exhibition or log-rolling could put some pep into events - but perhaps not enough to make it really sparkle. Mr. Edwards reflected the potential for Britain of synchronised swimming as it had developed in America - '*the performance of a variety of strokes and stunts, executed as a team*'. Stunts included somersaults, dolphins, porpoises, wheels and spurs, and were put to music and specially illuminated. Competition between teams was developed and marking systems similar to those used for diving were adopted. Canada had developed '*Floatation*' competitions from as early as 1925. America was in the lead in the 1930s and '40s in originating the huge water shows such as the San Francisco Water Follies of 1941. The shows played to massive audiences for several nights and did much to popularise the art of synchronised swimming through their magnificent displays. Much of this was suitable material for Hollywood film companies to build on. Esther Williams, an American Olympic swimmer, together with Johnny Weissmuller (the original film *Tarzan*) both starred in the Aquacade of 1940. Miss Williams' later successes in the lavish films, where large numbers of stars swam to music, made her one of Hollywood's richest women. The influence on young minds of such film stars in a swimming setting cannot be overestimated.

The 1940s witnessed the recognition in Canada and the USA of synchronised swimming as a sport alongside a set of rules to govern its administration and competition. In 1946 Cathy Gibson and Nancy Riach demonstrated some strokes in time to music at Motherwell in Scotland. The demonstrations which were spreading across Europe were having effect. E.H. Barton of New Kingston Swimming Club described how, in 1944, his club was threatened by closure because of fuel shortage. He organised his group of male swimmers into a team to perform synchronised strokes. His team, wearing red, white and blue costumes, subsequently performed at many galas including the United Nations Gala in London. He saw what he called *rhythmic swimming* as an outlet for those who were not so keen on racing, and it had saved his club from closure.

In 1953 Mrs. Beulah Gundling, USA Solo Synchronised Swimming Champion, and Mrs. Peggy Sellers, President of the Canadian Synchronised Swimming Association, together with two American champion divers, were invited by the ASA to tour England in an effort to popularise the sport. They demonstrated to huge crowds at fifteen locations between 18 August and 5 September. The Ilford event was televised and very soon tickets at all locations were sold out. As it was 1953, a special *Coronation Dance* routine was prepared by Mrs. Gundling. Her English tour was hailed as the real introduction of synchronised swimming in Britain and it left indelible memories. In the previous year Mrs. Gundling had demonstrated daily at the Olympic Games at Helsinki. On the closing night of the Games the FINA water show formed the climax of the event. Efforts were being made to have this sport included in the Olympic programme and her demonstration was a great added attraction at the event. Her convincing performance must have helped the FINA officials at Helsinki towards their decision to approve proposals for the insti-

tution of a set of international rules for synchronised swimming. The enthusiasts for the cause had worked hard for this recognition for the previous four years. Pat Besford Nievens commented that this new discipline was nothing to do with the earlier *group swimming* based on known strokes with rhymical routines and floating. Nor was it connected to the professional aqua show. It was, instead, to be a series of acrobatic figures arranged to music in a flowing routine, attractively costumed and performed in perfect unison by individuals, couples or teams. Competition officials would be a referee, seven judges and a scorer. Marks would be awarded for Execution 0/40 points; Synchronisation 0/20 points; Composition 0/20 points; and Showmanship 0/20 points - totalling 100.

The *Swimming Times* was a good advertisement for synchronised swimming. It continued to publish articles by experienced Americans and to print many illustrations of the movements and patterns connected with the sport. Although the activity was originally designed to be co-educational it was apparent that it was to be dominated by women. Beulah Gundling related that in earlier days boys and girls swam together and boys often won the stunt competitions. Since the sport had been recognised by the American Athletic Union it tended to be more girl orientated. Mrs. Gundling recognised that male and female swimmers brought different strengths to bear - the girls grace, smoothness and buoyancy - the boys strength and power. There were themes which were more male than female in character. Certainly there was recognition that between man and woman there were differ-

Beulah Gundling from the USA did much to popularise synchronised swimming in Britain particularly by her touring exhibitions.

ences of flexibility, muscle and floatation ability. It was noted that in France, unlike Britain, there were, and are, many men in mixed teams. It is, today, quite difficult for a boy in England to reach the District or National Championships.

During the 1950s there was great effort being made in the swimming world to further recognise the progress and potential of synchronised swimming. In 1956 an International Synchronised Swimming Committee was formed by FINA in Holland. The ASA was invited to send a representative but found no-one to be sufficiently qualified to attend. In 1956 the American *Athens Water Follies Team* came to England as guests of the Metropolitan Diving School which had a small but keen *synchronised group*. As with most foreign demonstrators they were a great inspiration and Metropolitan subsequently sent a team to Amsterdam to compete in 1958. Still Britain seemed slow to respond to the need to produce a form of administration for synchronised swimming. It needed to be nurtured as it was in so many countries abroad. The first synchronised swimming club in the country was founded at Seymour Hall Baths in London in 1961 by Dawn Zajac who had studied the activity in the USA with leading coaches. The Club had two nights a week for training and American films and books were the aids for the small group which was willing to learn the basics. Bathside sound-reproduction for the music was difficult at first because of electrical dangers. Transistorised equipment later solved the problem. The need for an underwater speaker system was yet to be met. As with many aspects of swimming this was a family activity. Parents supported their young, made costumes and raised funds. In the early 1960s the Club was visited by American, German and Dutch teams which helped to inspire it to greater things. By 1966 Seymour School had 100 members and was operating for five nights a week. One evening a week many of the girls attended the ballet training at the Royal Academy, and on the other evening took part in land and water training activities. In 1966 Dawn Zajac and Jo Smith produced a booklet *Beginning Synchronised Swimming* - the first home-grown publication.

Dawn Zajac, co-founder of the Seymour Synchronised Swimming Club in 1961, had earlier studied the sport in the USA. The impetus given by her efforts led to the ASA setting up a Synchronised Swimming Committee in 1964.

It was during this last five years of solid progress at the Seymour Hall Bath School that the ASA officially embarked on the development of synchronised swimming in this country. In 1964 it set up a specialist committee for the purpose consisting of Mr. R.A. Brown, Miss P. Jones, Mr. G. Rackham and Mrs. D. Zajac. Mrs. D. Rackham and Mr. F.C. Older were appointed later, and Miss H. Elkington joined in as National Technical Officer. Mr. Brown was appointed as secretary and without doubt became the ASA's foremost champion in the efforts to get the sport fully accepted and recognised. He fought against the prejudices of many administrators in his efforts to succeed. A new ASA Law regularised the Committee's powers to advise on how best to encourage synchronised swimming and to produce a manual on the subject. One of the Committee's first ventures was to stage an exhibition by American Ladies at the Crystal Palace Centre and it was a great success. The ASA Synchronised Swimming Committee acted quickly and mainly with the purpose of enlightening the English swimming world about the real meaning of the sport. There were still many people with very hazy ideas about the entire concept. A handout leaflet was prepared to put the matter right. A conference attended by 120 aficionados and organised jointly by the ASA, STA and CCPR was held with great success at Crystal Palace in June 1965. As very little printed material was available, the ASA brought in a stock of the American AAU *Handbook*. A Synchronised Swimming demonstration was arranged as an adjunct to the ASA National Diving Championships at Crystal

Clarity of music beneath the water, as well as above, contributed to its interpretation. This light submersible speaker provided the answer to the problem.

Helen Elkington, N.T.O., with special responsibility for Synchronised Swimming.

Palace. The Southern Counties ASA were the first District to form their own Synchronised Swimming Committee.

1966 was a year of great activity for this sport. A large number of courses and demonstrations were organised that year - some by clubs, but most following the pattern set by Miss Elkington, National Technical Officer, whose Rochdale course with 23 teachers, 65 swimmers and 8 staff was extremely successful. She also produced a number of teaching film loops on the subject. Other courses were initiated at Derby, Birmingham and Leicester. Dawn Zajac was prominent in many aspects of teaching and demonstrations. The difficulties of supervising a number of courses in different parts of the country cannot be overestimated. Miss Elkington's travelling schedule in all weathers must surely go into the ASA history of its NTOs as a legendary example of devotion to duty. An examiners' course at Crystal Palace had 34 candidates of whom 20 qualified. Dickie Brown, ASA Synchronised Swimming Secretary, urged all Counties and Districts to form their own committees and to follow the Southern District's example. The more the clubs learned to participate in the art of synchronised swimming, the more they threw out challenges to rival clubs to compete in friendly fixtures. This was proof that the message was getting through.

An additional ASA success for 1966 was the making of a Synchronised Swimming instructional film at Loughborough College of Education Bath in July. Here the skills could be filmed above and below water level. Helen Elkington, who was much involved with the project, was pleased with the result which would be very useful to exhibit at future courses. The ASA also had to concern itself with satisfying the rules of the Performing Rights Society because of the very wide use of tapes and recordings to produce poolside music. For public displays, fees were due to the Society and the Association tried to make sure that rules were observed. To illustrate the increasing prominence of synchronised swimming, the Annual ASA Education Committee Swimming Week at Crystal Palace included a whole week on the topic under the direction of George Rackham, Chairman of the ASA Synchronised Swimming Committee.

The existing ASA Award Scheme was extended in 1967 to include awards for synchronised swimming. It had not been easy to set this up over the previous year and necessitated panels of examiners being available to administer it. The awards ranged from Grades 1 to 5 and were an incentive for participants to progress. At the same time, these *proofs of success* enabled District and County Championship organisers to ensure reasonable entry standards for their events. Miss L. Cook, who organised the distribution of all awards from her home, now had this additional task and, of course, the ASA received an additional source of income. Mrs. P. Slater had overall responsibility for the scheme on behalf of the ASA. In 1968, 577 awards were made and in 1969, 1,823 awards. The Swimming Teachers' Association had successfully instituted its own awards scheme for synchronised swimming in 1962, so there was now very ample opportunity for large numbers of youngsters to show what they could do.

As the 1960s progressed it was obvious that most administrative aspects of this sport were coming into place in preparation for entry into competition at County, District, National and later International level. In 1967 the ASA set up its National Panel of Judges and the Southern District held its first official synchronised swimming competition. In the same year, LEN (League of European Swimming) held an International Match at Amsterdam but the ASA Committee did not send a team to compete. Instead it permitted the Metropolitan Diving School to enter under its own name. No doubt the experience was rewarding.

Beulah Gundling made an interesting comment in 1967 when she was deciding how best synchronised swimming could be considered as a serious Olympic sport. She was adamant that there must be the elimination of those elements associated with art and entertainment which could not be judged objectively and which gave too much of an appearance of a *show-type activity*. Thus fancy costumes, theoretical make-up, themes with no gymnastic elements and the use of deckwork or poolside routines (i.e. out of the water) would have no place in serious competition. Mrs. Gundling also suggested that in this discipline, which cannot be measured by stopwatches or tape measures, the judges were bound to be influenced subjectively by such aspects as *appearance, age, choice of music, their own personal ideas of perfection and their personal likes and dislikes.* She considered that if synchronised swimming was to be recognised by the Olympic organisation as a sport then it must be given the chance to develop along two separate lines either as an art form (or *aquatic art*) for those who did not aspire to serious competition or as a sport for those who did.

It was inevitable that a sport as complex as synchronised swimming would have initial problems at National and International levels. Great Britain was just about to tread into these waters. George Rackham had for long been a member and sometime Chairman of the ASA Synchronised Swimming Committee and had for years contributed a swimming page to the *Swimming Times.* He probably expressed the opinions of many when, in 1969, he saw the competition aspect still being very much at the embryo stage in what was a very sophisticated sport. Great Britain could benefit from the experience of the USA where many problems had already been voiced and by the experience of our own District competitors, where valuable knowledge had been gained. International FINA rules were also in existence and these would act as a guide to national development.

The ASA's first National Synchronised Swimming Championships were appropriately held in the 1969 Centenary Year at London's Marshall Street Baths and were considered to be a success. Afterwards, as expected, the subject of judging was discussed and there was concern about the marking of stunts and routines. So much of this aspect of assessment was, by the nature of the exercise, a subjective and personal opinion and some rules were able to be *interpreted*. This was not a criticism of the judges but a pointer to the fact that a greater measure of conformity was required. Also, in 1969, trials were held for team selection for an International match in Paris between Great Britain and France. The Team Manager was Dickie Brown and the Coach, Dawn Zajac. Although defeated, the team put up a good performance. It is to be noted that the ASA did not approve a Committee item that '*males could be permitted to take part in Synchronised Competitions*'. In 1967, Helen Elkington and Jackie Brayshaw visited the USA to study the organisation of synchronised swimming. They subsequently produced a *Treatise on Synchronised Swimming* for the ASA. Miss Elkington later extended her horizons in 1969 when she won a Winston Churchill Travelling Scholarship.

In 1970 the section of the ASA's Martin Report which dealt with synchronised swimming was published and made a number of recommendations. The report was commenting on an activity which had been part of the ASA for just six years and which '*had done great work often in the face of opposition and apathy*'. It identified a nucleus of competent, enthusiastic workers for the cause

The Queen met members of the Beefeater Syncho Display Team at the ASA's Centenary Gala at Crystal Palace on 15th May 1969. The team included international representatives, Jennifer Lane and Jennifer Gray (née Robb).

The Beefeater International Team of 1969.

and counted between 60 and 70 clubs or groups in existence in the country. In some schools it was part of the curriculum. Having listed the many positive developments in synchronised swimming since its inception the report pointed to problems: the limited number of officials and publications; a lack of water space; and time allocation. The suggested lines of development were predictable: *Working through Colleges of Education and Schools; Courses and Summer Schools; Propaganda; Publications; Competitions; Demonstrations; Encouragement of Spectator Interest.* Other lines of approach would be through Regional Sports Councils which could consult with local authorities about pool sizes, inspection windows, lighting, power points, etc. The great value of the Report was that it was in general analysing the many systems within the ASA which had been in place for a long period of time. With synchronised swimming still so young there was little to change but much to support.

The 1970s could be identified as a decade when the great efforts made throughout the '60s came to fruition. There were successes which could only have been dreams in earlier times and the ASA was, with the help of a nucleus of over-burdened enthusiasts, helping to make things happen across a whole range of developments. The Association's long awaited *Handbook on Synchronised Swimming* appeared in 1970, as did the first Easter Course for Synchronised Swimmers and Coaches at Crystal Palace. The following year the Easter Residential Course was arranged for those identified as top synchronised swimmers plus two from each District and two from each of Scotland and Wales. Helen Elkington was Course Director, with Dawn Zajac in charge of students and Miss Brayshaw supervising the dance aspect.

For four years from 1971 to 1974 Great Britain won the Four Nations Competition against Holland, France and West

Britain's National Squad of 1972 demonstrated one of the figures on a plastic sheet. (Copyright: North of England Newspapers, Darlington.)

Germany, and so received the Dolphin Trophy to keep. In 1973 Britain was fifth in the first World Championships at Belgrade and the experience was invaluable.

At home very few Counties had formed their synchronised committees and were strongly advised by the ASA to follow the Districts example to do so for the benefit of the sport and competition.

There was also a shortage of qualified national officials but courses were set up and, in 1973, 14 Grade A Examiners passed the Judges examination. Scorers examinations were initiated, a difficult aspect for this sport.

In 1973 the first Inter-District Competitions were held at Coventry and this improved the competitive potential and increased the experience for officials.

The first European Championships between seven countries were held at Amsterdam in 1974. Great Britain came first by taking Gold medals in solo, duet and team events. It was a busy year for the competitors who also entered the World Championships at Colombia and took part in Britain's first National Championships. A Synchronised Swimming Teachers' Certificate Course was also set up at Crystal Palace and a handbook published to go alongside it. Twenty-four teachers passed the first course. In the following years these courses were spread around the country and a growing number of teachers were added to the qualified list. In 1976 Jennifer Gray was appointed by the ASA as National Development Officer for Synchronised Swimming and Diving: she had previously been a member of the Great Britain Team and became a producer of a variety of publications on the subject. Part of her brief was to emphasise the fitness aspect of the sport and the need to develop programmes to condition the body anatomically and physiologically and to develop it psychologically in order to produce greater efficiency

The Dolphin Trophy which Great Britain retained in 1974.

Britain's Synchronised Team of 1978.

with less fatigue. It seemed apt that the ASA should consider creating this new post at a time when so much was happening in the world of synchronised swimming and when undoubtedly international competition would get harder. Mrs. Gray worked closely with teachers courses and liaised with local authorities.

In 1978 Great Britain was fourth in the World Championships in West Berlin and, in 1977 had won the European Championships in Sweden. In the same year the ASA was developing an Advanced Teachers' Certificate with a pilot course at Crystal Palace. Also a Preliminary Teachers' Certificate was initiated as a lead in to the main course. There were now three stages to pass through. Our National Championships were now big enough to become a two-day event. Every year the Judges and Referees Conferences were held at Bedford College of Higher Education [now De Montfort University] and every year the number of qualified officials increased although there were never enough of them.

To finish the decade, in 1979 the Great Britain Team won the Five Nations Contest and came fifth out of eight countries in the first FINA Synchronised Swimming World Competition event.

The first Synchronised Age-Group Competition was held at Nuneaton in 1980. In the 1980s, sponsorship of events by national companies was eagerly sought. It gave a good advertising outlet for the sponsors and enabled the ASA to spread its own financial assets to where they were most needed. The Mazda Car International between the USA, Canada and Great Britain at Coventry was televised. In 1982 a Philips/ASA Synchronised Swimming Festival was held at Crystal Palace as the first venture of its kind. Every year each District would attempt to get sponsorship for a specific event. Thus an Electricity Board or a City Council would be pleased to be seen to sponsor an event. One year the income from a Horlicks television advertisement, based on synchronised swimming, was sufficient to support one of Great Britain team's visit to Australia. In 1983 Britain's team won the European Championships in Rome. Throughout the 1980s Britain's Junior Teams competed at European level in a variety of age-groups and in 1984 won the Junior European Championships. In 1982 the ASA introduced a Synchronised Swimming Coaches' Certificate and held courses for it. This about completed the full circle of officials' courses. As an adjunct to this, the ASA brought out a booklet, two videos and an official handbook. Another form of aid for participants and coaches was the formation of a panel of physiotherapists who would be called upon to attend special team events. The use of sports psychologists was also a 1980's phenomena. It was recognised that there was a need for synchronised swimmers, as with other sports

Underwater action at the 5 Nations Match at Crystal Palace in 1984.

persons, to focus the mind and to *'tune in to the real aims and objectives of the competition.'* Other researchers, such as Professor Keating at the London Hospital, were looking at the effect on swimmers of the time spent under water and were also making a study of hyperventilation. Thought was given to integrating disabled swimmers into synchronised activities but this was to be a responsibility of the club and not of the ASA. As with all new ventures of this kind, a body of *useful practice and information* was built up within those clubs which had the experience and which were willing to pass this *good practice* on to others.

At long last in 1984 synchronised swimming was part of the Olympic Games programme. The road to admission had been arduous. Top Olympic officials had put obstacles in the way and no doubt, as it was a discipline which was not as easily judged as other sports, there had to be much thought given to the subject. The experience of official bodies gained at every level of competition, except Olympic level, must have helped to break the barrier of resistance. It seemed a long time since Beulah Gundling's demonstration at the ASA Helsinki Olympics. In 1986 the Commonwealth Games also accepted this form of sport competition and Great Britain won two Silver medals.

The ASA Awards Scheme had been operating since 1967 and needed some revision. Part of this was carried out in 1987 but in 1992 a completely new scheme emerged with three preliminary stages to go through before attempting the actual grades. In 1988 the *two mark* system for judging routines was introduced and required District conferences and training schemes to implement it properly. Examination criteria were also revised.

In 1992 Great Britain was placed sixth in the Olympics.

The ASA was pleased in 1993 to host the third World FINA Junior Synchronised Swimming Championships at Leeds. It was a measure, perhaps, of how far administration of the sport had come and was a credit to our officials. Comment was made in 1994 about how rapidly synchronised swimming had changed over the previous four years. Levels of competition had risen; FINA had adjusted a variety of rules; and figures were now more difficult to execute. The appointment of five ASA Regional Development Officers in 1993 was helpful to the sport. These experts were to be active in organising courses, planning useful contacts, and liaising with local authorities and clubs over matters such as pool space.

Research on performing synchronised swimming figures under water was still going on. Some competitors complained of dizziness, disorientation and momentary blackouts. The Physiology Department of Queen Mary and Westfield College, London University, showed that the concentration of oxygen in the lungs had been very low after exercise. The more intensive the exercise the faster low oxygen levels developed. The continuation of exercise in this condition could lead to unconsciousness. Heart rate also slowed but this was not considered to be of any great importance. Synchronised swimmers were shown generally to have greater vital lung capacity than the average person. This sort of research could help to answer the questions of those who trained vigorously under water and help them to realise their limitations.

The *ASA's Development Plan for 1993-96* helped to review synchronised swimming's situation in the 1990s - *'This highly demanding sport requires total watermanship, strength, flexibility, cardiac vascular endurances as well as artistic qualities and kinaesthetic awareness'.* The championship status attained by Great Britain between 1973 and 85 was not maintained between 1985 and 1990. This was not due to any decrease in the ability and skill of swimmers and coaches, but to the more positive developmental programmes of other European countries. The lost ground was slowly recovered in 1991 and 1992. To keep level with the competition, a strong English programme was necessary and entailed the integration of the *qualification system* and *opportunity* and *aims of swimmers.*

The total competitive structure, by then, included the International Programme, the National Synchronised Swimming Championships, the National Synchronised Swimming Age-Group Competitions in three groupings, the Inter-District Competition, District, County and Inter-County Competition and National Masters Competition. It is intended that synchronised swimming will be included in the World Masters for the first time.

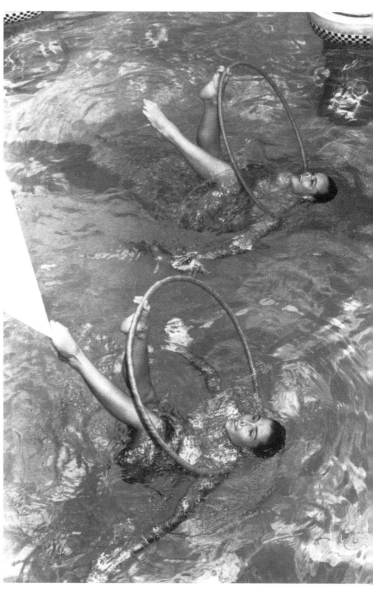

Reading Royals in 1988.

The *Development Plan* advocated as much participation in international events as possible, not just for prestige, but for swimmers, coaches and officials to evaluate their own performances alongside their opposite numbers. It also made a long list of suggestions of ways to achieve the plan's strategic aims to further the programme of education, propaganda, facilities, courses and the general extension of the sport. At the same time the ASA wished to find ways to support the development of synchronised swimming as one of the three minor disciplines, i.e. alongside Water-Polo and Diving. This would include special financial support of up to £10,000 for innovative proposals which could be confirmed as not being funded through the normal channels.

It was now 30 years since the ASA officially recognised the need to take synchronised swimming under its wing. Since then the sport had come a long way and had achieved much. The ASA had produced the conditions for the sport to grow. The quite small nucleus of those who had themselves become proficient and knowledgeable by studying American developments must, today, be seen as the real catalyst. Against many odds, the teachers, coaches and officials emerged to foster the progress of youngsters and adults towards goals, which in the 1970s and 1980s were the real reward as well as being a shining example.

The amount of pleasure that so many people have derived from participation and competition is immeasurable. Nor can the amount of fitness or the degree of education ever be truly estimated. Possibly in no other branch of swimming have so many people been involved with their children by acting as chaperones, making costumes, raising funds and just being part of the huge band of volunteers on which the ASA has built its empire.

Chapter 9

Water Polo

Comment by Frank Sachs, member of Otter SC and founder member of the ASA Committee, 1912.

'Of the many team-ball games that exist there is none less like polo than the game in which swimmers indulge...... Matches wherein the contestants sat astride a wooden horse or an inflated skin .... and played a ball with a wooden bat or with the hand, have frequently taken place at seaside regattas and in some swimming baths .... such titles as "Football in the water," "Water baseball," "Aquatic Polo," and "Aquatic Hand-ball" were some of earliest names used for the sport.'

The origins and development of water polo

What little historical evidence we have supports the idea that the original game of water polo was an attempt to translate field polo into an aquatic context. At galas during the 1870s, two teams of players sat astride wooden barrels, to represent the ponies, placed in the water and attempted to score goals by throwing a rubber ball. Little was said about rules, the object being to provide as much amusement for the spectators as possible. As the contests between two teams became more serious and the players moved to establish their game as an aquatic sport, the barrels have disappeared and the game became much more like handball in the water. Variations on this terminology were being used by players and in the press during the second half of the nineteenth century. Reports in the press used terms such as *Aquatic Handball* in Bournemouth, 1876 and *Water Baseball* at Crystal Palace, 1874. In 1870 we find the term *Football in the Water* used when the London Swimming Association (the forerunner of the ASA) set up a committee on 12 May to devise rules for the game, though no record survives to show whether the committee completed this task. William Wilson, the Glaswegian swimmer and publicist, wrote rules in 1877 for the game of *Aquatic Football* which was being played in the River Dee by the Bon Accord SC of Aberdeen. The term *water polo* was also used and by the later 1880s this name had gained general recognition.

Whatever the name used, a team game in the water, using a ball, became possible because new rubber technology made possible the development of inflatable balls at an affordable price. At galas the game provided fun for players and an entertainment for bystanders. The organisers published rules which enabled spectators to understand the aims of the game and to judge the skill of teams and the roles of the players. The game attracted adherents, particularly in Scotland and the Midlands of England, who wished to play on a regular basis. The Midland Counties Aquatic Football Association was in being by 1883. In the same year, at the Portsmouth Festival, a team representing All England played against a Birmingham Leander Club side. These teams were already playing within a framework of eleven rules which were specially published for the occasion. The first rule specified that the game should last for twenty minutes but there was no statement about team size. In 1884 the Torpedo Club of London published its seven rules which specified that a team should be not less than five or more than eleven in number, depending on the space of water available. An early indication of potential problems is indicated by their fourth rule which stated: *'When making for the ball or obstructing an opponent, rough play should be avoided if possible. The ball must be struck or pushed and in no case thrown'.* Rule five stated: *'Should the ball be thrown it must be returned to the spot where thrown from, the men forming into line either side for scrimmage'.* During the 1880s the rules of the game evolved so that team size was standardised at seven participants. William Henry, a pioneer in many activities related to swimming, devised the first rules adopted by the SAGB in 1885 and these were revised by the ASA in 1888. The first international water polo match took place in 1890 between England and Scotland.

MIDLAND COUNTIES AQUATIC POLO ASSOCIATION.

FINAL TIE FOR THE 20 GUINEA CHALLENGE CUP.

The association having decided that the final tie for the above trophy should be played in neutral water, selected Dudley Bath, and last Wednesday night the Birmingham Leander journeyed over to Dudley to meet Hanley Swimming Club, and played off the tie. At the commencement of the game it could be clearly seen that the Leanders were playing up to their best form, as the ball was kept continually in the Hanley quarters, and from a quick bit of passing Harris was enabled to secure a goal. Upon re-starting, the Leanders again pressed their opponents very hard, but were unable to raise the score, and at the call of time the Leander's were declared the winners by one goal to 0. In addition to having won the cup the association presents each of the winning team with a silver medal. Bravo! Leander, who are now able to say that they have not suffered defeat once this year, either in cup ties or friendly matches. Leander cup team: W. G. Bensly, goal; E. Deakin, J. Pritchard, backs; H. A. Warrington, E. T. Patstone, centres; H. Taylor, W. Harris, J. Johnson, forwards.

In October 1885 the match between Edgbaston and Hanley took place under the auspices of the Midland Counties Aquatic Polo Association.

Archibald Sinclair, also an enthusiast for all things related to swimming, recalled refereeing the game where the skill of the Scots more than compensated for the heaviness of the English players. Each side had been accustomed to different rules so that the match revealed the limitations of a lack of standardisation within the game. It was agreed to form an International Board of the ASA, which included Scottish representatives, to codify the rules and these were published in 1892. The first match between England and Scotland under the new rules resulted in a victory for England under the captaincy of William Henry.

This woodcut shows an early version of water polo, probably in the 1870s, which was played in the sea in an arena made by boats around the playing area.

Aston SC won the Midland Counties Water Polo Championship in 1905.

In the early 1890s spectators viewed the game from boats or from a bathing platform at the sea side.

In 1937 Joshua Payne, Honorary Secretary of the Nautilus Swimming Club between 1881 and 1889, reminisced in the *Swimming Times* about the 'Origins of Water Polo':

'It was about the year 1886 that I learnt that a Glasgow swimming club was playing with a football in their bath and I understood that they called their game "Aquatic Handball" or "Aquatic Football". This gave me the idea for an item in the programme of our Nautilus S.C. annual races in the Crown Baths, Kennington Oval (London), and having drawn up a few rules and got together two teams of our members, we played what proved to be a most interesting and exciting game - the goal posts being without the usual football nets.'

PORTSMOUTH ROYAL DOCKYARD REGATTA.

500 YARDS AMATEUR HANDICAP, decided at Southsea for four prizes, Aug. 15th.—J. Simmonds, H.M.S. St. Vincent, 35, 1 : J. R. Holley, 45, 2 ; E. H. Eason, 30, 4 ; H. H. Burton, 30, 0 ; A. F. Cooke, 60, 3 ; H. H. Oliver, 40, 0 ; N. I. Kingsbury, 120, 0 ; A. Sargeant, 45, 0 ; J. Daltrey, H.M.S. Vernon, 45, 0; young Cooke, who has been unfortunate in securing prizes of late, was expected to secure first place upon this occasion, but his friends were once again doomed to disappointment, as Holley and the St. Vincent lad caught him travelling too slowly in the last turn for the marked boat, and putting in all they knew passed him, and after a neck and neck struggle, urged on by the cheers of their respective partisans, finished in the order named, the sailor gaining first prize by a yard, Cooke about twice that distance behind the second man.

An AQUATIC POLO MATCH ON HORSEBACK, between the following teams, ended in one goal being obtained by each side and a division of the prizes. Red and White Caps : H. W. Fisk (captain), H. H. Burton, S. Warrell, G. Gould, B. Ward. F. G. J. Wright, J. Heffer-man (goal-keeper). T. Bailey (umpire). Blue and White Caps : J. Andrew (captain), A. Sargeant, C. F. Armstrong, A. W. Ward. A. W. Jones, A. J. Green, T. Dyer (goal-keeper), and E. Sigrist (umpire). The gigantic efforts of the riders to sit their watery steeds and at the same time do their best for their respective sides was the source of great amusement to about 10,000 spectators, who watched every movement of the players.

Water polo had several meanings as is evident in this item from Swimming Notes about the Portsmouth Royal Dock Regatta held in August 1884.

MIDLAND COUNTIES AQUATIC POLO ASSOCIATION.
EDGBASTON v. HANLEY.

The above match was decided at the Public Baths, Hanley, on the 7th inst., before a good audience. The teams met at Birmingham on September 23, but the game then ended in a draw, consequently great interest was shown in the match. The Association referee being unable to attend. Mr. Griffiths, of the *Midland Athlete*, was chosen referee. The ball was thrown in at 8.30, and was at once secured by Hanley, who immediately carried it to the visitors' goal, but were here met by a splendid defence. The play was kept well in the Edgbaston quarters owing to the good passing of the Hanley team. The visitors now attacked, but the defence proved equal to the occasion. Half time was called with no goals scored. The Hanley again obtained possession of the ball, and a determined rush was made, but without effect, Nicholls showing fine form. Some very even play ensued, and at last Mason for the home team placed a goal amidst great cheering. The referee, however, disallowed the point, saying he had blown for time. In accordance with the laws of the Association an extra ten minutes was ordered to be played. The Edgbaston men now appeared to be getting tired, but the home team seemed quite fresh. The first 5 minutes ended in a draw, but on again changing ends Hanley seemed to bewilder their opponents, who seemed useless against the rush made by the forwards, and half back and a goal was scored by Mason amidst tremendous applause. This seemed to incite the "Brums" to trying to equalise matters, but owing to the grand play of Smith, Nuttall, and Sockett, the ball was got away, and by a neat bit of passing by Heath and Simpson another goal was secured by Mason. The referee then called time the game thus ending in favour of the Hanley team by two goals to nil. The Hanley men will now have to meet Dudley in the final tie.

Midland Counties Aquatic Polo Association was one of the earliest water polo organisations. It was active in October, 1884.

ANNUAL SPORTS OF THE DUDLEY SWIMMING CLUB

On September 17 the annual sports of the Dudley Swimming Club took place in the Corporation Baths, in the presence of a large assemblage. In the unavoidable absence of the Mayor, Alderman W Walker presided, and he was supported by Councillor M Smith, Mr R G Walker, Mr W Waldron, Chief Superintendent Burton, Mr Finney (Brierley Hill), Mr J Nayler, Mr J Prince, Mr J Noonan, Rev W J Clarke, Mr J Davies, Mr M Fletcher, Mr H Perrins and numerous other residents in the town and district.

In commencing the proceedings, the Chairman regretted the absence of the Mayor, who had gone for a 10 days holiday, but who had written a letter expressing the hope that the sports would be successful. He, (the Chairman) regretted that the entries for the scholars race were so few, and trusted that in the future more interest would be taken in this particular branch of the art of swimming in order to encourage a love of it, and to encourage those who were always ready to give instruction to any who were desirous of learning. He was sure that the committee of the club would at all times be willing to give all the assistance they could, and there was nearly always someone at the baths who would instruct learners. He hoped next year a greater interest would be shown, and that a larger number would come forward and compete for the prizes which the committee were only too pleased to provide (applause.)

The following events were then commenced :-

Scholars' Handicap (two lengths).—Open to youths attending schools in the Borough of Dudley. First prize, microscope and case, value 10s.; second prize, pocket knife (presented by Mr Theedam) value 5s.—This was won by—Albert Willis 12 1, Richard Hancock 9 2.

Club Handicap (four lengths).—Open to members of the Dudley Club only. First prize, dressing case, value £2 2s. (presented by the ladies of Dudley) ; second prize, carriage clock, value £1 1s. (presented by the Mayor) ; third prize, gold solitaires, value 10s. 6d. (presented by Mr H Morris, builder). First and second in each heat to swim in the final.—Heat 1 : A Fincher 8 1, A Duce 14 2. Heat 2 : A Hughes 5 1, J Wood 12 2. Final : Fincher 1, Hughes 2, Duce 3.

Novice Race Handicap (four lengths).—Open to amateurs who have never gained a public prize for swimming. First prize, egg stand, value £1 1s. (presented by Brooke Robinson, Esq.); second prize, silk umbrella, value 10s. Four entered in each heat, first in each heat to swim in the final.—Heat 1 : J Clements (West Bromwich) 10 1, Heat 2 : W Dauncey (Walsall) 3 1. Heat 3 : A Hanson (Victoria) 20 1. Heat 4 : J Moss (Victoria) 5 1. Final : Moss 1, Hanson 2, Clements 3.

All England Amateur Handicap (six lengths).—First in each heat and second in fastest to swim in final. Heat 1 : H Pearson (Cheltenham) 25 1, F Edwards (Walsall) scratch 2. Heat 2 : L Hadley (Ashted) 24 1 ; E Patstone (Victoria) scratch 2. Heat 3 : W Hancock (Dudley) 18 1, F Arblaster (Victoria) 30 2. This was a most interesting race, good form being shown by all the competitors. Edwards (Walsall) scratch coming in about four strokes behind. The final was gamely struggled for, and resulted—Pearson 1, Hancock 2, Edwards 3.

Youths' Race Handicap (two lengths), open to youths under seventeen years of age residing within three miles of Dudley.—The only entries were—Ernest Newey (Dudley) scratch, Oliver Dudley 6 sec, S Bourne 10. Newey was over-handicapped, and had the misfortune to collide with the posts in the bath. Dudley came in first, Bourne second, Newey making a good third.

Variety Swimming Race (three lengths), open to members of the affiliated clubs of the Midland Counties Swimming Association. First length, swimming on the back ; second, swimming on the back ; third, go-as-you-please. Heat 1 : Alfred Duce 1, W Blocksidge 2. Heat 2 : A Fincher 1, Alfred Hughes 2. Final : Fincher 1, Hughes 2.

Grand Polo Match between the Cheltenham Club and Dudley Club, the teams being stationed as follows : Cheltenham—goal, Cardew ; backs, W Sadler, W Herbert ; half-backs, T Darby, Pearson ; forwards, H Ewbank (captain), H Cooper, G Norman. Dudley—goal, J Davies ; backs, J Hannay, A Deuce ; half-back, Fletcher ; forwards, S Hooper (captain), A Hughes, T Goodwin, Baggott. Umpires, Messrs. A Morton and A Taylor ; referee, Professor Bates. Some capital play was shown on both sides, but the Dudley team were too strong for their opponents. At half-time no goal had been obtained, although a good try had been made by Dudley, the umpire declaring it no goal. On change of ends, Hooper for Dudley planted the ball between the posts in fine style amid loud cheering, thus scoring the first goal to the home team. This was followed by a fine scrimmage, and the ball was thrown in by Hughes, it being ruled no goal, however. When the time was called, Dudley had won by one goal to nil. The competing team then gave three cheers for each other, and Alderman Walker having distributed the prizes, the gathering dispersed.

The following acted as officials : handicapper and starter, Professor Baths ; judges, Messrs, M Smith, H Hughes, T H Goodwin, and J Collett, timekeeper, Mr J Mitchell.

Swimming Notes devoted a column in September 1885 to the Annual Sports of the Dudley (West Midlands) SC. One event was the Grand Polo Match between Cheltenham and Dudley.

The Belgians playing against the British in the Water Polo Final of the Olympic games in London in 1908.

The British Olympic water polo gold medallists of 1908 - left to right standing in back row: Walter Brickett (trainer), F. Baxter (ASA), C.G. Forsyth, G. Hearn (President of the ASA); standing left to right middle row: Paulo Radmilovic, R. Cross (SCASA President), George Wilkinson, J.C. Hurd (Honorary Secretary of ASA): and seated left to right: George Cornet, Charles Smith (Captain), George Nevinson, Thomas Thould.

This entertainment took place on 28 October 1887. Two years later, 26 October 1889, an illustration of that first water polo match played at the Nautilus Club entertainment evening appeared in the *Illustrated Sporting and Dramatic News*. At a similar occasion on 16 October 1891 the participants were teams raised for the event, representing the Universities of Oxford and Cambridge. Oxford won.

Recalling the early days of organised water polo John Davenport wrote for the *Swimming Times* in 1948: 'Water polo training - a memory'. During the time he played the game he recollected many discussions of training and tactics. It was decided that the upper left hand side of the goal presented the greatest difficulty to goal keepers. Davenport's team practised aiming the ball at a target, a white patch about 18 inches square placed where the top left hand corner of the goal would be during a match. One club member, who taught physical education, assisted players with rubbing down and massage during and after games. The team called him '*Trainer*' and he attended matches always holding a folded white bath towel over his arm. During play he *happened* to stand behind the left hand side of the opponent's goal with the white towel hanging over his arm, just at target level. Davenport said of this ploy:

'It was not necessarily a match-winner, there being other

factors of course, but it certainly simplified and directed attacks at goal. All this happened 50 years ago, and since that time I have not seen or heard of similar "happenings"'.

Codified rules became essential as the game of water polo gained popularity and spread both within the British Isles and overseas. The ASA revised the rules in 1901, by which time the number had risen to twenty-three with some interpretative notes entitled *Hints for the Guidance of Referees*. These were so elaborate as to make use of the letters in the alphabet from A to O. The ASA Committee found itself having to provide rulings on the interpretation of the rules on various occasions before the outbreak of the First World War. Examples from the *Handbook* recorded decisions by the Committee and these give a flavour of how the ideas of fairness were maintained and how the rules were to be interpreted: in 1908, (Rule No. 69) referees in some matches in the NCASA were not using flags. Northern representatives said this would be remedied in future. In 1908, (Rule No. 71) SCASA asked:

'A player after starting to swim up, takes the ball and passes back to one of his own side. The latter player throws at his opponents' goal without crossing the half-way line, and the goal-keeper, in attempting to save, touches the ball with his hand, and puts it through. What is the Referee to give?

The committee rules that this should be considered a goal.'

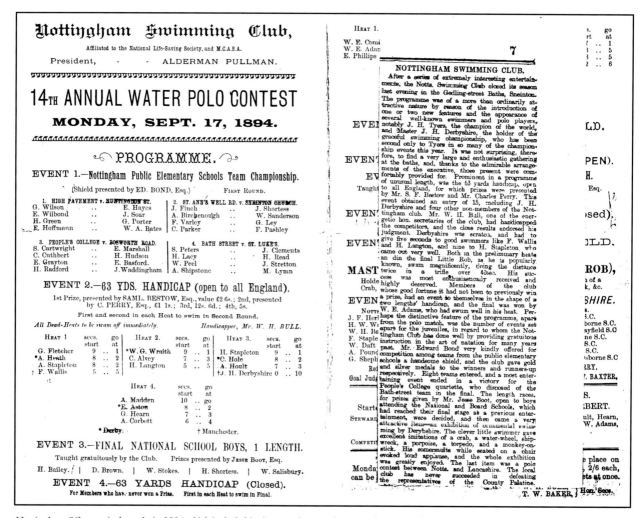

Nottingham SC organised a gala in 1894 which included its fourteenth annual water polo contest. The match between Nottinghamshire and Lancashire, event 12, ended with a victory for the visitors. H.M. Thomsett was the referee from the MCASA who subsequently served the ASA as President in 1902. Amongst the attractions was an event with cash prizes for professionals or those who did not value their amateur status. More mundane was the 1901 programme card of the St James SC (right).

St. James's Swimming Club.

Dulwich Baths, August 17th, 1901.

Programme:

WATER POLO

CHAMPIONS OF KENT	V.	CHAMPIONS OF SURREY.
WHITE CAPS.		BLUE CAPS.
A. H. Stevens	Goal	J. Jones
W. J. L. Milne } P. Abbott	Backs	H. S. Martin C. Botting
P. Plumstead	Half-back	G. Lever
L. Fenoulhet H. Tims O. E. Challis	Fowards	P. Kemp W. Cullen E. H. Byshe

Reserve : Clive Sharman.

Referee : H. Thomsett, Esq.,   Time-keeper; R. C. Beale.

INTERNATIONAL TRIAL MATCH.

NORTH	V.	SOUTH
WHITE CAPS		BLUE CAPS
S. Smith (Wigan S.C.)	Goal	R. E. Claridge (St. James's
T. Coe (Capt) (Osborne S.C.)	Backs	E. A. Paine (Worthing S.C.)
E. Robinson (Osborne S.C.)		R. Grey (Polytechnic S.E.)
T. T. Wildgoose (Hyde Seal S.C.)	Half-back	Graham Marshall (Capt. Nautilus S.C.)
P. Ripley (Ayde Seal S.C.) G. Wilkinson (Osborne S.C.) F. F. Swift (Wigan S C.)	Forwards	P. C. Robertson (Polytechnic) E. Hunt (Polytechnic) R. F. Cohen (Richmond)
A. G. Robertson (Warrington S.C.) W. Gallagher (Openshaw S.C.) J. W. Shaw (Osborne S.C.)	Reserves	P. Kemp (St. James's S.C.) G. Emerson (Amateur S.C.)

Referee : H. Thomsett Midland Counties A.S.A.

Time-keeper : R. B. Cross, Southern Counties A.S.A.

Goal Scorers { S. J. Monks (Amateur) W. J. Ellis (St. James's)

CUTTS AND CO , PRINTERS, VICTORIA ROAD PECKHAM

interval. In reality the duration of the game was much greater, often taking as much as 45 minutes. The discrepancy arose from the time taken for the resolution of fouls with the consequence that swimmers remained in the water throughout the period. The effects of such prolonged immersion might not only damage health, but limit the appeal of the game. On the health question the writer suggested that attacks of cramp were one of the manifestations of overexposure to cold water and highlighted the problem of cold in limiting muscular power and flexibility. According to the then current medical opinion, time spent in cold water should not exceed 15 minutes. In framing the rules the ASA and other governing bodies ignored this advice.

During the 1880s and early 1890s many counties formed water polo teams and during the 1890s matches were played in increasing numbers at county level. Other leagues besides the Midlands developed in various parts of the country. For example, the London Water Polo League was founded in 1889 and by 1909 had fifty nine clubs affiliated to it.

Water polo was also played in various parts of the British Empire as well as in many European countries. In 1900 Belgium received the credit for originating the game and codifying the rules when water polo was recognised as a sport for the Olympic Games held in Paris. The British version was that a team from Brussels had visited the Otter SC in the later 1890s and one of

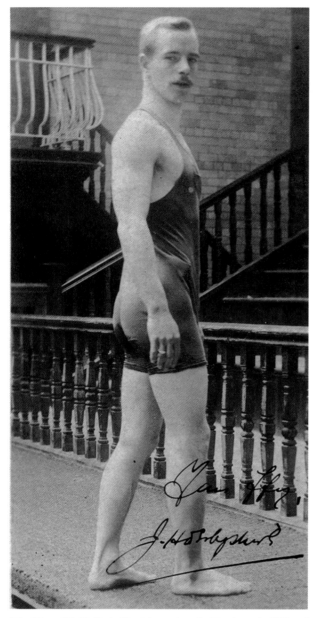

John Henry ('Rob') Derbyshire, who was born in Manchester in 1878 and died in 1933. He was an outstanding water polo player, being a gold medallist in the 1900 Olympic Games. He played for Manchester Osborne. Concurrently as a sprinter he won the ASA 100 yards freestyle championship six times between 1898 and 1904.

Again in 1908, (Rule No. 73) '*Championship matches must be played in a bath and not Open Water.*'.

In 1910 the ASA adopted a wholly revised set of rules for water polo which reduced the number to twenty two. The guidance for referees was simplified by requiring the letters from A to M to distinguish the points of interpretation. These rules were used in the Olympic Games of 1912. They remained unchanged until after the end of the First World War in 1918.

In contrast to other types of swimming activity, water polo often generated debate about the impact of the game on the players' health. An 'international captain' (almost certainly William Henry) wrote in *The Swimming Magazine* in 1915: 'The Drawbacks of Water Polo - Is the Game a suitable Physical Exercise?' He suggested that the duration of the game according to the rules might be supposed to be 14 minutes with a 3 minute their members, Monsieur Sounemann, obtained a copy of the Otter SC rules and translated them into French. In spite of not having credit for their contribution, the British team won the water polo event at the Olympic Games in Paris in 1900. No British water polo team went to the Olympiad of 1904 at St Louis, USA, but at the London Games of 1908 the British team beat the Belgians in the finals. At the Stockholm Games of 1912 the British team defeated the Austrians in the finals. Commenting in 1914 on this history of internationals, Archibald Sinclair said of Stockholm: *'The competition has, however, taught us that we must look to our laurels in the future'*.

Women and water polo

Women began playing water polo and they were already organised into teams before the end of the nineteenth century. One of the early accounts of the women's game appeared in the *Swimming Magazine* of October 1914. This referred to the Swansea Ladies Water Polo Club as one of the earliest, which had started in 1899 and played its first match against a Penarth team, on 17 July 1899. Swansea lost by three goals to two. Swansea won all its other matches in the early years, including the finals in 1900 against Jersey Ladies, for which they were awarded the Ravensbourne Shield. The shield was a gift of Sir George Pragnell to encourage the women's competition. Swansea suffered the second loss of its career only in 1907 against Leicester Ladies. Further detail is not available because women's water polo attracted little attention from the press during these years.

In the Ladies Section of the *Swimming Magazine* in 1915, the *Lady Dorothy* column stated:

> *'Water polo as regards ladies has received no support from official sources. The governing bodies in the swimming world have let it go its own way, and the clubs promote and control the game quite alone. It is true that some male players take a very practical interest in polo for ladies, and individually they help and encourage our play, but collectively they do not recognise us yet. Naturally, polo for ladies is in its infancy, and we must expect to go slowly'.*

Hammersmith Ladies' Swimming Club.

Annual Entertainment

THURSDAY, JULY 18th, 1929, at 7.30 p.m.

AT

LIME GROVE BATHS

SHEPHERD'S BUSH.

ATTRACTIVE PROGRAMME:

S.C.A.S.A. 200 Yards Ladies' Breaststroke Championship.

S.C.A.S.A. Ladies' Graceful Diving Championship.

WATER POLO MATCH

Welsh Ladies v. Hammersmith Ladies

DIVING DISPLAY by OLYMPIC DIVERS

SWIMMING RACES, Etc., Etc.

PRICES OF ADMISSION:

Reserved Seats 3/6, 2/4.   Unreserved 1/6

Tickets may be obtained from the Baths.

CROYDON LADIES' SWIMMING CLUB.

(Affiliated to the S.C.A.S.A., R.L.S.S., A.D.A. and C.B.S.A.)

The 35th Annual

AQUATIC GALA

(UNDER A.S.A. LAWS)

will take place at

THE CROYDON BATHS

on

WEDNESDAY, 24th JULY, 1929,

at 7 p.m.

Ladies' Diving Championship of the County of Surrey. Grand Diving Display by Members of the A.D.A. Invitation Two Lengths Handicaps for Ladies and Boys.

Team Races and Club Events.

Water Polo Match (London League)

Croydon S.C. v. Avondale S.C.

The Prizes will be presented by MRS. RIESCO, President of the Club.

TICKETS: Reserved 2/4; Unreserved 1/2 (including tax); School children (under 14) 6d.

Tickets can be obtained from the Assistant Hon. Secretaries (Mrs. Goodliffe, 68, Selwood Road, Croydon, and Mrs. Rose, 18, Morton Gardens, Wallington), any Member of the Committee, or at the Baths.

(Miss) ETHEL ROGERS,
Hon. Secretary.

Croydon Ladies' SC was an active fundraiser and had a water polo team. Prices for entry were high even allowing for tax and a levy to pay for entertaining guests of the club. Examples of water polo, contributing to events organised by Ladies' clubs in the London area, included galas arranged in 1929. The admission charges possibly reflected the drawing power of the ladies' water polo match as much as nearness to central London.

Incidents during the Universities Athletics Union competition for water polo between men's and women's teams representing Loughborough and Sheffield in February 1993. Loughborough's teams became overall winners of the competition. (Copyright: Loughborough Students Athlectics Union)

The columnist suggested that those swimming clubs listed in handbooks and catalogues, and having ladies water polo teams, should agree to indicate their existence in order to assist in creating fixtures and so promote the sport. Lady Dorothy commented on a view, attributed to trainers, that playing water polo destroyed the speed of racers. No evidence had been produced to support the point and Lady Dorothy asserted that players benefited by increasing their stamina and strength.

The Amateur Swimmer of June 1926 described ladies' water polo in terms which showed that the game had an enthusiastic following. Such comments in an ASA publication indicated that this minority activity was regarded as newsworthy and demonstrated that women had sufficient stamina for playing so demanding a sport. In 1928 Violet Cranston reviewed the state of ladies' water polo for the *Swimming Times*. She began: *'No branch of swimming has made greater or more surprising progress during recent years than ladies' water polo'*. However, she had found it necessary to assert:

'This is a far cry from the days (not so very long ago) when ladies' polo matches were regarded as comic relief, and when the players themselves were looked upon more in sorrow than in anger by their superior men-folk'.

Cranston related that the London Water Polo League had introduced a competition for affiliated ladies' clubs. Drawn from its membership, a London ladies' team had defeated a visiting Dutch ladies' side and had helped to raise greater interest in the sport. The popularity of the sport was such that it had already reached the level amongst women whereby the competition for the *Grose Cup* (George Grose and Company were a London-based sports outfitters) had already run for several years. A junior level competition was begun at the time of writing the article. The writer emphasised that the paucity of facilities for both practices and matches had held back the development of the sport for ladies. She hinted that some of the difficulties were the result of bath superintendents' placing obstacles in their way. She mentioned in passing that coaching and refereeing were provided by sympathetic men.

Even with enthusiastic supporters, women's water polo never attracted the same attention as the men's game from the press and it was ignored in the Martin Report. Many of the articles which appeared in the *Swimming Times* were about the game for boys and men with few explicit references to the women's game before 1975. Then David Reeves noted the development of water polo for women in the United States and some of the reasons for this. It was only in 1986 that the first international games played under FINA rules took place. British competitors showed considerable promise. Their coach, Duncan Faulkner, suggested how further improvements might by made. He concluded:

'One note on "man-up". It is probably weak at present as most club teams do not have either enough players or enough competent players to practice the situation properly. I think, therefore, they will have to practice against junior boys more'.

Water polo clubs for women amongst the British universities have had the dual effect of promoting the game amongst students and of improving the standards of play. In 1992 there were 60 women's clubs registered with the ASA with 260 players. They received a grant of £12000 from the ASA to assist them with the game. By the 1990s the women's game was recognised as demonstrating a high standard of commitment and performance. Indeed, in international matches the women's teams have been placed in a higher rank than those of the men.

Water Polo between the World Wars

The ASA undertook minor revisions of the rules of water polo in 1920 to ensure uniformity with international commitments, although the guidance for referees remained those made in 1911. The issue of rough play appears to have been a focus of concern for giving guidance for referees and for the swimming and general sporting press.

The question of roughness was a commonly reported issue in the *Swimming Times* between the two World Wars. From the beginning of the codification in the later nineteenth century, the rules were designed to cope with rough play. Winning at any cost or being revenged against a supposed or real grievance against an opponent were contrary to the code of true amateurism. Players did not always find it easy to reach these standards. By 1903, included within Rule 10 was the assertion: '*In baths no grease, oil, or other objectionable substance shall be rubbed on the body*'. More significant and ominous were the two rules, nos. 14 and 15 '*Ordinary Fouls*' and '*Wilful Fouls*' which were followed by rules relating to '*Free Throws*' (16), '*Penalty Throw*' (17) and '*Declaring Fouls*' (18). Referees had *Guidelines* for interpreting these rules which occupied more than a page of the *Handbook*. On rule no. 17, for example, guideline 'I' stated, optimistically, referees had great powers '*to stamp out at once the rough methods of tackling that are now practised*'.

During its short life '*as the official organ of the ASA*' The *Amateur Swimmer* carried articles about water polo. Some expressed displeasure at unsporting behaviour. One such appeared in October 1926 and it gave a graphic account of a game at Burslem baths where a fight broke out between the teams and enthusiastic spectators joined in the mêlée. The affair caused the baths to be closed.

In 1928 *Water Rat* wrote in the *Swimming Times* on the problem of roughness, claiming that it arose from '*players being physically unfit*', '*playing the man instead of the ball*', and '*cheating the referee*'. He asserted the cure for such evil was punishment and a member of the Welsh ASA wrote supporting this view:

'A few of our first grade referees got together, discussed this subject, and decided that as the players were making it difficult for the referees to keep the game spectacular, they, the referees, would make it difficult for the players to have a game. In other words they whistled and had men out of the water on every possible occasion, and one or two matches actually finished with fewer than five men in the water. This drastic measure had the desired effect, and I pass it on as a possible cure'.

In 1929 the problem of rowdyism and its cure was laid at the door of the incompetent referees by a contributor, P.H. Hardidge. The MCASA had proposed to Council the formation of a national water polo referees association with membership restricted to those who had qualified by examination. This idea had been rejected in 1926 on the grounds that it was in advance of its time by four years. Three years had elapsed and the problem of rowdyism remained. Hardidge noted that the proximity of spectators to the players probably contributed to the situation. Later in the same year, T.J. Kimber contributed a strongly supportive article on the need to have well-qualified referees. In the next few years the debate continued with examples of malpractices such as *'dragging on parts of costumes of a player so as to impede the progress of a move'*.

The *Swimming Times* carried a full report of a debate at the SCASA Council meeting held in December 1929 where a motion condemned the refereeing of an international match between England and Germany held earlier in the year. The conduct of some players, it was argued, suggested that wrestling was a more

important skill than being able to play the game. The conditions of a shallow and narrow bath added to the problems of the Germans who suffered from playing the man rather than the ball.

During the 1930s, attention to water polo seemed to arise as much from complaints about the continued roughness in the men's game as for their achievements in international contests. In 1934 P.H. Hardidge surveyed opinions from some players and administrators, and again concluded in his *Swimming Times* article that the major lack of discipline originated with the referees. Even so, the attitudes of players contributed to the atmosphere of violence and *'dirty'* behaviour. One officer responded to such an atmosphere by resigning from the Honorary Secretaryship of the Liverpool and District Water Polo Association saying: *'I have no desire to be associated with the so-called sport of water polo'*.

Water polo rules were capable of various interpretations as shown in a series of cartoons accompanying articles by E.J. Scott during the early 1950s in the Swim

A referee also resigned having attracted much adverse comment for not controlling a game. He particularly resented the taunt: '*A man is known by the company he keeps*'. Yet another referee wrote that the answer lay in better training for referees combined with a will to enforce the rules consistently.

In the years leading to the Second World War the *Swimming Times* continued to record complaints about the standard of refereeing, the calibre of referees, the absence of a water polo manual and concern about rough play. The British team did badly in the 1929 European Water Polo Tournament, so badly that no British side entered the Tournament of 1935. The level of the game improved somewhat and the British team acquitted itself competently at the Olympic Games of 1936, although it did not win any medals. It is impossible to know whether there would have been further improvement because the outbreak of war in 1939 truncated the regular activities of the game.

From 1945 onwards

During second half of the twentieth century and in contrast to the achievements of women's teams the international standing of water polo for British men's team declined. After the 1956 Olympics no British men's team reached the qualifying standard to enter Olympic competitions. Considerable effort has been spent in trying to analyse and explain how this disappointing state had occurred.

The development of water polo needs to be set in the context of what was possible and how far steps were taken to remedy

perceived shortcomings. The ASA sought to promote the sport at all levels by encouraging relevant qualifications and competitions. Repeatedly, reports to Council drew attention to the problems of facilities and of training and coaching. In each of these cases a vital component was lacking: money. In some respects this is a common theme for all swimming activities. However, critics of the game suggested that its image of roughness and the complexity of its rules and their enforcement combined to limit the interest of the general public. Such public indifference was not lost on politicians. It had the effect of making the case for finance to provide facilities more difficult.

Chapter five drew attention to the lack of investment in swimming pools between 1945 and 1960 when very few new pools were built. During the 1970s and after, the emphasis on investment in leisure pools by local authorities and more recently private companies, did not produce baths with the appropriate depths. Nor, equally importantly, were there sufficient facilities to allow for water polo practice as well as for matches themselves. When local authorities made their plans for annual budgets, even during the so-called free spending 1960s, there was no priority

given for meeting the capital costs of high standard pools to meet the needs of water polo. Likewise private sector investors in Britain saw no returns likely to justify expenditures on such pools. Often where new facilities came into being the purse had to be the state's. One good example of this was the splendid pool at RAF Cosford where excellent facilities were provided for cadets. Despite these signs of progress it was still possible for David Reeves to say in 1990:

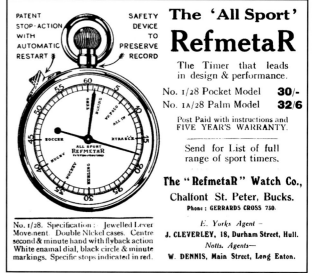

Time keeping was an essential part of water polo. Allowances had to be made for time lost from play because of fouls or other interventions. These advertisements for stop watches before the electronic age show the expense of precision engineering required in their manufacture. The prices from RefmetaR of 1930 and Smiths of 1956 illustrated the effects of both inflation and taxation. In 1959 Charles Frank sold naval surplus at a bargain price. By 1959 the Grose company had a long history of meeting water polo needs.

'With the almost non-existence of International-sized pitches and with limited finance available for competition and team training, it is not surprising that the quality of the play in Britain lags behind European and World standards'.

The story of the establishment of water polo teams is, by contrast, a success story. In the years immediately after the end of the Second World War the sport needed time to rebuild teams. Undoubtedly the Olympic Games of 1948 provided the spur for reconstruction. The Henleaze SC at Bristol offered its facilities to the ASA for preparations leading to the Olympics for both diving and water polo. Each District was invited to send a team to play in a tournament, at that time the most ambitious ever held in England. From these matches the ASA chose the members of the squad for more intensive training and from their number, together with players from Wales and Scotland, the British team was selected.

In 1949 the ASA instituted the Junior Inter-District Water Polo Championship. The intentions of this competition were to encourage the game in all Districts and in the longer term to benefit the senior game with the potential for finding outstanding players worthy of being trained for membership of international teams. By the late 1980s, 400 British clubs ran teams for men and concurrently there were 60 women's club teams.

Water polo remained a focus of debate. In 1960 Council was criticised for its policy regarding the game. Having congratulated the ASA for providing £1000 for training purposes Ernest Scott:

> *'.... deplored their decision to revert to the antique practice of allowing matches of importance to be played in shallow water baths, mainly because matches played at Blackpool last year failed to attract big gates'.*

However, the report in the *Handbook* for 1962 applauded improved performances in the international matches in 1961 and warned that new laws promulgated by FINA were to take effect in 1962. Reporting on the County Water Polo Championships in 1961 held at Cosford, David Barr drew attention in the *Swimming Times* to the shortcomings of the structure of the competition. It allowed some teams, whose inadequacies were displayed starkly, to reach quarter and semi-finals:

> *'Little can be said of the second semi-final, in which Gloucestershire were the victors over Cornwall by 18 goals to 0, other than that Cornwall were completely outclassed in the matters of fitness, of swimming, of ball-handling, of tactics, of team-play, and in appreciation of modern water polo concepts. What else is left?'*

Such a set of strictures highlighted the problems faced by water polo in some parts of England where there existed weaknesses in the facilities and the coaching system. Ironically, RAF Cosford was described by David Barr in 1961 as the *Loughborough of Water Polo*. He stressed the importance of recognising the twin problems and how RAF Cosford pointed the way forward.

The impact of changes in the FINA rules in relation to training, coaching and refereeing was a particular focus of concern. Squadron Leader Gerry Worsell, formerly national coach for the Great Britain teams at both European and Olympic Games, responded in 1967 to a plea to isolate Britain from the FINA

Rules issued in 1966, by saying *'Please don't stop the water polo clock'*.

He asserted that the FINA rules should be applied in Britain, that the health of the game depended on fostering it in schools, and that referees, trained by the ASA, should follow interpretations of rules consistently. He concluded:

> *'Then there will be no need to hark back to those mythical good old days. If two teams of 16 stoners (93 kg) punching it out in 20 by 8 yards (19 by 7 metres) of shallow water provided the character the game now lacks, we are best off without it'.*

Developing good coaches remained the ASA's continuing ambition. In 1975, this was advanced by the creation of the ISTC with water polo as one of its responsibilities. Improvement of coaching by itself could not compensate fully for the lack of training and practice facilities for high performance players. Not least among the requirements for water polo referees was total familiarity with the latest rule changes and their likely interpretation. The efforts to recruit and train women's coaches at the top levels failed. Men still undertook this task.

The health of water polo stimulated commentaries from time to time in the *Swimming Times*. It was reported that suggestions that the game was in the doldrums had been made at the ASA Council of 1963. In reporting on the first ever Universities water polo tournament in 1963 involving teams from Cambridge, London, Oxford, Wales, the Scottish universities and the Universities Athletic Union (which resulted in a win for Oxford), David Barr revealed his mixed feelings about the game:

> *'But if the general standard of team-play is low the potential in this sphere of water polo is high'.*

He accounted for the situation by identifying poor facilities, lack of top-class coaching, and competing demands on student time. Others were thinking along the same lines. There was a report of a conference held in March of 1963 where a paper outlined a series of ideas which were very similar to those which were later to be more thoroughly addressed in the Martin Report. David Barr continued to comment on the game. In a subsequent article, in 1963, he argued that the presentation of water polo games to the spectators left much to be desired ranging from the need to start on time, to having clear commentaries on the nature of fouls and the penalties enforced. By 1967 the *Swimming Times* was reporting that the dreary performances of the British men's water polo teams, and the difficulties confronting the game, had provoked suggestions to the ASA from Gerry Worsell and Hamilton Bland about what ought to be done. A lively correspondence followed these proposals with calls for a national technical officer to have special responsibility for the game.

The Martin Report, 1970

The basic reasons for setting up the Working Party on Water Polo as part of the Martin inquiry arose from the assessment of the situation as it was in 1969 and 1970. From the comments submitted to the Working Party, ten opinions related to the decline of the game were distilled:

1. It was not the same game as it used to be.

2. New concepts, mainly from continental Europe, altered the rules and bewildered those who did not see the need for changes.

3. The game was played at the top levels in large deep pools which had made rigorous swimming training an essential. Players needed to have as prerequisites, speed and stamina far above the standards attained before 1939.

4. Britain had too few pools of the sizes and depths, indoor or outdoor, for international standard matches. Spectators were not well served in the new environments.

5. Resistance to changes of rules had consequences for the way the game was played and so did not prepare British teams for international competitions.

6. British influence in water polo had waned.

7. The longer duration of the modern game cost money for bath hire and some clubs no longer allocated time for the game, sometimes because they could not afford to do so.

8. Water polo was once the life-blood of clubs which had either given it a lower priority or ceased to play.

9. The emphasis on swimming, especially for the young, had reduced the scope for many seniors who had dropped from club membership. At one time these people had kept water polo thriving.

10. Spectator interest in water polo had dwindled in contrast to swimming.

On the positive side evidence was acquired that 400 clubs continued to play the game.

The team from Cheltenham Swimming and Water Polo Club was the National Water Polo Champion in 1955. Standing (L to R) A. Auchterlonie, P. Jones, W.T. Tiver, P. McGonagle, D. Moss, and seated (L to R) D. Taylor, J.S. Jones (captain) and K. Phillips.

This was the starting point for the Working Party's investigation. The ASA could neither provide the finance to provide the necessary basic facilities for the game nor could it do more than keep the needs of water polo on its agenda. Lobbying pool providers and funding agencies for assistance with training, would improve the opportunities for the game to flourish. Clearly the ASA was already aware of most of these issues. As the Martin Report was being prepared the Association took an initiative to popularise and extend water polo playing so as to attract the young. Thus, in 1969 the ASA launched a Water Polo Proficiency award scheme which had three grades: bronze, silver and gold. These covered the basic techniques: swimming with the ball, catching, throwing, passing, treading water, turning and shooting at goal. The equipment required depended on the grade. The gold grade needed the use of a 21 metre pool whereas 16 metres were sufficient for the other grades. A structure the correct size of the goal was necessary but nets were not.

In 1970 Norman Sarsfield, the newly installed ASA secretary, devoted the first half of his first contribution in the *Swimming Times* to water polo. He indicated a strategy to obtain international success and thus to promote the game. He stressed the vital importance of

(1) playing together as a team,

(2) being physically fit and trained,

(3) possessing individually brilliant players.

He pointed out that as a relatively small country with good transport facilities it ought to be possible, given commitment, to attain a prominent place amongst the leading international teams. These comments encapsulated his attitude which he expressed to the Water Polo Working Party.

The recommendations of the Martin Report were made on the basis of the advice of a Working Party comprising Kenneth Martin as convenor, Jack S. Jones, Peter Churchley, Ronald Turner, David Barr, Hamilton Bland, and Graham Sykes and, from time to time, contributions from other prominent people in the water polo game. Women's water polo received no mention. Thus, the final proposals applied to the game for men although there were implications for women players who relied on male coaches and referees.

The recommendations of the working party indicate some of the deficiencies of the game in Great Britain and not just England. Amongst the proposals were that FINA rules had to remain the framework of the game so as to maintain international status, although it was recognised that the ASA might allow deviations to meet local needs. The organisation of the international programme for home teams should be on a 4 year cycle, making space for the European Games and the Olympic Games. Such a schedule might enable leading players to gain sufficient experience in overseas matches to benefit the national teams in competitions. Moreover, although the ASA did not organise the Premier League, the proposed programme of events should accommodate its matches.

Simultaneously, the English championships should adopt the LEN criteria for age registrations. Accompanying this, other competitions, including inter-District for younger players, ought to take account of the LEN age categories. The structure of competitions within the country should be reformed. Regional competitions should replace those based on counties. Regions should also replace divisions in the organisation of the Club Championships with the purpose of making it easier to identify players of national calibre. The junior championships should remain on a District basis.

The sections of the Martin report on water polo recognised that, although the ASA had agreed to revise many of its general polices in 1970, the sport had its own special requirements. For example the importance of international competition made it desirable to include within the membership of the Water Polo Committee, representatives from Scotland and Wales. This committee, to be effective, needed sub committees to advise on programme-planning, coaching, awards and examinations, selection, development of the game and refereeing, so that all facets of the game should be considered appropriately. In its conclusion the report said:

> *'It is strongly recommended that the personnel of these sub-committees should include as many knowledgeable persons actively interested in the game as possible, rather than their being composed of members of the Water Polo Committee'.*

The Martin Report urged a more effective use of resources by improved financial planning, the appointment of a full-time co-ordinator or National Technical Officer, and, in due course, a full-time national coach. Amendment of the First Claim Rule should take account of where players lived and worked.

In the analysis of the game the Working Party identified what it considered necessary to produce teams of world class standard. It proposed choosing a national squad with opportunities to train at a centre such as Crystal Palace. It acknowledged the problems of team members who did not have the ideal residential and financial circumstances. Part of the solution would be to have three training pools with squads at Senior, under 20 and under 18. To give effect to these proposals the ASA needed a scout system to find potential players.

Improving the game at all levels called for better training courses and awards, especially for club coaches, organised within summer schools such as at Loughborough, Jordan Hill and Crystal Palace. Other moves open to the ASA included seeking closer liaison with the armed services and student sports organisations in higher education. The Facilities Committee of the Association should press the needs of water polo in their negotiations. Swimming clubs should be encouraged to be more positive about water polo and devote more time to it.

The longer term viability of the game rested on attracting young players. To achieve this the recommendations included: Age Group water polo, the involvement of ESSA to promote the game in schools, and the development of water ball games leading to water polo. Water polo proficiency awards needed greater publicity. Given the problems faced by schools and clubs, the ASA might modify the rules to allow it to be played where facilities were inadequate and ignorance of water polo widespread. A defined pattern of progression should keep promising young players in the sport.

The Great Britain versus Spain Under Twenties match at Zaragoza in July 1971.

The British teams in 1980.

Undoubtedly water polo depended upon having an adequate financial basis. The ASA Honorary Treasurer reported to the Working Party his forecast that for the next few years the annual budget for water polo would be £6,500, a sum too small to meet the cost of most of the key proposals. To pay for reform required an increase of revenue for the game. Suggestions included seeking grants for training the national team, raising entry fees for competitions, obtaining sponsorship or television coverage for important matches. The sting came in the final observation:

'It has been said that "a radical question needs a radical solution". Without some radical thought being given to the whole question of the financing of the game, we shall not materially alter the present situation'.

Post Martin

The flow of debate about the condition of the game continued in the *Swimming Times* after the Martin Report. There are many examples: in February 1974, 'Is Water Polo Dying?', in April 1974, 'Water Polo Rules and Using Them', in February 1976, 'British Coaches can bring about a water polo revival'. These discussions continued to rehearse the opinions about why there had been a decline in interest and the diminished standing of British water polo internationally.

The first professional coach for the Men's Great Britain Water Polo team was appointed in 1981. The programme for training set out by the team manager showed that the training sessions were divided between Britain and overseas. Such arrangements were met with caution by one contributor, Richard Tate:

'We do not expect miracles, nor are we going to get them. We need a lot of help from all sections of the sport from very junior club level right up to the international player and whilst at the moment we can only hope to qualify for the Olympics, perhaps in two years time we can confidently say we are going to qualify for the Olympics'.

In 1984, writing in the ISTC section of the *Swimming Times* on the theme of 'Introducing Water Polo' J.M. Glover argued that one of the ways of increasing interest in the game was to make it accessible to children. He asserted that they take to it very easily and indicated how to teach the game to young beginners. He did this in the context of stating some problems of policy and attitudes which placed obstacles in the way of the game:

'The great pity is that over the years the restrictions imposed on its introduction by narrow minded local authorities and swimming teachers have retarded its growth.

The main reasons for this would appear to be:

(a) worry about damage to fittings and personnel, and

(b) fears that Polo ruins ones competitive swimming strokes'.

Ten years later, in 1994 Col. Andrew Morton, a member of the ASA Water Polo Committee for some years, was echoing the need to increase the game's appeal amongst school children. By that point only slow progress had been made in developing a simplified game for children although the Martin Report had identified the need twenty years before.

Rule changes

The game of water polo has been characterised by major changes in its rules since 1945. Some were dramatic: from a rule which forbade any movement by players once the whistle blew until the ball was put back into play, to a rule which allowed movement. Looking back in 1990, particularly on the rule changes authorised since 1950 by FINA, David Reeves said that such changes: *'have made it [water polo] unrecognisable from the earlier activity'.* He was commenting from detailed knowledge, having served the ASA as secretary of the Water Polo Coaches Committee for some years, and from playing experience. He listed the major innovations during the forty years from 1948 to 1988:

'.... the abolition of the 'no man moving' rule; control of the game by two referees; extension of the game to four periods of seven minutes of actual playing time; maximum ball possession time of 35 seconds without a shot at goal; and teams having access to six substitute players'.

He also commented that:

'With two referees, a constant changing of players, and tactics mainly based on scoring goals when one team has a player out of the water for fouling, the game had lost a great deal of spectator appeal'.

He added the interesting point that, whilst this appeared to be true for Britain, in the higher performing nations better informed crowds appreciated skill and good exhibitions of tactics.

All those closely involved in the game recognised the importance of rule changes. Col. Morton, looking back from 1994, observed that rule changes had had two important effects: they cleaned up the game in front of the goal and made the game a much more mobile one. The criticism of roughness which had validity in the more distant past but should be modified as a consequence of several developments in the rules during the 1950s and after. The changes in rules, including those agreed by FINA in Rome in 1978, provided a context whereby good refereeing had curbed the brutality of some players. Those players who had indifferent swimming ability but who used their strength to achieve advantages by playing the man, lost their prominence as technical skill in the game improved and took precedence. Such skill called for better swimming ability and a higher standard of physical fitness than had been the case for many players in earlier years. Moreover, something as practical as the provision of costumes in the newer man-made fibres, which could not be grabbed to constrain opposing swimmers, reduce the scope for cheating.

Overall, the potential of water polo as a spectator sport had not been realised by the 1990s for various reasons. There was little media coverage and sometimes hostile publicity. Col. Morton referred to the status of water polo as a minor sport whose value as a spectacle had been ignored by television. In addition even in some of the more modern arenas, the accommodation for pool side spectators was often indifferent. To add to problems, he suggested that the complexity of the rules, often inadequately explained, reduced the attractions of water polo as an exciting game.

Into the 1990s

That these problems did not result in the total demise of the game in England can be attributed to the success of the National Water Polo League, successor to the Premier League. It consisted of four divisions affiliated and closely allied to, the ASA, particularly in relation to calendar planning. Both playing and refereeing standards have improved and, contrary to the findings of the Martin report, players appeared to accept the increased cost of travel. The first men's water polo team from Britain for many years to earn a medal on the world stage did so at the World Masters Swimming Championships at Indianapolis in the United States in July 1992.

In the *ASA Development Plan, 1993/6* water polo was said to have suffered since 1960 from: (a) a gradual reduction in the number of clubs playing at regular league level, (b) the high costs of pool hire with only a small number of players able to use the pool at any one time compared with the normal swimming training sessions, and (c) a shortage of international standard facilities in Britain. Remedies recommended were to attract more players, teams and clubs to water polo. Apart from the desirability of investment in international standard facilities, the ASA hoped to gain more publicity for the game, raise finance to pay for some features including access to pools at appropriate times, and to develop a modified version of water polo for inclusion in the school physical education curriculum.

The issues identified in the ASA Development Plan are not dissimilar from those which have been recognised throughout the development of water polo as a competitive team game. As a sport water polo experienced many changes of fortune since its emergence as a recognisable team game in Great Britain during the late nineteenth century. In the first two decades of the twentieth century Britain dominated the international scene. At the same time the club game flourished, attracting both male and female players. After the First World War, British overseas performances were eclipsed by other European teams and, along with all British swimmers, water polo teams suffered a loss of prestige. After the Second World War water polo remained one of the minor sports in Britain. Its enthusiasts, both male and female, enjoyed their game but the support for it declined. Only women's water polo teams reached a high international status. In reviewing all aspects of the sport, the Martin Committee's Working Party on Water Polo had a great many comments and recommendations to make. Although the performance of British teams internationally was somewhat lack-lustre, it has to be recognised that this was not entirely the fault of the players and their coaches. There were also problems of administration. However, all these were in many ways related to the continuous and underlying problem of resources, in particular finance for facilities. As a consequence, even though during the period under discussion the ASA changed the rules relating to the sport in many radical ways, water polo did flourish as much as some other swimming activities.

The goalkeeper's perspective of a match in progress.

Chapter 10 :

Long Distance Swimming

Comment from Introduction to G. Forsberg's book of 1963.

'When Morecambe Bay was first crossed by Stearn in 1907, a positively gargantuan amount of food and drink was taken across with him in the pilot boat. Today, the average Bay contestant never thinks about refreshment. Even the Channel has been crossed on less than a couple of bottles of glucose and a few oatmeal biscuits. The pounds of thick grease once thought absolutely necessary, have dwindled down to a matter of ounces.

Introduction

Long Distance Swimming has been an admired but a minority sport throughout the history of organised swimming in Great Britain. It originally had a strongly professional flavour of money prizes and side-betting. However, the birth of the Serpentine SC in 1864, the founding in 1869 of the organisation which eventually became the ASA, and the enormous upsurge of support for all sorts of amateur sporting codes, came together in the late Victorian era to cause the decline and virtual disappearance of professionalism. Interestingly, a central body to organise long distance swimming did not emerge until the twentieth century.

No precise definition was ever formulated as to what constituted the minimum distance for which the title *Long Distance* was appropriate. Both the half mile and the mile championships at national, District and local levels were recognised as major feats and competitions for these distances were sponsored by the ASA throughout its history. With one exception, the greater distances were promoted by local clubs of like minded enthusiasts and they attracted swimmers of national stature. The exception was the ASA's Long Distance Championship for men which had begun in 1877, with a counterpart for women introduced in 1920. Both had a discontinuous history. Otherwise, the ASA, as did LEN and FINA, left events of more than a mile or 1500 metres out of their legislative and regulatory interest. Nonetheless an account of Long Distance swimming is relevant here because of the ASAs involvement in the Long Distance Championship and because after 1956 Long Distance Swimming became the direct concern of the Association.

The early years

Long distance swimming attracted strong public interest in Great Britain during the nineteenth century. Early in the century a few people had chosen to swim across estuaries or bays or along rivers. Retrospectively, Lord Byron acquired much fame for his swim in 1810 across the Hellespont in imitation of the classical exploits of Leander who swam from Sestos to Abydos. Awareness of such athletic achievements depended upon publicity and this is what cheap mass circulation newspapers provided during the second half of the nineteenth century. These events attracted spectators, including some gambers who betted on whether an endeavour was feasible, or, in a competition, which performer had the better form.

In the later years of the nineteenth century various long distance swims took place at different venues. In 1877 an annual competition began. It was this competition which was organised by SAGB and subsequently by the ASA. For the years 1877 to 1879 it had the name *Lords and Commons* because keen swimmers amongst members of both the Houses of Parliament had subscribed for the first cup to be presented to the winner. The regulations of the contest stipulated that the course should be between five and six miles long in fresh running water or in a tidal river. The organisers chose the River Thames because it satisfied the criteria. The first two races were from Putney to Westminster and the third in the reverse direction. From 1880 until 1889 the course was from Putney to Charing Cross Railway Bridge. In 1890 it was changed so as to run from Kew Railway Bridge to Putney Pier (the reverse direction to the Oxford and Cambridge Boat Race). In 1914 the race was scheduled to start at the Anglian Boat House at Kew and end at Putney Pier, a distance of 5 miles and 60 yards (approximately). The swim took place on the ebb stream which substantially reduced the effective length of the distance. This course was used each year until the outbreak of the Second World War. No competition was possible in the war years and in 1946 the Districts were invited to comment on the future of the Long Distance Championship. Only the South supported its continuance. Thus, the only competition immediately after the war was organised by the SCASA in 1947 and a triangular course in the Serpentine in Hyde Park was used. Pollution of the River Thames had forced the change of venue. The Serpentine proved unsatisfactory because swimmers from the public Lido entered the marked course during the race. Pollution had been a problem several times; as early as 1929 the start of the Ladies' Long Distance Championship was delayed for one hour on the advice of the Port of London Authority *'to allow the worst of the debris, dirt, etc. to be carried down stream'*. The course for women was the same as for men and Clarence Hatry donated a perpetual challenge trophy. From 1921 the rules stated that women had to be at least 16 years of age by the date of the race. It was held annually until 1939, and once in 1947. Both the men's and women's championships lapsed after 1947 and were not revived until 1963.

The start of the ASA's Long Distance Swimming Championship at Kew in 1911.

Any account of long distance events during the nineteenth century should also include the competitions and feats, arranged from time to time, along rivers and across estuaries. These drew large numbers of spectators and received wide coverage in the press. Matthew Webb, for example, swam across the Thames estuary and some of the leading swimmers of the time, both professional and amateur, took part in unusual swimming exploits. Horace Davenport, a great contributor to the work of the ASA, later serving as its President, swam from Southsea Pier to Ryde Pier on the Isle of Wight in 1884. The first recorded crossing of this difficult course had been made a year earlier by George White of the Portsmouth SC. Achievements of intrepid athletes between the two world wars included the Guernsey to Sark swim, a geographical distance of 9 miles, by John Heyward in 1927. Strong currents and tides extended the distance to about 11 miles which he covered in 4 hours 55 minutes. He accomplished the feat solo and used the trudgen stroke. In the same year, Kathleen Thomas of Penarth became the first person to swim across the Bristol Channel.

In many respects one of the greatest long distance swimming contests during the years between the world wars was the chal-lenge issued annually by the Morecambe Cross Bay Swimming Association. This organisation was affiliated to the NCASA and was established to administer the race across the bay from Grange to Morecambe. It usually succeeded in attracting most of the major amateur swimmers. Its celebration of the twenty-fifth anniversary involved six separate contests in the summer months of 1932 and all, except the event devoted to team relay race, were open to individual competitors.The actual course seems to have varied in length. In 1932 it was advertised as being of 14 miles from Grange to Morecambe. In 1947 the course was between 10 and 12 miles. In 1958 Gerald Forsberg wrote of the fifty-first year of the swim that it '*is geographically 10 miles in length but is reduced by a favourable tide to five*'. He reported that the *Manchester Guardian* devoted half a page to the contest '*the best national-newspaper coverage I have seen of the event*'. In that year the men's race was won in 2 hours 32 minutes by A.E. Ayres (Coventry SC) and the women's by A. Johnson (Grange SC) in 2 hours 52 minutes. Comparisons of times in open sea races present formidable problems because of the need to take into account the variable winds, tides and temperatures.

There were 15 entrants at the River Thames start of the Ladies' Long Distance Championship of England in 1930. The winner was Miss M.J. Cooper (extreme left) of Mermaid SC in 72 minutes 57 seconds.

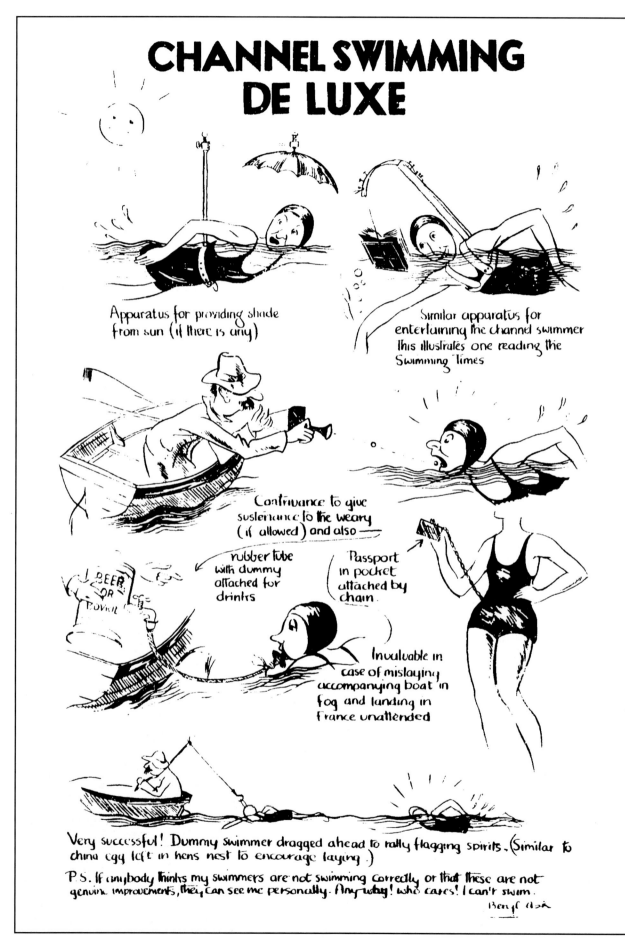

Although the Channel Swims were organised separately from other Long Distance competitions, the techniques of sustaining competitors attracted a cartoonist in 1936.

Preparations for a Long Distance Swim.

In August 1974 ten girls of Stratford School with their coach, Mrs Olive Bowles, were training at Folkestone for a relay swim of the English Channel to be undertaken by six of the pupils.

Swimming the English Channel

Undoubtedly the most celebrated long distance swim was Captain Matthew Webb's crossing of the English Channel from the Admiralty Pier at Dover to the Sands at Calais. His successful swim took from 12.56 in the afternoon of Tuesday, 25 August, 1875 until 10.41 in the morning of Wednesday, 26 August. Other swimmers had undertaken crossings of the English Channel in the preceding few years but they had used buoyancy aids. Webb used no such aids and his achievement gave him the status of a popular hero. Although many attempts were made by prominent professional and amateur swimmers to emulate Webb, it was not until 1911 that Thomas Burgess succeeded in swimming the Channel. Webb's was the first recorded Channel swim and his time remained unbeaten until 1934 when E.H. Temme crossed in 15 hours 34 minutes.

THE GREATEST SWIM IN BRITAIN

THE SWIMMING EVENT OF THE YEAR

For twenty-nine years Lancashire and Yorkshire swimmers have been conquering MORECAMBE BAY, until 1935, when the winner hailed from the Midlands. All Amateurs should attempt this 12 Miles Swim across Morecambe Bay.

MORECAMBE
CROSS BAY SWIM

Organised by the Morecambe Bay Swimming Association (Affiliated to the N.C.A.S.A.) Under A.S.A. Laws.
OPEN TO ALL AMATEUR SWIMMERS.
1937 is the 30th Year of the Swim.

SWIMS THIS YEAR

Saturday, July 10th.	Time : 1.40 p.m.	Tide : 28ft. 10in.
Saturday, July 24th.	12.50 p.m.	27ft. 0in.
Saturday, Aug. 7th.	12.40 p.m.	28ft. 10in.
Saturday, Aug. 21st.	12.12 p.m.	27ft. 2in.
Saturday, Sept. 4th.	11.43 a.m.	28ft. 3in.

Certificates for all who succeed in crossing.

PRIZES :—Magnificent ASHTON Challenge Shield (value 50 gns.) "KILLI" Challenge CUP and Solid Silver Replica. FIRST PRIZE value £10-10-0, SECOND value £8-8-0, THIRD value £4-4-0, FOURTH value £2-2-0.

LADIES' CHAMPIONSHIP (Fastest Time). "CHRISTIE" Challenge CUP (value 35 gns.), and FIRST PRIZE value £5-5-0, SECOND value £3-3-0, THIRD value £2-2-0.

ACCEPT THE CHALLENGE NOW.—Write for all particulars and Entry Form. **Make a Holiday in Morecambe and swim "BRITAIN'S BONNIEST BAY."**

Headquarters : Crown Hotel, Morecambe.

Write to-day to the Hon. Secretary, Cross Bay Swim. R. K. WRIGHT. 88, Ulleswater Road, Lancaster.

MORECAMBE CROSS-BAY CHAMPIONSHIP

(10-12 Miles across Morecambe Bay from Grange-over-Sands to Morecambe)
Organised by the Morecambe Cross-Bay Swimming Association
Affiliated to the N.C.A.S.A) Under A.S.A. Rules.

OPEN TO ALL AMATEUR SWIMMERS

SWIMS FOR 1947

Will take place on the following
SATURDAYS

JUNE 21 —Dive in at Grange	3.0 p.m. Tide—28 ft. 7 ins.
JULY 19— " "	2.0 p.m. Tide—29 ft. 0 ins.
AUG. 2— " "	1.41 p.m. Tide—25 ft. 7 ins.
" 16— " "	Noon Tide - 28 ft. 6 ins.
" 30— " "	11.45 a.m. Tide - 25 ft. 6 ins.
SEPT. 13— " "	11.3 a.m. Tide 27 ft. 3 ins.

Certificates to all who succeed in crossing

ENTRANCE FEE 10/-   This includes Cost of Pilot

Entry form and prospectus from :
The Hon Secretary, JACK HACKETT, "Visitor," Office, Morecambe   Tel. : 392

PRIZES :

Magnificent Ashton Challenge Shield (Value 200 Gns.)
"Killi" Challenge Cup and Solid Silver Replica (Value 100 Gns).

FIRST PRIZE	Value	£10 10 0
SECOND PRIZE	"	£8 8 0
THIRD PRIZE	"	£4 4 0
FOURTH PRIZE	"	£2 2 0

LADIES' CHAMPIONSHIP

"Christie" Challenge Cup (Value 100 Gns.)
and FIRST PRIZE Value £5 5 0

SECOND PRIZE Value £3 3 0   THIRD PRIZE Value £2 2 0

"BIRTLE" Cup (Value 30 gns.) presented by W. BIRTLE jun., for best first attempt

---

Morecambe Bay Swimming Championship

PRELIMINARY NOTICE

It has been decided to hold this swim during 1946. The distance is approximately eleven miles, from Grange to Morecambe. Further particulars later or enquiries to:

Hon. Secretary : N. L. Nevison, 327, Lancaster Road, Morecambe.

Long Distance events were regularly reported and advertised in the Swimming Times. The Morecambe Cross-Bay Championship attracted much attention before and after the Second World War.

The English Channel swim was never organised by the ASA. Nonetheless the sport of swimming benefited from the publicity surrounding these events. From the crossings made in the 1870s until 1927 the arrangements were informal, being made by the swimmers and their small party of assistants who made the crossing possible: pilot, boatmen and trainer. The person attempting the swim was honour bound to stay in the water without any artificial aid to buoyancy or to motion. Refreshment had to come by hand from the support boat. This expectation of fair play by swimmers, either amateur or professional, remained without a challenger until Dr Dorothy Logan claimed to have swum the Channel. She subsequently revealed that she had spent part of the crossing in a boat. Her purpose was to highlight the possibilities of cheating. As a consequence the Channel Swimming Association was formed in 1927. This association appointed observers to travel in the boat of any swimmer who wanted to register the swim as completed according to the rules.

English Channel swimming received separate official recognition from 1927 onwards through the specialist Channel Swimming Association (CSA). Although in its early years it was almost entirely administered by loyal Kent and Southern ASA officials, it was not considered appropriate for the CSA to be affiliated to the ASA. The stumbling block was that the CSA dealt with professionals as well as amateurs and with all nationalities. It also accepted sponsorship and prizes of kinds which were not acceptable to the ASA at the time. Diplomacy and careful wording enabled the CSA to work alongside the ASA to the extent that the CSA stationery carried the words '*Recognised by the Amateur Swimming Association*'. This continued until the early 1960s when the CSA's secretary removed the wording on discovering that the ASA stationery carried no reciprocal notice.

During the twentieth century comparatively large numbers of swimmers attempted the English Channel challenge. By 1939 about two dozen people had achieved the notable crossing and E. Temme had the distinction of having swum the Channel in each direction. The first woman to complete the crossing was Gertrude Ederle in 1926. Her time was 14 hours 34 minutes, the fastest time ever. The speed of the swims increased, with the passage from France to England proving the faster crossing. After the Second World War and by the early 1980s the pace of the faster swimmers had reduced crossing times to less than nine hours. A few swimmers undertook the crossing each way without stopping, the first being in 1961 when A. Abertondo of the Argentine, did so in 43 hours 10 minutes. By 1987 P. Rush from New Zealand had reduced the time to 16 hours 10 minutes. Three-way crossings were successfully undertaken in the 1980s by J. Erickson (USA) and P. Rush, the latter having the faster time of 28 hours 21 minutes.

The acceleration of times in crossing the Channel and in other long distance events since 1950 not only showed the skill and stamina of the swimmers but that they had benefited from changes which had consequences for speed swimmers in general. They had the advantages of developments in systematic training, appropriate nutrition and advances in navigation. Improvements in crossing times also owed much to the ease of access to detailed knowledge about the relationship of speeds of tides and of movements of currents and to more reliable and sophisticated weather forecasts.

Channel swimming always had prestige. Ovaltine, for example, borrowed some of the glory in 1928.

Matthew Webb's crossing of the English Channel probably involved him in swimming a much longer course than his counterparts a century later. Many of the failures of eminent swimmers to emulate Webb's example in the last years of the nineteenth century probably arose from the exhaustion of having to swim a much greater distance than had been expected. How the improvements in navigation techniques played their part was explained by Gerald Forsberg in 'Navigate the English Channel' in the February, 1961 issue of the *Swimming Times*. He also wrote about 'Weather Aspects of Channel Swimming' in the Meteorological Office's *Marine Observer* of July 1961. Since that time, technological advances have brought into being satellite navigation instruments at comparatively low cost which have made it possible to find the position of a swimmer to within a few metres. Computers have made it possible to predict crossings and for adjustments to be made at 'way points' so that guesswork and the anxieties of the past have all but disappeared.

Personal fitness for long distance swimming owed much to the effect of training and lifestyle. Practice in distance swimming on a regular basis had to be matched with training regimes. During the second half of the twentieth century notable advances were made in understanding the relationships of nutrition, physiology and psychology in athletic success including swimming. The consequences for performers in long distance events can be seen in the contrast between Webb's refreshments of beef tea and brandy in 1875 during his 21.75 hours Channel crossing. Bill Pickering's diet in 1955 when, in 14 hours 6 minutes, he consumed green salads and raw peaches. By 1990 most swimmers drank nutrient enhanced liquids to prevent dehydration and ate carbohydrates to supplement energy stocks.

One of the images of long distance swimming during the later twentieth century has been the hardiness of the participants. Their capacity to swim in cold water stands in marked contrast to the practice of most swimmers of using heated pools whether for learning, for competition or for recreation. In the early twentieth century most Channel swimmers covered their bodies with a thick layer of grease as thermal insulation. The knowledge of medical researchers indicated the nature of protection necessary for long immersion in sea water; towards the end of the twentieth century swimmers were using lighter products such as olive oil. They also used goggles to protect their eyes from pollutants in either fresh or sea water. In 1980 the ASA's Scientific Committee recommended that all long distance competitions should provide medical supervision and facilities to treat hypothermia.

British Long Distance Swimming Association

After many years of local based organisations, the British Long Distance Swimming Association (BLDSA) was set up by enthusiasts in 1956. It reviewed many features, including such matters as general safety aspects, uniformity of starts and finishes, publicity, and ways of encouraging the growth of the sport. Because many of the long distance swimmers of the era were Yorkshire

people, and almost entirely amateur, the BLDSA affiliated immediately to the Yorkshire ASA but soon after left the umbrella of Yorkshire to affiliate directly with the ASA. .

Founder members of BLDSA were John Slater, Fred Oldman, Trevor Smith and Lewis Craven, all with formidable achievements to their credit. They had concluded that their sport needed an organisation capable of improving its position. In 1956 the inaugural meeting elected the distinguished Yorkshire ASA official, Philip Rising, as President. He also had a distinguished record, including crossing the English Channel in 1951 in 15 hours 55 minutes and, in the following year, the first ever swim of the double length of Windermere (20 miles) in 17 hours 38 minutes. His work with other devoted members of the committee gave a firm basis to the sport. The first officers were John Slater, sometime record holder for Windermere, as Secretary and Trevor Smith, the Morecambe Cross Bay Champion of 1948, as Treasurer. In 1957 BLDSA organised the first National Long Distance Championship at Windermere over a 10 mile course, which was recognised as one of the great swimming events of the year. In the following year, 1958, BLDSA organised the first National Long Distance Sea Championship at Torbay, a venture supported by Torquay Corporation.

By 1958 Gerald Forsberg, a member of BLDSA and himself a competitor, reported in the *Swimming Times* on the calendar of events open to amateurs. He grouped them by approximate duration of swim. In category 1, swims of half hour duration, there were a number of events supported by seaside resorts such as the Southsea Pier to Pier, and the Brighton Pier to Pier. In category 2, of slightly longer swims, there were events at Douglas Bay (Isle of Man), Morecambe Inshore, Clyde Firth, and Humber. In category 3, of longer swims, usually won in times between two and three hours, there were events covering the distances from Ryde to Southsea, Morecambe Cross Bay, and Torbay. In category 4, Windermere ten mile race and the English Channel. A year later the twenty one and a half mile Loch Lomond race was added to the calendar.

Although the BLDSA remained operationally independent of the ASA until 1986, it had affiliated, as already noted, soon after its formation. In 1963 the BLDSA persuaded the ASA to reinstate its Long Distance Championship awards and undertook to organise the contests in order to bring the magnificent trophies back into circulation. The first of the revived series for both men and women was swum in the River Ouse at York. Later venues were the River Wear at Durham (1964 and 1965), Trentham Lake, Stoke-on-Trent, Staffordshire (from 1966 to 1981), National Water Sports Centre, Holme Pierrepont, Nottinghamshire (from 1982 to 1989), Rother Valley, Sheffield (1990 and 1991), and Rudyard Lake, Leek, Staffordshire (1992 and 1993). From 1990 the distance was reduced from approximately five miles to five kilometres in order to attract more entries.

In 1986, the BLDSA and ASA decided to work even more closely together so as to benefit long distance swimming. The ASA continued to have responsibility for relationships with LEN and FINA (which inaugurated the first world cup event for long distance swimmers in 1986, and the first European competition under FINA rules in 1989). The ASA also remained the final authority responsible for National and District Championships.

BRITISH LONG DISTANCE SWIMMING ASSOCIATION

EIGHTH ANNUAL TORBAY
CHAMPIONSHIPS

(Held under A.S.A. Rules, by permit of the Devon County A.S.A. and Yorkshire A.S.A., and by permission of the Torquay Corporation and Brixham U.D.C.)

COURSE: From TORQUAY to BRIXHAM and back to TORQUAY
(approximately 8 miles)

MEN'S CHAMPIONSHIP	WOMEN'S CHAMPIONSHIP
(1964 Champion:	(1964 Champion:
Norman Trusty, Kent)	Elaine Gray, St. Albans)

SATURDAY, July 3rd, 1965

Start at 11.00 a.m., Beacon Cove, Torquay.

Sponsored by TORQUAY CORPORATION—who have kindly donated perpetual Challenge Trophies and Plaques for competition in both Championships.

Entry Forms, Championship Rules and further details from :—
Hon. Torbay Championship Secretary,
F. C. Oldman, Esq.,
163 Handley Road, New Whittington, Derbyshire.

(FINAL Closing Date for Entries: May 24th, 1965)

The BLDSA regularly promoted Long Distance events such as its prestigious Torbay Championship.

BLDSA representation on the ASA Committee made it possible for the Association to draw upon its experience and knowledge of the practicalities of organising the Championships. BLDSA continued to organise and operate its traditional championships, its own network of club events, and generally to care for and encourage grass roots support. In 1994 the ASA established its Technical Open Water Swimming Committee, which included BLDSA membership, and was designed to maximise the opportunities available for Long Distance competition.

Long distance swimming attracted men and women as competitors. By 1990 there were eleven senior and three junior national competitions. Competitors came from most age groups, particularly the Masters age group. These older swimmers combined their enthusiasm with stamina and endurance. Competitors demonstrated great skill and provided consistently good publicity for swimmers and for the Association.

Promotion of the sport

Long distance swimming, like all sports, benefited from publicity. The glamour of English Channel swims in the interwar period owed much to the publicity associated with contests organised by the *Daily Mail* and Butlins. However, such events formed only a part of the interest created by the achievements of sustained swimming. Reports of any unusual or spectacular swimming feats were given wide coverage in popular newspapers, especially during the summer months. In the serious press, the most consistent support for the sport came from the *Swimming Times* which carried advertisements for competitions and reports of events from its earliest days.

Advocacy of long distance swimming had an indefatigable champion in Commander Gerald Forsberg, OBE, RN. His personal achievements qualified him to provide strong guidance on the subject. Amongst these achievements was the 1957 Cross English Channel record from England to France, of 13 hours 33 minutes and success in winning the first three BLDSA championships at Windermere, Torbay, and Loch Lomond. He wrote the first major manual on the subject in 1957: *Long Distance Swimming*. He later revised this work to take account of advances in knowledge and it was published in 1963 with the title *Modern Long Distance Swimming*. It had not been superseded by 1994. Undoubtedly his regular column, 'Long Distance Swimming', in the *Swimming Times* had an important part to play in keeping the sport in the eyes of the swimming public. His contributions began in November 1957 at the start of the BLDSA. When the ASA became proprietors of the magazine in 1971 Gerald Forsberg continued his monthly column. Among the many posts he held in the organisation of his sport was President of the CSA from 1963 until the time of going to press. His commitment was such that in 1982 *The Observer* nominated him its *'Sports Nut of the Year'*. His enthusiasm has never waned and communicates itself to the reader through his vigorous presentation of events and topics.

The particular character of long distance swimming has attracted a small but dedicated group of participants. It has also attracted the interest and admiration of the wider public and the popular press. Until the closer association of the ASA. They BLDSA in the mid twentieth century, the ASA itself was involved in the organisation of only one long distance championship which had its origins in the nineteenth century. Nonetheless the ASA benefited from the prestige of long distance swimming, especially since most swimmers belonged to clubs affiliated to the ASA. They swam in competitions whose rules and regulations were guided by the ethos fostered by the Association. The closer links between BLDSA and the ASA provided an opportunity to consolidate available knowledge and experience.

Commander Gerald Forsberg being congratulated after completing the 1000 metres freestyle race at Lyn Padarn in 1994. (Copyright: Jim Stitt, Barrow-in-Furness)

The triumph of Bill Pickering who swam from Penarth (South Glamorgan) to Weston-super-Mare (Somerset) on 27 August 1969.
This was the first successful crossing for 40 years from Wales to England and it took six hours and twenty minutes. (Copyright: Press Association.)

Afterword

At the beginning of the 1990s several publications provided information about facilities for and participation in swimming. Kit Campbell Associates undertook a study for the Sports Council which was published in 1992: *Provision for Swimming. A National Strategy for Swimming and Swimming Provision.* This focussed on the adequacy of the numbers of pools in England and on their modernity. In 1991 the public had access to about 1,300 indoor pools of which just over four fifths were constructed between 1960 and 1990 and of which almost one half dated from the 1970s. A major part of this stock was owned by local authorities and required maintenance and refurbishment to keep it safe and usable, representing a demand on local authority finance. Pools in private ownership, but accessible to the public, usually formed part of leisure complexes and accounted for about a tenth of the total provision. Such leisure pools catered for casual swimming rather than for the needs of divers, water polo or racers. The Department of Education and Science in 1990 published statistics for England showing pool facilities were available in 13 per cent of primary schools and in 23 per cent of secondary schools. *Sport in the Nineties - New Horizons,* published in 1993, drew attention to the *General Household Survey* of 1990 which had found swimming was placed third amongst the most popular sports by men and women over the age of 16 years. A survey by Mintel in 1992 showed that in Great Britain one fifth of the population of all ages swam at least once a month. Participation in swimming was much greater than in any other sports including all kinds of football, golf, and lawn tennis or any indoor games.

This survey evidence establishes that swimming is a highly popular leisure activity even though facilities of the appropriate standards are not generally available. However, such information does not make clear the complexities of the struggle to ensure that facilities for swimming should be made available and that opportunities of learning to swim should exist for all. In addition, such surveys say little about competitive swimming at local, national and international levels. Much of the detail of these activities is revealed in a close study of the ASA. By tracing its emergence and the development of the Association it has been possible in some measure, to tell the story of amateur swimming in England.

A summary of the work of the ASA could focus on three themes. First, the experiences of the swimmers themselves whether swimming for pleasure or in competition. Second, an account of those people and organisations which facilitated all aspects of swimming, whether the opportunity to learn, coaching for competition, or the provision of pools. The third theme is the development of the ASA itself since the mid nineteenth century and the Association's responses to successive challenges. This book has attempted to record each of these themes, drawing upon the documentary evidence of minutes, *Handbooks*, and other materials. Not least are the recollections of many of the stalwarts who have supported and carried out the work of the ASA over the years. These chapters aim to clarify the many struggles and successes and to show the reader that, even at the end of 125 years of operation, there is work still to be undertaken if the goals of the ASA are to be attained.

Chronology

The insignia of the President of the ASA.

This chronology is intended to show major developments in the history of the ASA.

The convention adopted for persons is to give titles but without stating honours, professional qualifications and academic degrees.

The holders of principal offices are listed after the following abbreviations: P. for President; H.T. for Honorary Treasurer; H.S. for Honorary Secretary; and, S. for Secretary and C.E. for Chief Executive.

1868 Advertisement calls "Swimming Congress" at the Turnhalle (German Gymnasium) at Kings Cross, London

1869 **Associated Metropolitan Swimming Clubs** forms in January and in February becomes the **London Swimming Association.** (L.S.A.)
P.: J. Warrington; H.T.: G.H. Vize; H.S.: W.W. Ramsden
First Men's English Mile Championship

1870 From January L.S.A. is renamed the **Metropolitan Swimming Association**
P: S. Bullett; H.T.: J.F. Moultrie; H.S.: H.J. Bradley

1871 P.: S. Bullet; H.T.: J. Cole; H.S.: H.J. Bradley

1872 P.: Capt. H. Woods; H.T.: J. Fawcitt; H.S.: H.J. Bradley

1873 P.: H.G. Smith; H.T.: J. Fawcitt; H.S.: W.J. Everton, John Trudgen swims the Trudgen stroke in London
Changes title to Swimming Association of Great Britain

1874 P.: H.G. Smith; H.T.: G. Price; H.S.: W.J. Everton

1875 Captain Matthew Webb swims English Channel
P.: A.C. Heeps; H.T.: – H.S.: W.J. Everton

1876 P.: - H.T.: – H.S.: A.G. Lupton

1877 ASA Long Distance Championship for Men begins
P.: R.H. Watson; H.T.: A.G. Lupton; H.S.: W.W. Ramsden

1878 P.: G. Williams; H.T.: A.G. Lupton; H.S.: W.W. Ramsden

1879 P.: G. Williams; H.T.: A.G. Lupton; H.S.: W.W. Ramsden

1880 P.: H. Davenport; H.T.: A.G. Lupton; H.S.: H.J. Barron

1881 Professional Swimming Association established.
P.: H. Davenport; H.T.: A.G. Lupton; H.S.: H.J. Barron

1882 P.: H. Davenport; H.T.: A.G. Lupton; H.S.: H.J. Barron

1883 First ASA Plunging Championships established.
P.: H. Davenport; H.T.: H.F. Strange; H.S.: H.J. Barron

1884 Cygnus and seven other clubs do not accept the definition of "amateur" accepted by the SAGB and form the **Amateur Swimming Union.**
P.: H.J. Barron; H.T.: C.A. Itter; H.S.: H. Weaver

1885 P.: H.J. Barron; H.T.: C.J. Davison; H.S.: H. Weaver

1886 Reform of constitution and laws creates the **Amateur Swimming Association** when the SAGB and ASU agree on a definition of amateur.
P.: A. Clark; H.T.: C.J. Davison; H.S.: W.W. Ramsden

1887 Queen Victoria consents to be Patron of the ASA
P.: Lord C. Beresford; H.T.: R. Sandon; H.S.: E.J. Tackley

1888 National Water Polo Championships begin.
P.: Lord C. Beresford; H.T.: R. Sandon; H.S.: E.J. Tackley

1889 Agreement to form the Northern, Midland and Southern Districts with a revised constitution taking effect in 1890.

P.: Lord C. Beresford; H.T.: C.E. Macrae; H.S.: E.J. Tackley

1890 ASA makes first law on Costume. First International Water Polo Match (England – Scotland)
P.: H. Davenport; H.T.: C. Plumpton; H.S.: E.J. Tackley

1891 P.: H. Davenport; H.T.: C. Plumpton; H.S.: E.J. Tackley

1892 ASA's International Committee issues first codified rules for Water Polo.
P.: H. Davenport; H.T.: W.J. Read; H.S.: E.J. Tackley

1893 ASA publishes first Annual Handbook.
P.: H. Davenport; H.T.: W.J. Read; H.S.: Sir G. Pragnell

1894 P.: H. Davenport; H.T.: W.J. Read; H.S.: Sir G. Pragnell

1895 First National Graceful Diving Championships at Highgate.
P.: W.J. Read; H.T.: W.J. Read; H.S.: Sir G. Pragnell

1896 First Modern Olympic Games at Athens includes swimming
P.: H.E. Cashmore; H.T.: J.H. Fisher; H.S.: Sir G. Pragnell

1897 P.: G.H. Rope; H.T.: J.H. Fisher; H.S.: Sir G. Pragnell

1898 P.: J.H. Fisher; H.T.: J.H. Fisher; H.S.: Sir G. Pragnell

1899 Inauguration of the first Professional Certificate for Teachers of Swimming.
P.: J.F. Herbert; H.T.: J.H. Fisher; H.S.: Sir G. Pragnell

1900 First Olympic Water Polo Tournament
Revision of Constitution – Five Districts to come into being in 1901 – South, Midland, North, North East and West.
P.: H. Benjamin; H.T.: J.H. Fisher; H.S.: Sir G. Pragnell

1901 First English Ladies' Championship is for 100 yards freestyle
Inauguration of the Amateur Diving Association to regulate and promote the sport in England
P.: R. Williams; H.T.: J.H. Fisher; H.S.: Sir G. Pragnell

1902 P.: H. Thomsett; H.T.: J.H. Fisher; H.S.: Sir G. Pragnell

1903 P.: Sir G. Pragnell; H.T.: J.H. Fisher; H.S.: G.W. Hearn

1904 First Olympic Diving event is the Spring Board
P.: A. Mosley; H.T.: J.H. Fisher; H.S.: G.W. Hearn

1905 P.: W.N. Benjamin; H.T.: J.H. Fisher; H.S.: G.W. Hearn

1906 Supplementary Olympic Games at Athens includes High Diving events
P.: F. Baxter; H.T.: J.H. Fisher; H.S.: G.W. Hearn

1907 P.: J.T. Hinks; H.T.: J.H. Fisher; H.S.: G.W. Hearn

1908 Ladies Diving Association inaugurated in London.
Formation of Fédération Internationale de Natation Amateur [FINA]
Charles Daniels wins Olympic 100 metres showing the advantage of the crawl over the trudgen
P.: G.W. Hearn; H.T.: J.H. Fisher; H.S.: H.C. Hurd

1909 P.: A. Atkinson; H.T.: J.H. Fisher; H.S.: H.C. Hurd

1910 Revision of ASA Professional Certificate.
P.: E.J. Tackley; H.T.: J.H. Fisher; H.S.: H.C. Hurd

1911 P.: F.R. Edwards; H.T.: J.H. Fisher; H.S.: H.C. Hurd

1912 First Olympics to include women's swimming and diving events
P.: F.G. Wraith; H.T.: J.H. Fisher; H.S.: H.C. Hurd

1913 P.: E.W. Jordan; H.T.: J.H. Fisher; H.S.: T.M. Yeaden

1914–18 First World War severely restricts ASA activities
P.: H.J. Johnson; H.T.: J.H. Fisher; H.S.: T.M. Yeaden

1919 Teachers Swimming Certificate awards for both amateurs and professionals
P.: A. StP. Cuffin; H.T.: J.H. Fisher; H.S.: T.M. Yeaden

1920 First Long Distance Championship for Women.
P.: W. Hammond; H.T.: J.H. Fisher; H.S.: T.M. Yeaden

1921 P.: C.N. Milner; H.T.: T.M. Yeaden; H.S.: H.E. Fern

1922 P.: R.W. Jones; H.T.: T.M. Yeaden; H.S.: H.E. Fern

1923 P.: A.J. Tucker; H.T.: T.M. Yeaden; H.S.: H.E. Fern

1924 P.: T.M. Yeaden; H.T.: T.M. Yeaden; H.S.: H.E. Fern

1925 P.: H.T. Bretton; H.T.: T.M. Yeaden; H.S.: H.E. Fern

1926 First European swimming championships
Captain Cummins issues first *Swimming Times*
P.: F. Isherwood; H.T.: T.M. Yeaden; H.S.: H.E. Fern

1927 P.: G. Newton; H.T.: T.M. Yeaden; H.S.: H.E. Fern

1928 Olympic Games introduces Plain and Fancy Diving for women but for men the Plain and Fancy Competition is amalgamated
P.: W.H.A. Buller; H.T.: H.T.: T.M. Yeaden; H.S.: H.E. Fern

1929 P.: R.A. Colwill; H.T.: T.M. Yeaden; H.S.: H.E. Fern

1930 First British Empire (later Commonwealth) Games including swimming
P.: H. Crapper; H.T.: T.M. Yeaden; H.S.: H.E. Fern

1931 P.: W.S. Hankins; H.T.: T.M. Yeaden; H.S.: H.E. Fern

1932 National Association of Swimming Instructors founded.
P.: F. Harrison; H.T.: T.M. Yeaden; H.S.: H.E. Fern

1933 P.: T. Jebb Lee; H.T.: T.M. Yeaden; H.S.: H.E. Fern

1934 P.: H.E. Fern; H.T.: T.M. Yeaden; H.S.: H.E. Fern

1935 First demonstration of the 'Butterfly' stroke in the USA
ASA assumes control of Diving when the Amateur Diving Association dissolves itself
P.: R.G. Jordan; H.T.: T.M. Yeaden; H.S.: H.E. Fern

1936 P.: W.H. Darke; H.T.: T.M. Yeaden; H.S.: H.E. Fern

1937 Physical Training and Recreation Act.
P.: G.T. Evershed; H.T.: R.A. Colwill; H.S.: H.E. Fern

1938 P.: J. Hodgson; H.T.: R.A. Colwill; H.S.: H.E. Fern

1939–45 Second World War severely disrupts work of the ASA
P.: H.P. Leverton; H.T.: R.A. Colwill; H.S.: H.E. Fern

1946 P.: Capt. B.W. Cummins; H.T.: R.A. Colwill; H.S.: H.E. Fern

1947 First Loughborough Summer Training Course
P.: J.D. de Lancey; H.T.: R.A. Colwill; H.S.: H.E. Fern

1948 NASI is renamed STA.
P.: R.J. Pryde; H.T.: R.A. Colwill; H.S.: H.E. Fern

1949 ESSA founded.
P.: A.J. Perring; H.T.: R.A. Colwill; H.S.: H.E. Fern

1950 P.: Lt.Col. E. Read; H.T.: R.A. Colwill; H.S.: H.E. Fern

1951 P.: C.W. Plant; H.T.: R.A. Colwill; H.S.: H.E. Fern

1952 ASA elects its first woman President. ASA begins Proficiency Awards.

P.: Mrs A.M. Austin; H.T.: R.A. Colwill; H.S.: H.E. Fern

1953 HM Queen agrees to become Patron of the ASA.
FINA separates 'Butterfly' and 'Breast' strokes
P.: Brig. G.deV. Welchman; H.T.: R.A. Colwill; H.S.: H.E. Fern

1954 FINA recognises individual medley world records
P.: A. Mothersdale; H.T.: R.A. Colwill; H.S.: H.E. Fern

1955 P.: R. Murray; H.T.: G. Matveieff; H.S.: H.E. Fern

1956 FINA bans underwater breast stroke and limits world record list to long course events
FINA recognises the sport of Synchronised Swimming
British Long Distance Swimming Association founded.
P.: R. Hodgson; H.T.: G. Matveieff; H.S.: H.E. Fern

1957 P.: K.B. Martin; H.T.: G. Matveieff; H.S.: H.E. Fern

1958 P.: Sir H. Parker; H.T.: G. Matveieff; H.S.: H.E. Fern

1959 ASA starts Scientific Advisory Committee.
P.: C.F. Clark; H.T.: G. Matveieff; H.S.: H.E. Fern

1960 Wolfenden Committee Report on Sport.
A.D. Kinnear appointed as first NTO.
Learn to Swim Campaign launched.
First Olympics to include Medley relay events
First Paralympics (Parallel Olympics) held in Rome for some disabled athletes included swimming events
P.: H. Dixon; H.T.: G. Matveieff; H.S.: H.E. Fern

1961 Inauguration of the Harold Fern Award for the best effort in popularising the sport of swimming at national or international level
P.: A.C. Price; H.T.: G. Matveieff; H.S.: H.E. Fern

1962 ASA Proficiency Awards for Personal Survival
P.: L.H. Koskie; H.T.: G. Matveieff; H.S.: H.E. Fern

1963 ASA starts the Synchronised Swimming Committee.
P.: H.R. Walker; H.T.: G. Matveieff; H.S.: H.E. Fern

1964 ASA established National Age Group Committee.
First Olympics to include Individual Medley events
P.: G. Matveieff; H.T.: G. Matveieff; H.S.: H.E. Fern

1965 Government founds the Sports Council.
P.: W.T. Tiver; H.T.: G. Matveieff; H.S.: H.E. Fern

1966 P.: N.W. Sarsfield; H.T.: C.W. Plant; H.S.: H.E. Fern

1967 ASA/Coca-Cola launches a Training Scheme.
ASA founds its Public Relations Committee.
P.: E.J. Scott; H.T.: C.W. Plant; H.S.: H.E. Fern

1968 P.: A. Rawlinson: H.T.: A.H. Turner; H.S.: H.E. Fern

1969 ASA Centenary Year.
P.: J. Jordan; H.T.: A.H. Turner; H.S.: H.E. Fern

1970 ASA publishes the Martin Report
Last National Championships to be held at Derby Baths, Blackpool.
First National Age Group Championships in England
ASA publishes first Handbook on Synchronised Swimming
P.: E.W. Keighley; H.T.: A.H. Turner; S.: N.W. Sarsfield

1971 In January ASA company takes over publication of the *Swimming Times*
ASA adopts metric in place of imperial measurements for all championships and events
P.: T.A. Thomdale; H.T.: A.H. Turner; S.: N.W. Sarsfield

1972 Munich is the first Olympic Games to use electronic timing and place measuring equipment
P.: J. Wilson; H.T.: A.H. Turner; S.: N.W. Sarsfield

1973 First World Swimming Championships at Belgrade includes swimming, diving and water polo
23 March official opening of Harold Fern House in Derby Square, Loughborough, Leicestershire
P.: C.P. Parkin; H.T.: A.H. Turner; S.: N.W. Sarsfield

1974 Ligue Europénne de Natation(LEN) introduces Synchronised swimming events into the European Games where Great Britain wins the Solo, Duet and Team championships
Norman Sarsfield elected secretary of LEN
P.: E. Warrington; H.T.: A.H. Turner; S.: N.W. Sarsfield

1975 World Championships introduces Synchronised Swimming events
P.: M. Rutter; H.T.: A.H. Turner; S.: N.W. Sarsfield

1976 12 March ASA founds the Institute of Swimming Teachers and Coaches (ISTC) with its headquarters in Loughborough
P.: G.R. Eddowes; H.T.: A.H. Turner; S.: N.W. Sarsfield

1977 P.: T. Elsom-Rhymes; H.T.: A.H. Turner; S.: N.W. Sarsfield

1978 P.: F.W. Latimer; H.T.: A.H. Turner; S.: N.W. Sarsfield

1979 P.: J.H. Zimmermann; H.T.: A.H. Turner; S.: N.W. Sarsfield

1980 P.: D.F. Scales; H.T.: A.H. Turner; S.: N.W. Sarsfield

1981 First English National Masters Championship
P.: F.E. Collins: H.T.: A.H. Turner; S.: H.W. Hassall

1982 Alfred H. Turner award inaugurated for the most outstanding contribution to swimming at national or international level.
ASA Enterprises Ltd set up for commercial work
P.: A.H. Turner: H.T.: A.H. Turner; S.: H.W. Hassall

1983 P.: E.E. Warner; H.T.: A.H. Turner; S.: H.W. Hassall

1984 Drug testing starts in National Championships
Synchronised Swimming becomes one of the Olympic Games
ISTC becomes a company wholly owned by the ASA
P.: Mrs S.W. Margetts; H.T.: A.H. Turner; S.: H.W. Hassall

1985 P.: R.R. Garforth; H.T.: A.H. Turner; S.: H.W. Hassall

1986 Commonwealth Games includes its first Synchronised Swimming events
P.: Mrs Y.M. Price; H.T.: A.M. Clarkson; S.: D.A. Reeves

1987 P.: H. Booth; H.T.: A.M. Clarkson; S.: D.A. Reeves

1988 P.: T.G. Thomas; H.T.: A.M. Clarkson; S.: D.A. Reeves

1989 P.: J.J. Lewis; H.T.: A.M. Clarkson; S.: D.A. Reeves

1990 P.: E. Dean; H.T.: A.M. Clarkson; S.: D.A. Reeves

1991 P.: E. Wilkinson; H.T.: A.M. Clarkson; S.: D.A. Reeves

1992 Paralymics held at Barcelona and Madrid included swimming events for athletes with all disabilities for the first time
P.: L.G. Howe; H.T.: A.M. Clarkson; S.: D.A. Reeves

1993 ASA appoints 5 Regional Development Officers.
P.: T.H. Cooper; H.T.: A.M. Clarkson; S.: D.A. Reeves

1994 P.: R.H. George; H.T.: A.M. Clarkson; S.: D.A. Reeves

1995 P.: T.G. Handley; H.T.: A.M. Clarkson; C.E.: D. Sparkes

Acknowledgement of Sources

Manuscript and Interviews

Minute Books of the LSA, SAGB, and ASA in the ASA library.

We are grateful to have had the opportunity to interview the following specialists – often at length. Many of the interviews were taped for future reference.

Hamilton Bland, Richard Brown, Paul Bush, Professor J.M. Cameron, Anne Clark, Wendy Cole, Alan Donlan, Helen Elkington, The Misses Fern, C.G. Forsberg, Professor Susan Glyptis, Colin Hardy, Margaret Hohmann, Bert Kinnear, John Lawton, Andrew Morton, Austin Rawlinson, David Reeves, Brian Relf, Norman Sarsfield, David Sparkes, Derek Stubbs, Alfred Turner, John Wardley, Aileen Williams.

Printed materials
ASA Official Published Records

We have made full use of the ASA *Handbook* published annually from 1904 until 1994 except for the years of the First World War (1914 to 1918) when the 1919 volume reported on the war period and for the years of the Second World War (1939 to 1945) when a composite volume in 1946 covered the war years.

The format of the handbooks had altered from time to time to cover the years of the major wars when the normal activities of the ASA dropped to a low ebb, with the consequence that the years 1914 to 1918 were reported in the volume for 1919 and those from 1940 to 1945 in the volume for 1946.

Until 1970 *Handbooks* recorded the laws of swimming, arrangements for championships, results of ASA competitions, and of the international games in which the ASA participated. Normally, the principal meetings of the ASA committee were reported together with the Annual Report and Accounts submitted to the yearly meeting of the ASA Council.

Bound with each handbook were handbooks of the five districts.

Various changes took place in the organisation of the *Handbook* the most significant being that from 1970 the ASA issued its *Annual Report and Accounts* separately. These included reports from the ASA Committee on the work of the previous year together with other matters of record including reports from the committees on Swimming, Diving, Synchronised Swimming and Water Polo. Illustrations on the cover and as the years passed within the text added to the interest of the publication.

From 1989 the *Annual Accounts* became a distinct publication and the format changed to accommodate the current conventions of keeping accounts for a much larger organisation.

In 1989 the editor altered the *Handbook* in page size and style where photographs and colour illustrations became the norm. Each district still had its handbook bound with the ASA's national record.

Newspapers

The Times – published in London and until after the middle of the nineteenth century. Its focus on British news was on what happened in London and the neighbouring counties. It did not cover swimming events systematically unlike some other sports.

Magazines about Swimming and Swimmers in England

The Swimming, Rowing and Athletic Record
Published by Robert Watson it began in 1873 but its appeal was mainly to Londoners.

The Swimming Record and Chronicle of Sporting Events
A weekly begun by Robert Watson in 1884. It foundered and was replaced in a few months by
Swimming Notes
This was expanded from Octavo to a larger format as a fortnightly called
The Swimmer.
Watson replaced this in early 1886 with
National Sports
This paper failed to attract readers and advertisers in sufficient numbers and for its final number appeared as *National Hygiene*.

Swimming
This weekly magazine was an "offshoot" of English Sports issued in 1895 and its subheading made it clear that it was aimed at the London public.

The Swimming Magazine
Published as its official organ by the Royal Life Saving Society as a monthly. Its first number came out in June 1914. ASA library collection (not complete) begins October 1914 and ends in September 1917. It contains a few line drawings and photographs associated with articles and columns of news items complied by a small number of dedicated contributors including William Henry.

The Amateur Swimmer
Published by the ASA as its official organ it first appeared in May 1926 but copies do not survive in the ASA library beyond early 1927.

The Swimming Times
Published from 1926 as a bimonthly and then monthly every year by Captain B.W. Cummins who was editor except for the war years when Janet Bassett-Lowke replaced him. The ASA became owner of the magazine on 1 January 1971. It appeared without a break although its Octavo size was changed in 1989 to A4 page size. Throughout it carried photographs and illustrations although colour was not used often until the 1970s.

Illustrations

Souvenir Programmes of the Ravensbourne Swimming Club for 1896 and 1898 issued for the September Entertainments.
Deposited memorabilia including some ASA event programmes and photographic albums.
Photographs and newspaper cuttings in the ASA Library.
Swimming Times – photographic collection.

Other Sources

Nestlé UK Ltd.
Omega Electronics
Speedo (Europe) Ltd

Select Bibliography

Amateur Swimming Association, 1898, 1901 – on, *Handbook*, London, Amateur Swimming Association

Amateur Swimming Association, 1964, *Notes on the construction of Swimming Pools, and the requirements for teaching, competitive swimming, diving, and water polo*, second edition, London, ASA.

Amateur Swimming Association, 1991, *ASA Handbook of Synchronised Swimming* , Loughborough, ASA Swimming Enterprises

Amateur Swimming Association Education Committee, 1919, *School Swimming Baths*, Manchester, ASAEC

Anon, 1923, *The Original Bath Guide* (established 1762), Bath, William Lewis and Son, The Herald Press

Arlott, J. (editor), 1985, *The Oxford Companion to Sports*, Oxford, Oxford University Press

Association of Swimming Therapy, 1981, *Swimming for the Disabled*, Wakefield, E.P. Publishing

Atkinson, P. 1985, 'Strong Minds and Weak Bodies: Sports, Gymnastics and the Medicalisation of Women's Education', *British Journal of Sports History*, vol. 2, no. 1, London

Auger, A. 1995, 'Mrs Bloomer's Finest Hour', in *The Lady*, London, The Lady

Bailey, P. 1978, *Leisure and Class in Victorian England, Rational recreation and the contest for control, 1830-1885*, London, Routledge and Kegan Paul

Barron, F. 1993, *Swimming for a Century : Irish Amateur Swimming Association celebrates 100 years of Achievement*, Dublin, Irish Amateur Swimming Association

Baxter, F., Fern, H.E., Fisher, J.H., Leather, H., Wilson, J., Wraith, F.G., Yeaden, T.M. 1914, *Teaching of Swimming in Elementary Schools: Report of Sub-committee appointed by ASA committee*, London, ASA

Bellhouse, E.T. 1877-78, 'On Baths and Wash-houses for the People of Manchester' Item 9, *Transactions of the Manchester Statistical Society*, 241-252, Manchester, Manchester Statistical Society

Berridge, V. and Edwards, G. 1981, *Opium and the People Opiate Use in Nineteenth-century England*, London, Allen Lane

Besford, P. 1975, *Encyclopaedia of Swimming*, London, Robert Hale

Borton, D.L. 1977, *Swimming Pools, Requirements for Competition*, Loughborough, ASA

Cameron, J.M. 1990, *The History of Kent County Amateur Swimming Association*, Kent, Kent Amateur Swimming Association

Cameron, J.M. 1993, *The History of the Beckenham Swimming Club*, Beckenham, Brooklyn Press for Beckenham S.C.

Campbell, A. 1918, *Report on Public Baths and Wash-houses in the United Kingdom*, Edinburgh, The Carnegie United Kingdom Trust

Carter, E.J. and Goldfinger, E. 1945, *The County of London Plan Explained*, Harmondsworth, Penguin Books

Champions of the World, 1915, *The ASA Book on Swimming*, London, Simpkin, Marshall, Hamilton, Kent and Co.

Clarke, J. and Critcher, C. 1985, *The Devil Makes Work, Leisure in Capitalist Britain*, London, Macmillan

Cook, A. 1993, 'Sponsorship in Sport', in R. Saw (editor) *The Spread of Sponsorship in the Arts, Sport, Education, the Health Service and Broadcasting*, Newcastle, Bloodaxe Books

Cook, T.A. 1908, *The Fourth Olympiad being the Official Report of the Olympic Games of 1908 celebrated in London*, London, The British Olympic Association

Coombs, M. 1989, *Southern Counties Amateur Swimming Association 100 Years - 1889-1989*, London, Southern Counties ASA

Cross, A.W.S. and K.M.B. 1930, *Modern Public Baths and Wash-houses*, London, ASA and Simpkin Marshall

Cross, K.M.B. 1938, *Modern Public Baths*, London, ASA

Cunningham, H. 1980, *Leisure in the Industrial Revolution, c.1780-c.1880*, London, Croom Helm

Daniels, C.M., Johansson, H., and Sinclair, A. 1907, *How to Swim and Save Life*, London, British Sports Publishing

Daniels, C.M., Olsson, J. 1908, *How to Swim and Save Life, including the Rules of Water Polo*, London, British Sports Publicity Company

Davenport, J. 1947, *Planning and Design of Covered Baths, Part II, Design and Equipment*, Liverpool, Davenport

Defoe, D. [Reprint of First Edition of 1697], 1969, *An Essay Upon Projects*, Menston, The Scolar Press

Elliott, M. 1979, *Victorian Leicester*, Chichester, Phillimore

Fern, H.E., Wilson, J., Wraith, F.G. 1911, *The Promotion of Swimming*, London, ASA

Fletcher, S. 1985, 'The Making and Breaking of a Female Tradition: Women's Physical Education in England, 1880-1980', *British Journal of Sports History*, vol. 2, no. 1. London

Forsberg, G. 1963, *Modern Long Distance Swimming*, London, Routledge and Kegan Paul

Granville, A.B. 1971, *Spas of England and Principal Sea-bathing Places* with new introduction by G.II. Martin, Bath, Adams and Dart

Gray, J. 1977, *Synchronised Swimming*, London, A. and C Black

Gray, J. 1993, *Coaching Synchronised Swimming: Figure Transitions*, London, Standard Studio

Gray, J. with ASA Synchronised Swimming Committee, N.D. (?1976), *Teaching Synchronised Swimming*, Wakefield, E. P. Publishing

Gurney, J.D. 1984, 'Swimmerabilia', *The Antique Collectors' Club Journal*, June, 39-42, London, Antique Collectors' Club

Halladay, E. 1990, *Rowing in England: A Social History, The Amateur Debate*, Manchester, Manchester University Press

Hamilton, Lady. 1970, *Sport and Physical Recreation for the Disabled*, London, Disabled Living Foundation

Harding Payne, E. 1912, *Suggestions on the General Arrangements, Structure, and Equipment of Public Baths and Bathing Places*, London, Southern Counties Amateur Swimming Association

Hardy, C.A. 1985, 'Development of Swimming in England: the important years', in *In the Swim*, Loughborough, ISTC

Hardy, C.A. 1991, 'The Female and Competitive Swimming', in J.M. Cameron, editor, *Aquatic Sports Medicine*, London, Farrand Press

Hargreaves, J. 1994, *Sporting Females, Critical Issues in the history and sociology of women's sports*, London, Routledge

Hargreaves, J. 1992, 'Sex, Gender and the Body in Sport and Leisure: Has there been a civilizing process?' in E. Dunning and C.J. Rojek, editors, Sport *and Leisure in the Civilizing Process, Critique and Counter-critique*, London, Macmillan

Hargreaves, J.A. 1985, 'Playing Like Gentlemen While Behaving Like Ladies', *British Journal of Sports History*, vol. 2, no. 1. London

Harris, J. 1993, *Private Lives, Public spirit, A Social History of Britain, 1870-1914*, Oxford, Oxford University Press

Hawthorne, L. 1994, 'Women in newspapers' in *The Blackcountryman* vol. 28, no. 1. Stourbridge, Black Country Society

Heatly, P. 1950-1951, 'The Planning and Design of Modern Swimming-Baths' in *Journal of the Institution of Civil Engineers*, 89 - 131

Heatly, P. 1961, 'Indoor Swimming Pools, Their Design and Planning' in

Journal of the Institution of Municipal Engineers

Holt, R. 1989, *Sport and the British, A Modern History*, Oxford, Oxford University Press

Hugman, B. (editor) with Cranfield, L. (consultant), 1989, *Hugman's Swimming Year Book, 1990, in association with the Amateur Swimming Association*, London, Hugman's Sporting Publications

Institute of Baths Management, 1971, 'Baths Service' (Golden Jubilee Number), *Journal of the Institute of Baths Management*, vol. 30. no. 9

Institute of Baths Management, 1977, *Swimming Pools, Design Guide no. 1*,

London, Institute of Baths Management

Jarvis, A. 1975, *Captain Webb and One Hundred Years of Channel Swimming*, Newton Abbot, David and Charles

Jarvis, J.A. 1902, *The Art of Swimming, with notes on water polo and aids to life saving*, London, Hutchinson

Jones, S.G. 1986, *Workers at Play. A Social and Economic History of Leisure, 1918-1939*, London, Routledge and Kegan Paul

Juba, K. 1972, *All About Water Polo*, London, Pelham

Leahy, 'Sergeant' J. 1875, *The Art of Swimming in the Eton Style*, London, Macmillan

Lennard, R. 1931, 'The Watering Places', in R. Lennard, editor, Englishmen *at Rest and Play*, Oxford, Clarendon Press

Levy, S. and members of the Club,1964, *Breaking the Ice, A publication to commemorate the Centenary of the Serpentine Swimming Club, 1864/1964*, London, Serpentine Swimming Club

Margetson, S. 1969, *Leisure and Pleasure in the Nineteenth Century*, London, Cassell

Martin, K.B. and ASA special committee,1970, *Report and Recommendations of A.S.A. Special Committee on Competitive Swimming*, London, ASA

Mason, A. 1988, *Sport in Britain*, London, Faber and Faber

Mason, A. 1981, *Association Football and English Society, 1863 - 1915*, Brighton, Harvester Press

McIntosh, P.C.1952, *Physical Education in England since 1800*, London, Bell

Meller, H.E. 1976, *Leisure and the Changing City, 1970-1914*, London, Routledge and Kegan Paul

Morgan, E. 1972, *The Descent of Woman*, London, Souvenir Press

Morris, R.J. 1990, 'Clubs, Societies and Associations', in The *Cambridge Social History of Britain, 1750-1950*, vol. 3. *Social Agencies and Institutions*, Cambridge, Cambridge University Press

Munting, R. 1993, 'Social Opposition to Gambling in Britain: An historical overview', in *International Journal of Sports History*, vol. 10, no. 3. London

National Association of Bath Superintendents, N.D. (?1960), *Modern Baths and Laundries*, London, National Association of Bath Superintendents Inc.

Oppenheim, F. 1970, *The History of Swimming*, New York, Swimming World

Orme, N.I. 1983, *Early British Swimming, 55 B.C. to A.D.*

1719, Exeter, Exeter University Press

Rackham, G. 1959, *Diving*, London, ARCO Publications

Rackham, G. 1968, *Synchronised Swimming*, London, Faber and Faber

Rodger, N.A.M. 1986, *The Wooden World. An Anatomy of the Georgian Navy*, London, Collins

Rowntree, B. S. 1941, *Poverty and Progress, A Second Social Survey of York*, London, Longmans, Green and Company

Sachs, F. 1912, *The Complete Swimmer*, London, Methuen

Sands, M. 1987, *The Eighteenth-Century Pleasure Gardens of Marylebone, 1737-1777*, London, The Society for Theatre Research

Shimmin, H. 1986, *Liverpool Life: The Courts and Alleys of Liverpool*, (reprint of original works of 1856 and 1864), New York, Garland

Sinclair, A. and Henry, W. 1893, *Swimming*, in The Duke of Beaufort and A.E.T. Wilson, editors, The Badminton Library Series, London, Longmans, Green

Sporting Life, The, 1908, *Olympic Games of London*, London, The Sporting Life

Sports Council, The, 1976, *Building Cost Study: 25m Indoor Swimming Pools*, Technical Unit for Sport, *Bulletin 3*, London, Sports Council

Sports Council, The, 1993, *Sport in the Nineties - New Horizons*, London, The Sports Council

Sports Trader, The, 1904 - on, *The Sports Trader and Sidelines Review*, London, The Sports Press

Stokes, H.G. 1947, *The Very First History of the English Seaside*, London, Sylvan Press

Swimming and Bathing Pool Review Monthly, The, June 1935 -September 1936, London, Olympic Publications

Thomas, R. 1904, *Swimming*, London, Sampson Low, Marston

Thompson, A. 1985, *Callander through the Ages*, Callander, Callander Printers

Veal, A.J.1974, *Multi-Purpose Recreation Centres in Britain: Some Observations*, Working paper, Centre for Urban and Regional Studies, University of Birmingham

Walter, F. 1971, *Sports Centres and Swimming Pools, A study of their design with particular reference to the needs of the physically disabled*, London, The Thistle Foundation

Walvin, J. 1984, *English Urban Life, 1776-1851*, London, Hutchinson

Wolfenden, J.F. (chair of committee), 1960, *Sport and the Community*, London, Central Council for Physical Recreation

Wroth, W. and Wroth, A.E.1979, *The London Pleasure Gardens of the Eighteenth Century* (Reprint of 1896 edition), London, Macmillan

Zajac, D. and Smith, Jo. N.D. (?1966), *Beginning Synchronised Swimming*, London, The Seymour Synchronised Swimming School

Index